D1001349

COMPREHENSION INSTRUCTION

COMPREHENSION INSTRUCTION

PERSPECTIVES AND SUGGESTIONS

Gerald G. Duffy
Laura R. Roehler
Jana Mason

Longman
New York & London

Comprehension Instruction
Perspectives and Suggestions

Longman Inc., 1560 Broadway, New York, N.Y. 10036
Associated companies, branches, and representatives
throughout the world.

Copyright © 1984 by Longman Inc.

All rights reserved. No part of this publication may be
reproduced, stored in a retrieval system, or transmitted
in any form or by any means, electronic, mechanical,
photocopying, recording, or otherwise, without the prior
permission of the publisher.

Developmental Editor: Lane Akers
Editorial and Design Supervisor: Frances A. Althaus
Production Supervisor: Ferne Y. Kawahara
Manufacturing Supervisor: Marion Hess

Library of Congress Cataloging in Publication Data

Main entry under title:

Comprehension instruction.

   Includes bibliographical references.
   1. Reading comprehension—Addresses, essays,
lectures. 2. Teacher participation in curriculum
planning—Addresses, essays, lectures. 3. Teachers—
Attitudes—Addresses, essays, lectures. 4. Academic
achievement—Addresses, essays, lectures. I. Duffy,
Gerald G. II. Roehler, Laura R., 1937–
III. Mason, Jana.
LB1050.45.C68 1983   428.4′3   82-23944
ISBN 0-582-28406-6

Printing: 9 8 7 6 5 4 3 2   Year: 91 90 89 88 87 86 85 84

Manufactured in the United States of America

ECC/USF Learning Resources
8099 College Parkway, S.W.
Fort Myers, Florida 33907-5164

Contents

Foreword / *vii*
Preface / *ix*

PART I   BACKGROUND   1

1 The Reality and Potential of Comprehension Instruction /
   Gerald G. Duffy, Laura R. Roehler and Jana Mason   3
2 The Reader's Perceptual Processes / *George McConkie*   10
3 A Schema-Theoretic View of the Reading Process as a Basis
   for Comprehension Instruction / *Jana M. Mason and the Staff of
   the Center for the Study of Reading*   26
4 A Question about Reading Comprehension Instruction / *Jana M.
   Mason*   39

PART II   CONSTRAINTS ON INSTRUCTION   57

5 Teacher Planning and Reading Comprehension / *Christopher M.
   Clark*   58
6 The Teacher as Thinker: Implementing Instruction / *Jere
   Brophy*   71
7 The Environment of Instruction: The Function of Seatwork in a
   Commercially Developed *Curriculum* / *Linda Anderson*   93
8 The Environment of Instruction: The Forms and Functions of
   Writing in a Teacher-Developed Curriculum / *Susan Florio and
   Christopher M. Clark*   104
9 Schools as a Context for Instruction / *Lawrence Lezotte*   116
Summary / *125*
Selected Bibliography / *125*

PART III   TEXT AND COMPREHENSION INSTRUCTION   127

10 Readability Formulas and Comprehension / *Alice Davison*   128
11 Content of Basal Text Selections: Implications for

Comprehension Instruction / *William H. Schmidt, Jacqueline Caul, Joe L. Byers and Margaret Buchmann* 144

12 Workbooks That Accompany Basal Reading Programs / *Jean Osborn* 163

13 Children's Preconceptions and Content-Area Textbooks / *Charles W. Anderson and Edward L. Smith* 187

14 The Problem of "Inconsiderate Text" / *Bonnie B. Armbruster*... 202

Summary / 218
Selected Bibliography / 218

PART IV   COMPREHENSION AS VERBAL COMMUNICATION

.... 221

15 Direct Explicit Teaching of Reading Comprehension / *P. David Pearson* 222

16 Question-Related Activities and Their Relationship to Reading Comprehension: Some Instructional Implications / *Taffy E. Raphael and James R. Gavelek* 234

17 The Quest for Meaning from Expository Text: A Teacher-Guided Journey / *Annemarie Sullivan Palincsar* 251

18 Direct Explanation of Comprehension Processes / *Laura R. Roehler and Gerald G. Duffy* 265

19 Verbal Patterns of Teachers: Comprehension Instruction in the Content Areas / *Kathleen J. Roth, Edward L. Smith and Charles W. Anderson* 281

Summary / 294
Selected Bibliography / 295

PART V   IMPLICATIONS FOR RESEARCH AND PRACTICE   297

20 A Practitioner's Model of Comprehension Instruction / *Jana Mason, Laura R. Roehler and Gerald G. Duffy* 299

Foreword

When the Institute for Research on Teaching and the Center for the Study of Reading were established in 1976 by The National Institute of Education (NIE), their scholarly agendas were quite different. Nevertheless, they were thought in principle to be compatible and complementary.

The Institute was to study the processes of teaching with special reference to the manner in which teachers' thought and action were coordinated in effective instruction. In contrast with the then prevailing mode of research on teaching, which entailed discovering relationships between teacher behavior and pupil performance, the Institute was to study how teacher planning, judgment, decision making, and other cognitive aspects of teaching related to teacher behavior and student performance. If these relationships were better understood, then they could be facilitated through improved programs of preservice and inservice teacher education. This program of research would draw upon the emerging "cognitive revolution" in the social sciences and would involve the collaborative efforts of interdisciplinary research teams made up of scientists and practitioners from education, the social sciences, and the public schools.

The Center, too, was to ground its work in the cognitive revolution, especially as manifested in psychology, computer science (the two forming the exciting new hybrid dubbed "cognitive science"), linguistics, and education. The research agenda was to progress beyond an understanding of the elementary process of decoding in reading to an understanding of the complex processes of reading comprehension. It was expected that from this work would emerge models of how pupils come to understand written materials in many subject areas, how they learn to think about their reading comprehension and strategies for its improvement, and how teachers could improve such processes through instruction.

Despite the apparent concordance of interest and theoretical perspective between the two institutions, almost no interaction occurred between our staffs during the first four years. Only through the efforts of the editors of this volume was serious communication between the Institute and the Center initiated. The present volume has resulted from that collaboration. We have come to recognize the insufficiency of studying teaching without learning or learning without teaching when the ultimate goal is the understanding and improvement of practice. But each research effort demands a high level of scholarly expertise. It is difficult merely to dictate that scholars broaden their focus. Instead, we need to foster the "marriage of insufficiencies," to paraphrase Charles Osgood's apt formulation in another context. Such marriages bring together those specializing in the investigation of teaching with others who inquire into the processes of learning. This disciplined eclectic can lead to levels of understanding and utility that far transcend what any one group of investigators could accomplish alone.

This set of collected papers authored by leading members of the research staffs of the Institute for Research on Teaching and the Center for the Study of Reading testify to the vigor of their respective research enterprises and the promise this marriage holds for adding to our understanding of the processes of instruction and learning in schools.

Lee S. Shulman
Richard C. Anderson

Preface

A pedagogy of reading comprehension has long been needed but has not been forthcoming. Instruction has been investigated; reading has been investigated. Never have the two been studied together. Now, new ways of investigating the theories, strategies, and processes of reading comprehension plus the trend toward using the classroom as a research site for teaching have made the combining of comprehension and instruction possible. We can examine reading comprehension as an interactive process and simultaneously examine how instruction occurs in the fluid, complex workplace of the classroom. This combination is the basis of the present book.

A sabbatical leave provided an opportunity for the three editors to discuss comprehension and instruction at the Center for the Study of Reading at the University of Illinois. We were struck by the converging paths of the Center's work and that of the Institute for Research on Teaching at Michigan State University. After discussions with the codirectors of the CSR and the IRT, a jointly offered colloquium series that examined the nature of reading comprehension instruction was established. The colloquia were offered during 1982 by both IRT and CSR researchers. Their presentations reflected their particular research and its implications for comprehension instruction. These presentations, transformed into chapter form, make up the content of this book.

We would like to thank the following: the National Institute of Education; by sponsoring the CSR and the IRT, it made this book possible. The codirectors of the IRT (Doctors Jere Brophy and Andrew Porter) and the CSR (Doctors Richard Anderson and Tom Anderson) recognized the importance of this collaborative effort and supported it. The contributors prepared their manuscripts under considerable time pressure.

Gerald G. Duffy
Laura R. Roehler
Jana Mason

COMPREHENSION
INSTRUCTION

PART I

Background

1

The Reality and Potential of Comprehension Instruction

Gerald G. Duffy

Laura R. Roehler

Jana Mason

We stand at an important point in the history of reading instruction. After decades of emphasis on word recognition and lip service to the importance of comprehension, we are on the brink of an important breakthrough that promises an emphasis on reading comprehension and how to teach it in classrooms. Credit for this developments goes to a new research emphasis on both comprehension and instruction. Since 1965, the Institute for Research on Teaching (IRT) at Michigan State University and the Center for the Study of Reading (CSR) at the University of Illinois have been leaders in this research. The IRT, by virtue of its charge to investigate teaching, has examined instruction; the CSR, because of its concern with reading, has studied comprehension. As a result, researchers at the two institutions now possess unique insights about what to teach in comprehension and how to teach it.

This book brings together researchers from both institutions. It synthesizes their emerging understandings regarding the nature of comprehension and the complexities of instruction and provides perspectives and suggestions useful to classroom teachers, administrators, policy makers, and educators responsible for improving classroom practice. By so doing, this book can help bridge the gap between research and practice, and move us closer to achieving the breakthrough in classroom instruction that is so sorely needed.

THE CURRENT STATE OF COMPREHENSION INSTRUCTION

The need for improved instruction in reading comprehension is clear, as four major studies of current classroom practice may illustrate. Durkin (1979) studied 24 fourth-grade classrooms searching for evidence of comprehension instruction. After more than 7,200 minutes of observation, she reported a prevalence of teacher assessment (question asking) and "mentioning" (generalized nonexplicit statements). Instruction for comprehension accounted for less than 1 percent of the time.

Duffy and McIntyre (in press) studied six first- and second-grade teachers looking for descriptions of what teachers do when they show pupils how to perform various reading tasks. The results were similar to Durkins's. The teachers seldom showed pupils how to do tasks. Instead, they monitored pupils through basal textbook activities and supplied correctives in response to errors. Further, teacher interviews indicated that they believed this was what they were supposed to do.

A third study[1] provided similar data. It focused on student responses to reading seatwork in eight classrooms. A major conclusion was that pupils, particularly those in the low group, view seatwork as something to get done, not something designed to help them make sense of the reading process. Such student responses seemed to reflect the fact that teachers seldom provided purposes, sense-making strategies, and suggestions for self-monitoring during either the instruction or the directions for seatwork.

In 1981 Durkin attempted to explain the absence of comprehension instruction in her earlier study. Noting that all her teachers used basal textbook series, she analyzed the directions to teachers in five commercial programs. She found little that could be categorized as comprehension instruction. Her conclusion was that the basal textbook recommendations were similar to what she observed teachers doing in her earlier study. Hence teachers who "assessed" and "mentioned" were probably following prescribed procedures.

In sum, these studies, as well as others by Brophy, Joyce, and Morine-Dershimer,[2] suggest that classroom reading instruction is often mechanical, activity dominated, and basal text driven. There is little evidence that comprehension is taught at all, much less taught well.

WHY DOES THIS SITUATION EXIST?

Why do studies of classroom practice paint such a dismal picture about reading instruction? Three reasons come to mind. First, until recently we have had little specific knowledge regarding the nature of comprehension. It has not been the subject of intensive study, and as a result, there has been no substantive direction regarding *what* one teaches in comprehension or why it is sensible to teach it. Instead, recommendations to teachers often have consisted of vague encouragement to create learning environments that value meaningful reading activities or of "tricks of the trade" viewed as technical aids to be implemented in routine and mechanical ways. It is difficult to provide effective comprehension instruction without a curriculum that specifies the elements, operations, experiences, processes, skills, and attitudes associated with successful comprehension and how these work together in a systematic and sensible way.

Second, until recently we have had little data regarding the nature of classrooms. Research designed to determine how to teach reading in classrooms has often been conducted with college students in laboratories, and scholarly studies of classroom life have been rare. Our understandings of the complexities of classroom life and the constraints on teachers have been based almost entirely in conventional wisdom. As a result, we have generally been insensitive to the restrictions posed by class size, the pressure for activity flow and smooth management, the impact of accountability, and the reality that teachers teach from basal texts with little choice regarding *which text* they will use. Without a clear concept of the environment in which learning takes place and an appreciation of the way various aspects of the environment constrain instruction, it is difficult to improve the teaching of comprehension.

Finally, there has been debate regarding the nature of instruction. For instance, Duffy and Roehler point out that reading educators argue among themselves about what instruction is:

> ... researchers of reading instruction, having been less than precise in our use of the term "instruction," are now having trouble defining what it is we are studying. For instance, there is a debate over what Durkin (1978–79) really meant when she reported that the teachers she observed spent little time instructing comprehension; Hodges (1980) argues that instruction is more than what Durkin said it was while Heap's[3] critique of Durkin is based on yet another definition of what instruction is. There are other examples of instruction meaning something different to different researchers.[4]

At the same time, there is concern that the various functions of instruction—management, explanation, practice, and application—have not been distinguished clearly. As a result, it has been suggested (Duffy and Roehler 1981) that what seems to be a diversity of teaching suggestions for reading comprehension are "an illusion masking a conceptual sparcity about teaching" because all rely on a model of "repeated exposure." In short, there are many teaching suggestions for *practicing* comprehension but not many for explaining or applying comprehension. Without a clear concept of what instruction is, it is difficult to provide teachers with substantive assistance to improve the teaching of comprehension.

THE CONTRIBUTION OF THE TWO CENTERS

In the past we have had little knowledge about comprehension, classrooms, and instruction, but this is no longer true. To the contrary, researchers at the Institute for Research on Teaching and at the Center for the Study of Reading, as well as a wide variety of other researchers across the nation, have studied comprehension and comprehension instruction from a variety of perspectives. This spirit of intense scholarly study has resulted in unique insights and important understandings that promise to alter the face of classroom reading instruction.

The Center for the Study of Reading

The Center for the Study of Reading has contributed to a potential breakthrough in reading instruction by articulating a largely new theory of reading that is already accepted by a majority of scholars in the field. In broad outline, the theory has four central tenets:

1. The mature reader derives information more or less simultaneously from *many levels of analysis* including the graphophonemic, morphemic, semantic, syntactic, pragmatic, schematic, and interpretive.

2. Reading is an *interactive process*; analysis does not proceed in a strict order from basic perceptual units through to the overall interpretations of a text, but hypotheses at any level may facilitate or inhibit hypotheses at any other level.

3. Reading is a *contructive process*. A text does not "have" a meaning by virtue of its wording and syntax; rather, the text is an abbreviated recipe from which the reader elaborates a meaning based on analysis of the author's intentions, the physical and social context, and the reader's knowledge of the topic and the genre.

4. Reading is a *strategic process*. Skillful readers continuously monitor their comprehension; they are alert to breakdowns and selectively allocate attention to difficult sections as they progressively refine their interpretation of the text.

This theoretical framework suggests tentative answers to several questions about comprehension instruction. One is the relative emphasis to be placed on text meaning as opposed to word decoding. The theory that reading is an interactive, constructive process suggests a balanced perspective: Every level of analysis is necessary; none is sufficient. From this perspective, the hypothesis endorsed by some reading educators that readers "sample" from the text in order to confirm "guesses" based on context can be seen as too extreme. Indeed, the Center for the Study of Reading has provided direct experimental evidence that such is the case. This is but one illustrative example of the insights available from this line of research; others could be cited.

Hence the work of the Center for the Study of Reading, while based in a theoretical framework, has produced findings that have practical applications for the teaching of comprehension. These applications relate to the nature of the text, the nature of the reader's cognitive processing, and the interaction of text and reader.

The Institute for Research on Teaching

The Institute for Research on Teaching has contributed to the potential breakthrough in reading comprehension instruction by placing a priority on studying classrooms and teachers in order to build a pedagogical psychology of teaching, including the teaching of reading comprehension. This emphasis has resulted in three important areas of findings.

First, we now have a better understanding of teacher *effectiveness*. Studies that focused on carefully defined teacher instructional behaviors and how these correlated with achievement outcomes have given rise to "direct instruction," a general concept that places a premium on academic focus, pupil engaged time on task, and careful teacher monitoring of pupil response (Rosenshire 1976, 1979). Experimental studies have provided further evidence of the importance of these findings, particularly in primary grade reading. There is now a general sense that we have made a significant start toward understanding what makes certain teachers more effective than others. As described by Brophy (in press) and Duffy (1981), the effective teacher (1) allocates most of the classroom time to instruction and enhances student use of time through efficient classroom management; (2) sets positive expectancies for pupils and backs these up by engaging students in academic activities that result in high success rates; and (3) assumes responsibility for actively teaching and avoids simply managing instruction through the distribution, monitoring, and correcting of assignments.

Second, researchers at the IRT have demonstrated a growing interest in classroom context. The resultant studies have shown classroom instruction to be dynamic and fluid, occurring within a collective setting involving structural subtleties of environment and interactional subtleties of communication. As a result, we are beginning to understand that teachers emphasize materials management rather than explanation because the context constrains instructional practice, limiting teacher options and encouraging the use of routines and mechanical monitoring procedures that simplify the task of working in a complex environment. In addition, it has become clear that a teacher's classroom management skills are crucial to effective instruction. Failure to get pupils engaged and to keep them engaged not only results in low achievement but also makes the teacher's working environment intolerable.

Third, IRT researchers have focused on how teachers, despite the complexities of classroom context, can provide instruction that emphasizes substantive assistance to pupils while it minimizes mechanical monitoring. The focus here is how the teacher talks to students when explaining, assigning, practicing, and applying; how the teacher makes decisions about interactive instructional talk and the interaction of the instructional environment, the teacher, and the processing of students.

Hence the Institute for Research on Teaching has created knowledge of what classrooms are like, the ingredients of effective instruction in classrooms, and what needs to be done if we are to understand the teacher-student interaction called "instruction." The psychology of instruction emerging from the IRT's work is much more than simply looking at what we know about reading comprehension and trying to apply it to the classroom. It is, rather, a set of questions based on findings of classroom teaching as it really occurs.

THE FOCUS OF THIS BOOK

Both the Center for the Study of Reading and the Institute for Research on Teaching are making unique contributions that have the potential to improve the reading comprehension of schoolchildren. To utilize these contributions, however, the findings from the two centers must be synthesized in a way that is usable to professionals charged with translating research findings into classroom practice.

This book is designed to accomplish this. While it may also hold interest for researchers, it is primarily directed to public school personnel and teacher educators responsible for training and supervising teachers and to classroom teachers who are responsible for delivering instruction. As such, it is not a book about comprehension—it is a book about comprehension *instruction*. It is not a book about theory—it is a book about how to improve *practice*.

Various chapters are written by leading researchers who are experts in comprehension, instruction, or both. Each researcher describes his or her research findings. However, each chapter is written to put the particular research findings into a perspective that practitioners can use to improve classroom instruction of reading comprehension.

Specifically, the book has two purposes:

1. To describe the "common ground" among the research findings relating to comprehension instruction so that they can be used as a foundation for building effective instructional programs.
2. To provide suggestions for school personnel and teacher educators so that they can create improved comprehension instruction in today's classrooms.

To accomplish this, the book is organized into five sections. The remainder of this section (Part 1) provides further introduction to the book. Specifically, it sets the stage for examining comprehension instruction by summarizing what we know about how children perceive written text, what we know about the nature of comprehension, and what we know about current comprehension instruction in many American classrooms. Part 2 focuses on constraints on instruction. It creates an understanding of the variables that restrict and shape instructional practice by reporting findings on teacher thinking, classroom environments, school effects, and teacher communication, among others. Part 3 examines various kinds of text. It focuses on the readability of basal text stories and workbooks and content-area textbooks and the implications for comprehension instruction. Part 4 emphasizes how to go about *instructing* comprehension. It includes descriptions of studies on teacher questioning, instructional strategies, direct explanation, and others. Each chapter is based on a slightly different concept of what constitutes instruction and as such provides a variety of ways to go about teaching comprehension. The last section consists of a single chapter. It summarizes the findings from Parts 2, 3, and 4, synthesizes them, and provides answers to the two purposes stated above.

The organization reflects the three central themes of the book: (1) improvement in instructional practice in reading requires the collaboration of researchers of reading and researchers of teaching; (2) successful reading comprehension instruction requires as careful attention to *instruction* (the constraints, tools, and strategies thereof) as to comprehension; (3) the true test of the utility of educational research is its applicability to classroom practice.

NOTES

1. L. Anderson. *Student responses to seatwork: Implications for the study of student's cognitive processes*. Research Series No. 102, Institute for Research on Teaching, Michigan State University, 1981.

2. J. Brophy. *Potential policy implications of recent research in teaching*. Paper presented at the Summer Institute of Learning and Motivation in the Classroom, University of Michigan, Ann Arbor, June 1981. B. Joyce. *Toward a theory of information processing in teaching*. Research Series No. 76, Institute for Research on Teaching, Michigan State University, 1979. G. Morine-Dershimer. *Teacher plans and classroom reality: The South Bay Study Part IV*. Research on Teaching, Michigan State University, 1979.

3. J. Heap. *Understanding classroom events: A critique of Durkin, with an alternative*. Paper presented at the State of the Art Conference, State University of New York—Albany, November 1981.

4. G. Duffy. and L. Roehler. *An Exploration of Teacher Explanation Behavior*. Paper presented at the Annual Conference of the International Reading Association, May 1982.

REFERENCES

Brophy, J. How teachers influence what is taught and learned in classrooms. *Elementary School Journal*, in press.

Duffy, G. Teacher effectiveness: Implication for reading education. In M. Kamil (Ed.), *Directions in Reading: Research and Instruction*. Thirtieth Yearbook of the National Reading Conference. Washington: National Reading Conference, 1981.

Duffy, G., & McIntyre, L. A naturalistic study of instructional assistance in primary grade reading. *Elementary School Journal*, in press.

Duffy, G., & Roehler, L. The illusion of instruction. *Reading Research Quarterly*, 1982, *17* (3), 438–445.

Durkin, D. What classroom observation reveals about reading comprehension instruction. *Reading Research Quarterly*, 1978–79, *14*, 481–533.

Hodges, C. Commentary: Toward a broader definition of comprehension instruction. *Reading Research Quarterly*, 1980, *15*, (2).

Rosenshine, B. U. Classroom instruction. In N. Gage (Ed.), *The Psychology of teaching methods*. 75th yearbook of the National Society of the Study of Education. Chicago: University of Chicago Press, 1976.

Rosenshine, B. U. Content, time and direct instruction. In H. Walberg and P. Peterson (Eds.), *Research on teaching: Concepts, findings and implications*. Berkeley: McCutchan Publishing Company, 1979.

2

The Reader's Perceptual Processes

George W. McConkie

Reading has always been recognized as the first of the "three Rs," and teaching people to read has been seen as a primary responsibility of the educational system. Because of this, research investigating the reading process has been continuing since before the turn of the century. Many issues studied today, especially those concerning perceptual processes in reading, are dealt with in Huey's (1908) book, which contains many insightful observations about reading.

Progress in understanding the mental processes involved in reading has been slow, because reading is a complex mental activity that takes place rapidly and privately within a person's mind, making it difficult to study. Not only is the activity unobservable to others, but readers themselves hardly know what they are doing. Readers, desirous of understanding, pass their eyes over a text and in the process gain meaning and knowledge. Even though they may comprehend the text, they are unable to shed much light on how they did it: What were they seeing? How frequently did their eyes stop? How did they decide on word meaning when a word had more than one potential meaning? How did a series of words call a new, complex thought to mind? Decades of research on reading have only begun to give us an understanding of what the mind is doing as it carries out this remarkable activity.

Recently a series of advancements has aided our understanding of perception in reading. The application of computer technology to reading research has made it possible to study the perceptual processes taking place as people read with a level of precision never before possible. This chapter describes some of this research, including techniques used to study perception in detail and some of the discoveries that have resulted. First, however, it is necessary to recognize that in reading, as in most visual tasks, perception occurs by means of a rapid series of eye movements, taking the eyes to different locations. It is worthwhile describing some of the characteristics of these eye movements.

EYE MOVEMENTS DURING READING

As people read they have the feeling that their eyes are moving most of the time. In reality, the eyes move less than 10 percent of the time. About four times per second, the average reader's eyes make quick movements, referred to as *saccadic eye movements*, or *saccades*, which center the eyes on some new location in the text. Saccades can take from 20 to 80 milliseconds (msec), with a saccade of average length (eight to ten letter positions) requiring about 35 msec. In making saccadic movements, the eyes can reach velocities up to 800 degrees of visual angle per second (Alpern 1971). In the periods between saccades, which are referred to as fixations, the eyes are relatively still, showing only small drifts and tremors. Incidentally, although these movements are so small that they can be observed only with the most sophisticated equipment, they are critical to proper vision. Without them, the objects we are looking at would fragment and disappear. The average fixation is about 250 msec, or about one quarter of a second. Such factors as reading ability, text difficulty, and reading purpose can change the average saccade length and fixation period somewhat. However, these changes are small in comparison to the variation that exists within the eye movement record of a single person reading a single passage.

Several techniques are used to monitor a reader's eye movements. In one, the reader's eyes are illuminated with infrared (invisible) light, and small photo cells are mounted about one quarter of an inch from the eyes' surface to measure the amount of this light reflected. These photocells are aimed at the boundary between the iris and the sclera (the white part of the eye), one on each side of the iris, as shown in Figure 2.1. Since the sclera is whitish, it reflects more light than does the iris. As the eyes rotate to the right, more of the sclera falls within the field of view of one of the photo cells, thus increasing the light reflected to that cell, while more of the iris falls within the field of view of the other photo cell, reducing the light reflected to it. The relative amount of light reflected to the two

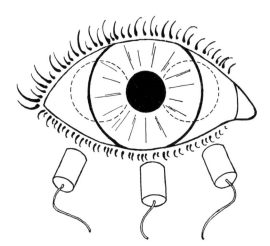

FIGURE 2.1   Example of Scleral Reflection Technique for Monitoring Eye Movements. The center cylinder illuminates the eye with infrared light, and the two side cylinders are photosensors that respond to infrared light reflected from the surface of the eye indicated by dotted lines. If the eye moves to the left, the light level drops at the left photosensor because more of the iris moves into its field of view, while the light level at the right photosensor increases because more of the sclera moves into its field of view. Changes in these intensities indicate relative eye position.

photo cells can be used to obtain an indication of the rotational position of the eyes, or the direction of gaze.

Other common techniques include taking pictures of the eye with a television camera and having the computer analyze the image of the pupil, and the location of a highlight within the pupil region, to identify the direction of the eye. A very accurate indication of eye position can be obtained with highly sophisticated equipment that tracks reflections from the front surface and the back of the lens of the eye. While these techniques differ in their degree of accuracy, none of them requires direct contact with the eyes, as other techniques do (for instance, requiring specially made contact lenses that do not slip on the surface of the eyes). Methods of monitoring eye movements have been reviewed by Young and Sheena (1975).

The most basic data obtained from eye-movement equipment is shown in Figure 2.2, which presents an eye-movement record (about 3/4 second) of a college student reading a passage. The figure shows the relative horizontal position of the eyes at each msec (each 1/1000 second). Time is represented along the x axis, with a vertical line of the grid occurring at each 1/10 second. Eye position on

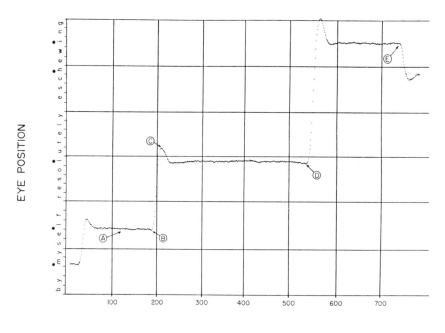

TIME (msec)

FIGURE 2.2 Example of .8 Second of Raw Eye Movement Data (horizontal movement component only). Time is represented along the X axis, and eye position along the Y axis. Points are plotted indicating the eye's position at each msec. When the curve is flat (as at A), the eyes are in a fixation. Movement of the eyes rightward is reflected in an upward movement of the curve (as at B), and movement of the eyes leftward is reflected in a downward movement of the curve (as at E). The location of each fixation on the line of text is represented by a dot over the corresponding letter position on the Y axis.

the line of text is represented along the *y* axis, with a horizontal line of the grid occurring each five-letter position. The part of the line of text being read is also shown on the *y* axis. When the curve is flat, as at point *A*, the eyes are in a fixation. Here the eyes are centered between the *e* and *l* in *myself*. At point *B*, where the curve begins to rise, the eyes have begun to move to a new location; at point *C*, about 21 msec later, the eyes have completed a saccade and are coming to rest for a new fixation, centered on the first *l* in *resolutely*. The eyes then remain at that location for about 325 msec before beginning a new saccade at point *D*. Finally, at point *E*, the eyes begin a regressive movement, moving leftward back along the line to examine something that might have been seen earlier. This figure illustrates how the eyes remain in position during fixations and how the eyes speed up, then slow down as they travel to each new location. The hump at the end of each saccade is a period of time during which the eyes are settling into position for the new fixation after having been subjected to tremendous forces exerted by the ocular muscles to pull them quickly to their new position.

A more common method of illustrating eye-movement data is shown in Figure 2.3. In this figure the text the person was reading is shown. The reader's eyes stopped for fixations centered on those letters under which there is a numeral. The numerals in turn indicate the sequence in which fixations occurred. Finally, under each numeral is a number indicating the number of msec the eye stayed at that location. From this figure, it can be seen that the reader's first fixation was centered on the letter *h* in the word *ship* and that this was a short fixation, lasting only 122 msec. Following this, the eyes moved farther to the left for the second fixation and remained there for a longer period of time. Such small regressions are common at the beginning of each line; the eyes seem to be finding an appropriate initial position after having made the long movement from the end of the prior line of text. This fixation is then followed by a series of fixations, each farther to the right along the line. It should be noted that fixation 5 is a regression, the eyes having briefly moved leftward again for some reason.

```
built a ship and set sail in 1728.  They discovered Saint Lawrence
      2     1 3      5 4          6          7    8         9    0   1
    253   122 139   24 339      280        296  214       268  235 102
```

FIGURE 2.3 Eye Movement Record Showing Where One Reader Fixated in Reading a Line of Text. Each fixation is indicated by a digit under the line of text, with the digits indicating the order of the fixations. The number under each digit indicates the number of msec. the eyes stayed at that location.

Several points should be made about this figure. First, it is apparent that while the average fixation for this subject was about 235 msec as she read the passage, there is considerable variability from fixation to fixation as to how long the eyes remain in each location, ranging from 24 to 339 msec on this one line. This variability is probably related to the nature of the mental processes required at each position in the text. Second, the lengths of the saccades vary considerably. Again, while the reader's average for this passage was about eight letter positions (where a letter occupies about $\frac{1}{3}$ degree of visual angle), the saccades actually range from two to 12 letter positions on this line alone. Thus there seem to be moment-to-moment differences in how far the mind needs to send the eyes. Third, even relatively good college-level readers fixate over half the words in a passage when they are reading carefully (Hogaboam and McConkie 1981). Finally, whereas the eye-movement record indicates with considerable precision (within less than one letter position in this record) where the eyes were centered during a fixation and how long the eyes remained at that location, it does not indicate what was seen during that fixation. For example, while fixation 9 was centered directly on the word *Saint*, we do not know whether that word was seen on that fixation, and if it was, whether it was the only word seen on that fixation. It is conceivable that the word was seen on two or more fixations. This takes us into questions about the nature of perception during reading.

PERCEPTION DURING READING

It has long been known that people see most precisely that which they look at directly. Looking directly at a small object causes the eyes to rotate to a position where the image lies on the part of the retina known as the *fovea*, the region that has the greatest density of visual receptors and where the smallest details can be seen. Thus, what is seen during a fixation depends on three things: (1) where the eyes are centered during that fixation, (2) what the visual region is within which stimuli of interest can be resolved or seen, and (3) what the person attends to during that fixation. Even though someone may direct his gaze toward a particular pattern, and its image may lie on the retina at a location where it could be seen, the person may fail to attend to it and thus fail to see it. In studying perception in reading, then, we must investigate where the mind chooses to send the eyes for fixations (eye-movement control), what region is typically seen during a fixation (perceptual span), and what is attended to within that region (attention to text). Finally, we must consider how the mind integrates the information it receives on successive fixations.

Most of the research to be described has been done with relatively skilled readers, not with children or disabled readers. Thus the extension of this research to studying the behavior of younger readers is needed before statements can be made about changes in the mental processes that occur as reading skill develops.

Eye-Movement Control

It seems clear that much of the time during reading the mind is sending the eyes to rather precise locations in the text. If the eyes do not go to the specific locations to which they were sent, changes are observed in the eye-movement pattern. This was established by studies in which people read text from a computer display (cathode-ray tube, or CRT) as their eye movements were monitored (O'Regan 1981).[1] These studies used an experimental technique in which the entire line of text was shifted two letter positions to right or left on the CRT during certain saccades while the eyes were moving. When the eyes stopped for the next fixation, they were directed toward a text position that was two letter positions away from where they normally would have been in the text under normal conditions. This is illustrated in Figure 2.4, which presents a line of text as it may have appeared during one fixation, with the eyes centered on the letter marked by *A*. The location to which the eyes were sent on the next fixation is marked by *B*.

```
North America were connected by land.   In 1725, he commissioned Bering,
                              A       B

  North America were connected by land.   In 1725, he commissioned Bering,
                                C
```

FIGURE 2.4   Nature of Change in Text Used in Text-Shift Study. The location of one fixation is indicated on the first line by *A* under the line. During the following saccade, the text was shifted two letter positions to the right, as shown in line 2. The following fixation, which normally would have been at the location marked *B* in line 1 was thus misplaced to the location marked *C* in line 2.

During the eye movement, however, the text was moved, as shown in line 2 of the figure. Now the *C* indicates the location in the text where the eyes were actually centered during the next fixation, two letter positions away from where they normally would have been centered. Shifting the text in this manner causes a misplacement of the eyes in the text. When this happens, readers are totally unaware that the text has been moved, but their eye movements are definitely affected. A large number of short saccades occur, taking the eyes closer to the location where they would have been had the text not been moved. Thus, displacing the location of a fixation just two letter positions seems to have an effect on the perceptual system that leads to changes in the eye-movement pattern, though this is not something of which the reader is conscious. There seems to be some good reason why the eyes are sent to the exact location at which they are aimed in a saccade.

   Since we know that the eyes are precisely controlled, we would like to know the rules the mind uses in determining where to send the eyes and how long to leave them at each location. We are far from having the full answer to this question, but a few facts have become apparent. First, there is a tendency for the eyes to be sent to the centers of words (O'Regan 1981, Rayner 1979, Zola 1981) and to avoid such less informative areas as blank areas (Abrams and Zuber 1972–73) and the region between sentences (Rayner 1975). There is evidence that the word "the" tends not to be fixated as frequently as other three-letter words (O'Regan 1979, Rayner 1977), though highly predictable longer words receive just as many fixations as less predictable words (Zola 1981). How long the eyes remain in a fixation is related to characteristics of the word on which it is centered, with more unusual words causing longer fixations (Rayner 1977)[2] and with more highly constrained words receiving shorter fixations (Zola 1981). Fixations also tend to be longer on words containing spelling errors (Zola 1981) and words in regions of the text regarded as being more important.[3]

   The important message here is that the eyes are responding sensitively to the mental processes of the reader. The language processes involved in comprehending the message of the text require information from the visual system. The visual system in turn must ensure that the eyes are appropriately centered to provide this information when it is needed. A full description of how the eyes are moved in reading will probably require a description of the language comprehension processes, of how they depend on visual information from the text, and on how the perceptual system controls the eyes in response to the need for this information. Observing an aberrant eye-movement pattern produced by a person with reading disabilities indicates that the flow of processing is not proceeding fluently, as it does in better readers, but does not at present indicate the nature of the problem. It is likely that a strange pattern is reflecting the fact that problems are being encountered in comprehending the text, to which the reader must respond by doing further analysis and reanalysis of the text, thus requiring an unusual pattern of encountering the visual stimulus. It certainly is not necessarily the case that there is any problem with the reader's perceptual abilities or ability to control the eyes, though among a few disabled readers this may be a problem (Elterman, Abel, Daroff, Dell'Osso, and Bornstein 1980; Pavlidis 1981; Pirozzolo and Rayner 1978; Zangwill and Blakemore (1972).

The Perceptual Span

When the eyes stop for a fixation, what region of text is seen? Does the reader see only a word or two, or is an entire phrase or clause seen? Or does this depend on the level of a person's reading skill? These are critical questions in understanding reading, and recent research is providing some relatively clear answers. Skilled readers utilize visual information no farther than four letter positions to the left of the letter at the center of vision (McConkie and Rayner 1976; Rayner, Well, and Pollatsek 1980), and they do not appear to identify letters more than about four to eight letter positions to the right.[4] Word-length information may be perceived slightly farther to the right than this (McConkie and Rayner 1975; Rayner, Inhoff, Morrison, Slowiaczek, and Bertera 1981).

These conclusions have come from studies in which the text, displayed on a CRT, is changed in specific ways as people read from it. For instance, if on certain fixations all letters outside this region are replaced by other letters, as shown in Figure 2.5, this does not produce any disruption in the normal reading process.[5]

```
Fixation                 Appearance of text

1  One  night,  a demanding  customer  returned  Crum's  fried  potatoes  to
                   *

2  One  night,  a demanding  customer  returned  Crum's  fried  potatoes  to
         *

3  One  night,  a demanding  customer  returned  Crum's  fried  potatoes  to
            *

4  Zen  ebyfh,  a tnamnding  customes  snhosent  Jsoa'r  isbnt  juhmhunr  hu
                   *

5  One  night,  a demanding  customer  returned  Crum's  fried  potatoes  to
                                         *

6  Zen  ebyfh,  a tnametbey  customer  retusent  Jsoa'r  isbnt  juhmhunr  hu
                                *

7  One  night,  a demanding  customer  returned  Crum's  fried  potatoes  ot
                                           *

8  Zen  ebyfh,  m tnametbey  vorhuans  snhosent  Jsoa'r  isbed  potatoes  tu
                                                                    *
```

FIGURE 2.5 Appearance of Text during Each of Several Fixations in Underwood and McConkie Study. On certain fixations, all letters more than a certain distance to the left and right of the fixated letter were replaced with other letters, as seen on the lines indicating the appearance of the text on fixations 4, 6, and 8. Fixation location is indicated on each line.

Another technique makes it possible to specify exactly the fixation on which a given letter was acquired. In this technique the experimenter identifies pairs of words that differ by a single letter, then writes a sentence into which either of the two words fits appropriately, as shown in Figure 2.6. As the person reads the sentence from the CRT, each time a saccade is made, the critical letter is changed. Thus, the critical word changes from one fixation to the next as the person reads. The reader is not aware that the word is changing, and there is no evidence from the eye-movement pattern that this manipulation has any effect on the reading. Thus it appears that words are usually identified only on a single fixation, unless there is a later regression to the word and it is examined again. After a person has read such a sentence, he indicates which of several words he saw in the sentence. Knowing which word the reader saw allows the experimenter to identify the fixation on which the critical letter was seen.[6] Initial studies using this technique indicate that readers are attending to the text in word units. That is, whether a letter lying two letter positions to the left of the fixation point is seen on that fixation depends on whether or not it is in the word fixated (Rayner, Well, and Pollatsek 1980).

```
Fixation                    Appearance of text

6   His friends became concerned over what they thought were sighs of despair.
                                                      *

7   His friends became concerned over what they thought were signs of despair.
                                                         *

8   His friends became concerned over what they thought were sighs of despair.
                                                            *

9   His friends became concerned over what they thought were signs of despair.
                                                                    *
```

FIGURE 2.6   Appearance of Text during Each of Several Fixations in McConkie Study. During each eye movement, one of the letters changed, causing one word to be different from one fixation to the next. Fixation location is indicated on each line.

The picture that is emerging from these studies is that the skilled reader, at least when reading carefully, encounters the text almost a word at a time. It is not true that phrases or larger units are perceived at once, as some have suggested. Nor does it seem to be true that increasing reading skill broadens the region seen during a fixation. When fifth graders reading at the third-grade level are compared to fifth graders reading at or above grade level and skilled college readers, no differences are observed in their perceptual spans, the region from which they acquire and use visual information during a fixation.[7] These studies have also demonstrated that during a fixation people do not identify all the words that are within the visual region where they could be seen. Once a word is read on one fixation, for instance, even though it may lie at a retinal region on the next fixation that would allow it to be read once again, it appears not to be seen. For instance, if a word is read during one fixation, the fact that the word is changed for the next fixation is not noticed by the reader. Thus, in reading as in other situations, we see only what we attend to, and learning to read must involve learning to attend to the words at the right time and in the right way. This theme leads to the next issue.

Attending to the Text

It has been proposed that an efficient reader develops the ability to use his knowledge of the language to reduce the degree to which he must do a visual analysis of the text. This proposal amounts to the suggestion that the reader can avoid attending to many aspects of the text that he can predict from his knowledge of the language (Goodman 1976). A recent careful test of this hypothesis has failed to provide evidence for it (Zola 1981).

In this study, nouns were identified that could be highly constrained by preceding them with some particular adjective. For instance, when given a passage about a football game indicating that a player sustained a "compound ———," nearly all readers predict that the next word will be *fracture*. However, if "compound" is replaced by "serious," few if any readers predict that the next word will be "fracture." Thus, by manipulating a single preceding adjective, the following word can be very highly constrained, or constrained to a much lower degree. The question investigated was whether constraining the word would change what information was used in perceiving it. In the high-constraint condition, common notions of reading would suggest that a skilled reader would hardly need to look at the word.

The study yielded three important results. First, it found that making the word highly predictable did not cause people to fixate on the word less often. Thus they did not skip over it when it was highly constrained, as might be expected. Second, when spelling errors were placed in the word (which should be missed if little visual analysis of the word was performed), they had just as much effect under the high-constraint as under the low-constraint condition. Apparently constraint was having little effect on the degree to which the word was perceived. Third, fixations on the word were slightly longer when it was less constrained. Apparently it took the mind slightly less time (in the neighborhood of .02 sec) to perceive and assimilate the meaning of the word when it was highly constrained by the preceding language. However, from the other findings, this did not seem to be because of any tendency to skip either the word or letters in it.

Present research provides little evidence that more highly skilled readers depend less on visual information from the text. There are recent suggestions that the truth may be just the opposite, that greater reading skill allows one to depend more heavily on the visual information in reading, in the process of identifying the words[8] (Stanovich, 1981). Of course, prior knowledge is very important for comprehending the message of the text.

A recent study has investigated when it is during the fixation that visual information is attended to.[9] For example, it may be that only the early part of the fixation is used for seeing the visual pattern and that the remainder of the fixation period is used for identifying the meaning of the word or words seen during that fixation (Rayner, Inhoff, Morrison, Slowiaczek, and Bertera 1981). This question is being studied by changing letters in the text partway through the fixation so that a particular word is different during the latter part of each fixation than it was during the earlier part. When the reader reports which word he saw in the text, this indicates whether a specific letter was seen in the early or late part of the fixation.

Results clearly indicate that readers see words at different times during fixations, not always just at the beginning. Sometimes they report seeing the word that was present early in the fixation, and sometimes they can only report the word that was present later in the fixation. Thus it seems that readers attend to different things at different times during the fixation and that attending to the letters, or the words of which they are part, can occur at various times. In fact, it seems possible that part of the process of developing reading skill is learning to attend to the text in an efficient manner from moment to moment. But this must be a topic for future research.

The point to be made from these findings is that although the eyes may be still during a fixation, the mind is actively attending to the text in some sequence not currently known. This attention to visual details takes place even when the words are so highly constrained that the reader could guess them if he were asked to do so.

Integrating Information across Fixations

In reading as in other visual tasks, the person makes several fixations per second, each providing a slightly different view of the stimulus. Although these fixations are discrete, the reader has no experience of discontinuity from one fixation to the next. In fact, there is a feeling of a smooth flow through the text; the reader is not only unable to report the number of fixations made but is even unaware that such a process is taking place. This raises the question of how information from successive fixations is being brought together and integrated into a single flowing experience.

A common proposal has been that the person builds in his mind a single unitary visual image of the page, with each successive fixation simply adding more visual detail to it. Thus the experience is said to be based on this mental image, which maintains continuity across fixations and assimilates detail from successive fixations, rather than on the individual fixations themselves. If this were the case, we would think of the reader as reading from this mental image rather than directly from the text. It should be noted that this view conflicts with the earlier reported evidence suggesting that letters are typically seen only within a narrow region.

In order to test the possibility that an integrated visual image exists, people were asked to read text printed in AlTeRnAtInG cAsE, where every other letter was capitalized (McConkie and Zola 1979). Skilled readers were able to do this with very little difficulty after practicing for a short time. Then, as they were reading from the CRT, during certain eye movements the shape of every letter was changed. Every upper-case letter was replaced by its corresponding lower-case form, and vice versa, as shown in Figure 2.7. We reasoned that if the images from the two successive fixations were being brought together into a single mental image, they would now not fit together properly, and this would cause consider-

```
a DaNiSh SeA cApTaIn, To ExPlOrE tHe NoRtH pAcIfIc ReGiOn.   BeRiNg AnD
                                   1
A dAnIsH sEa CaPtAiN, tO eXpLoRe ThE nOrTh PaCiFiC rEgIoN.   bErInG aNd
                                   2
```

FIGURE 2.7   Appearance of Text during Two Successive Fixations in McConkie and Zola (1979) Study. The text was printed in alternating case. During the saccade from fixation 1 (shown on line 1) to fixation 2 (shown on line 2), the case of each letter was changed.

able difficulty to the reader. However, in conducting the study, we found that not only did this manipulation not cause any difficulty but that readers were actually unaware that anything had changed, and their eye-movement records showed no indication of difficulty. Although the shape of every word and every letter was different on one fixation than it had been on the prior one, they had no awareness that any change had occurred. Thus it seems that there must not be any integrated visual image of the text in the reader's mind. Rather, any information carried over from one fixation to the next must be some encoding that does not distinguish between whether individual letters were in upper-case or lower-case form. Apparently during the short period of the fixation, the word and letter information gives rise to some higher level of code, and the visual images are not preserved. The nature of this code must now be explored, as well as how one develops the ability to carry out this encoding in a rapid and automatic fashion (LaBerge and Samuels 1974). This also must be a key in understanding the development of perception that occurs in learning to read fluently.

Summary

Recent research leads to a view of the reader as actively engaged in attending to the text in response to the needs of the comprehension processes. The task is to comprehend the message; the goal of the perceptual system is to provide the visual information needed to keep this mental activity moving smoothly. Apparently this comprehension process proceeds on a word-by-word basis with the individual words perceived and having their effect on the mind. This perception occurs as it is needed, not just at the beginnings of fixations, and the visual information available for it to occur is that which is currently available from the retina, not that which is aggregated across a series of prior fixations. How long the eyes remain in a location, and how far they move next, are determined by the needs of comprehension processes and the control of the eyes seems to be both precise and delicate. Small differences in the text, or changes in the stimulus pattern, have effects on the perceptual or higher processing activities, which are then reflected in small but detectable differences in the eye-movement pattern.

Using Eye Movements to Study Other Aspects of Reading

We turn now to a consideration of how eye-movement data might be used in studying other aspects of reading. If the mind directs the eyes in response to the needs of the higher mental processes, then it seems reasonable that the eye-movement pattern should reveal certain aspects of those processes. This has been an appealing notion to researchers investigating the cognitive processes, partly because there are so few other external indicators by which it is possible to observe what the mind is doing during cognition. It has also attracted the attention of those who wish to diagnose reading difficulties. Even a cursory comparison of the eye-movement data of a very good versus a relatively poor reader shows striking differences, with the poor reader typically showing shorter forward saccades, many more regressions, and a generally more erratic-looking pattern. While such data may be used to distinguish better from poorer readers,[10] there is at present no good evidence that it provides a better indicator of reading ability than do the commonly used standardized tests. The problem is that while the differences in eye-movement patterns are obvious, it is not clear what these differences mean, other than that some people read more fluently than others. There are certainly instances in which problems of the visual or oculomotor systems can be detected through eye-movement data (Pavlidis 1981, Zangwill and Blakemore 1972). But in most cases of reading difficulties, these are not the problems. The problem lies in the ability to properly identify words and interpret the meaning encoded in word sequences.

There was a period in the history of reading research when it was thought that poor eye-movement patterns might be causing reading problems; that is, if people were taught to move their eyes like good readers do, they would be good (or at least better) readers. Attempts to do such training were sometimes successful in improving the eye-movement pattern, but improved reading did not seem to result (Gibson & Levin 1975). The commonly accepted view today is that while erratic eye-movement patterns may be a symptom of reading difficulty, attempting to deal directly with this symptom is unlikely to have any beneficial effects for most people.

This is not to say that eye-movement patterns cannot be useful for diagnosis. Indeed, it still seems likely that they can be a rich source of information about characteristics of a person's reading. However, to realize this potential first requires an understanding of the relationship between the higher mental processes and the control of the eyes during reading. The research investigating perception during reading, described earlier, begins to lay the groundwork for this understanding. But, much research is needed before we will have a deep enough understanding of this relationship to be able to do detailed diagnosis of comprehension difficulties from individual eye-movement records.

Measuring the Time Needed to Process Different Aspects of Language

One major attempt has been made to use eye-movement data as a measure of the time required to carry out various mental processes involved in the act of reading (Just and Carpenter 1980). It was assumed that the time spent fixating a word corresponded exactly to the time required to process it. Thus an average processing time for each word was calculated by finding the average amount of time a group of readers spent fixating it as they read the passage. Each word was then classified by its length, frequency in the language, function in the language, and so on. Regression analysis techniques were then used to find how much processing time was required by words of different lengths, of different frequencies, and of different functions. Some of the assumptions made in producing the processing time measure are probably faulty (Hogaboam and McConkie 1981).[11] For instance, it is frequently the case that a word other than just the one fixated is being processed during a fixation,[12] characteristics of a word can be seen on fixations on other words,[13] and it is probably inappropriate to simply sum the time on a word resulting from multiple fixations on it.[14] While these problems make it likely that the actual processing times obtained in the study are not accurate, the general approach has considerable promise. Once there is a better understanding of exactly how to derive a measure of processing time for different segments of language from the eye-movement data of people reading it, it may be possible to determine the relative amount of difficulty different language constructions cause readers and to compare different groups of readers in what produces difficulties for them.

Diagnosing Sources of Reading Difficulty

The development of techniques to study the perceptual processes occurring during reading, as people are actually engaged in reading a passage, has been an important step in reading research. The extension of these techniques to the study of language processing, now being attempted, is an important further development. In these studies, eye-movement information has played a central role both as a basis for making experimental manipulations (changing the text in specific ways as the person is reading it) and as a source of data that indicate whether stimulus changes or language characteristics are creating difficulty for the reader. This raises the question whether these same techniques might be useful for diagnostic purposes.

The most noteworthy characteristic of these eye-movement-based research techniques is that they have been successful in providing rather precise information about specific aspects of perceptual and language processes in reading. That makes it likely that they will be very useful for diagnosis. Once a groundwork of research has been laid concerning the normal course of development in learning to read, it is likely that these techniques can be used to identify rather precisely whether a person is showing normal development in specific ways. Thus they will allow a reading specialist to test whether various aspects of a child's reading behavior are developing normally and to detect deviations from a normal pattern. This will take place by having the student read a few carefully prepared passages with specific language characteristics built into them, and perhaps with certain changes taking place in the text during the reading, while his eye movements are being monitored. After the reading, the eye-movement records will be analyzed, and precise conclusions can be made about specific aspects of that child's perceptual and language processing. For instance, the data may indicate whether or not more time was taken at the point in the text where an inference is required for comprehension, or from what visual region words are being identified, or whether an entire word is perceived during a single fixation or is assembled from subword units acquired on successive fixations, or how attention is deployed during fixations. Such information can be of use to the remedial teacher in suggesting courses of action that might help the student overcome obstacles that are holding back the development of reading skill. This might be done in much the same way that a good violin teacher can help a student overcome limitations by changing hand or bowing arm positions that are limiting progress. Knowing very specific facts about how the child is processing the text, either perceptually or for language characteristics, is likely to provide the basis for selecting exercises that will help him change his approach in the manner needed. The development of such diagnostic systems must await further research on reading development and disorders, but is likely to come into existence at some time in the not too distant future.

Perceptual Processes and Comprehension Instruction

Research on the perceptual aspects of reading, as reviewed here, has reached some conclusions important to reading comprehension instruction. It is the theme of other chapters in this book that to help a reader become more effective in comprehending, a teacher must spend time teaching how to comprehend. Some instructional activities, other than teaching to comprehend, that have been believed to contribute to comprehension have involved trying to change perceptual processes. Instructional time has sometimes been devoted to trying to broaden the perceptual spans of readers, with the rationale that seeing more text at once facilitates comprehension by allowing the reader to process in larger units. Others have attempted to teach children to identify words on the basis of fewer visual cues, believing that this would free up more mental capacity that could be used for higher-level comprehension activities. Recent perceptual research indicates that the assumptions on which these instructional activities are based are probably incorrect. Rather, skilled readers seem to be very efficient at attending to the text and using the visual information for their reading while encountering the text only a word or two at a time. However, the research does not yet indicate how teachers can help students achieve this ability, or even whether it should be taught directly. It may be that, for children with properly functioning perceptual abilities, this develops normally as they read to understand, just as they learned to attend to the subtleties of the sounds of their mother tongue and interpret speech smoothly and with little effort, in the absence of instruction on how to do it.

Thus knowledge about the perceptual aspect of reading may be helpful to classroom teachers mainly through freeing them from myths about the necessity of perceptual training, allowing them to focus their effort on helping children to seek meaning from printed language. In the future, as research progresses and eye-movement technology becomes more widely available, research in this area may play a more prominent role through providing diagnostic techniques for use with children who fail to show normal progress.

NOTES

1. G. W. McConkie, D. Zola and G. S. Wolverton. *How precise is eye guidance?* Paper presented at the annual meeting of the American Educational Research Association, Boston, April 1980.

2. R. Kliegl, R. K. Olson, and B. J. Davidson. *Eye movements in reading: Separation of cognitive and perceptual factors.* Unpublished manuscript, University of Colorado, 1981.

3. W. L. Shebilske and D. F. Fisher. *Eye movements reveal components of flexible reading strategies.* Unpublished manuscript, University of Virginia, 1981.

4. N. R. Underwood and G. W. McConkie. *The effect of encountering errors at different retinal locations during reading.* Unpublished manuscript, University of Illinois, 1981.

5. Ibid.

6. G. W. McConkie. *Where do we read?* Paper presented at the annual meeting of the Psychonomic Society, San Antonio, Tex., November 1978.

7. N. R. Underwood. *The span of letter recognition of good and poor readers.* Urbana: University of Illinois, Center for the Study of Reading, 1982.

8. J. R. Frederiksen. *Word recognition in the presence of semantically constraining context.* Paper presented at the annual meeting of the Psychonomic Society, San Antonio, Tex., November 1978.

9. H. E. Blanchard, G. W. McConkie, D. Zola and G. S. Wolverton. *The timing of utilization of visual information during a fixation in reading.* Paper presented at the annual meeting of the Midwestern Psychological Association, Minneapolis, Minn., May 1982.

10. S. E. Taylor. *The dynamic activity of reading: A model of the process.* Research Information Bulletin No. 9. New York: Educational Developmental Laboratories, 1971.

11. R. Kliegl, R. K. Olson, and B. J. Davidson. *Perceptual and psycholinguistic factors in reading: Comment on Just and Carpenter's eye-fixation theory.* Unpublished manuscript, University of Colorado, 1981.

12. T. W. Hogaboam. *The relationship of word identification and eye movements during normal reading.* Paper presented at the 20th annual meeting of the Psychonomic Society, Phoenix, Ariz, November 1979.

13. Underwood and McConkie, note 4. See also Kliegl et al., note 2.

14. Kliegl et al., note 2.

References

Abrams, S. G., & Zuber, B. L. Some temporal characteristics of information processing during reading. *Reading Research Quarterly*, 8, 1972–73, 42–51.

Alpern, M. Effector mechanisms in vision. In J. W. Kling & L. A. Riggs (Eds.), *Woodworth & Schlosberg's experimental psychology, 3rd edition.* New York: Holt, Rinehart & Winston, 1971. Pp. 369–394.

Elterman, R. D., Abel, L. A., Daroff, R. B., Dell'Osso, L. F., & Bornstein, J. L. Eye movement patterns in dyslexic children. *Journal of Learning Disabilities*, 13, 1980, 16–21.

Gibson, E. J., & Levin, H. *The psychology of reading.* Cambridge, Mass.: MIT Press, 1975.

Goodman, K. S. Behind the eye: What happens in reading. In H. Singer & R. B. Ruddell (Eds.), *Theoretical models and processes of reading.* Newark, Del.: International Reading Association, 1976.

Hogaboam, T. W., & McConkie, G. W. *The rocky road from eye fixations to comprehension.* Tech. Rep. No. 207. Urbana: University of Illinois, Center for the Study of Reading, May 1981.

Huey, E. H. *The psychology and pedagogy of reading.* New York: Macmillan, 1908.

Just, M. A., & Carpenter, P. A. A theory of reading: From eye fixations to comprehension. *Psychological Review*, 1980, 87, 329–354.

LaBerge, D., & Samuels, S. J. Toward a theory of automatic information processing in reading. *Cognitive Psychology*, 1981, 6, 299–314.

McConkie, G. W., & Rayner, K. The span of the effective stimulus during a fixation in reading. *Perception and Psychophysics*, 1975, 17, 578–586.

McConkie, G. W., & Rayner, K. Asymmetry of the perceptual span in reading. *Bulletin of the Psychonomic Society*, 1976, 8, 365–368.

McConkie, G. W., & Zola, D. Is visual information integrated across successive fixations in reading? *Perception and Psychophysics*, 1979, 25, 221–224.

McConkie, G. W. Eye movements and perception during reading. In K. Rayner (Eds.), *Eye movements in reading: Perceptual and language processes.* New York: Academic Press, in press.

O'Regan, K. Saccade size control in reading: Evidence for the linguistic control hypothesis. *Perception and Psychophysics*, 1979, 25, 501–509.

O'Regan, K. The "convenient viewing position" hypothesis. In D. F. Fisher,

R. A. Monty, & J. W. Senders (Eds.), *Eye movements*: Cognition and visual perception. Hillsdale, N.J.: Erlbaum, 1981.

Pavlidis, G. T. Sequencing, eye movements and the early objective diagnosis of dyslexia. In G. T. Pavlidis & T. R. Miles (Eds.), *Dyslexia research and its applications to education.* New York: Wiley, 1981.

Pirozzolo, F. J., & Rayner, K. Disorders of oculomotor scanning and graphic orientation in Developmental Gerstmann Syndrome. *Brain and Language*, 1978, *5*, 119–126.

Rayner, K. The perceptual span and peripheral cues in reading. *Cognitive Psychology*, 1975, *7*, 65–81.

Rayner, K. Visual attention in reading: Eye movements reflect cognitive processing. *Memory & Cognition*, 1977, *4*, 443–448.

Rayner, K. Eye guidance in reading: Fixation locations within words. *Perception*, 1979, *8*, 21–30.

Rayner, K., Inhoff, A. W., Morrison, R. E., Slowiaczek, M. L., & Bertera, J. H. Masking of foveal and parafoveal vision during eye fixations in reading. *Journal of Experimental Psychology*: Human Perception and Performance, 1981, *7*, 167–179.

Rayner, K., Well, A. D., & Pollatsek, A. Asymmetry of the effective visual field in reading. *Perception and Psychophysics*, 1980, *27*, 537–544.

Stanovich, K. E., Attentional and automatic context effects in reading. In A. M. Lesgold, & C. A. Perfetti (Eds.), *Interactive processes in reading.* Hillsdale, N. J.: Erlbaum, 1981. Pp. 241–268.

Young, L. R., & Sheena, D. Survey of eye movement recording techniques. *Behavior Research Methods & Instrumentation*, 1975, *7*, 397–429.

Zangwill, O L., & Blakemore, C. Dyslexia: Reversal of eye movements during reading. *Neuropsychologia*, 1972, *10*, 371–373.

Zola, D. *The effect of redundancy on the perception of words in reading.* Tech. Rep. No. 216. Urbana: University of Illinois, Center for the Study of Reading, September 1981.

3

A Schema-Theoretic View of the Reading Process as a Basis for Comprehension Instruction

Jana M. Mason
and
The Staff of the Center for the Study of Reading,
University of Illinois

At the heart of reading is the process of comprehension. Yet, of all aspects of reading, comprehension has been the least adequately explained and, as a result, the most difficult to teach.

This situation exists not because of a lack of attention. Since the turn of the century, the reading comprehension process has been analyzed and discussed. Early writers believed that comprehension was allied closely to thinking. To wit:

Huey (1908): Reading is "thought-getting and thought manipulation."
Thorndike (1917): "Reading is reasoning."
Gray (1925): "Reading is a form of clear vigorous thinking."
Dewey (1938): Comprehension is "an effort after meaning."

Despite the assumption that reading comprehension is tied to thinking, inspection of guidelines to practitioners about what and how to teach reading reveals a curious neglect of this relationship. Instead of stressing thoughtful analysis of written information, teachers were presented with long lists of other instructional concerns and aims. See, for example, Part 1 of the *Twenty-Fourth NSSE Yearbook* (1925), the writings of W. S. Gray, the country's most eminent reading educator, or a summary of reading practices by Zirbes (1928).

Gray's position was still ambiguous in the 1930s. In 1937 he served as a spokesperson for a committee of reading educators in the *Thirty-Sixth NSSE Yearbook*. At this time, he firmly rejected the notion that reading is restricted to "the process of recognizing printed or written symbols" or that it is simply extended to "the recognition of the important elements of meaning in their essential relations, including accuracy and thoroughness in comprehension." Instead, he asserted that "the reader not only recognizes the essential facts or ideas presented, but also reflects on their significance, evaluates them critically, discovers relationships between them, and clarifies his understanding of the ideas apprehended" (pp. 25–26).

Unfortunately, this clear statement featuring the notion that reading is thinking suffers in his later chapter on instruction. There he breaks instructional suggestions into the following "aims":

1. To arouse keen interest in learning to read.
2. To promote increased efficiency in both silent and oral reading.
3. To extend and enrich experiences and to satisfy interests and needs.
4. To cultivate strong motives for and permanent interest in reading.
5. To elevate tastes in reading and to promote discrimination in selecting books, magazines, and newspapers to read.
6. To acquaint pupils with the sources and values of different kinds of reading material and to develop ability to use them intelligently and critically. (p. 66)

Then he lists "fundamental attitudes, habits and skills [that] are common to practically all reading situations":

1. "A thoughtful reading attitude and the participation of the sequence of ideas in sentences and paragraphs.
2. Accuracy in recognizing words and groups of words . . .
3. The recognition and interpretation of typographical devices . . .
4. Conformity to hygienic requirements for reading. . . ." (p. 67)

Finally, and standing at the center of his instructional guidelines, is a detailed description of "stages of development in reading":

1. "The stage at which readiness for reading is attained . . .
2. The initial stage in learning to read . . .
3. The stage of rapid progress in fundamental attitudes and habits . . .
4. The stage at which experience is extended rapidly and increased power, efficiency, and excellence in reading are acquired . . .
5. The stage at which reading interests, habits and tastes are refined. . . ." (p. 76–77)

Problems are apparent in his attempts to extend reflective thinking to reading instruction. Reasoning is never described as an aim of reading. While listings of attitudes and habits include the phrase "thoughtful reading," this is not elaborated on except as the simple act of predicting sequences of information. Finally, only one of the "specific aims" listed with a description of each stage of development (pp. 93, 101, 110, 122) provides the teacher with particular advice about relating thinking to reading. He labels this the development of study habits, elaborating (pp. 117–18) with a list of thirty-one abilities and twelve types of knowledge. These range from the mundane ("ability to use an alphabetical arrangement") to the thought-provoking ("willingness to suspend judgment until sufficient evidence is at hand"). Even this listing does not help the teacher by distinguishing between those abilities that are critical for reflective thinking and those that merely represent good work habits. Moreover, the guidelines are descriptions of accomplishments or goals rather than descriptions of information about how to instruct students. Without advice about procedures, materials, ordering of skills, or differences in difficulty, teachers have inadequate instructional guidelines.

Despite the pronouncement by Gray and others that reading is a form of thinking, comprehension was not reflected in early descriptions about reading instruction. One reason for this was that such guidelines dealt with the broader social, psychological, and developmental aspects, diverting practitioners from the central aim of reading. Another was that their conceptualization of instruction assumed that skills and knowledge could be derived from listings of reading purpose and explanations of reading development. As a result, practitioners more often than not were misled into isolating and practicing skill-based reading activities instead of attending to their students' background knowledge and providing opportunities for expanding, understanding, interpreting, and evaluating written information.

A similar attitude prevailed thirty years later. In the *Sixty-Seventh NSSE Yearbook* (1968), Clymer outlined the then current conceptions of reading instruction. He noted that reading was still to be considered a thinking process and that although "models" of the reading process had been developed, lists of skills and abilities continued to dominate conceptualizations about comprehension. For example, Spache (in Clymer 1968) transformed two dimensions of Guilford's three-dimensional model of the intellect to obtain a list of 30 reading skills and behaviors. Similarly, Barrett (in Clymer 1968) modified Bloom's Taxonomy of Educational Objectives to construct a set of 33 "cognitive and affective dimensions of reading comprehension"; these were subsumed under the skill categories literal comprehension, reorganization, inferential comprehension, evaluation, and appreciation. Robinson (in Clymer 1968) modified a late-appearing model by Gray, classifying the skill dimensions of reading as word perception, comprehension, reaction to what is read, assimilation of new and old ideas, and speed or rate of reading.

Clymer's presentation of work in that era does not show a great change in conceptualization about reading comprehension instruction except that sets of skills were interrelated to a greater extent than before. Most descriptions, even though they were called "models," continued to be lists of skills or abilities thought necessary for skillful reading. It is apparent that while educators spoke of the reading process, they continued to itemize its assumed components, thereby ignoring its relationship to the classroom environment, to students' background for thinking and learning, and to the comprehension process.

In recent years, however, there has begun to emerge a new perspective of reading that centers on the process so that thoughtful acts of the reader are paramount. This view, called "schema-theoretic," is influencing current conceptions of comprehension instruction. It has two key components: (1) that skilled readers draw simultaneously on several different sources of knowledge as they peruse text sources ranging from letter information and words to high-level concepts and from interpreting facts to constructing strategies and planning how to read; and (2) that skilled readers construct progressively refined hypotheses about a text in order to understand, learn, or remember it. The first component pinpoints the interactive nature of reading, while the second describes the meaningfulness of the reading process and the necessary active involvement by the reader.

INTERACTION BETWEEN KNOWLEDGE SOURCES

With an interactive view of the reading process (Adams and Collins 1979, Rumelhart 1977), it is assumed that the reader collects evidence as he or she reads along about what the text might mean. This evidence comes both from information in the text and from the hypotheses in the reader's mind (Bobrow and Norman 1975). Text information, in coordination with the reader's hypotheses, is processed at many different levels of analysis: lexical, syntactic, schematic, planning, and interpretive. While all these levels of processing must be available to the reader at all times to form possible explanations about the contents of the text, particular explanations will gain credence as they tend to facilitate or inhibit evidence at other levels of analysis (Collins and Loftus 1975). A description of the three higher levels follows to help clarify this theoretical position.

Schematic Knowledge

People have a vast amount of conceptual knowledge about the world that they remember and think about in order to understand any text. This knowledge is assumed to be stored in structured networks described as *schemata* (Adams and Collins 1979, Anderson 1977, Rumelhart and Ortony 1977), or *frames* (Charniak 1978, Minsky 1975) or *scripts* (Schank and Abelson 1977). We will use *schema* (singular) or *schemata* (plural) here. Schemata, which are structured into meaning-oriented clusters, compete with each other in both a top-down (e.g., gist-type analysis first) and bottom-up (e.g., word analysis first) process to account for a coherent view of the text.

A brief text from Collins, Brown, and Larkin (1980) illustrates this process. In the study from which these and later interpretations are drawn, readers were shown the following text sentence by sentence and asked to report their interpretation.

> He plunked down $5 at the window. She tried to give him $2.50, but he refused to take it. So when they got inside she bought him a large bag of popcorn.

When shown only the first sentence, most adults report that they invoke a schema for a racetrack, a movie, or a bank. Bottom-up and top-down processing lead to the invocation of such schemata; the act of "plunking down $5" suggests the idea of "giving" or "buying," and the word "window" activates all different kinds of windows, such as those in a house, a car, a bank, or a ticket office. This is bottom-up processing. At the same time, different schemata are competing to fill their conditions for invocation. People do not plunk down $5 at a house or car window; however, someone might deposit $5 at a bank window, or at a movie window someone might pay $5 for tickets, or at a racetrack window someone might make a $5 bet. This is top-down processing. These competing schemata act to inhibit other schemata, and they tend to interact with the interpretation of other elements in the text to form several tentative hypotheses, which are resolved on reading the remaining two sentences.

Planning Knowledge

Much of the world knowledge needed to understand texts (nonfiction as well as fiction) invokes people's plans, goals and social interactions (Bruce and Newman 1978*a*,*b*; Wilensky 1978). Knowledge about such high-level goals interacts with knowledge about actions. To illustrate, we can use an example from a study by Adams and Collins (1979) about constructing an interpretation for one of Aesop's fables.

Stone Soup

> A poor man came to a large house during a storm to beg for food. He was sent away with angry words, but he went back and asked, "May I at least dry my clothes by the fire, because I am wet from the rain?" The maid thought this would not cost anything, so she let him come in.
>
> Inside he told the cook that if she would give him a pan, and let him fill it with water, he would make some stone soup. This was a new dish to the cook, so she agreed to let him make it. The man then got a stone from the road and put it in the pan. The cook gave him some salt, peas, mint, and all the scraps of meat that she could spare to throw in. Thus the poor man made a delicious stone soup and the cook said, "Well done! You have made a wonderful soup out of practically nothing."

Various actions occur in the fable: The man begs for food, the maid sends him away, he asks to dry himself by the fire. These actions operate in a bottom-up way to activate in the reader different high-level goals. For example, begging for food could activate either that the man is hungry or his family is starving. The maid sending him away could be because she dislikes him or because she wants to preserve her master's goods. The man's asking to dry himself by the fire could be because he wants to be comfortable or he wants to get inside. During the reading these high-level goals are considered as ways to account for the events that occur in the fable. Eventually, the reader decides that the maid is only protecting her master's goods, because she later lets the man in, and that the man asks to dry himself by the fire in order to get inside, because he later makes stone soup. The goals finally chosen then are the ones that fit all the actions best.

Interpretive Knowledge

The skilled reader brings to bear high-level knowledge about the structure and intent of different genres in reading. Work on story grammars (Mandler and Johnson 1977 Rumelhart 1975) is an attempt to characterize people's general knowledge about the structure of stories. But skilled readers invoke much more specific knowledge as they read different kinds of texts.

The Stone Soup fable can be used again to illustrate how some of the knowledge about text genre can influence comprehension. If the reader knows about fables, Stone Soup will be much easier to interpret. This is because fables are constructed according to a regular formula. A fable is a short story. Its characters, which are often animals, are stereotypes (e.g., maids are subservient, rabbits are frivolous, foxes are self-serving and cunning). Fables are generally based on the theme that life requires that we be flexible: Individuals who are too nearsighted are liable to suffer ill consequences—their goals will be thwarted or they will be outsmarted; individuals who are adaptive and resourceful will be successful even in the face of adversity. Any particular fable is intended to convey a more specific lesson or moral within this theme. The moral is often summarized by the last line of the fable. All this knowledge is organized in a general fable schema.

For purposes of interpreting the Stone Soup story, the reader's first task is that of recognizing that it is a fable. If this information is not explicitly given, it may be signaled in bottom-up fashion from the structure of the story or from the fact that it was authored by Aesop. Once the fable schema has been suggested, top-down processes will be initiated in the effort to satisfy the reader's expectations about how a fable is written. Most important, the fable schema must (1) find either a flexible successful character or a rigid, foiled character; and (2) interpret the events leading to this character's success or failure in terms of some general lesson of conduct. In Stone Soup, the main character is flexible, and so the moral will be a positive suggestion of how to deal with the world rather than a negative lesson of how not to. To determine the moral, we can summarize the event structure as the following: If one method fails, you can often reach your goal by a more circuitous method that is clever but not immoral. There are several underlying aspects to this moral: (1) initial failure; (2) persistence or repeated trying when you fail; (3) changing methods when you fail; (4) devising multistep plans; (5) using clever means; (6) not using immoral means, such as stealing or threatening; and (7) succeeding. The avoidance of immorality can only be realized from the reader's knowledge of alternative methods, which were not used in Stone Soup. This ability to evaluate another person's plan derives from the reader's own ability to plan.

Furthermore, if readers know that the points of fables are often proverbs, they might be able to select the correct proverb for Stone Soup. This is done by matching the various aspects of the moral against the parallel aspects of any candidate maxims. For example, "If at first you don't succeed, try, try again" matches the two aspects of initial failure and repeated trying. "Where there's a will, there's a way" matches four aspects fairly well: persistence, changing methods, using a circuitous multistep plan, and ultimate success. Neither of these proverbs matches perfectly or includes the cleverness aspect, but that is why we have fables.

Summary

The interactions at different knowledge levels discussed in this section illustrate how reading comprehension depends as much on the reader's previously acquired knowledge as on the information provided by the text. Moreover, comprehension depends on readers' ability to interrelate appropriately their knowledge and the textual information both within and between levels of analysis. The power of the interactive view of reading lies in the capacity to support these analyses through a single, stratified knowledge structure and a few basic processing mechanisms.

PROCESSING TEXT INFORMATION

A schema-theoretic view of the reading process involves two components. The first, construction of hypotheses through an interaction between reader and text, has been described. The second component, a progressive refinement of hypotheses in order to comprehend, interpret, or evaluate text information, is discussed next. Four ways to refine hypotheses are presented: modifying hypotheses, evaluating a text model, comprehension monitoring, and creating author-reader relationships. These are intended to serve as examples of the processes that occur; they do not represent all possible processing strategies and procedures.

Modifying Hypotheses

The notion of construction of competing hypotheses as one reads demands an explanation of how an initial interpretation of a text is rejected, modified, or accepted. Collins, Brown, and Larkin (1980) proposed a set of five strategies, similar to those found in human problem solving (Fikes 1970, Newell and Simon 1972, Winston 1977). Each of the strategies is briefly described in reference to reinterpreting the story about plunking down $5 at the window.

1. *Rebinding.* If the bank-teller schema were invoked after reading the first sentence in the window text, in which the $5 is first interpreted as a deposit and then is changed to buying a lottery ticket, rebinding has occurred.

2. *Questioning a direct or indirect conflict.* This is like rebinding except that when the notion of change does not fit, as upon presentation of the second sentence, the reader may question the interpretation that the man was buying a lottery ticket.

3. *Questioning a default interpretation.* In the window text, this occurs if the reader questions whether the "she" offering the $2.50 is the woman behind the window, or whether this is in fact a bank.

4. *Shift of focus.* This could happen upon presentation of the third sentence in the window text if a reader failed to get meaning by thinking of questions about intentions (e.g., "Why did she buy popcorn?") and instead jumped to trying to answer questions about the locale (e.g., "Where did this take place?").

5. *Case analysis and most likely case assignment.* Case analysis might occur if the reader considered several possible things the $5 was for (e.g., to get change, to buy a lottery ticket, to make a deposit) and tested the implications of each. Most likely case assignment occurs if one chooses an alternative (e.g., to get change) and works from there.

Evaluating a Model of the Text

Evaluating a text model is another way to increase comprehension. Collins, Brown, and Larkin (1980) found that subjects evaluated their interpretations while trying to make sense of the texts. There were at least four different tests that subjects applied in evaluating the plausibility of the interpretations they constructed. The evidence from all these tests appeared to be weighed together in evaluating the plausibility of an interpretation.

1. *The plausibility of the assumptions and consequences of the model.* When a default assumption or a consequence of the interpretation seems implausible, then subjects tend to reject the interpretation. For example, one subject rejected the idea that "she" referred to the woman behind the window because the idea that "she" would go inside with the man was implausible.

2. *The completeness of the model.* Interpretations are evaluated in terms of how well the assumptions and consequences of the model answer all the different questions that arise. For example, the "date" interpretation answers questions

such as why the woman offered the $2.50 (i.e., she did not want to feel obligated to the man) and why the man refused (i.e., he had a conventional notion of the man paying), whereas other interpretations leave these questions unanswered.

3. *The interconnectedness of the model.* The assumptions or consequences of an interpretation are weighed with respect to how they fit together with other aspects of the model. For example, if "she" had bought the man a beer, instead of popcorn, this would have fit less well into the notion of a date at a movie. But popcorn is a staple at movie theatres; $2.50 is a reasonable price for each ticket; one "goes inside" at a movie. In short, everything hangs together.

4. *The match of the model to the text.* Occasionally subjects seem to weigh the model in terms of how well its assumptions or consequences match certain surface aspects of the text. For example, one subject said he choose the racetrack schema rather than the movie schema because it is a window at the racetrack (i.e., a betting window) whereas it is a box office at the movie.

Comprehension Monitoring

A third ability for evaluating ongoing comprehension requires that readers be able to monitor their understanding of a text as they read. The notion of comprehension monitoring comes out of the recent research on metacognition (e.g., Brown 1978; Flavell, in press; Markman 1979).

Comprehension monitoring skills range from handling local world-level failures to global text-level failures. That is, they include failures to understand (1) particular words, (2) particular sentences, (3) relations between sentences, and (4) how the text fits together as a whole.

Collins and Smith (1981) outline a number of actions readers can take if they fail to understand a word or passage. Six possible remedies are listed below, roughly in the order of increasing disruptiveness to the flow of reading.

1. *Ignore and read on.* If the word or passage is not critical to understanding, then the most effective action is to ignore it. For example, failures within descriptions and details usually can safely be ignored.

2. *Suspend judgment.* This is a wait-and-see strategy that should be applied when the reader thinks the failure will be clarified later. For example, new words or general principles are often explained in subsequent text. The structure of the text should tell the reader when an idea is likely to be clarified later.

3. *Form a tentative hypothesis.* Here the reader tries to figure out from context what a word, sentence, or passage means. The hypothesis may be a general hypothesis or a specific hypothesis. It acts as a *pending question* (Collins, Brown, Morgan, and Brewer 1977) that the reader tests as he or she continues reading.

4. *Reread the current sentence.* If the reader cannot form a tentative hypothesis, then it often helps to reread the current sentence or sentences, looking for a revised interpretation that would clarify the problem.

5. *Reread the previous context.* Jumping back to the previous context is even more disruptive to the flow of reading. But it may be necessary if there is a contradiction with some earlier piece of the text or the reader is overloaded with too many pending questions.

6. *Go to an expert source.* The most disruptive action the reader can take is to go to an outside source, such as a teacher, parent, dictionary, or other book. But this is sometimes required, for example, when a word is repeatedly used and

the reader cannot figure out what it means, or when a whole section of text does not make sense.

Creating Author-Reader Relationships

A final example of comprehension processing is based on the tenet that meaning does not reside in the text, but is created by a reader from clues provided by the author (see Adams and Bruce, in press; Bruce, in press). A reader processes new information only as it relates to information acquired previously (Anderson and Pichert 1978; Kintsch and Greene 1978; Rumelhart and Ortony 1977; Reder 1979; Steffensen, Jogdeo, and Anderson 1978). This means that the inferences we draw in reading, the portions of the text we remember, the way we summarize—indeed, our very perceptions of a text—are all functions of what we already know about texts. An important aspect is our knowledge about how stories work. The examples presented here are excerpted from Bruce (1980 in press), Bruce and Newman (1978), Newman (1980), and Steinberg and Bruce (1980).

1. *Conflict.* Conflict is a major source of complexity for stories. Understanding it implies understanding characters' goals, how their goals interrelate, and how plans to achieve those goals mesh or clash. Characters' goals and actions are not just physical movements but social actions (Bruce 1975, 1980) designed to have effects on other characters. Most goals and actions are conditioned by respective beliefs about the world, about one another, and about others' beliefs. The act of interpretation then depends upon the reader's beliefs about the characters' beliefs.

The fact that readers must infer beliefs or, in other words, come to understand a character's model of the world in order to understand social interaction among characters, is one reason why conflict often induces greater involvement for the reader with characters. This involvement with the characters in turn makes the conflicts more important to the reader and thus the story itself becomes more engaging.

2. *Inside view.* The need to understand characters' beliefs, which is vital to conflict development, has the side effect of complicating the reader's task. Through a variety of devices, including inference from a character's utterances or other actions, inferences from what other characters say or do, and direct or indirect quotation of thoughts, the reader obtains an inside view about a character's values and feelings.

The extent to which an author lets us see inside a character in this way greatly affects how much we are able to empathize with the character. It also adds to the processing load for reading because it permits, and then requires, the reader to keep track of multiple, often conflicting, views of the world.

3. *Point of view.* The amount of inside view is but one example of a more general phenomenon of stories: The reader is not permitted to see everything that pertains to the events of the story. Instead, he or she sees the story world as it might be perceived from a particular perspective.

Under point of view, a distinction can be made between a *focus character* and a *point of view character*. Essentially, the former is one the reader watches, the latter is one watched through. In most children's stories, one character plays both these roles, that is, the reader learns what happens to the "main character" as he or she would see it. In some stories, these two roles are separated so that the focus characters are observed through another's eyes, though there are also stories in which the point of view is not allied with that of any character.

For focus characters and point of view characters (where there is one), two dimensions seem to be of paramount importance: consistency and group size. *Consistency* relates to the fact that a character in focus (or a point of view character) may not remain so. Three levels of consistency are useful for story coding: *consistent*, if there is virtually no change throughout the story; *inconsistent*, if there are small shifts; and *shifting*, if there are so many changes that it becomes difficult to identify the appropriate character. *Group size* most usefully breaks down into *single* (as in a story in which we see only what one character would see), *double* (in which the point of view alternates between two characters), and *group* (in which an identifiable group provides the pretext for our perspective in the story).

An aspect of traditional point of view classifications is covered by *rhetorical form*, the relationship between the author and the reader. Briefly there are five forms to be considered: (1) *diary*, in which the author is the reader; (2) *argument*, in which the author and the reader are both explicitly engaged in the discourse (applies to many essays, letters, and author commentary on a text); (3) *immersion*, in which the reader is engaged (as in the rare second person form of narration as well as in instructions); (4) *participant account*, in which the author relates events he or she was engaged in; and (5) *observer account*, in which neither author nor reader are involved. This categorization allows a distinction to be made between the surface point of view form (e.g., person) and the underlying author-reader-discourse relationship. For example, one device used in many children's stories is narration by one of the characters.

Once a distinction is made between formal features, such as person and rhetorical forms, it becomes apparent that a story may be narrated at more than one level. For example, if a character narrates the story, then there must be an author (the *implied author*) who has created the narrator. Multiple levels of rhetorical structure add variety and increase the range of possibilities for text interpretation.

CONCLUSION

At the core of schema-theoretic approaches to reading is the constructivist assumption that comprehension consists in representing or organizing information in terms of one's previously acquired knowledge. This assumption is held to be equally applicable at all levels of analysis, from elementary sensory features to complex social interactions. However, the perceiver's knowledge is assumed to be organized in such a way that stimulus information is automatically processed upwards through increasingly comprehensive levels of interpretation (bottom-up processing) and extended downward to satisfy partially activated higher-order knowledge complexes (top-down processing).

Through the interactions between top-down and bottom-up processes, the flow of information through the system is constrained. Nevertheless, given a knowledge base as rich as the one in a human mind, these interactive processes are not in themselves enough to ensure apt comprehension. Because of this, schema-theoretic models have adapted from theories of human information processing the notion that a central processor is responsible for refining hypotheses and interpreting goals. In addition, the way in which hypotheses generated by the interaction of top-down and bottom-up processes are modified and refined determines whether and how the text will be understood.

Problems that plagued earlier models of reading are easily reconciled within a schema-theoretic approach. It makes sense, for example, that difficulties at the level of letter and word recognition will be prevalent among young readers. The knowledge and processes required at this level are unique to the printed medium and are uniquely foreign to the beginner. As a result, difficulties at the level of letter and word recognition should be a pervasive impediment to fluent reading because, in the reading situation, letters and words are the basic data. If, at this level, the upward flow of information is obstructed or requires much active attention, comprehension must suffer. Also, it makes sense that skilled readers should rely on both bottom-up and top-down processes. It is to be expected that more complex modes of processing will operate, with interpretations appearing through judgment and evaluation of competing hypotheses about text meaning and that tryouts and experiences with different texts will lead to the creation of a rich set of procedures and strategies for understanding and remembering written information.

The most significant aspect of this new conception of the reading process lies with its impact on comprehension instruction. The description of comprehension described here is much more representative of the complex interaction between reader and text than the static list of skills and abilities which typically represented descriptions of comprehension in the past. This book, with its focus on comprehension instruction, is influenced throughout by the principles of this new view of the reading process.

REFERENCES

Adams, M. J., & Collins, A. A schema-theoretic view of reading. In R. Freedle (Ed.), *New directions in discourse processing*. Norwood, N.J.: Ablex, 1979.

Anderson, R. C. The notion of schemata and the educational enterprise. In R. C. Anderson, R. J. Spiro, & W. E. Montague (Eds.), *Schooling and the acquisition of knowledge*. Hillsdale, N.J.: Erlbaum, 1977.

Anderson, R. C., & Pichert, J. W. Recall of previously unrecallable information following a shift in perspective. *Journal of Verbal Learning and Verbal Behavior*, 1978, *17*, 1–12.

Bobrow, D. G., & Norman, D. A. Some principles of memory schemata. In D. G. Bobrow & A. Collins (Eds.), *Representation and understanding: Studies in cognitive science*. New York: Academic Press, 1975.

Brown, A. L. Knowing when, where, and how to remember: A problem of meta-cognition. In R. Glaser (Ed.), *Advances in instructional psychology*. Hillsdale, N.J.: Erlbaum, 1978.

Bruce, B. C. *Belief systems and language understanding*. BBN Report No. 2973. Cambridge, Mass.: Bolt Beranek and Newman, 1975.

Bruce, B. Plans and social actions. In R. J. Spiro, B. C. Bruce, & W. F. Brewer (Eds.), *Theoretical issues in reading comprehension*. Hillsdale, N.J.: Erlbaum, 1980.

Bruce, B. C. A social interaction model of reading. *Discourse Processes*, in press.

Bruce, B. C., & Newman, D. Interacting plans. *Cognitive Science*, 1978, *2*, 195–233.

Bruce, B. C., & Newman, D. *Interacting plans*. Tech. Rep. No. 88. Urbana: University of Illinois, Center for the Study of Reading, June 1978. ERIC Document Reproduction Service No. ED 157 038.

Charniak, E. On the use of framed knowledge in language comprehension. *Artificial Intelligence*, 1978, *11*, 225–265.

Clymer, T. What is "reading"?: Some current concepts. *The Sixty-seventh Yearbook of the National Society for the Study of Education: Part II*. Chicago: University of Chicago Press, 1968.

Collins, A., Brown, A. L., Morgan, J. L., & Brewer, W. F. *The analysis of reading tasks and texts*. Tech. Rep. No. 43. Urbana: University of Illinois, Center for the Study of Reading, April 1977.

Collins, A., Brown, J. S., & Larkin, K. M. Inference in text understanding. In R. J. Spiro, B. C. Bruce, & W. F. Brewer (Eds.), *Theoretical issues in reading comprehension*. Hillsdale, N.J.: Erlbaum, 1980.

Collins, A., & Gentner, D. A framework for a cognitive theory of writing. In L. Gregg & E. Steinberg (Eds.), *Processes in writing*. Hillsdale, N.J.: Erlbaum, in press.

Collins, A., & Smith, E. E. Teaching the process of reading comprehension. *Intelligence*, 1981.

Dewey, J. *Experience and education*. New York: Macmillan, 1938.

Fikes, R. F. REF-ARF: A system for solving problems stated as procedures. *Artificial Intelligence*, 1970, *1*, 27–120.

Flavell, J. H. Cognitive monitoring. In W. P. Dickson (Ed.), *Children's oral communication skills*. New York: Academic Press, in press.

Gray, W. S. *The twenty-fourth yearbook of the National Society for the Study of Education: Part I*. Bloomington, Ill.: Public School Publishing, 1925.

Gray, W. S. *The thirty-sixth yearbook of the National Society for the Study of Education: Part I*. Bloomington, Ill.: Public School Publishing, 1937.

Huey, E. B. *The psychology and pedagogy of reading*. Cambridge, Mass.: MIT Press, 1968. (Originally published in 1908.)

Kintsch, W., & Greene, E. The role of culture-specific schematic in the comprehension and recall of stories. *Discourse Processes*, 1978, *1*, 1–13.

Mandler, J. M., & Johnson, N. S. Remembrance of things parsed: Story structure and recall. *Cognitive Psychology*, 1977, *9*, 111–151.

Markman, E. M. Realizing that you don't understand: Elementary school children's awareness of inconsistencies. *Child Development*, 1979, *50*, 643–655.

Minsky, M. A. Framework for representing knowledge. In P. H. Winston (Ed.), *The psychology of computer vision*. New York: McGraw-Hill, 1975.

Newell, A., & Simon, H. *Human problem solving*. Englewood Cliffs, N.J.: Prentice-Hall, 1972.

Newman, D. *Children's understanding of strategic interaction*. Unpublished manuscript, University of California, San Diego, 1980.

Reder, L. M. The role of elaborations in memory for prose. *Cognitive Psychology*, 1979, *11*, 221–234.

Rumelhart, D. E. Toward an interactive model of reading. In S. Dornic (Ed.), *Attention and performance VI*. London: Academic Press, 1977.

Rumelhart, D. E., & Ortony, A. The representation of knowledge in memory. In R. C. Anderson, R. J. Spiro, & W. E. Montague (Eds.), *Schooling and the acquisition of knowledge*. Hillsdale, N.J.: Erlbaum, 1977.

Schank, R. C., & Abelson, R. P. Scripts, plans and knowledge. *Proceedings Fourth International Joint Conference on Artificial Intelligence*. Tbilisi, Georgia: USSR, 1975.

Steffensen, M. S., Joag-Dev, C., & Anderson, R. C. A cross-cultural perspective on reading comprehension. *Reading Research Quarterly*, 1979, *15*, 10–29.

Steinberg, C., & Bruce, B. C. *Higher-level features in children's stories: Rhetorical structure and conflict*. Reading Education Rep. No. 18. Urbana: University of Illinois, Center for the Study of Reading, October 1980.

Thorndike, E. L. Reading as reasoning: A study of mistakes in paragraph reading. *Journal of Educational Psychology*, 1917, *8*, 323–332.

Wilensky, R. Why John married Mary: Understanding stories involving recurring goals. *Cognitive Science*, 1978, *2*, 235–266.

Winston, P. H. *Artificial Intelligence*. Reading, Mass.: Addison-Wesley Publishing Company, Inc., 1977.

4

A Question about Reading Comprehension Instruction

Jana M. Mason

OVERVIEW

What is the nature of reading comprehension instruction in our elementary schools today? How frequently is it taught, and with what sorts of activities? Is there a shift from word recognition and phonics activities to text analysis and text-level comprehension instruction at about the fourth grade? A common belief of many teachers is that most of the instructional time in the first three grades is spent in teaching students how to recognize print, whereas in the upper elementary grades it centers on learning from texts by analyzing, evaluating, outlining, and interpreting written information (Martin and Chambers 1974). There is little direct evidence to support a belief in such an instructional change. Even if the belief could be supported, it ignores questions about why fourth grade should be chosen for initiating comprehension instruction. It also ignores the fact that shifts in the use of learning materials, classroom organization, or procedure could give an appearance of an instructional change.

If this belief has any basis, we can assume that learning goals for younger children are intended to help them achieve fluency and establish good habits in reading; goals for older children aim to show them how to acquire knowledge from written information. This change must be differentiated from policy shifts that occur at about the fourth grade, such as initiating formal grading, using students from two or more classrooms to form instructional groups, or utilizing different types of instructional materials. Thus there are three possibilities: (1) The belief may have no instructional basis whatsoever because there are no changes; (2) teachers are only modifying social and managerial dimensions of classroom instruction; or (3) there may be instructional goal shifts, or both organizational

A complete report of this study can be found in J. Mason, and J. Osborn. When do children begin "Reading to Learn": A survey of classroom reading instruction practices in grades two through five. Tech. Rep. No. 261, Center for the Study of Reading, University of Illinois.

and goal changes may be made. Which situation actually exists should be known, for improvement in instructional practice requires an understanding of the implicit forces that guide it as well as the explicit cognitive demands made of students.

Thus, understanding when and how instruction shifts to text-level comprehension was the purpose of this work. The problem reflects a larger concern regarding the nature of comprehension instruction. It is reflected in three ways. The first is the lack of specific suggestions. Twenty years ago, when the author was a fourth-grade teacher, she bemoaned the difficulty of relating instructional materials to text-level comprehension and the paucity of effective suggestions from teacher guides about teaching comprehension. Questions and projects for students often were trivial, not closely related to the text being read, or did not facilitate a serious analysis of written information. It is not apparent that the situation has changed substantially or that teachers better understand how to teach comprehension.

Second, there is a lack of clarity about what *constitutes* comprehension instruction. If comprehension instruction is interpreted globally to include any sort of meaning activity related to written text (Austin and Morrison 1963), then primary and intermediate-level teachers seem to devote a good part of their reading instruction time to comprehension instruction. If comprehension instruction is narrowly defined (e.g., Durkin 1979, Goodlad 1977, Guszak 1967), then the amount of comprehension instruction that occurs is seen to be very limited, and is as limited in the upper grades as in the lower grades.

Third, there is a problem regarding how to gather information about comprehension instruction. When comprehension instruction is assessed by teacher questionnaires, as in the Austin and Morrison survey, intermediate-grade teachers report more attention to higher-level aspects of comprehension instruction than do primary teachers. Similarly, from the Martin and Chambers study, teachers think reading instruction in the intermediate grades can be characterized by the phrase "reading to learn," whereas in the primary grades the students are "learning to read." Yet the observational studies indicate little attention to comprehension instruction at any time, and above all, do not reveal a shift to "higher-level" questioning activities in the intermediate grades.

Perhaps an explanation for this unclear picture of comprehension instruction lies in the considerable confusion about the nature of comprehension instruction. The questionnaire survey and classroom observations of the present study represent an attempt to clarify the issue by probing more deeply into teachers' beliefs about comprehension instruction and how those beliefs are manifested in classroom instructional activities.

THE STUDY

The study has two parts. For the first part, teachers described how they teach reading in their classrooms by filling out a questionnaire. For the second part, what 20 of the same teachers did when they taught reading in their classrooms was documented. An instrument was designed for each part of the study, a teacher questionnaire for Part 1 and a classroom observation form for Part 2.

The Setting and the Subjects

The study took place in a small industrial city in the Middle West during the spring of 1978. The city was chosen because it is representative of medium-sized industrial cities in the United States. The population of the city is about 90,000 and has an enrollment of 19,000 students in four high schools, five middle schools, and 25 elementary schools. There are other students enrolled in Catholic and other private schools.

The largest proportion of the employed adult population work in manufacturing and processing plants. Clerical and other skilled workers in offices, professionals, and the staff of the public schools and two community colleges form another group of employed adults. Black and other minority-group members make up about 15 percent of the population. Except for a recent immigration of some additional minority families, the population has been relatively stable for the past decade.

According to information obtained from the teachers on the questionnaire, the wage earners in the families of students are professional or managerial, 22 percent; clerical or skilled, 29 percent; unskilled, 29 percent; and unemployed, 19 percent.

Over 90 percent of the public school teachers in grades 2 through 5 responded to the questionnaire survey. Of these teachers, 6 percent had taught one year or less, 18 percent had taught for two to five years, 23 percent for six to ten years, 33 percent for 11–20 years, and 20 percent for more than 20 years.

The Instruments

We were concerned that instructional terms appearing on the questionnaire and the observation form would be understood by the teachers filling out the questionnaires and the observers using the observation forms. The teachers were to fill out the questionnaires in an unsupervised setting, and the observers, once trained, were to code the type and duration of instructional events without our supervision. We were well aware of the confusion surrounding the words and phrases used to describe reading instruction, especially comprehension instruction.

We met the problem of varying interpretations of the terms used to describe reading instruction by incorporating the labels for the teaching of decoding and comprehension that typically appear in the manuals that accompany basal reading materials. Then we piloted the forms in third- and fourth-grade classrooms and discussed the observation and questionnaire forms with several teachers. After several revisions, we were satisfied that the questionnaire and observation procedure would be interpreted by the teachers and the observers as we intended it. We ended up using labels on both instruments that we found teachers to understand.

Procedures

The Questionnaire Survey. The questionnaire was passed out to all grade 2 through 5 teachers during a district meeting. A good number of the completed questionnaires were collected at a subsequent meeting by a representative of the district's central administration. Follow-up notices were sent to teachers who did not turn in the questionnaires at that meeting. Ultimately, over 90 percent of the teachers who received questionnaires returned them.

Responses to the questionnaire were tabulated separately for teachers from each grade. Teachers who noted that they taught two grades were classified with the lower grade because in almost every mixed-grade class, most of the children were reading texts from the lower grade. For some questions, teachers could add other information. In those cases, the fixed responses to the questions were adjusted by the teachers' added comments.

The Classroom Observations. Observations were made in 20 classrooms, ten classrooms each of grades 3 and 4. Classrooms were not chosen at random from the entire district but were selected by the curriculum supervisors. (The supervisors selected rooms in which they thought observers would be able to work in an unobtrusive way). Most of the classrooms were in schools in middle-class neighborhoods. Two retired teachers from the district were trained as observers and collected all the data. Within a two-week period three different reading periods were observed in each of the 20 classrooms. The observations took place early in the second semester.

Two separate sets of observations were collected simultaneously by one observer. The first set included a detailed description of the teacher's activities, the mode of instruction, the number of students with the teacher, the materials being used, the kinds of tasks the teachers and students were engaged in, as well as the time spent on each segment of the reading period. The second set of observations documented what students working independently were doing.

The observation form had been tried out in a pilot by pairs of observers in four classrooms before this study. Revisions were then made so that essentially all kinds of classroom activities could be recorded and so that observers using the schedule had a high degree of agreement about the recorded classroom activities. As a final check, four classroom lessons were simultaneously observed by a regular observer and one of our staff. The few disagreements (on task type) were resolved by rechecking the listed assignment.

Results from Part 1 of the Study

The responses to the first part of the questionnaire, which deal with how teachers set up their classrooms, are reported in Mason and Osborn (1982). They indicate substantial grade-to-grade differences in classroom organization, grouping for reading instruction, distribution of time, evaluation of students, and use of published materials. However, contrary to the notion that an abrupt change in comprehension instruction occurs at about fourth grade, the responses suggest there is a gradual change over the four grades in classroom organization, method of evaluation, and the use and kind of materials.

Evidence of change in the content of reading lessons. Three questions were asked to determine teachers' perceptions of which instructional tasks were foremost at each grade level:

1. What do you consider the most important reading activities at each grade level?
2. What reading activities could most of your students do at the beginning of the school year?
3. What reading activities are you emphasizing in your grade this semester?

Each of these questions utilized one set of 14 reading activities. They are listed in Table 4.1 as part of the analysis of question 2, and for reporting convenience are grouped into three categories: (*a*) text-level comprehension activities, (*b*) word- and sentence-level comprehension activities, and (*c*) word recognition activities.

The responses to the three questions were analyzed to determine teachers' perceptions of what should be taught at each grade level in comparison to what they were teaching and what they thought their students already knew. The analyses considered whether teachers' perceptions differ over grade, whether teachers are consistent in their answers to the three questions, and whether their plans vary over student achievement as well as over grade.

The first question was designed to find out what teachers think ought to be taught at each grade level. The teachers were asked to check the three activities they considered most important from the 14 listed. Each teacher was asked to do this separately for each of the grades. The teachers were to also rank order the

TABLE 4.1   Teachers' Reports of Activities Students Could Do with Ease at Beginning of Semester

Activity	Grade			
	2	3	4	5
Text-level comprehension activities				
Grasp main idea of most written passages	51%	50%	59%	66%
Draw appropriate inferences from texts	40	17	18	26
Recognize author's purpose	4	5	9	18
Sequence and summarize information from texts	13	9	18	34
Understand cause-and-effect relationships in texts	17	17	6	24
Use study skills effectively	2	5	30	39
Locate information in texts	4	28	23	47
Word- and sentence-level comprehension activities				
Recall important facts and details from texts	55	59	56	63
Understand and follow directions	55	52	53	47
Use context to figure out new words	55	59	59	50
Understand meanings of most words encountered in classroom materials	51	57	79	63
Word recognition activities				
Read fluently (orally)	57	76	73	66
Recognize by sight most words encountered in classroom materials	60	86	91	100
Use phonetic skills or structural analysis to decode most unfamiliar words	91	90	82	74

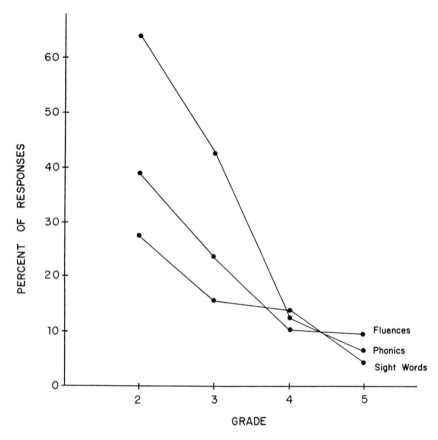

FIGURE 4.1   Teachers' Beliefs about Importance of Word Recognition Activities.

three activities they selected for each grade level. Tallies of checks for each activity were then transformed to a percentage of checks made at each grade level.

Teachers checked fewer word recognition activities for fourth- and fifth-grade students than they did for second- and third-grade students (Figure 4.1), suggesting that decoding and phonics instruction and reading fluency practice is thought less important instructionally in the upper grades than in the lower grades. They checked somewhat fewer word- and sentence-level comprehension activities in the upper than lower grades (Figure 4.2), but they checked far more text-level comprehension activities for upper-grade students than for lower-grade students (Figure 4.3). This suggests that instruction on inferencing, sequencing, summarizing, locating information, understanding an author's purpose, and understanding cause-and-effect relationships is thought to be increasingly important over the four grades. Of the seven text-level comprehension activities listed, only one, understanding the main idea of a passage, was thought important in the early grades.

Hence, responses to the question about what *ought* to be taught suggests that teachers believe that a shift over grade in the instruction of reading is appropriate. They believe that word recognition activities should become less important after

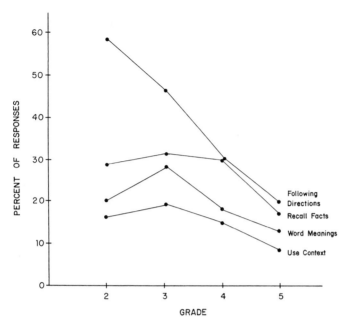

FIGURE 4.2 Teachers' Beliefs about Importance of Word Comprehension
Activities.

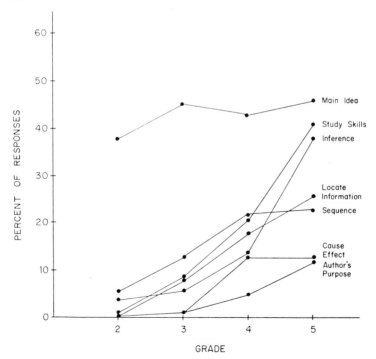

FIGURE 4.3 Teachers' Beliefs about Importance of Text-Level Comprehension
Activities.

third grade, word- and sentence-level comprehension activities should become somewhat less important in the upper grades, and text-level comprehension activities should become increasingly more important over the four grades.

In the second question, teachers were asked to check from among the 14 listed activities any which they thought their students "could do with ease at the beginning of the school year." Teachers checked information for only the grade they taught and could check as many activities as they wished so that reported percentages for each grade sum above 100 percent. Second-grade teachers typically checked five or six activities; third-grade teachers checked six activities; fourth-grade teachers, six or seven activities; and fifth-grade teachers, seven activities.

Figure 4.4 displays grade-by-grade percentages for the averaged values for activities within each of the three categories. It is readily apparent that teachers perceive their students as being much less competent on comprehension activities than on word recognition activities and that text-level comprehension activities are least well understood. Table 4.1, which provides a breakdown for each category, shows that except for main idea, teachers perceive activities within each category in a similar way. That is, word recognition activities are thought to be well understood, while text-level comprehension is generally not well understood. What is surprising is the lack of increase over grade. Very few activities are perceived as being more understandable by upper- than by lower-grade students. Most change little or else fluctuate in an uninterpretable manner.

An explanation for the (relatively flat) character of these responses over the four grades is that the terms are general code names for a wide assortment of decoding and comprehension tasks. In lower grades, when vocabulary in stories is

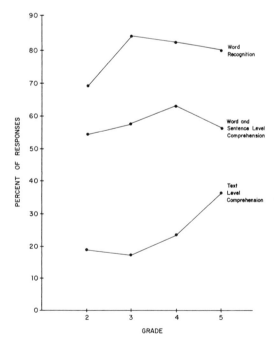

FIGURE 4.4   Teachers' Perceptions about Students' Reading Competencies.

controlled, there are fewer new words and simpler letter patterns. As text and workbook materials increase in difficulty over grades, the real tasks that are similarly labeled also increase in difficulty. This may explain the reported competency decrease for "use phonetic skills or structural analysis." These skills may not be considered mastered even by fifth grade because the words in stories are longer and demand syllabic analysis skills rather than the letter-sound analysis of the lower grades. Similarly, teachers at succeeding grade levels are likely to require students to perform more complex interpretations or analyses on comprehension tasks. For example, second graders might only be asked to report the first or last sentence of a text as the "main idea," while fifth graders might be asked to construct one using their own words.

An explanation for the low percentages on text comprehension tasks is that teachers are correctly perceiving that their students are not yet competent. Comparing, for example, the reported percentages of the text-level comprehension activities in Table 4.1 shows that only main idea activities were thought by second-, third- and fourth-grade teachers to be as well understood as the word recognition and word- and sentence-level comprehension activities in those grades. It is also the only text-level comprehension activity that teachers indicated in the previous question was as important to teach in the early grades as word recognition. It is conceivable, then, that the belief that few text-level comprehension activities ought to be taught in the early grades is generally matched by little text-level comprehension instruction and thus by realistic, low-student-competency assessments.

The responses to the third question stand in definite contrast to the responses to the question about what teachers think *ought* to be taught at each grade level, as well as to the question about what students know at the beginning of the school year. This question asked about the reading activities the teachers emphasized at the grade level they were teaching. The teachers were asked to check those activities they were emphasizing during the current semester. They were also asked to report this information separately for their high-, middle-, and low-achieving students. If teachers taught only one group of students, these responses were classified according to the grade level of the text being used for instruction (i.e., above-grade text, high group; on-grade text, middle group; below-grade text, low group). The teachers could check as many activities as they wished so that percentage figures sum above 100 percent. The average percent of checks for each activity per grade and for each reading achievement group are reported in Table 4.2. From those percentages, two sets of summaries are reported, one looking at the results over grade (Figure 4.5) and the other over student reading achievement (Figure 4.6).

Figure 4.5 presents the average percent of checks made by teachers at each grade, collapsed over achievement and type of activity. Very small changes are apparent. Text-level comprehension activities are given slightly more emphasis in the upper grades than in the second grade. Word recognition and word- and sentence-level comprehension activities are given gradually less emphasis over the four grades. By fifth grade text-level activities are emphasized a little more than word recognition activities, but throughout the four grades word- and sentence-level comprehension activities are emphasized the most.

Figure 4.6 presents teachers' perceptions of instruction as a function of students' reading achievement, collapsing over grade and activity. These data reveal

TABLE 4.2   Teachers' Reports of Emphasized Activities for Students

Activity	Reading Achievement	Grade 2	Grade 3	Grade 4	Grade 5
Text-level comprehension					
Main idea	High	97%	100%	100%	91%
	Middle	82	79	88	89
	Low	78	75	91	95
Inference	High	87	100	83	100
	Middle	74	82	60	77
	Low	56	56	52	55
Author's purpose	High	66	56	83	83
	Middle	26	35	36	27
	Low	16	22	09	25
Sequencing	High	87	97	100	83
	Middle	74	91	84	77
	Low	56	75	78	60
Cause and effect	High	74	62	83	74
	Middle	50	35	44	58
	Low	25	19	22	45
Study skills	High	97	100	100	87
	Middle	68	85	76	92
	Low	25	50	57	65
Locating information	High	92	100	91	70
	Middle	53	100	80	89
	Low	31	56	61	75
Word- and sentence-level comprehension					
Recall facts	High	97%	97%	87%	83%
	Middle	87	97	88	81
	Low	94	97	96	70
Follow directions	High	97	97	87	96
	Middle	90	100	88	96
	Low	100	100	100	100
Use context cues	High	79	79	87	65
	Middle	76	82	76	77
	Low	75	78	83	60
Word meaning	High	95	94	91	65
	Middle	95	91	76	73
	Low	72	81	74	50
Word recognition					
Fluent reading	High	76%	68%	57%	39%
	Middle	90	65	60	58
	Low	72	81	70	65
Sight-word recognition	High	79	74	83	61
	Middle	71	85	60	71
	Low	66	84	83	70
Phonetic skills	High	87	71	65	52
	Middle	87	85	88	65
	Low	94	100	100	75

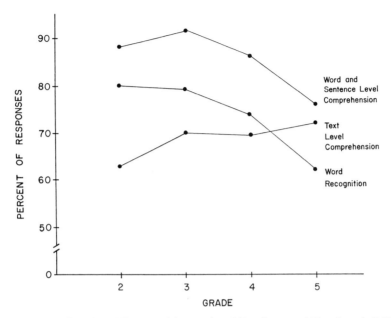

FIGURE 4.5   Teachers' Reported Instructional Emphases of Reading Activities as a Function of Grade.

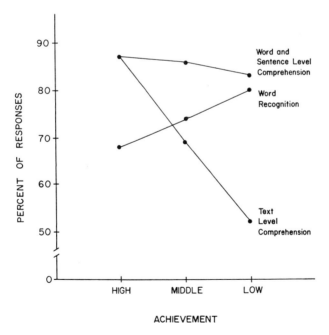

FIGURE 4.6   Teachers' Reported Instructional Emphases of Reading Activities as a Function of Student Reading Ability.

that teachers make, or believe that they make, greater adjustments for differences in students' reading ability than they do for differences in grade. High-achieving students are given instruction that emphasizes comprehension; average-achieving students receive more word- and sentence-level comprehension than word recognition and text comprehension, low-achieving students receive mostly word recognition and word- and sentence-level instruction.

According to teachers' own reports, there is little difference over grade in the stress they place on most reading activities, but there is a substantial difference in emphasis as a function of achievement. The result is that teachers stress word- and sentence-level comprehension for all their students. Differentiation of instruction occurs over student achievement within grade rather than across grade such that high-achieving students receive more text-level comprehension instruction and low-achieving students receive more word recognition instruction.

Summary of Part 1 results. There is a striking incongruity between what teachers say *ought* to be emphasized at different grade levels and what they say they *do* emphasize. While teachers believe there ought to be a substantial grade-to-grade shift in emphasis from word recognition to text-level comprehension activities, they then acknowledge only a small increase in instructional emphasis of text-level comprehension over word and sentence comprehension. However, they do differentiate their instruction, for when responses are coded in terms of whether the students are reading above, at, or below their grade level, high-performing students are said to receive appreciable instruction on text-level comprehension, while less able students obtain mostly word recognition and word- and sentence-level comprehension instruction. Scanning Table 4.2 confirms in an impressive way this agreement among teachers. At every grade level, every text-level comprehension activity (except main idea) is given more emphasis to higher-achieving than to lower-achieving students.

There is also an incongruity between what teachers say they are teaching now and what they say their students could do with ease at the beginning of the school year. Teachers report higher competence on word recognition and word-level comprehension activities than on text-level comprehension activities. We had then expected, at least in the upper grades, to find greater emphasis on text-level comprehension activities. Yet, except in grade 5, these activities are given *less* emphasis than all other activities. It is not surprising now that teachers report such low competence among their students on text-level comprehension. They are apparently not providing the instruction that they acknowledge implicitly is needed.

Thus, the questionnaire responses suggest that the learning to read–reading to learn belief is just that, and no more. Instead of describing actual practice, it indicates an attitude about what practices ought to occur.

Results from Part 2 of the Study

To determine whether teachers' reports coincide with actual instructional practice, a procedure was developed for recording events in reading periods. As noted, the procedure requires the observer to alternate between watching the activities of the students the teacher is working with, and watching the activities of students working alone. The observer records all audible teacher-student interaction events and at ten-minute intervals scans the room to note the behaviors of students working on their own.

General observation results.   Twenty teachers were observed, each on three occasions, making a total of 60 observed reading periods, 30 for third grade, and 30 for fourth grade. Third-grade reading periods lasted an average of 55 minutes; fourth-grade periods lasted 51 minutes. Within each lesson there were averages of 11.2 interaction events of instructed students and 5.6 scans of students working independently. There were about 29 third-grade students and 32 fourth-grade students in each classroom. At any given time in third-grade rooms about 22 students were working independently while seven were being instructed by the teacher. In fourth grade about 20 students were working independently and 12 were with the teacher.

Observations of teachers working with students.   The activities of the teacher and instructed students are reported in Table 4.3. Five aspects of the analysis are presented: (1) lesson characteristic, (2) interaction pattern, (3) student response mode, (4) instructional materials, and (5) reading activities. Since each is an independent analysis, each sums to 100 percent of the total reading period. The first two analyses that follow describe how the teacher presents lesson material. What is taught and how the student interacts with the teacher during the lesson appear in the last three analyses.

Lesson characteristics.   Table 4.3 indicates that more than 25 percent of the available time is spent preparing students for work, while less than half the time is devoted to the presentation of new work. New and review work engage third-grade students for a longer percent of the time than fourth-grade students (70 vs. 53 percent). By contrast, fourth-grade teachers spend a greater percent of time checking assignments and working with individuals.

Interaction patterns.   Both third- and fourth-grade teachers most often use a teacher-question/student-response interaction pattern in which the teacher asks a question and calls on a student to answer. Nearly as frequent is the lecture pattern in which the teacher either calls on students to discuss information or has students listen to a presentation of information. These two interaction patterns take 70 percent of the class instruction time in both grades. The two grades differ in that third-grade teachers more often use a round-robin format in which students read or answer questions in a fixed order, while fourth-grade teachers more often talk to individual students.

Student response mode.   The response mode describes the interactional behaviors of those students who are working with the teacher. In both grades nearly 50 percent of the time involves a verbal interaction with the teacher and 20 percent involves listening to the teacher. These sum to nearly the 70 percent of the reading period, as noted above. Hence, nearly 50 percent of the reading period is utilized by answering or discussing information with the teacher. Twenty percent of the time has students listening to the teacher. Of the remaining 30 percent of the time, in third grade most of it is spent in oral reading, while in fourth grade most is spent in reading and writing answers (usually worksheet exercises). Very little silent reading occurs in either grade.

TABLE 4.3 Percent Time by Teachers and Instructed Students of Reading Activities, Materials, and Tasks

	Grade 3	Grade 4
Lesson characteristic		
Preparation for work	23.6	27.4
Presentation of new work	45.8	36.9
Reviewing	23.8	15.8
Checking individual work	3.4	13.8
Other	3.3	6.0
Interaction pattern		
Question-answer	38.9	41.2
Lecture-dicussion	31.6	29.7
Round robin	23.3	10.3
Private (one-to-one) interaction	3.4	13.8
Other	3.3	6.0
Student response mode		
Verbal interaction with teacher	47.6	45.7
Listening to teacher	18.2	19.6
Silent reading	3.3	6.1
Oral reading	19.2	7.0
Reading and writing answers	8.2	19.0
Writing or drawing	2.4	0.1
Other (includes 1% off-task time)	1.1	2.4
Student material		
Workbook	30.9	38.4
Textbook	32.7	16.2
No material	17.1	27.2
Chalkboard, chart	11.9	10.0
Paper and pencil	3.3	3.7
Dictionary	2.2	1.4
Tradebook	1.0	1.7
Other	1.0	1.4
Student task		
Reading	14.8	15.8
Following teacher directions	19.4	19.8
Word recognition and word attack	15.8	8.5
Word- and sentence-level comprehension		
Word meaning	14.4	24.9
Recalling or locating facts and details	11.6	10.0
Interpreting sentences	3.7	2.7
Text-level comprehension		
Interpreting paragraphs or stories	7.8	4.8
Sequencing, information	2.3	0.3
Summarizing or finding main ideas	1.2	0.8
Learning study skills or using reference materials	3.0	4.7
Learning punctuation, capitalization, sentence structure, or grammar	1.1	0.7
Analyzing paragraph or poem structure or writing reports, stories, or poems	0.4	0.5
Analyzing literary forms, devices, or author's purpose	0.6	1.8
Other (unclassifiable worksheet exercises)	4.0	4.9

Lesson material. The analysis of student material indicates that basal reading materials, workbooks or textbooks, are being used around 60 percent of the time, with textbooks in greater use in third grade and workbooks in greater use in fourth grade. To our surprise, for an appreciable amount of time students in both grades are not using materials (nearly 20 percent of the time in third grade and almost 30 percent in fourth grade). Chalkboard and chart work occur for about 10 percent of the time. Trade books, dictionaries, or other reading materials are seldom used in either grade.

Student task. While the materials analysis would lead one to expect that third-grade students are reading 31 percent of the reading period time and fourth graders are reading 16 percent of the time, the task analysis indicates that half of that time third graders are locating information, recalling, or interpreting information rather than reading in a continuous fashion. Thus, in both grades, text reading occurs about 15 percent of the time. Following directions, which are occasions when students listen to directions for activities they will carry out later, take about 20 percent of the time in both grades. This helps to explain the time spent with no materials in hand.

Task differences between the two grades are more evident after grouping them as reading, following directions, and the three content areas of word recognition, word- and sentence-level comprehension, and text-level comprehension. One difference, which was expected by the responses to the questionnaire, is that word recognition tasks occur for nearly twice as long in third as in fourth grade (16 percent of the time in third grade and 8.5 percent of the time in fourth grade).

The other difference, which was not expected, is that fourth-grade students spend more time on word- and sentence-level tasks than do third graders (38 percent versus 30 percent). The difference is due entirely to vocabulary instruction. Fourth-grade students devote one quarter of their instructional time to locating, discussing, or recalling word meanings. Confirming teachers' questionnaire reports about what they teach rather than what they think ought to be taught, both grades spend about 15 percent of the time on text-level comprehension tasks. However, the greater part of that time is devoted to discussion of story content rather than to analysis of the content. Unaccountably, since teachers believe that they ought to spend time teaching main ideas and think that they do emphasize it, almost no time is spent with main idea tasks. In other respects, though, observation of the reading lessons conforms to what teachers say they emphasize and not to what they believe ought to be emphasized.

Observations of students working independently. Observations of students working at their seats yields three analyses: (1) student response mode, (2) materials, and (3) activities. The data, which were transformed to percent of time values, are presented in Table 4.4.

Student response mode. Students working at their desks devote much more of their time to writing than to reading. Writing is interpreted broadly in this analysis to indicate filling out a worksheet or creative writing. Third graders are writing more than fourth graders; fourth graders are reading more than third graders. Third graders spend over half their work time writing; fourth graders spend over one third of the time writing. For third graders, it is three times as frequent as

TABLE 4.4   Percent Time of Reading Lesson Activities, Materials, and Tasks of Students
Working Outside Teacher-Instructed Group

	Group 3	Group 4
Student response mode		
Writing	54.2	39.4
Silent reading	14.9	26.8
Oral reading	2.6	0.0
Listening to tapes	2.3	0.0
Painting or drawing	0.4	10.2
Other	25.7	23.6
Materials		
Workbook or ditto	50.7	41.5
Textbook	10.0	10.0
Tradebook	9.8	16.4
Dictionary	1.5	0.0
Paper and pencil	2.3	13.6
Chalk, games, audiotape	8.4	1.0
No materials	17.3	17.1
Student tasks		
Reading	20.5	25.6
Word recognition or word attack	10.5	7.4
Word- and sentence-level comprehension		
Word meaning	19.0	7.1
Recalling or locating fact and details	7.7	8.1
Interpreting sentences	1.2	0.5
Text-level comprehension		
Interpreting paragraphs or stories	5.2	6.0
Sequencing, summarizing, or finding main idea	2.3	3.6
Study skills or using references	3.7	1.2
Punctuation, capitalization, sentence structure, grammar	3.0	0.0
Literary forms and devices or author's purpose	0.0	0.0
Writing reports, stories, poems	1.6	4.9
Other work (math, spelling, drawing)	5.3	15.8
Off task	17.7	17.1

reading. For fourth graders writing or painting and drawing occur almost twice as
often as reading.

In this analysis a larger percent of time categorized is "other." It was
assigned if students were looking around, talking to other students, or were working on nonreading or unclassifiable academic tasks. The last analysis distinguishes
among these categories.

Student materials.   The materials analysis defines further the reading and writing
response modes. It is now apparent that most writing activities are carried out
with worksheet exercises. For both grades, worksheets are being filled out for
about half of students' seatwork time. Textbooks, dictionaries, or trade books are
used for about 25 percent of the time, though fourth graders are using tradebooks
for more time than are third graders.

Student activities. Comparing these results with percentages obtained for instructed students indicates that more reading occurs as seatwork in both grades, that much less time is spent by fourth graders as seatwork on word- and sentence-level comprehension tasks, and that time spent on text-level comprehension tasks remains the same, about 15 percent of time in both grades. In both grades, a large amount of seatwork time is not well spent. Students are not working on any academic task for about 17 percent of their seat time and are engaged in nonreading work for an additional 5 to 15 percent of the time. Grade comparisons indicate that third graders spend more time on word meaning exercises, while fourth graders are reading more and using the period for math and other nonreading work.

Summary. Observation of grades 3 and 4 reinforces the conclusion that a shift from learning to read to reading to learn is a belief that teachers share but do not practice. While the observation reveals instructional as well as organizational differences between third and fourth grades, these are not related to an increase in emphasis on text-level comprehension.

DISCUSSION

Are there differences between the earlier and later grades in reading comprehension instruction? Do upper-grade teachers teach more text-level comprehension? The answer from the questionnaire survey and reinforced by the observation is no if the definition of instruction is limited to *tasks* being carried out as opposed to *procedural* and *organizational* characteristics. Although there are very large grade-to-grade differences in teachers' beliefs about what ought to occur and in the kinds of materials used and the way to which they are put and in classroom organization patterns, there are few differences over grade in instruction of text comprehension.

The understanding of when and how comprehension instruction occurs was the purpose of this project. The central issue was whether there is an instructional shift from learning to read to reading to learn. There is not, even though teachers believe it ought to occur and even though changes in classroom organization, evaluation of student progress, and use of materials would seem to be providing support for such a change. Explanations for this situation, whether due to an inherent difficulty of providing text-level comprehension instruction to most children or to a basic conflict between text-level instruction and other commonly favored instructional materials, procedures, or practices, is not forthcoming from this research. But future studies ought to be directed to understanding why teachers, in the face of advice they are given and even their own beliefs, do not teach a majority of their students about how to learn from texts.

REFERENCES

Austin, M., & Morrison, C. *The first R: The Harvard Report on Reading in Elementary Schools.* New York: Macmillan, 1963.

Durkin, D. What classroom observations reveal about reading comprehension instruction. *Reading Research Quarterly,* 1979, *14,* 481–533.

Goodlad, J. What goes on in our schools? *Educational Researcher*, 1977, *6*, 3–6.
Guszak, F. Teacher questioning and reading. *Reading Teacher*, 1967, *21*, 228–234.
Martin, M., & Chambers, L. *Evaluation of the elementary reading survey K–5, 1973–1974*. ERIC ED 101 320.
Mason, J., & Osborn, J. *When do children begin "reading to learn": A survey of classroom reading instruction practices in grades two through five*. Urbana: University of Illinois, Center for the Study of Reading, 1982.

PART II

Constraints on Instruction

As noted in Chapter 1, researchers on teaching have in the past spent much effort trying to determine what makes one classroom teacher more effective (usually defined in terms of achievement outcomes) then other teachers. These efforts have identified the correlates of effectiveness to be academic focus, efficient classroom management, high amounts of pupil engaged time on task, and positive teacher expectations.

While these findings have been important, many researchers now consider such correlates to be *prerequisites* to effectiveness—that once an academic focus, efficient management, pupil engagement and positive expectancies have been established, other, more subtle elements become important in determining teacher effectiveness.

Research has been initiated to understand these other elements. Three broad areas have been emphasized: the teacher as a thinker whose decisions affect instruction, the classroom as an environment where instruction occurs, and the school as a social context for instruction. Although these new research efforts have not yet identified additional correlates of teacher effectiveness, they have provided a rich data set regarding the complexity of instruction.

This complexity is reflected in the chapters in this section. Chapters 5 and 6 examine the teacher as an instructional planner and an implementer of plans; Chapters 7 and 8 examine classroom environments, one where standard curricula are used and another where nonstandard curricula are used; and Chapter 9 examines the interactive nature of the school social system and how its instructional subsystems influence the nature of instruction.

These chapters on the teacher, the classroom, and the school form a framework because each constrains instruction. As we learn more about teachers, classrooms, and schools, we become more sensitive to the fact that instruction, whether comprehension instruction or some other kind of instruction, cannot be whatever we want it to be. Rather, instruction exists within constraints imposed by, among others, the limits of the teacher's thinking about instruction, the implicit and explicit messages communicated by the classroom environment, and the social system of the school.

Consequently, Part 2 provides background on the constraints placed on comprehension instruction. The various studies, when considered as a whole, demonstrate how instruction is shaped and sometimes limited by teachers, classrooms, and schools.

5

Teacher Planning and Reading Comprehension

Christopher M. Clark

Teacher planning is one of the central topics of study in the domain of research on teacher thinking (Clark and Yinger 1977, Shavelson and Stern 1982). Planning comes into play as the link between thought and action, and as such can exert a profound influence on what is taught, how it is taught, and ultimately on what is learned in schools. Since 1970, when the first studies of teacher planning were published, a considerable amount has been learned about the variety of teacher planning, the processes by which teachers plan, and the functions of the planning process. This chapter provides a review of the research on teacher planning, describes a recent study of teacher judgment exercised during the planning process, and concludes with suggestions about how this work might contribute to research on and the teaching of reading comprehension.

PRIMARY THEMES

Three themes are interwoven in the studies of teacher planning reviewed in this chapter. The first concerns the kinds and functions of planning—what teacher planning is and what purposes it serves. The second theme deals with models of the planning process—how planning operates. And the third theme is the relation between planning and subsequent action in the classroom—how it can operate to activate curriculum and produce a framework to guide both teacher and student behavior. Since all three themes are often addressed within a single study, the review is organized in a roughly chronological fashion rather than thematically.

Publication of this work is sponsored by the Institute for Research on Teaching, College of Education, Michigan State University. The Institute for Research on Teaching is funded primarily by the Program for Teaching and Instruction of the National Institute of Education, U.S. Department of Education. The opinions expressed in this publication do not necessarily reflect the position, policy, or endorsement of the National Institute of Education. (NIE Contract No. 400–81–0014.) Parts of this paper were presented in the Colloquium Series on Reading Comprehension jointly sponsored by the Institute for Research on Teaching and the Center for the Study of Reading, February 4, 1982.

Research on Teacher Planning

Zahorik (1970) did an early empirical study of classroom planning when he examined the effect of structured planning on teacher classroom behavior. He provided 6 of 12 teachers with a partial lesson plan containing behavioral objectives and a detailed outline of content to be covered two weeks hence. He requested the remaining six teachers to reserve an hour of instructional time to carry out a task for the researchers, not telling them that they were going to be asked to teach a lesson on credit cards until just before the appointed time. Zahorik analyzed recorded protocols of the 12 lessons focusing on "teacher behavior that is sensitive to students" (p. 144). He defined this behavior as "verbal acts of the teacher that permit, encourage, and develop pupil's ideas, thoughts, and actions" (p. 144). Upon examining the protocols of the planners and nonplanners, Zahorik judged that teachers given plans in advance exhibited less honest or authentic use of the pupils' ideas during the lesson. He concluded from this that the typical planning model—goals, activities and their organization, and evaluation—results in insensitivity to pupils on the part of the teacher.

Unfortunately, Zahorik did not determine the degree to which teachers who received the lesson plans in advance actually planned or elaborated the lesson. A competing explanation of these findings is that teachers who had no advance warning about what they were to teach were forced by the demands of the task to concentrate on their students' ideas and experiences, while teachers who knew the expected topic of instruction for two weeks prior to teaching were influenced to focus on the content rather than on their students.

Taylor (1970) conducted a study of teacher planning in British secondary schools. This study was directed toward examining how teachers planned syllabi for courses. Using group discussions with teachers, analyses of course syllabi, and a questionnaire administered to 261 teachers of English, science, and geography, Taylor came to the following general conclusions: The most common theme found across all modes of data collection was the prominence of the pupil, especially pupil needs, abilities, and interests. Following this, in order of importance, were the subject matter, aims (goals), and teaching methods. In planning for courses of study, evaluation emerged as of little importance, as did the relation between one's own course and the curriculum as a whole. Taylor concluded that most course planning was unsystematic and "only general" in nature and that most teachers appear far from certain about what the planning process requires.

Through teacher ratings of the importance of various issues in curriculum planning and a factor analysis of their responses, Taylor identified four primary factors of interest to his sample of teachers. The results generally indicated that when planning, teachers tended to consider in order of importance (1) factors associated with the teaching context (e.g., materials and resources); (2) pupil interest; (3) aims and purposes of teaching; and (4) evaluation considerations. Rather than begin with purposes and objectives and move to a description of learning experiences necessary to achieve the objectives, as rational planning theorists propose, these teachers began with the context of teaching, next considered learning situations likely to interest and involve their pupils, and only after this considered the purposes their teaching would serve. Also, unlike the planning of the theorists, criteria and procedures for evaluating the effectiveness of their course of teaching was an issue of only minor importance to these teachers. These findings led Taylor to conclude that curriculum planning should begin with the content to be taught and accompanying important contextual considerations (e.g., time, sequencing, resources). This should be followed by considerations of pupil interests and attitudes, aims and purposes of the course, learning situations to be created, the philosophy of the course, criteria for judging the course, the degree of pupil interest fostered by the course, and evaluation of the course.

Zahorik (1975) continued this line of inquiry by examining the use of behavioral objectives and the "separate ends-means" model of planning, as well as the use of the "integrated ends-means" model proposed by MacDonald and Eisner. He asked 194 teachers to list in writing the decisions that they make prior to teaching and the order in which they make them. He classified these decisions into the following categories: objectives, content, activities, materials, diagnosis, evaluation, instruction, and organization. He found that the kind of decision used by the greatest number of teachers concerned pupil activities (indicated by 81 percent of the teachers). The decision most frequently made first was content (51 percent), followed by learning objectives (28 percent).

Zahorik concluded from this study that teacher planning decisions do not always follow logically from a specification of objectives and that, in fact, objectives are not a particularly important planning decision in terms of quantity of use. He also argued, however, that the integrated ends-means model does not appear to be a functioning reality because of the relatively few teachers (only 3 percent) who reported beginning their planning by making decisions about activities.

More recently, researchers on teacher planning have turned their attention to describing teacher decision making in actual planning situations. Peterson, Marx, and Clark (1978) examined planning in a laboratory situation as 12 teachers prepared to teach a new instructional unit to groups of junior high school students with whom they had had no previous contact. These units were taught to three different groups of eight students on three different days. During their planning periods, teachers were instructed to "think aloud," and their verbal statements were later coded into planning categories such as objectives, materials, subject matter, and process. The following results were obtained from this study: (1) Teachers spent the largest proportion of their planning time dealing with the content (subject matter) to be taught; (2) after subject matter, teachers concentrated their planning efforts on instructional processes (strategies and activities); (3) the smallest proportion of their planning time was spent on objectives. All three findings were consistent with those by Zahorik (1975) and Goodlad et al. (1970). The third finding was also similar to results reported by Joyce and Harootunian (1964) and by Popham and Baker (1970).

As was done in the Zahorik (1970) study, task demands on teachers should be taken into account in interpreting these results. Researchers provided teachers with unfamiliar materials from which to teach and limited preparation time to the 90 minutes immediately preceding teaching on each day of the study. Since the teachers did not know their students in advance, it follows that the emphasis in their planning would be on content and instructional processes. Finally, the researchers did provide the teachers with a list of six general teaching goals, expressed in terms of content coverage, process goals, and cognitive and attitudinal outcomes for students. Under these circumstances, it is not surprising that the teachers devoted little planning time to composing more specific objectives, and used the largest fractions of their planning time in studying the content and deciding how to teach it.

The place of learning objectives in teacher planning was examined in a study by McLeod (1981) of 17 kindergarten teachers. McLeod did a stimulated recall interview with each teacher, using a videotape of a 20- to 30-minute lesson taught earlier the same day. The purpose of the interviews was to determine when intended learning outcomes were formulated in terms of four stages: preactive stage 1, before planning activity or selecting materials; preactive stage 2, after planning but before teaching; interactive stage 3, during the act of teaching; and postactive stage 4, during reflection after a teaching episode (Pylypiw 1974). The interviews also revealed how different kinds of intended learning outcomes (cognitive, social, and psychomotor) were distributed.

Averaging the responses across the 17 teachers, McLeod found that the largest percentage of intended learning outcomes (45.8 percent) was identified during the interactive stage. This was followed by preactive stage 1 (26.5 percent), preactive stage 2 (19.5 percent), and by the postactive stage (8.2 percent). The data also indicated that 57.7 percent of the intended learning outcomes were categorized as cognitive, 35 percent were classified as social or affective, and 7.2 percent as psychomotor or perceptual. Interestingly, the social/affective intended learning outcomes were primarily identified during the interactive stage, while cognitive outcomes predominated in the preactive and postactive stages.

The McLeod study can be criticized on the grounds that possibly excessive weight was placed on the stimulated recall interviews. These data could have been supplemented to good effect by observations and teachers thinking aloud during the preactive stages. But this research does much to broaden the concept of goals, objectives, or intended learning outcomes and their roles in planning and teaching. Earlier research tended to dismiss learning objectives as a rare and therefore unimportant element in teacher planning, even characterizing teachers as interested in process rather than outcomes. McLeod's study suggests that teachers can and do think about and act to support both specific and general learning outcomes for their students and that it is hazardous to study the process of teacher planning in isolation from interactive teaching and postactive reflection.

A study by Morine-Dershimer (1976) and Vallance in a classroom setting found results consistent with those of Peterson, Marx, and Clark. Morine-Dershimer collected written plans for two experimenter-prescribed lessons (one in mathematics and one in reading) taught by teachers in their own classrooms to a subset of their students. Teacher plans were described in terms of (1) specificity of written plans, (2) general format of plans, (3) statement of goals, (4) source of goal statements, (5) attention to pupil background and preparation, (6) identification of evaluation procedures, and (7) indication of possible alternative procedures. Morine-Dershimer found that teachers tended to be fairly specific and use an outline form in their plans. Their written plans reflected little attention to behavioral goals, diagnosis of student needs, evaluation procedures, and alternative courses of action. However, the teachers reported that writing plans for teaching researcher-prescribed lessons was not typical of their planning, and observations of their classroom teaching behavior revealed that much of what the teachers had planned was not reflected in their written outlines (Morine-Dershimer 1979).

The results of the Morine-Dershimer and Vallance study, together with those of a later study by Morine-Dershimer (1979), suggest that teachers' plans are seldom fully reflected in their written lesson plans. Rather, details recorded on a written plan are nested within more comprehensive planning structures, called "lesson images" by Morine-Dershimer. These lesson images, in turn, are nested within a still larger construct called the "activity flow" by Joyce (1978–79). For elementary school teachers the activity flow encompasses the year-long progress of a class through each particular subject matter and also the balance of activities across subject matters in a school day or week.

Yinger (1977) studied the planning decisions of a single first/second-grade teacher over a five-month period. Using interviews, thinking aloud, and extensive classroom observations, Yinger determined that this teacher engaged in five different levels of planning: yearly planning, term planning, unit planning, weekly planning, and daily planning. The "activity" was found to be the basic unit of short-range planning (e.g., daily and weekly). The teacher drew heavily on "routines" established early in the school year that incorporated intended learning outcomes for students. These routines were seen as functioning to reduce the complexity and increase the predictability of classroom activities.

Yinger also generated a theoretical model of the process of teacher planning, summarized in Clark and Yinger (1977):

> Three stages of planning were represented in the planning model. The first stage, problem finding, was portrayed as a discovery cycle where the teacher's goal conceptions, her knowledge and experience, her notion of the planning dilemma, and the materials available for planning interact to produce an initial problem conception worthy of further exploration. The second stage in the planning process was problem formulation and solution. The mechanism proposed for carrying out this process was the "design cycle." In this cycle, problem solving was characterized as a design process involving progressive elaboration of plans over time. Elaboration, investigation, and adaptation were proposed as phases through which plans were formulated. The third stage of the planning model involved implementation of the plan, its evaluation, and its eventual routinization. This stage emphasized the contribution of evaluation and routinization to the teacher's repertoire of knowledge and experience which in turn play a major role in future planning deliberations. (p. 285)

Further support for the idea that teacher planning is a nested process comes from a study by Clark and Elmore (1979). They interviewed and observed five elementary school teachers during the first five weeks of the school year and found that their planning was primarily concerned with setting up the physical environment of the classroom, assessing student abilities, and establishing the social system of the classroom. By the end of the fourth week of school a system of schedules, routines, and groupings for instruction was established. These structural and social features of the classroom persisted throughout the school year and served as the framework within which particular activities were planned. Other studies of the first weeks of the school year also support the claim that, to a significant degree, the problem space (after Newell and Simon 1970) within which teacher and students operate is defined early, changes little during the course of the year, and exerts a powerful if subtle influence on thought and behavior (e.g., Anderson and Evertson 1978, Buckley and Cooper 1978, Shultz and Florio 1979, Tickunoff and Ward 1978).

Planning and the Content of Instruction

Although schedules, routines, and the social system of an elementary classroom seem to be products of teacher planning and classroom interaction during the first weeks of the school year, the content of instruction is likely to be determined well before school begins. In one of the only studies of yearly planning to date, Clark and Elmore (1981) had a teacher of second grade think aloud while doing her yearly planning for mathematics, science, and writing. The primary resources used in yearly planning were curriculum materials (especially teacher's guides), the teacher's memory of classroom interaction during the previous year, and a calendar for the coming school year. The process of yearly planning, typically done during the summer months, consisted of the teacher reviewing the curriculum materials she would be using during the coming year, rearranging the sequence of topics within curricula, and adding and deleting content to be taught. A broad outline of the content to be taught, and to a lesser extent how it would be taught, emerged from a process of mental review of events of the past year, combined with adjustment of the planned sequence and pace of teaching to accommodate new curriculum materials and new ideas consistent with the teacher's implicit theory of effective instruction.

While changes in the content and sequence of instruction were not extensive in this case of yearly planning, the process served to integrate the teacher's own experiences with the published materials, establishing a sense of ownership and control of content to be taught (Ben-Peretz 1975). Yearly planning sessions satisfied this teacher that she had available the resources to provide conditions for learning at least equal to those she had provided during the previous year. Yearly planning decreased the uncertainty and unpredictability that attend every teaching situation.

The Clark and Elmore study of yearly planning supports the idea that published curriculum materials have a powerful influence on the content and process of teaching. In a series of studies of teacher planning for sixth-grade science instruction, Smith and Sendelbach (1979) pursued this idea at the level of unit planning. Working with the SCIS science curriculum, Smith and Sendelbach compared the explicit directions for a unit of instruction provided in the SCIS teacher's manual with four teachers' transformations of those directions into plans, and finally with one of the four teacher's actual classroom behavior while teaching the unit.

Observation of the four teachers during planning sessions combined with analysis of think aloud and stimulated recall interview data revealed that the principal product of a unit planning session was a mental picture of the unit to be taught, the sequence of activities within it, and the students' probable responses. These mental plans were supplemented and cued by sketchy notes and lists of important points that the teachers wanted to be sure to remember. Smith and Sendelbach characterized the process of activating a unit plan as one of reconstructing the plan from memory rather than carefully following directions provided in the teacher's guide.

Smith and Sendelbach are critical of the loose coupling between curriculum and instruction because of the potential they see for distortions or significant omissions in the content of science instruction. From their classroom observations of one experienced teacher implementing her unit plan, they concluded that the quality of instruction was degraded by both planned and unintended deviations from the SCIS curriculum, which they attributed to the teacher's limited subject-matter knowledge, difficulty in finding information in the teacher's guide, and the presence of inherently complex and confusing concepts. The researchers suggest that the quality of instruction could be improved by revising teacher's guides to make them more clear, more comprehensive, and more prescriptive.

A series of three related studies of teacher planning is reported in a paper by Clark and Yinter (1979). The three studies were (1) an analysis of teachers' written descriptions of their planning practices, (2) a field study of the relationship between teacher planning and teacher implementation of instruction, and (3) a study of teacher judgment while evaluating curriculum materials.

In the study of teachers' written descriptions of their planning practices, 68 elementary school teachers described the general characteristics of their planning and selected and described three examples of plans representing the three most important kinds of planning that they did during the year. The results include the following findings:

1. Learning objectives were seldom the starting point for planning. Instead, teachers began planning by considering their students and activities.
2. Teachers tend to limit their search for ideas to resources that are immediately available, such as teacher editions of textbooks, magazine articles, films, and suggestions from other teachers.
3. Teachers indicated that most of their planning is done for reading and language arts (averaging 5 hours/week), followed by math (2.25 hours/week), social studies (1.7 hours/week), and science (1.4 hours/week).
4. Teacher planning is more explicit and involves a longer lead time in team-teaching situations than in self-contained classrooms.
5. The most common form of written plans was an outline or list of topics to be covered, although many teachers reported that the majority of planning was done mentally and never committed to paper.
6. Planning seems to operate not only as a means of organizing instruction, but as a source of psychological benefits for the teacher. Teachers reported that plans gave them direction, security, and confidence. (p. 15)

The study of teacher planning and instruction involved asking five teachers to plan a two-week unit on writing that had never been taught before. Teachers kept journals documenting their plans and their thinking about planning during a three-week period, and they were interviewed twice each week. The journal keeping and interviews continued and were supplemented by observations during the two-week period when the plans were being implemented.

Analysis supported the idea that unit planning was not a linear process moving from objectives through design of activities to meet objectives. Rather, it was a cyclical process, typically beginning with a general idea and moving through phases of successive elaboration. Some teachers spent a great deal of time and energy at the *problem-finding* stage, generating topics or ideas for their unit. The search process typical of this stage was distinctly different from the elaboration and refinement of the idea that took place in the subsequent problem-formulation/solution stage. These data are consistent with the planning process model developed by Yinger (1977).

Two of the unit plans consisted of a short problem-finding stage, brief unit planning, and considerable reliance on trying out activities in the classroom. This approach to planning was called "incremental planning" and described teachers who employed a series of short planning steps, relying heavily on day-to-day information from the classroom. The remaining three unit plans were characterized as products of "comprehensive planning," in which the teachers developed a thoroughly specified framework for future action. Comprehensive planning involves more attention to the unit as a whole and more time and energy invested in specifying plans as completely as possible before beginning to teach. Both approaches to unit planning seemed to work well for the teachers who used them. Incremental planning saved time and energy while staying in touch with changing student states. Comprehensive planning provided a complete and dependable guide for teacher-student interaction for the whole course of a unit, reducing uncertainty and increasing the probability of achieving prespecified outcomes.

Teacher Judgment during Planning

The third study in the Clark and Yinger series concerned the operation of teacher judgment during the planning process. Twenty-five upper elementary teachers read and made judgments about the quality and usefulness of 32 different writing activities. The researchers' initial interest was in the activity features or "cues" that the teachers took into account as they made judgments about the attractiveness, appropriateness, likelihood of use, and predicted effectiveness of these curriculum materials. Like many other studies of human judgment, this was a policy-capturing study. The 32 writing activity descriptions varied systematically on the level (high or low) and combination of five activity features (student involvement, difficulty, fit between the aim of the activity and the process described, demand on the teacher, and integration). Regression equations were generated to describe the teachers' policies, expressed in terms of the weightings given each of the five manipulated variables that played a part in predicting their judgments (see Clark, Wildfong, and Yinger 1900; and Yinger, Clark, and Mondol 1981 for a full account of these analyses).

In addition, six of the 25 teachers in this study were asked to think aloud during the process of reading the activity descriptions and making judgments about them. This provided an opportunity to compare the results of the policy-capturing analysis with a process-tracing analysis. It was hoped that by creating descriptions of the judgment process derived from the teachers' own reports of their deliberations, a rich and appropriately complex picture of this aspect of teacher planning would develop.

Comparison of the policy-capturing and process-tracing representations of teacher judgment support the conclusion that teacher judgment in a realistic planning task is much more complex than the simplified policy-capturing design can portray (Yinger and Clark 1982). The main differences between the two methods of describing teacher judgment were that the process-tracing analysis revealed that the teachers attended to many more features of the activity descriptions (about 20) than the five that were manipulated (although four of the five manipulated features were considered) and that the teachers cited an average of about six features per activity in coming to a judgment. Furthermore, analysis of the think-aloud protocols revealed that the teachers used seven "heuristic operators" or information processing routines in preparing for the act of judgment. They were Reading, Interpreting, Mental Trying Out, Categorizing, Editing, Evaluating, and Justifying. The teachers used these heuristic operators to move through a four-step process. The process began with an attempt to understand the activity description by constructing a mental representation of it. This representation was then analyzed and evaluated through visualization of the activity in use or comparison with a similar activity drawn from the teacher's professional memory. During the process of comprehending the activity descriptions, the teachers also tended to edit and revise them into forms more suited to their own teaching styles and classroom situations.

Although this study dealt primarily with the process of teacher judgment, it also has implications for reading comprehension. The task set for the teachers could be characterized as one of comprehending each of the writing activity descriptions before rendering judgment. The think-aloud protocols, therefore, are transcripts of adults performing the act of reading comprehension. The materials they were comprehending were meaningful to them in several senses. First, these activity descriptions were instances of plans of the kinds with which these teachers were already familiar. Second, the materials were meaningful because they were embedded in a task on which the teachers presumably wanted to do well. And third, the teachers actually kept several activity descriptions for subsequent use in their own classrooms. Therefore, they had a strong incentive to comprehend plans that they might enact at some future date. So the meaningfulness of this reading comprehension task can be expressed both in terms of overlap with the teachers' past experiences and in terms of immediate and delayed consequences for them.

Figures 5.1 and 5.2 present an example of the data from the Yinger and Clark process-tracing study of teacher judgment during planning to demonstrate how reading comprehension played a part in the teachers' task. Figure 5.1 is a writing activity description typical of the 32 such descriptions that each teacher read and judged. Figure 5.2 is the transcript of what one experienced teacher of fourth grade said as he read and evaluated the activity description. The left side of Figure 5.2 consists of coding categories by which the researchers described the operations used by the teacher in comprehending the activity description and readying himself for judgment. Labels for these heuristic operators are nested to indicate how they seem to relate to one another for each section of the activity description. Reading of a new section of the activity description demarcates the four sequences of heuristic operators in this protocol.

In reading the purpose of the writing activity (transcript lines 1–6), the teacher experienced some difficulty, probably because the purpose is stated as a lengthy and complex sentence. To deal with this problem, he used the strategy of rereading the first half of the sentence (with considerably more inflection than he had the first time through), evaluating it, rereading the second half of the sentence (again with inflection), and evaluating it in relation to the first half. After a short pause, he then began reading the next section of the activity description (line 18 of the transcript). However, he jumped ahead in his reading when he encountered the expression "see below" to skim the list of objects provided (transcript lines 18–22). Rather than return to where his reading was interrupted, the teacher began reading a new section of the activity description (transcript lines 24–26). This new section did not make sense because understanding it depended on prior understanding of the skipped section of the description. The teacher then

MAROONED!

Purpose: *After completing this activity, the student should be able to identify several creative uses of common objects, and should gain increased facility in the processes required for critical thinking and making mature judgments.*

1. Ask your students to imagine this situation: You have been in a shipwreck and are floating alone in a rubber raft containing five objects (see below). You see an island far off, but the raft is sinking, and you will have to swim. You can hold only one of the objects while you swim.

> A baseball bat
> An eggbeater
> A book of fairy tales
> A jump rope
> A tablecloth

2. Ask students to indicate which one object they would pick and explain their choices in writing. They must tell how they expect to use the object and what advantage it might be to them while marooned on an uninhabited island.
3. Let students exchange their written work with one other student. Have them read and correct the paper for punctuation and spelling.

FIGURE 5.1   Writing Activity Description No. 32.

Hueristic Operators	Transcript
	1. Marooned! 32. After completing this activity
	2. the student should be able to identify
Reading	3. several creative uses of common objects and
	4. should gain an increased facility in the
	5. processes required for critical thinking and
	6. making mature judgments. Uhh . . . .
Evaluating	7. Sounds nice.
	8. After completing this activity, the student
Re-reading	9. should be able to identify several creative
	10. uses of common objects.
Evaluating	11. Okay
	12. . . . should gain increased facility in the
Re-reading	13. processes required for critical thinking and
	14. making mature judgements.
Evaluating	15. I'm wondering how that relates to the
	16. creativity . . . how it relates . . . .
	17.
Reading	18. Ask your students to imagine this situation
	19. you have been shipwrecked, floating along in
	20. a rubber raft containing five objects
Reading Skip	21.
Skimming	22. . . . a baseball bat, eggbeater . . . .
	23.
Reading	24. Ask students to indicate which object they
	25. would pick and explain their choices in
	26. writing.

FIGURE 5.2   Coded Think-Aloud Protocol for Activity No. 32.

Reading (backtrack)	27. Oh, I see, they can only hold one.
Evaluating	28. Alright.
Reading Skip	29.
	30. Let students exchange their written work
Reading	31. with one other student. Have them read
	32. and correct the paper for punctuation and
	34. spelling.
Evaluating	35. That's good.
Interpreting	36. Plus, it looks like they can choose their
	37. own student.
Editing	38. And for the kids who don't have anybody to
	39. choose, the teacher is always a good choice.
	40. Oh, I'm not sure all of these things up here
Evaluating	41. in the objective would take place.
	42. especially . . . .
Processing Shift	43. Oh . . . .
	44. . . . should gain increased facility in the
Re-reading	45. processes required for critical thinking and
	46. making mature judgements.
Evaluating	47. I think these last objectives are nice,
	48. and I think you have to have a lot more
Interpreting	49. experience. But if you are just talking
	50. about increasing a little bit, yeah,
	51. probably.
	52. Nevertheless, I think that this is an
Interpreting	53. activity that . . . a language activity which
	54. does not get anywhere near the attention
	55. that it should.
Evaluating	56. And this is really good.
	57. I think the fourth and fifth graders would
Justifying	58. love it. And they would probably be able
	59. to come up with some pretty interesting
	60. rationales for why they chose what they did.
Evaluating	61. I like it.

FIGURE 5.2 *continued*

backtracked in his reading to pick up the missing information and make sense of the activity description up to that point. Again he skipped over a section of the activity description (the second sentence of paragraph 2) to read the final section of the activity description (transcript lines 30–34). The transcript after line 34 shows that the teacher then focused on evaluating, editing, and interpreting the activity description, bringing to bear his own experiences with fourth-grade students to support and justify his positive evaluation. Rereading of part of the purpose statement (transcript lines 44–46) was also employed to help reach a final judgment.

Implications for Reading Comprehension

The Yinger and Clark study has a number of implications for research on and instruction of reading comprehension, as does the more general literature of teacher planning reviewed here. First, it may be that reading comprehension researchers could employ the think-aloud procedure to good effect. The aim of this kind of research would be to describe directly the processes and sequences of processes that accomplished readers use to comprehend text. A second and related implication is that using a task and material that are meaningful to the comprehender seems sensible. Just as decoding is not an end in itself, neither is comprehension. With meaningful materials and tasks we are more likely to see comprehension at its best, and see how the reader brings his or her prior experience to bear in making sense of a text. Descriptions of plans that readers can themselves envision carrying out may be a particularly appropriate form for reading comprehension studies.

Concerning direct instruction of reading comprehension strategies, one could consider use of the think-aloud procedure as a modeling device by teachers. Using this method, a teacher could illustrate how he or she moves through the sometimes complex, convoluted, and even confusing process of comprehending a challenging passage. And the teachers who try this approach might also learn more explicitly how they practice a process that has long since become automatic and unconscious.

The research on teacher planning more generally suggests that an important function of yearly, term, weekly, and daily planning is to allocate time for covering particular content. Reading comprehension takes time, and unless it is specifically planned for, it will tend to be slighted in favor of decoding (especially in the primary grades). Perhaps time and opportunity should be planned for students to alternate between reading aloud and commenting on what they have read. The habit of interrogating a meaningful text may come naturally to some readers, but others may be so driven by demands for flawless, continuous, linear decoding that deeper levels of processing never have a chance.

REFERENCES

Anderson, L. M., & Evertson, C. M. *Classroom organization at the beginning of school: Two case studies.* Paper presented to the American Association of Colleges for Teacher Education, Chicago, 1978.

Ben-Peretz, M. The concept of curriculum potential. *Curriculum Theory Network*, 1975, 5 (2), 151–159.

Buckley, P. K., & Cooper, J. M. *An ethnographic study of an elementary school teacher's establishment and maintenance of group norms.* Paper presented to the American Educational Research Association, March, 1978.

Clark, C. M., & Elmore, J. L. *Teacher planning in the first weeks of school.* Research Series No. 56. East Lansing: Michigan State University, Institute for Research on Teaching, 1979.

Clark, C. M., & Elmore, J. L. *Transforming curriculum in mathematics, science, and writing: A case study of teacher yearly planning.* Research Series No. 99. East Lansing: Michigan State University, Institute for Research on Teaching, 1981.

Clark, C. M., Wildfong, S., & Yinger, R. J. *Identifying cues for use in studies of teacher judgment.* Research Series No. 23. East Lansing: Michigan State University, Institute for Research on Teaching, 1978.

Clark, C. M., & Yinger, R. J. Research on teacher thinking. *Curriculum Inquiry*, 1977, 7 (4), 279–394.

Clark, C. M., & Yinger, R. J. *Three studies of teacher planning.* Research Series No. 55. East Lansing: Michigan State University, 1979.

Goodlad, J., et al. *Behind the classroom door.* Worthington, Ohio: Charles A. Jones, 1970.

Joyce, B. Toward a theory of information processing in teaching. *Educational Research Quarterly,* 1978–79, *3* (4), 73–77.

McLeod, M. A. *The identification of intended learning outcomes by early childhood teachers: An exploratory study.* Unpublished doctoral dissertation, University of Alberta, 1981.

Morine-Dershimer, G. *Teacher plan and classroom reality: The South Bay study, part IV.* Research Series No. 60. East Lansing: Michigan State University, Institute for Research on Teaching, 1979.

Morine-Dershimer, G, & Vallance, E. *Teacher planning.* Beginning Teacher Evaluation Study, Special Report C. Far West Laboratory, California, 1976.

Newell, A., & Simon, H. A. *Human problem solving.* Englewood Cliffs, N.J.: Prentice-Hall, 1972.

Peterson, P. L., Marx, R. W., & Clark, C. M. Teacher planning, teacher behavior, and student achievement. *American Educational Research Journal,* 1978, *15* (3), 417–432.

Popham, J. W., & Baker, E. L. *Systematic instruction.* Englewood Cliffs, N.J.: Prentice-Hall, 1970.

Pylypiw, J. *A description of classroom curriculum development.* Unpublished doctoral dissertation, University of Alberta, 1974.

Shavelson, R. J., & Stern, P. Research on teachers' pedagogical thoughts, judgments, decisions, and behavior. *Review of Educational Research,* Winter 1981, *51* (4), 455–498.

Shultz, J., & Florio, S. Stop and freeze: The negotiation of social and physical space in a kindergarten/first grade classroom. *Anthropology and Education Quarterly,* 1979, *10,* 166–181.

Smith, E. L., & Sendelbach, N. B. *Teacher intentions for science instruction and their antecedents in program materials.* Paper presented at the American Educational Research Association, 1979.

Taylor, P. H. *How teachers plan their courses.* Slough, Bucks: National Foundation for Educational Research, 1970.

Tikunoff, W. J., & Ward, B.A. *A naturalistic study of the initiation of students into three classroom social systems.* San Francisco: Far West Laboratory for Educational Research and Development, Report A-78-11, 1978.

Yinger, R. J. *A study of teacher planning: Description and theory development using ethnographic and information processing methods.* Unpublished doctoral dissertation, Michigan State University, 1977.

Yinger, R. J., Clark, C. M., & Mondol, M.M. *Selecting instructional activities: A policy-catpuring analysis.* Research Series No. 103. East Lansing: Michigan State University, Institute for Research on Teaching, 1981.

Yinger, R. J., & Clark, C. M. *Understanding teachers' judgments about instruction: The task, the method, and the meaning.* Paper presented at the annual meeting of the American Educational Research Association, 1982.

Zahorik, J. A. The effect of planning on teaching. *Elementary School Journal,* 1970, *71,* 143–151.

Zahorik, J. A. Teachers' planning models. *Educational Leadership,* 1975, *33,* 134–139.

6

The Teacher as Thinker: Implementing Instruction

Jere Brophy

The previous chapter dealt with teachers' planning for instruction. The present chapter considers the thinking and decision making that occurs as teachers interact with their students in the process of instructing them. Clark and Yinger (1979) describe studies in this domain as follows:

> Interactive decision making refers to decisions made during the act of teaching. The teacher is seen as constantly assessing the situation, processing information about the situation, making decisions about what to do next, guiding action on the basis of these decisions, and observing the effects of the action on the students. The fundamental question underlying this work is: How much teaching is reflective, and how much is reactive? The portion of teaching that is reflective is what interests those who study the interactive decision making of teachers.
>
> All studies of interactive decision making by teachers depend on the teacher's self-report of the decision made. The most common method of obtaining self-report data is some variation of a procedure in which a videotape of the teacher's teaching performance is replayed to stimulate recall of the teaching situation. In some studies only short segments of the videotape are replayed while in other studies the entire videotape is replayed. In the latter case, the videotape may be stopped by the teacher when he or she remembers having made a decision, or the researcher may control the identification of "critical incidents." In most cases, the teacher is asked a standard set of questions after viewing each videotape or segments, (pp. 247–48).

This research is still very new. So far, they have not yielded consensus on the "reflective vs. reactive" issue mentioned by Clark and Yinger (1979). There are conflicting reports about both the quantity and the quality of teacher decision making. Quantity estimates range from a low of ten decisions per hour (Marland 1977) to a high of 24 decisions per 35-minute lesson (Wodlinger 1980). These differences are due to differences in definition, in particular whether the term "decisions" should be restricted to those in which two or more alternatives are considered, or whether it should also include so-called null decisions (Wodlinger 1980), in which the teacher implicitly decides to continue with the lesson, although without actively considering any alternatives.

Regardless of its frequency, most studies of teachers' interactive decision making portray it as more reactive than reflective, more intuitive than rational, and more routinized than conscious. However, two caveats should be kept in mind in considering these data. First, Joyce (1978–79) has shown that interactive decision making occurs with reference to an "activity flow" established by prior planning, including not only planning for this specific lesson but planning and decision making done at the beginning of the school year that led to the establishment of certain routines that provide the context within which the lesson is taught. Studies that attend to this "big picture" usually portray teachers as more rational and impressive decision makers than studies that attend only to events occurring within the lessons observed. Second, differences in stimulated recall methodology affect the numbers and kinds of decisions brought to attention. In general, investigators who question teachers about every apparent decision point develop more information about decision making than investigators who confine their attention to only those decisions that teachers remember on their own while viewing the tapes or investigators who accept teachers' initial responses to their questions. In short, the amount and quality of interactive decision making revealed in stimulated recall studies varies with the kinds of questions asked by investigators and the degree of persistence they show in probing for responses.

SUMMARIES OF DECISION-MAKING STUDIES

Eight major studies are presented here. They are discussed separately and are organized logically (rather than chronologically). None of these studies focused on comprehension instruction in particular, but the implications affect comprehension as well as other subject areas. These are discussed later in the chapter.

Peterson and Clark (1978)

Peterson and Clark (1978) studied interactive decision making by 12 experienced teachers who were observed teaching an experimental social studies unit to three different groups of eight junior high students (with whom they were previously unacquainted). The teachers were shown four brief videotaped segments of their interactions and then asked about what they were doing during the segment, what they noticed about the students, whether they had objectives in mind, whether they considered alternative strategies, and whether situational factors had caused them to change their planned strategies.

The findings revealed that the teachers considered alternative strategies only when the teaching was going poorly. The primary cues they used to judge this were student participation and involvement. In 65 percent of the taped segments sampled, the teachers said that they were not thinking about alternatives because things were going well. In 10 percent, they noted problems but could not think of alternatives. In 7 percent, they noted problems, thought about alternatives, but ended up staying with their original plan nevertheless. Finally, for 18 percent of the segments, the teachers reported changing to alternative strategies. Thus the teachers changed to alternative strategies only about half the time that they noted problems, sometimes because they could not think of alternatives and sometimes because they apparently believed that the alternatives were even less acceptable than persisting with the original plan. In any case, most of the interactive decision making of these teachers involved relatively minor fine tuning of their basic plans and adaptation of these plans to situational events that are not totally predictable (such as student responses to questions). Major changes in plan were infrequent.

Peterson and Clark reported that teachers' experience and verbal ability were related to the quality of decision making. Teachers with higher verbal ability (assessed by a vocabulary test) reported more available alternative strategies and fewer instances in which they could not think of alternatives when the lesson was going poorly. Also, across teachers in general, instances in which lessons went poorly but the teachers could not think of alternatives dropped across the three replications.

Correlations with outcome measures indicated that teachers who stayed with their plans even when they were not working were less successful in producing student achievement and positive attitudes. Teachers who stayed with their plans because they were working tended to produce higher student achievement on lower-level cognitive objectives, but teachers who recognized problems and shifted to alternative strategies tended to produce higher student achievement on higher-level cognitive objectives.

It is difficult to evaluate these data because they are correlational and because they did not allow separation of issues regarding the need for change in plans and the reasons for this need from issues regarding the availability and implementation of effective alternative strategies. Even so, like other data to be discussed, they are provocative in suggesting that lessons that go entirely according to plan may be less successful, at least in some respects, than lessons that go generally according to plan but that require some interactive decision making involving shifting to alternative strategies to respond to unforeseen developments.

Morine-Dershimer and Vallance (1975)

Morine-Dershimer and Vallance (1975) used stimulated recall procedures to study decisions made by second- and fifth-grade teachers categorized as either more or less effective. They found that very few decisions related to activities not originally planned for the lessons. Most related directly to preactive decisions made during planning or else involved responding to instantaneous verbal interaction. The teachers focused on instructional processes when discussing the substance of their decisions, but shifted to pupil characteristics when asked about the basis for these decisions.

Teachers classified as *less* effective mentioned taking into account *more* items in their decision making. This may seem counterintuitive because we might expect teachers who process more information to be more perceptive in the immediate situation and/or more able to bring relevant concepts and experiences to bear in making their decisions. However, Newell and Simon (1972) have shown that it is important to cut down on the complexity of decision making by carving out a small "problem space" within which to work, especially when engaged in complex and continuously shifting tasks such as teaching. Also, Shulman and Elstein's (1975) studies of medical decision making indicated that experienced diagnosticians do not methodically work through all possible alternatives, but move quickly to testing their hypotheses about the most likely sources of the problem. Often they generate only a single hypothesis and stay with it until it is either confirmed or rejected.

The Morine-Dershimer and Vallance (1975) data suggest that something similar may happen with teachers. That is, the more effective or experienced teachers may have learned to cut through the complexities so as to be able to identify (and thus have to monitor) only those aspects of the teaching situation that are most reliable and relevant for interactive decision making. Furthermore, they may have honed down their lists of viable alternatives by eliminating those that have been found to be ineffective. If so, their information and processing and decision making would be less complex but yet more efficient than that of less effective or experienced teachers.

Morine-Dershimer (1979)

More recently, Morine-Dershimer (1979) used stimulated recall techniques to study interactive decisions by elementary teachers during reading lessons taught to high- and low-ability groups. Interviews were conducted at four points across the school year so that changes over time could be investigated.

The teachers were asked about the degree to which they were surprised or disturbed by events occurring at decision points in their lessons, and this information was used to classify lessons into three types. The first involved little or no discrepancy between what teachers had planned and what was occurring. In these lessons, most decision points were handled by previously established routines (and thus did not lead to conscious choice between recognized alternatives), and most of the teachers' information processing involved responding to their own preformed "images" of the flow of the lesson and the responses anticipated from the pupils. The teachers later explained or justified their behavior at decision points on the basis of their beliefs about the kinds of treatment that students needed or about how they were likely to respond to the content or the teachers. These beliefs apparently were correct, or at least were not contradicted by what happened during the lesson, so that the teachers were not forced to change either their plans for the lesson or their images about the students and how the lesson should be adapted to them. Few decisions involving active consideration of alternatives were reported in these lessons, because they were not needed (only 25 percent or less of the decision points involved unexpected events, and these were not especially disturbing to the teacher).

The second type of lesson featured frequent minor (not critical) discrepancies between plans and reality. Here, 50 percent or more of the decision points involved unexpected events, but less than 25 percent of these were disturbing to the teachers. Most of the unexpected events were minor problems such as pupils' understanding a question in a way different from that intended by the teacher, and not major problems such as showing boredom or irritation with the lesson. Morine-Dershimer found that these minor problems could be handled through immediate "inflight" decisions. Information processing for these "inflight" decisions had to become "reality oriented" rather than "image oriented" because the teachers had to observe what the students were actually doing rather than continue to respond to their own preformed images and expectations. There was no need for major shifts in approach or activities, however, because the unexpected pupil reactions did not threaten learning nor invalidate the basic plan.

The contrast between these two lesson types is interesting because it suggests that teachers may observe, and perhaps learn, more when forced to deal with minor deviations from expectation than when they are able to implement their plans smoothly. Apparently, there is literally more reality contact when things go generally but not entirely according to plan than when they go entirely according to plan. Like Peterson and Clark's (1978) data reported above, these findings suggest that lessons that go entirely according to plan may be somewhat less useful than lessons in which unanticipated events arise that require some shifting in plans (assuming, of course, that the teacher has appropriate alternatives readily available and can shift to these alternatives smoothly).

Too much unexpected response is counterproductive, however. Morine-Dershimer's third type of lesson included those in which 50 percent or more of the decision points were described by the teachers as not only unexpected but disturbing. Here the problems were major ones that threatened student learning and challenged the validity of the lesson plan itself (e.g., the material may have been too difficult for the students, or so removed from their experience that they could not respond very meaningfully to it). The teachers who experienced these critical discrepancies between their plans and the realities of their lessons were clearly aware of the problems and could describe them in some detail, but typically had little to say about how to respond to them (and in fact, they seldom responded successfully during the lessons in question). Morine-Dershimer speaks of the decisions in these lessons as being handled by "postponement" because the teachers did not have readily available any acceptable alternative strategies, and so their choices were usually restricted either to aborting lessons or continuing with the original plan even though it was clearly not working. Thus, whether the problem is lack of appropriate plans in the first place or lack of readily available and appropriate alternatives to shift to when generally appropriate plans must be adjusted, studies agree in suggesting that teachers who experience frequent and major discrepancies between their plans and the realities of their lessons tend not to be able to adjust to these problems effectively.

McNair (1978–79)

McNair (1978–79) presents information on the content of teachers' interactive decisions. The data are from the same high-and low-ability reading groups studied four times across the school year by Morine-Dershimer (1979).

Of 1,249 decisions coded, 291 dealt with pupil learning (whether or not pupils understood the concept or fact being taught). Another 188 concerned the task (what to require of pupils), 170 concerned facts and ideas (decisions based on perceptions of how difficult the facts or ideas would be for the group, or how to teach them), and 128 dealt with pupil attitudes (decisions based on pupil attitudes, attentiveness, etc.). Smaller numbers of decisions dealt with such matters as the instructions that the pupils would need, the materials, or student conduct. Only 3 percent of the decisions concerned instructional objectives. These percentages are very similar to those obtained in preactive planning studies (see previous chapter).

Comparisons of the content of decisions across the four times studied during the school year and across the two levels of ability of the reading groups yielded no significant differences, although there was a trend toward more decision making in the low-ability groups, especially concerning pupil attitudes and conduct.

This would be expected from Morine-Dershimer's (1979) findings if it is assumed that teachers are more likely to encounter problems in teaching low ability groups than high ability groups.

Both sets of findings, along with findings on preactive planning discussed by Joyce (1978–79), come from a single large study called the South Bay Study. In discussing the study as a whole, these investigators note their surprise in finding that conscious decision making during interactive instruction is less frequent and apparently less important than they expected. Joyce (1978–79) points out that the activity flow set up early in the year during preactive planning determines what occurs during lessons much more than interactive decision making typically does. McNair (1979–79) and Morine-Dershimer (1979) note that most teacher thoughts during interactive instruction involve only minor fine tuning of previously established plans. No major changes in direction occur so long as the lesson goes well, and plans typically are refined in small ways but not scrapped in favor of alternatives.

Wodlinger (1980)

Wodlinger (1980) studied 242 decisions made in ten lessons (averaging 35 minutes each) taught by a sixth-grade teacher with four years of experience. The frequency of decisions noted in this study is much higher than usual because it includes so-called null decisions in which the teacher implicitly decides to continue or resume the lesson, but does not actively consider any alternatives.

Wodlinger reports that most decisions were instance-specific: There was no master plan guiding all or even most decision making. The teacher cited a variety of cues, often more than one per decision, in explaining her decisions. These included both low-inference student behaviors (walking around, shouting out, gross movement) and high-inference student behaviors (facial expressions, voice tones, changes in body stance). The behavioral cues themselves were mentioned most frequently in explaining managerial decisions, but instructional decisions were justified more often on the basis of inferences about students' cognitive or affective states rather than on the basis of direct evidence. Furthermore, once estimates of students' states of mind and behavior were formed, they tended to be acted upon without any attempt to check their validity. Presumably they were "validated" by previous experience and/or beliefs about teaching and learning.

Most (86 percent) of the interactive decisions were formulated after consideration of only one alternative. However, the author suggests that many of these decisions had become routinized, based on earlier experience in which alternatives were considered more actively but then rejected for good reasons. Thus he suggests that this teacher may have been acting like the medical diagnosticians studied by Shulman and Elstein (1975). That is, perhaps the teacher was able to move immediately to the most promising alternative without actively considering less promising ones, or at least to be able to reject less promising alternatives subconsciously, and thus maximize efficiency in responding to ongoing events. There is no direct evidence to support this interpretation, however, and in fact, Wodlinger's data are very similar to those of other investigators who have concluded that teacher interactive decision making is mostly reactive and unimpressive.

Some of the other data from Wodlinger's study support his interpretation, and some do not. First, almost all (97 percent) of the teacher's decisions were judged to be congruent with her intentions. However, this meant only that the teacher was not conscious of any feedback that disconfirmed the wisdom of her decision (and given that she seldom sought feedback actively, it is likely that the actual effectiveness of her decisions was considerably lower than the 97 percent figure implies). Also, more than twice as many (164) of the teacher's decisions were instructional rather than managerial (78), suggesting that the teacher had good control of her class and was able to concentrate on academic instruction. In general, these data make the teacher appear to be an effective instructor (and by inference, an effective decision maker).

However, the teacher's quotes in which she explains her decisions do not make her appear to be particularly insightful or articulate, and evidence of confusion and anxiety or frustration appears frequently.

Also, the teacher reported getting feedback following only 25 percent of her decisions (19 percent of the instructional decisions and 36 percent of the managerial decisions). Wodlinger suggests that the instructional decisions may be based more on beliefs and principles of teaching that have been validated through previous experience and that they may be more highly routinized than managerial decisions, so that their consequences can be more predictable and certain. That is, the teacher may be more confident and thus able to act more "automatically" when responding to attentive but confused students with instructional behavior than when responding to inattentive or disobedient students with managerial behavior. In any case, it was clear that many of the teacher's decisions were based on inferences about, rather than direct evidence of, students' cognitive or affective states and that the teacher seldom sought evidence to verify her inferences or feedback to validate her decisions.

In addition, it was clear that the teacher often relied on what Tversky and Kahneman (1974) call "heuristics" (implicit rules that people use, without conscious awareness, for making sense of their environment and making decisions in complex situations). One of these is the "representativeness heuristic," in which a given cue is taken as representative of a larger class of behavior and is treated as automatically representative of that behavior. This teacher equated students' shuffling at their desks with restlessness and equated sitting quietly while looking at open books with engagement. The teacher also used the "availability" heuristic, in which decisions are made based on the most easily available information (such as observable student behavior) rather than necessarily the best available information (such as student responses to questions intended to clarify their cognitive or affective states). Such heuristics are useful because they enable teachers to simplify the complexities of teaching enough to enable them to make reasonable (if not totally rational) decisions (Shavelson and Stern 1981). Another example of such heuristics in action is Lundgren's (1972) demonstration that teachers use the responses of subsets of students that he called "steering groups" (usually the students who range from about the 10th to about the 25th percentile in achievement in the classroom) in deciding when a point has been understood sufficiently so that they can then move on to the next topic in the lesson. Teachers assume that if the students in the steering group understand the content, so will the majority of students who are higher achievers than those in the steering group to begin with (presumably the students in the bottom 10 percent will not be expected to understand the content, at least not without individualized assistance).

Given the complexities of the teacher's task, reliance on such heuristics is probably necessary, at least to some degree. However, heuristics are overgeneralized rules of thumb that work reasonably well most of the time but sometimes lead to false impressions or incorrect decisions. This is especially likely if teachers proceed as if they were working with factual information rather than inferences that should be validated by feedback. The teacher studied by Wodlinger, for example, often seemed to be responding more to her expectations of students than to the students' actual behavior in the situation. To the extent that those expectations were inaccurate and remained uncorrected by feedback, the teacher would be prone to inappropriate decision making in general and behavior likely to produce self-fulfilling prophecy effects in particular.

Shroyer (1981)

Shroyer (1981) studied the decision making of three elementary mathematics teachers, concentrating on their information processing and decision making at critical moments when things did not go entirely to plan. As did Morine-Dershimer, Shroyer describes the teacher as working on "automatic pilot" when things are going well but maintaining a more active and reality-oriented stance when unanticipated events occur. Many of these unanticipated events are student difficulties in learning, student inattention, or other problems, but critical moments can include potentially positive events as well. That is, students may give unanticipated responses to the teacher's questions, or may ask questions or make comments of their own, that represent achievement of important insights or present "teachable moments" that tempt the teacher to depart from the plan in order to take advantage of the unanticipated opportunity. Thus, when student "occlusions" (as she called them) occur, teachers can choose among three general courses of action. First, they can exploit the potential advantages that the occlusion presents. Second, they can do what is necessary to alleviate the problem (give an answer or brief explanation but then quickly get back on track). Finally, they can avoid responding to the occlusion altogether (ignore it, declare it to be irrelevant to the task at hand, state that it will be dealt with at some future time, etc.).

As a group, the three teachers studied by Shroyer encountered 421 student occlusions. They exploited only 8 percent of these, while alleviating 78 percent and avoiding the remaining 14 percent. The teacher who was most concerned about promoting student understanding did the most exploiting, and the teacher who was most bound to lesson plans and obtaining right answers did the most avoiding.

Only 14 (3 percent) of the student occlusions led to critical moments involving teacher cognitive difficulty or emotional discomfort. Another six critical moments occurred due to accumulated problems and pervasive patterns rather than single occlusions. In general, then, most of the teaching was business as usual, based on successful routines. The 20 critical moments included nine instances of inability to correct student difficulty, six instances of inability to accept or exploit a student insight, three pacing dilemmas that occurred because one or more students were not keeping up with the group, and two instances of unexpected success by the group as a whole that made the teacher realize that the lesson was probably unnecessary. The teachers generally responded poorly to these critical moments. As in other studies, they were marked by cognitive confusion and affective anxiety or frustration at these times, and not by rational consideration of clear cut alternatives. Shroyer believes that the lack of available alternatives is related in turn to a lack of immediately applicable mathematical knowledge (both knowledge of the mathematics itself and of how to teach it). Thus, like some of the studies reviewed earlier, this study suggests that experience alone (without new input) will not necessarily enable teachers to become more effective decision makers.

In this case, in fact, experience had been somewhat counterproductive. Shroyer reports that these teachers had learned that their attempts to deal with the unexpected usually only made things worse unless they achieved immediate success. They believed that this was especially true in dealing with problems presented by slower students. Thus, these teachers found it difficult to make changes in their planned activities. They planned their activities anticipating limited success and thus did not consider or plan for excessive difficulty or remarkable success. Alternatives were not available unless the teachers had planned for other activities. Their ability to develop alternative plans spontaneously was limited due to limited knowledge about how to teach the context.

Shroyer notes that teachers who seek to promote student understanding will encounter more critical moments than those who stick to the plan and concentrate on getting correct answers to preset questions. This will present them with more opportunities, however, if they are willing and able to exploit them. The teachers' response in these situations will depend on both their attitudes and their competence as subject matter instructors. The more willing and effective teachers are likely to see student occlusions and similar events as opportunities to exploit, but other teachers are likely to see them as disruptions to be avoided or suppressed. Shroyer concludes that teachers do not so much need more general information as they need task- and topic-specific mathematical knowledge and situation-specific pedagogical advice. They need to be made more aware of the student difficulties and insights that may arise in a particular lesson, what these might indicate, and what the possible courses of action in response to them may be.

Marland (1977)

Marland (1977) used stimulated recall techniques to study the interaction thinking of two first-grade and two third-grade teachers during language arts and mathematics lessons, and two sixth-grade teachers during language arts lessons. He classified teachers' thoughts not only according to content but according to function. The most common functions concerned correcting or adjusting lessons when they were not going smoothly, dealing with parts of the lesson that were unpredictable in principle (deciding how to respond to a student who gives a partially correct answer), regulating one's own behavior by reference to teaching principles, and adapting instruction to individual students. Other functions that were logically possible but did not appear often in teachers' thoughts were self-monitoring, verifying interpretations of student behavior, considering alternative teaching tactics, and optimizing instruction. As others have found, Marland's teachers did not give much direct consideration to their teaching style or its effectiveness or impact on students, but operated on the basis of hunches or intuitions about how students were responding. Impressions about students were taken as fact rather than as hypotheses to be tested. Tactical moves were considered with respect to whether or not to make them at all or to make them at this time, but there was little consideration of alternative tactics. Thoughts about improving instruction usually did not occur unless the lesson was going poorly.

Marland went beyond these descriptive findings to analyze teachers' behaviors and rationalize in order to induce explanatory principles. Five of these principles or implicit theories were mentioned by at least six teachers and seemed to influence their behavior: compensation, strategic leniency, power sharing, progressive checking, and suppressing emotions.

The principle of compensation involved trying to compensate for the limited initiation and participation of students who were shy, introverted, limited in ability, or culturally disadvantaged. Teachers referred to this principle to explain why they went out of their way to call on, encourage, or create success experiences for students they saw as needing this kind of help. Strategic leniency was a variation of the compensation principle, under which teachers would ignore or respond less sharply to the inappropriate behavior of students seen as needing special attention.

The principle of power sharing referred to sharing classroom leadership, responsibility, and authority with students. Teachers referred to this principle in discussing their beliefs about student involvement in classroom decision making and in explaining how and why they gave special attention to the students they perceived as class leaders. In particular, they tried to reinforce desirable behavior by these students in the hope that they would be a positive influence on the rest of the class. The principle of progressive checking was invoked to explain why teachers made a point of periodically checking on the progress of certain students, especially low ability students during independent work times. They saw these students as needing more structure, assistance, and encouragement and relied on frequent, systematic checking as a way to meet those needs.

The principle of suppressing emotions was mentioned by teachers who explained why they consciously suppressed their emotional reactions while teaching. One reason for this was that they were conscious of their roles as models, and feared that too much emotional expression on their part might lead to unacceptable emotionality among the students. Another reason was that they felt obligated to treat all their students professionally, courteously, and essentially equally. Consequently they made conscious efforts to mask their emotional reactions when they became aware that they particularly liked or disliked certain students.

Connors (1978)

By going beyond pure description in order to infer general principles that underlie teachers' decision making, Marland (1977) was able to show that even interactive decision making can be proactive and rational. His findings were replicated and extended by Connors (1978) in another dissertation study done at the University of Alberta. Connors's descriptive findings replicate those of others: Most interactive thoughts were about pupils and activities rather than objectives, and the teachers used pupil response and level of participation most often in judging the success of their lessons. Unlike Marland, however, Connors analyzed the teachers' behavior and rationales inductively to identify principles that guided their behavior and the beliefs that supported those principles. He identified three general types: overarching principleŞ; general pedagogical principles; and more specific principles from learning theory, motivational theory, and human growth and development. Three overarching principles were used by all nine of the teachers in his study: teacher authenticity, suppressing emotions, and self-monitoring.

The principle of teacher authenticity involved the teachers' presenting themselves to their students as ordinary adults who do not know everything and who make mistakes. This principle is cited as important in building good relationships with students and promoting a relaxed classroom atmosphere.

The principle of suppressing emotions was the same one described by Marland. This principle was invoked to protect pupil self-concept by avoiding harsh chastisement, and was used as a management strategy when teachers deliberately maintained controlled silence in order to gain the attention of the class. Connors notes that the teachers did not always adhere to this principle, even though they espoused it. Sometimes they could not contain their emotions, and occasionally they deliberately violated the principle in order to use a display of emotion as "the ultimate management strategy."

The principle of self-monitoring refers to the fact that the teachers were more or less continously aware of their own behavior and were assessing it critically (even though they could not be certain of how the pupils perceived this behavior). This principle is one of several aspects of Connors's findings that indicate a greater degree of self-awareness and reality contact seen in his teachers than has been reported by other investigators.

In addition to the three overarching principles, Connors identified five general pedagogical principles. Three of these (cognitive linking, integration, and general involvement) were used by all teachers, and two others (equality of treatment and closure) were used less frequently.

The principle of cognitive linking involved teacher recognition that new knowledge should be related to the information that pupils already possess. It was cited especially often during explanations for lesson introductions and reviews. The principle of integration involves teacher recognition that transfer of training can be facilitated by crossing subject-area boundaries to enable students to practice skills and concepts learned in one subject area when they are involved in activities in another subject area. The principle of general involvement referred to attempts to involve all pupils in lessons and to even use the lessons to develop aspects of their personalities when the teachers believed that this was desirable. This principle was invoked especially often to explain teachers' attempts to draw shy students into discussions and lessons. The principle of equality of treatment involved attempts to treat all pupils equally and consistently. Finally, the principle of closure involved teacher recognition of importance of reviewing, summarizing, and evaluating key points. It was especially relevant to teacher behavior at the close of lessons.

Connors also identified principles of learning theory, motivation theory, and human growth and development that individuals or subgroups of teachers invoked to explain their behavior. Learning theory principles included repetition, reinforcement, motivation, feedback, active pupil involvement in the learning process, and transfer of learning. Other teacher thinking in relation to learning was organized around major learning processes: problem solving, association, discrimination, and the importance of using a variety of modes of presentation. There were also various motivational principles mentioned, dealing with maintaining or enhancing student self-concept, creating a good classroom atmosphere, and catering to individual differences. Finally, various teacher thoughts were related to developmental principles or stages. After discussing these principles themselves, Connors discusses the teachers' beliefs that provided rationales for the principles. These included beliefs about learning, motivation, and development, as well as teacher role conceptions and associated beliefs about appropriate classroom rules.

Along with the study by Marland, Connors's study illustrates the value of going beyond descriptions of teachers' thinking and behavior in order to induce the general principles that seem to be guiding them. It also provides striking examples of the richness and variety in teachers' perceptions, thinking, and decision making during interactive instruction. It may be that teachers are more aware, observant, and rational during instruction than previous research has suggested.

Consider these examples given by Connors. Two teachers varied the difficulty level of questions in order to involve certain pupils in the discussion without embarrassing them. Another knew which pupils she could rely on to keep answering questions, so she often delayed asking these pupils questions in order to concentrate on nonvolunteers and those who infrequently contributed to discussions. All teachers knew which pupils did not contribute to discussions because of shyness, and made special efforts to involve them. They were also aware of pupils who tended to dominate discussions, and made efforts to minimize their influence (often by ignoring some of their comments and questions). When teachers knew that the lesson had to move along at a good pace, they would call on pupils that they knew would give correct answers. Teachers' reactions to inappropriate conduct varied according to their knowledge of the likelihood that the student would become disruptive and of how the student would respond to soft vs. sharp reprimands. Teachers were usually aware of pupil movement in the class such as walking around the room or raising hands to seek attention. They also monitored students' facial expressions, and sometimes used this information in deciding when to end an activity.

In general, Connors reports more teacher self-awareness and reflection, and more correspondence between beliefs and behavior than most other investigators. Even so, most of the thinking and decision making he uncovered dealt with general aspects of lesson presentation (especially beginnings and endings), group management, and regulation of the participation of individual pupils. There was little or no mention of instructional activity unique to the subject matter being presented, awareness of or attempts to probe individual students' preconceptions about the content or comprehension of the basic principles being taught, or awareness of and attempts to deal with what Shroyer calls "student occlusions."

SUMMARY: WHERE IS THE TEACHERS' SUBJECT–MATTER–SPECIFIC INSTRUCTIONAL EXPERTISE?

The research reviewed above can be summarized as follows (cf. Shavelson and Stern 1981). Based on preactive planning and prior experience, teachers enter lessons with plans, "scripts," or "images" that structure their expectations about the flow of activities and the responses of the students. Much of their instructional activity is accomplished through previously developed routines that minimize the need for conscious decision making during interactive teaching and that tend to be played out once they are begun. Using these images and routines, teachers proceed on "automatic pilot" as long as events develop as expected, with emphasis on keeping the activity flow moving at a good pace, managing the group, and monitoring the involvement of individuals. As long as the lesson proceeds smoothly and pupil response remains within expected and acceptable tolerance levels, group monitoring can be accomplished mostly automatically using routines and heuristics (relying on nonverbal behavioral cues as indicators of attitude toward the lesson and comprehension of its content).

Sometimes, however, unexpected events occur that preclude "business as usual" progression through the activity flow (inattention, disruption, or failure to respond to a question), or that indicate the need for a repetition or shift in activities (indications that students do not understand; student questions or responses that raise issues that the teacher did not plan on taking up but that may be worth pursuing once they have been raised). At these points, teachers' monitoring of students must become more active and "reality based," and their behavior may become temporarily determined by on-the-spot decision making rather than images and routines. At minimum, the teacher will have to decide whether to continue with the lesson as planned or whether to deviate from the plan. Most teachers seem to be reluctant to change their routines even if they are not working well, and when they do make changes, these tend to be minor adjustments rather than major revisions. This may occur mostly because teachers simply lack readily available alternatives, at least alternatives that they perceive to be preferable to the original plan. Thus teachers often make "null" decisions to continue with an activity even after they have become aware that the activity may not be necessary or that it is not going well, simply because they have time to fill and are not prepared to fill it any other way. Another possible motive, especially for teachers who fear loss of control of the students (Cooper 1979, Doyle 1980), is that established routines provide structure and predictability for both teacher and students. Abandoning or changing these routines not only introduces greater cognitive complexity and the need for on-the-spot decision making, but introduces ambiguities and breaks the flow of the lesson, and thus greatly increases the chances for escalation of student inattention or disruption (Kounin 1970).

Even teachers who do not experience serious classroom management problems and who appear to be generally effective instructors do not seem to be able to respond consistently and effectively when events dictate a major shift in plans or when students present them with "teachable moments" that could be exploited. The reasons for this are not yet clear, but several investigators have suggested that the teachers they studied lacked sufficiently specific and detailed knowledge of the subject matter (both the content itself and how to teach it) to enable them to diagnose learning problems on the spot and respond immediately with prescriptive instruction.

One reason for the relative absence of subject-matter-specific instructional expertise in existing research on teachers' interactive decision making may be that this research has concentrated at the elementary level. Perhaps studies of secondary teachers, who are trained as subject-matter specialists, would yield more impressive evidence of teacher thinking and decision making related to diagnostic and prescriptive aspects of instruction.

Another possibility is that the teachers included in these studies were considerably below average in sophistication and expertise. This is unlikely, however. Data presented in many of the studies make it clear that some of the teachers were average or better, and in any case, several studies by different investigators working at widely dispersed locations have all failed to produce much evidence of subject matter-specific instructional expertise. Thus, there is every reason to believe that most teachers (or at least most elementary teachers) do not have such expertise, at least not in a readily available form that would allow them to make effective on-the-spot instructional decisions during interactive teaching.

My own belief is that very few teachers become expert enough to function as effective decision makers regarding the whole range of content and method selection, adaptation, supplementing, evaluation, remediation, and adjustment of plans for the next time. Some of this probably represents cognitive limitations, at least in some teachers, in dealing with inherently complex tasks. However, I believe that most of it stems from the combination of a very limited knowledge base that would support teachers' decision making about selecting and presenting content, and the tendency of teacher education institutions to stress affective and interpersonal factors over content presentation factors in their courses for future teachers.

IMPLICATIONS FOR INSTRUCTION IN READING COMPREHENSION

The research reviewed here will be troubling to anyone concerned about effective content instruction in our schools. It is especially troubling to those concerned about instruction in reading comprehension because such instruction must necessarily depend squarely on the teacher (attempts to develop reading comprehension abilities through curriculum materials that students are to read and react to on their own are likely to be useful only to those students whose reading comprehension abilities are already well developed). Another cause for concern is that reading comprehension is a high-level, complex subject matter, and most reading comprehension activities require the teacher to concentrate on higher-level questions that require students to draw inferences or develop informed opinions about the material they have been reading. In contrast to the more factual questions that typify other aspects of reading instruction, the kinds of questions stressed during comprehension activities are more open to varying interpretations, can be answered with varying degree of completeness or relevance, may admit to a variety of acceptable responses, and are especially likely to elicit unexpected responses or prompt unexpected student comments. In short, reading comprehension activities are especially likely to assume and make demands on subject-matter-specific instructional expertise that teachers may not possess, and to invite "student occlusions" that many teachers view as threatening and that few teachers seem prepared to exploit.

In view of these complexities, no short or simple route to effective reading comprehension instruction is likely to be discovered. However, a comprehensive approach might be successful if it included a firm foundation in basic teaching skills and followed up by providing the teacher with both a well-developed reading comprehension curriculum and detailed, well-organized information about instructional methods.

Teacher Education

Effective instruction in a subject like reading comprehension, and in particular, effective on-the-spot decision making during interactive instruction, assume a critical mass of rather high-level teaching competencies that the teacher must be able to use "effortlessly" to adapt instantaneously to emerging developments during lessons. It is unclear at this point what percentage of teachers can attain this level of competence. It does seem clear that those who do so will first have to master and integrate a broad range of competencies in classroom organization, group management, and lesson preparation.

I believe that teacher decision making must be viewed developmentally. Beginning teachers are consumed with survival concerns, although these usually dissipate soon if the teachers receive good instruction in classroom organization and management. Once past initial survival issues, most teachers become concerned primarily about mastering the mechanics of instruction—learning to present lessons and activities "correctly" (Fuller 1969). At this stage, it may be necessary for many teachers to write out lesson plans or have a teacher's guide available for frequent reference during the actual teaching of the lesson. To reduce complexity and minimize the need for decision making (which they are not yet prepared to do efficiently), they may find it necessary to stick to a detailed script or to rely on instructional procedures or algorithms that are routinized to the point of rigidity. (This is intended as description, not criticism. I believe that most beginning teachers should be encouraged to rely on detailed lesson plans and instructional algorithms for the same reason that we encourage young children learning arithmetic to rely on counting sticks and Cuisenaire rods: The structure and simplification that they provide enable learners to deal with complexities that might be too much for them to handle otherwise.)

As teachers gain in knowledge and experience, more of these basic teaching functions become routinized, and heuristics are developed for monitoring student response efficiently and chunking information input at higher levels of sophistication. These events are accompanied by development of ease and confidence in teaching situations. No longer consumed by lower-level survival and procedure-oriented concerns, teachers become emotionally free to shift from control concerns to interest in explicating the content and promoting desired student outcomes. These emotional changes are accompanied by changes in cognitive functioning and potential: As instructional activities and monitoring become more routinized, the sense of cognitive strain associated with these activities recedes, and a greater proportion of the teacher's cognitive capacity becomes available for adapting to unanticipated events.

If this portrayal of teachers' professional development is accurate, it has at least three implications for reading comprehension instruction. First, the research on teachers' planning discussed in the previous chapter and the research on teachers' interactive decision making discussed in the present chapter both suggest that many teachers never get to the point where they are sufficiently freed from affective or cognitive prohibitions against deviating significantly from the planned activity flow as to be able to capitalize on unanticipated "teachable moments" or respond effectively to unanticipated student comments. Thus, not only preservice teachers but many inservice teachers need training in basic teaching skills of classroom organization, group management, and lesson preparation.

Second, teachers probably cannot be expected to teach reading comprehension activities effectively until they have reached higher levels in the progression outlined above. Unless they are emotionally free of survival and control concerns, they are unlikely to be able to sustain attention to comprehension objectives, and unless sufficient information processing capacity has been freed up by routinization of lower-level teaching functions, they will be unable to sustain the thinking and decision making that comprehension activities appear to require. Thus, for many teachers, development of effectiveness in reading comprehension instruction may not be possible until remedial training in more basic teaching functions has been completed.

Third, given the demands on teachers' time, the tendency of teachers to rely on curriculum materials to define the content of instruction, and the apparent complexities of reading comprehension instruction, it seems important to provide teachers with as much help as possible in the form of well-developed curriculum materials and instructional guidelines. Chances are that this level of support will prove to be necessary to enable most teachers to conduct effective reading comprehension instruction. As described below, what I have in mind are curriculum materials and instructional guidelines that are in many ways more elaborate than those developed for so-called teacher-proof curricula, and yet designed to encourage and facilitate teacher decision making and preparedness to capitalize upon unforeseen "teachable moments."

Reading Comprehension Curricula

Because most teachers depend on the curriculum to provide guidance about the content of instruction and materials with which to teach, it is clear that we must provide teachers with well-developed reading comprehension curricula if we are to expect them to conduct regular and effective reading comprehension instruction. Espousal of reading comprehension goals will not have much effect if it is supported only by occasional exercises in sequencing or main idea and vague instructions telling teachers to "discuss" the stories with the students. Only a comprehensive reading comprehension curriculum, integrated with the rest of the reading program, is likely to do the job effectively. This need not be discussed in detail here because it is covered in Parts 3 and 4 of this volume. What I have in mind, however, is the kind of instruction advocated by Duffy and Roehler (see Chapter 17) and by Pearson (see Chapter 16), backed by the kinds of materials and assignments advocated by Osborn (see Chapter 12).

To the statements of these authors I would add only one more point, stimulated by the research reviewed in the present chapter and by the research of Smith and Anderson (see Chapter 13) on improving students' comprehension of science constructs by improving the content and format of the teacher's manual accompanying science curricula. Smith and Anderson point out that instruction does not involve inserting content into a vacuum, but involves changing students' existing conceptions by moving them from whatever they are now toward the "goal conceptions" that correspond to the objectives of the lesson. They have shown that certain goal conceptions are much more difficult to achieve than others because they conflict with students' preconceptions that are incorrect but nevertheless widely believed and difficult to change. For example, students find it hard to abandon the notion that we see objects because the sun brightens them (rather than because they reflect sunlight to our eyes), or the notion that plants take in "food" from the soil in the form of water, minerals, or fertilizer (rather than that plants make their own "food" from sunlight through the process of photosynthesis). Smith and Anderson have shown that science instruction relating to these concepts can be improved by revising and elaborating the teacher's manual to call attention to misconceptions that the teacher probably will encounter; provide examples of questions and answers that help determine whether students have grasped the goal conception or are confused by one of the common misconceptions; and suggest analogies, explanations, or demonstrations likely to be effective in counteracting misconceptions.

Similarly elaborate teacher's guides would likely facilitate effective reading comprehension instruction. Here I would foresee attention not only to student misconceptions (which could be identified in the pilot testing stage) but to some of the other complexities inherent in reading comprehension instruction. One of these is that there is no single "correct" answer to many of the questions raised in reading comprehension instruction. Also, even when there is a correct answer to the question as phrased ("What did the story say was the hero's motive?"), a different question on the same topic might admit to a broad range of acceptable answers ("What might explain the hero's actions?"). It would be helpful if teacher's manuals were clear about when students were to be questioned for comprehension of what the story said, and when they were supposed to be invited to give their personal reactions to the story (and for what purpose, and with what expected outcome).

I would also like to see teacher's manuals written to help teachers remain aware that reading comprehension skills are tools rather than ends in themselves. Not all paragraphs have (or should have) a single main idea. Some material is more suited than others to outlining or sequencing. Sometimes two or more different sequences would be equally appropriate (although with different advantages and disadvantages). Most stories have more than one "moral." To the extent that teacher's manuals call these distinctions to teachers' attention, they will enable teachers to be more balanced and comprehensive in their instruction and more prepared to exploit the "teachable moments" that students present to them during lessons.

Guidelines for Decision Making

In addition to what has already been discussed, preparation of teachers to be effective decision makers during interactive instruction will require development of a much larger knowledge base about the options available to teachers in typical teaching situations, and the tradeoffs involved in selecting one option over another. So far, research on interactive decision making suggests that teachers usually cannot articulate two or more options available to them at a choice point in a lesson, let alone explain the relative merits of pursuing such options. Clearly, a great deal of research and development is needed in this area.

One strategy that has not been tried yet is to identify those (apparently few) teachers who are able to generate more than one feasible option for dealing with unforeseen events occurring in their lessons, to engage in rational on-the-spot decision making, and to articulate their rationales for this later in stimulated recall interviews. So far, research on teachers' interactive decision making has concentrated on elementary level teachers selected randomly or on the basis of convenience (easy access to their classrooms). It is possible that efforts to identify highly effective or impressive interactive decision makers would succeed and that systematic study of these teachers (most of whom would probably be subject-matter specialists at the secondary level or beyond) would yield useful information that could lead to improvement in the interactive decision making of teachers in general.

Even without such data, much can be done to improve teachers' interactive decision making by making them more aware of available options for responding to frequently encountered decision points. Lundgren's (1972) research, for example, provides a great deal of information about the tradeoffs involved in pacing decisions. He shows, for example, that pacing will be brisker and progress through the curriculum more rapid and complete if the teacher uses average-achieving rather than low-achieving students as the steering group for decision making about when to continue with further explanation about a topic and when to move on to the next topic. A drawback to this strategy, of course, is that it will increase the percentage of students (low achievers) who do not fully comprehend the content and therefore are destined to fall farther behind the rest of the class every day. This can be prevented by using the lowest achievers as the steering group, of course, but at the cost of considerably slowing the pace of progression through the curriculum and thus minimizing the progress of the average and especially the high achievers.

Lundgren also shows how time constraints (as perceived by teachers) affect pacing decisions. Early in a unit (and early in the school year) when teachers are usually less conscious of time constraints, they are likely to move at a leisurely pace, concentrate on low achievers, attempt to get everyone to participate, and be more patient in waiting for responses to questions. Late in the unit (or late in the year), awareness that time is running out leads to preoccupation with getting through the curriculum. Content coverage rather than individual participation becomes the primary concern, and the teacher is more likely to concentrate on the high-achieving students and to call on students judged to be most likely to supply correct answers that will sustain the brisk pacing of the activity. For the most part, the teachers studied by Lundgren, like the teachers in other interactive decision-making research, acted intuitively rather than on the basis of on-the-spot conscious decision making. However, it seems likely that other teachers who are made aware of this information will be able to think more consciously about the options involved in pacing and the tradeoffs associated with these options, and thus become able to be more planful and proactive in dealing with these options.

Similar improvement can be expected as information is developed about other common decision points in teaching. How long should teachers wait for a response to a question? When students fail to respond or give an incorrect answer, should teachers simply supply the correct answers, or should they try to elicit an improved response from the student by rephrasing the question or giving a clue? If they do give the answer, when will the answer itself suffice, and when will a more extended explanation be necessary? When should modeling with (first person) verbalization of self-instructions be used instead of the more typical (third person) verbal explanation or (second person) instructions designed to guide the student through the process?

To the extent that theory and data about these options are developed, this information can be included in teacher education programs. Even better, it can be included in the teacher's manuals that accompany curricula and instructional programs, where general principles can be adapted to the specific contexts (grade level, subject matter, etc.) within which they are going to be actually used. This should foster decision making not only by calling relevant decision options to teachers' attention, but also by presenting these options to them in concrete, immediately applicable form (thus eliminating the need to deduce specific applications from abstract general principles, a task that most people find difficult and that in any case is highly time-consuming, and so will not often be done systematically by teachers acting on their own).

By their very nature, the decision points that teachers commonly encounter are not amenable to simple, algorithmic solutions. The relative appropriateness of various options will depend on the subject matter, the students involved, the purpose of the activity (introduction of new content, provision of practice, review, application), the familiarity vs. novelty of the content or the task, time constraints, and numerous other factors. Despite this complexity, it is possible to identify some general principles and to facilitate decision making by organizing these principles into a hierarchical system capable of providing specific guidance for specific situations that may develop during lessons.

This approach was used in developing guidelines for teachers involved in Anderson, Evertson, and Brophy's (1979) experimental study of first-grade reading instruction. These guidelines concerned the organization and management of small group reading lessons. Some of these guidelines were to be followed under all circumstances, so that no decision-making options were involved (i.e., teachers should sit with their backs to the wall so that they can monitor not only the students in the reading group but also the rest of the students who are simultaneously involved in independent activities at various locations around the classroom). Most of the guidelines, however, involved decision making about when or under what circumstances they should be followed. The recommended strategies were described as specifically as possible, but were presented with detailed rationales emphasizing the relationships among the strategies and especially the effects on students that the strategies were planned to achieve. Thus the strategies were clearly presented as means to these higher ends, not as ends in themselves. They were also presented with embedded options, with the explicit understanding that factors like time constraints or group management concerns might take precedence over instructional concerns in certain situations. For example, one basic principle was that first-grade students need individualized opportunities to read and respond to questions overtly—that teachers need to see that each student in the group participates frequently and roughly equally, that this participation is monitored carefully, and that appropriate feedback is provided. Thus it is recommended that students be called on to participate in a standardized order and that the students be trained to respect one another's turns (by remaining attentive and listening to the student who was called on, but not by calling out answers themselves or waving their hands in an effort to get the teacher to call on them). Another part of this general principle calls for the teacher to wait patiently for a response when the student does not answer or begin to read immediately. However, it is recognized that situational factors will determine how this principle is applied in practice. It is recognized that teachers sometimes will be unable to wait long for a response because time constraints require that the activity be concluded shortly or lesson pacing/group management concerns indicate that signal continuity or momentum (Kounin 1970) will be lost if the teacher does not resume the activity flow. Also, the guidelines recognize that teachers should ordinarily wait longer when a student seems comfortable and is trying to think about the question than when the student seems stumped or is becoming anxious or embarrassed.

Guidelines are also provided to promote decision making about when and how to attempt to improve a student's response by rephrasing questions or giving clues. In addition to the criteria mentioned in the previous paragraph, these guidelines take into account the nature of the question. Many questions concern facts that have to be acquired through rote learning (letter-sound relationships, irregular pronunciations). There usually is not much point to trying to improve the responses of students who fail to answer these questions or answer them incorrectly because the kind of help that ordinarily would be useful does not apply (attempts to sound out words using the rules that fit regular words will not succeed with irregular words and may even compound the confusion of the student) and because the clues that do apply are of dubious benefit to the student ("It's one of our new words"). In these situations, then, it is probably better for teachers to give the student the correct answer than to try to elicit it through rephrasing or clues.

The opposite is true for complex questions that can be broken down into simpler questions or for questions that can be solved by applying a logical reasoning process that can be stimulated with a clue or a new question. Thus it is often appropriate for teachers to suggest that students sound out words that they do not recognize on sight (when the word is regular and can be sounded successfully using previously acquired phonetic knowledge), or to follow up failed comprehension questions with new questions that cue the student to a path that can lead to an acceptable response. Reading comprehension activities provide frequent opportunities for teachers to improve students' responses in these ways. The degree to which teachers actually do so, however, will probably depend on the degree to which the teacher's guide suggests this behavior directly, both in general guidelines about how to conduct reading comprehension activities and in specific suggestions for follow up questions to the primary comprehension questions suggested for each individual activity. The general guidelines described above should be applicable to most reading comprehension activities, especially those conducted in small groups in the early grades. They are clearly rather general and do not address the kinds of decision making that will be necessary if teachers are to succeed in meeting the goals of reading comprehension activities. Designers of reading comprehension curricula should be able to provide such guidelines if they are willing to take the time to do so.

CONCLUSION

The literature on teachers' interactive decision making is still very new, and some findings seem to tell us more about the methodologies used to develop the data than they do about the present functioning or future potential of teachers. Even so, it seems clear at this point that the inherent complexity of the teaching task, especially instruction in reading comprehension, coupled with the time constraints and group management concerns within which it is conducted in typical class-rooms, minimizes the opportunities that teachers get to conduct rational decision making involving the weighing of two or more clear-cut alternatives (even for those teachers capable of generating such alternatives on the spot). There may be some significant improvement in this situation as research on teachers' interactive decision making accumulates and as teachers and teacher educators become more sensitized to the topic. Even if this should occur, the potential for improving teaching through increasing the quantity and quality of interactive decision making seems limited because the degree to which teachers can interrupt the activity flow of lessons in order to contemplate alternatives is limited.

Consequently, I believe that the major part of any improvement in teachers' ability to respond effectively to decision points that arise in the process of teaching lessons in reading comprehension will come not through improved on-the-spot decision making but through routinization of hierarchically organized sets of instructional principles. Assuming the development of the needed knowledge base in comprehension (or even the development of logical and face valid sets of principles), some of this can probably be accomplished through improved preser-vice education. Most of it, however, probably will have to be accomplished through vastly expanded and improved teachers' reading manuals accompanying published curricula. Few people can routinely deduce the implications of abstract general principles for behavior in specific, context-bound situations, let alone do it on the spot in circumstances such as those under which teachers function routine-ly. However, if teacher's reading manuals accompanying packaged curricula were to be clear and somewhat detailed about the general principles of instruction ex-pected to be used with the curricula (taking into account not only the philosophy behind the curricula but also grade level, etc.), and if this general information were backed by more specific information alerting teachers to the particular deci-sion points that might arise in each activity and providing suggestions for dealing with them, we might begin to see a vast improvement in teachers' responses to such decision points. I do not believe that anything short of this level of support for teacher planning and decision making will be successful.

REFERENCES

Anderson, L., Evertson, C., & Brophy, J. An experimental study of effective teaching in first-grade reading groups. *Elementary School Journal*, 1979, *79*; 193–223.

Clark, C., & Yinger, R. Teachers' thinking. In P. Peterson and H. Walberg (Eds.), *Research on teaching*. Berkeley, Calif.: McCutchan, 1979.

Connors, R. *An analysis of teacher thought processes, beliefs and principles during instruction*. Unpublished doctoral dissertation, Department of Elementary Education, University of Alberta, 1978.

Cooper, H. Pygmalion grows up: A model for teacher expectation communication and performance influence. *Review of Educational Research*, 1979, *49*, 389–410.

Doyle, W. *Student mediating responses in teaching effectiveness: Final Report*. Proj-ect No. 0–0645. Department of Education, North Texas State University, March 1980.

Fuller, F. Concerns of teachers: A developmental conceptualization. *American Educational Research Journal*, 1969, *6*, 207–226.

Joyce, B. Toward a theory of information processing in teaching. *Educational Research Quarterly*, 1978–1979, *3*, 66–67.

Kounin, J. *Discipline and group management in classrooms*. New York: Holt, Rinehart and Winston, 1970.

Lundgren, U. *Frame factors and the teaching process*. Stockholm: Almquist and Wiksell, 1972.

Marland, P. *A study of teachers' interactive thoughts*. Unpublished doctoral dissertation, Department of Elementary Education, University of Alberta, 1977.

McNair, K. Capturing inflight decisions: Thoughts while teaching. *Educational Research Quarterly*, 1978–1979, *3*, 26–42.

Morine-Dershimer, G. *Teacher plan and classroom reality: The South Bay Study, Part IV*. Research Series No. 60. Institute for Research on Teaching, Michigan State University, 1979.

Morine-Dershimer, G., & Vallance, E. *A study of teacher and pupil perceptions of classroom interaction*. Technical Report No. 75–11–6, Beginning Teacher Evaluation Study. San Francisco: Far West Laboratory for Educational Research and Development, November, 1975.

Newell, A., & Simon, H. *Human problem solving*. Englewood Cliffs, Prentice-Hall, 1972.

Peterson, P., & Clark, C. Teachers' reports of their cognitive processes during teaching. *American Educational Research Journal*, 1978, *15*, 555–565.

Shavelson, R., & Stern, P. Research on teachers' pedagogical thoughts, judgments, decisions, and behavior. *Review of Educational Research*, 1981, *51*, 455–498.

Shroyer, J. *Critical moments in the teaching of mathematics: What makes teaching difficult?* Unpublished doctoral dissertation, College of Education, Michigan State University, 1981.

Shulman, L., & Elstein, A. Studies of problem solving, judgment, and decision making. In F. Kerlinger (Ed.), *Review of Educational Research*, vol. 3. Itasca, Ill.: Peacock, 1975.

Smith, E., & Anderson, C. Plants as producers: A case study of fifth grade science teaching. Unpublished research report, College of Education, Michigan State University, 1982.

Tversky, A., & Kahneman, D. Judgment under uncertainty, heuristics and biases. *Science*, 1974, *195*, 1124–1131.

Wodlinger, M. *A study of teacher interactive decision making*. Unpublished doctoral dissertation, Department of Educational Administration, University of Alberta, 1980.

7

The Environment of Instruction: The Function of Seatwork in a Commercially Developed Curriculum

Linda Anderson

There! I didn't understand that, but I got it done.
DONALD, AGE SIX

In addition to death and taxes, we might include *seatwork* in elementary class-rooms as a certainty in life, at least in present-day American schools. Think back to your own elementary school days. Remember the smell of the purple dittos? The excitement of a brand new workbook that would be your very own? The seemingly endless passage to be copied from the front board? They are all still there, although (at least in the author's memory) the ditto ink is now less pungent and the workbooks are more colorful.

A recent study of time use suggested that, in many classrooms, students may spend up to 70 percent of their allocated instructional time doing seatwork: reading or written tasks completed without immediate, direct teacher supervision (Fisher et al. 1978). Although individual products and individual effort are expected with seatwork assignments, such work is usually done in a social setting; that is, other students are doing seatwork at the same time, often working on the same assignment. This social setting affects how (and sometimes if) individual students complete their assignments.

Publication of this work is sponsored by the Institute for Research on Teaching, College of Education, Michigan State University. The Institute for Research on Teaching is funded primarily by the Program for Teaching and Instruction of the National Institute of Education, United States Department of Education. The opinions expressed in this publication do not necessarily reflect the position, policy, or endorsement of the National Institute of Education. (NIE Contract No. 400-81-0014 and NIE Grant No. 90840.) This work was done in collaboration with Gerald Duffy, Nancy Brubaker, and Janet Alleman-Brooks. Their contributions and participation are gratefully acknowledged.

The use of seatwork allows the teacher time to concentrate on face-to-face instruction with small groups and individuals. Another advantage of seatwork (at least when assignments are appropriate) is that students receive individual practice in applying skills and concepts. Thus, the pervasiveness of seatwork can be attributed to valid instructional goals.

The universality, frequency, and rationale of seatwork suggest that it is an appropriate topic for investigation. However, with the exception of studies focusing on "time on task," little research has been done on ways that seatwork affects students' learning. Time-on-task studies suggest that greater achievement on standardized tests occur when students spend more time engaged with tasks at appropriate levels of difficulty (Fisher et al. 1978); that seatwork settings typically yield less time on task than teacher-led small groups (Good and Beckerman 1978); and that teachers' management practices, including accountability for completed seatwork, affect the overall level of engaged time (Emmer and Evertson 1980).

Such findings are important because they confirm the bare minimum conditions that must exist if seatwork is to affect students' learning. Obviously, if students are not attentive to and engaged with their seatwork tasks, those tasks can have little effect.

However, given that students are on task and thus mentally engaged with seatwork, questions may be asked about the quality of that engagement: What mental processes occur while students are doing seatwork? How are these mental processes affected by variations in classroom and task structures? How do these mental processes that occur in response to daily assignments affect cumulative outcomes such as reading fluency?

This paper describes a study that addresses some of these questions about seatwork within the framework of a classroom environment using standard basal text approaches to instruction. While it was not focused on reading comprehension per se, the study *was* conducted during reading periods in primary classrooms and therefore included whatever comprehension instruction occurred there. Because the study was limited in scope and population, it did not provide generalizable statements about relationships, but it did suggest some ways to look at and wonder about children's comprehension of seatwork and the effect of seatwork on cumulative comprehension skills.

Background of the Study

The Student Responses to Classroom Instruction Study examined the "short-term" responses of children to daily classroom tasks, especially seatwork tasks. Some types of short-term responses are attention, initiative to participate, initiative to resolve difficulty, successful completion of tasks, and understanding of how and why to do daily assignments. The rationale for the study was that discrete experiences in response to instruction determine whether and how that instruction contributes to cumulative, or "long-term" outcomes, such as reading achievement (Anderson 1981). Two lines of research were influential in the design of the study. First, Doyle's (1980) work on the student as a mediator of instruction suggested that students' perceptions of classroom tasks (what is the goal, how is it reached, and what is risked in pursuing it) will determine *how* they select and use information from the classroom environment. The second line of work that led to the

Student Response Study was teacher effectiveness research, especially investigations of more and less effective classroom managers, where a distinguishing feature was the teachers' apparent sensitivity to the students' attention, involvement, success, and need for information while instruction was proceeding (Anderson, Evertson, and Emmer 1979). More effective managers acted as if they believed that the student was indeed the critical mediator of their teaching, and thus they remained aware of indications that the students were responding in ways that facilitated learning.

SAMPLE

Eight first-grade classrooms in four Title I schools in an urban district were observed. Classrooms were selected on the basis of teacher willingness to participate. Ten teachers were approached, and eight were interested.

In each classroom, four target students (one male and one female high achiever, and one male and one female low achiever) were selected for focused observation from all students whose parents had given permission. During the year, two high-achieving females moved, resulting in a final sample of 30 target students. Achievement classifications were based on the teacher's report of reading group placements, because no entering test scores were available. Thus, the labels "high" and "low" refer to relative position within each classroom, not performance judged on a common scale.

All classrooms were self-contained and taught primarily by one teacher, although aides were present in four classes. In five of the eight classes, reading instruction was presented in small ability-based groups. In the other three classes, little or no group instruction was given, and the teacher met with individuals to hear them read. In all classes, however, students spent some time each day doing reading-related seatwork.

METHODOLOGY

The study produced detailed descriptions of the target students performing seatwork assignments at five different times during the year (usually at one-month intervals). Observations lasted about three hours, during which time an observer alternated her attention between two target students, usually switching from one to the other at ten- or 15-minute intervals. However, this time sampling method was used flexibly in order to see beginnings and endings of certain events. Several instructional settings were observed, but the data collected in seatwork settings are emphasized in this paper.

The observer took notes on what the target child did, what he or she seemed to be attending to, how seatwork was approached, what the student did when he or she encountered a problem, and how successful the student was. The observational record also included as much information as possible about instructional stimuli (teacher's movements, types of materials, role of other students). Copies of the seatwork were obtained or described in detail. Teacher explanations of assignments were audio-recorded.

After an observation was completed, the observer taped a detailed narrative record of the morning's observation that included times. Also noted were the final performance of the child on assigned work that day and any teacher feedback that occurred while the observer was present.

The resulting data provided a very detailed record of the child's activities on a minute-to-minute basis. For example:

> 9:51   J. looks back at the board and writes "te" (copying *yesterday*) and then looks around some and then writes "day," all at once, without looking at the board for each letter. Then he glances over toward A. reading, but does not interact with her. (She is reading aloud "to herself," about three feet from J.).
>
> 9:52   He goes back to his writing and writes without distraction: "*Matt /ha/ d*" (the slashes indicate where he looked up at the board while he was copying) and then looks up at S. (sitting across the table from him) as the teacher is elaborating on a fact in the story that S. has just read.

The observational data was supplemented with informal conversations with students about work done that morning, in order to tap the student's understanding of how and why he or she was doing the work. For example, the child might have been asked to "show me how to do this page" or "how did you know to choose this word instead of that word?" Questions designed to elicit the child's understandings of the purpose of the work were, "What are you learning about when you do this work?" and "Why do you think your teacher wanted you to do this page?"

RESULTS

Qualitative analyses so far have focused on questions about general trends and exceptions to those trends. That is, in what ways were the classrooms and the students similar to one another? In what ways were they different, and could these differences account for some students benefitting from seatwork more than others?

We have found among these eight classes and 30 students some notable similarities in the seatwork done and in the students' apparent understanding of why they are doing seatwork. In fact, these two patterns of similarity may be reflective of one another, as described below.

Despite the similarities across classes and students, significant differences among students were also apparent. There was a group of students whose responses to seatwork frequently were not facilitative of learning. This subgroup included at least one child from each class and sometimes two. In at least a third of their observations, they revealed a lack of understanding of the content or skills featured in the seatwork, and they used strategies that were not likely to strengthen their understanding. In general, they did not seem to "make sense" of their seatwork tasks in ways that might further their learning. Although not all the low achievers fell into this group, all members of the group were originally labeled as low achievers.

Recognizing the prevalence of these "poor responders," our analysis efforts have focused on describing an environment that may create and support such patterns of responses to seatwork. The first step in describing that environment was to look at what all classes and students had in common.

The Nature of the Work: Similarities across Classes

The seatwork used and the ways that it was assigned were similar across the eight classrooms. For example, in all classes, from 30 percent to 60 percent of the students' allocated reading instructional time was spent doing some form of seatwork related to reading. In most of the classes (all but one), there was a strong reliance on commercial workbooks and/or dittos taken from commercial packages. At least 50 percent and in some cases almost 100 percent of seatwork assignments were based on commercial products. In many cases, the workbooks, dittos, and readers were all part of the same basal series.

Most of the reading seatwork from the commercial materials observed in this study emphasized discrete reading skills, with each page emphasizing a single skill. For example, every sentence on a page might include a word that has a soft *g* sound.

In all eight classes, at least part and sometimes all of the formal reading instruction consisted of moving in order through a reader, a reading workbook, or both. That is, the sequence of the book was important, and one book was completed before another one was begun.

Within each class, certain forms of seatwork assignments became very familiar to the students and were used from two to five times a week, although the classes differed on what forms were used. For example, there might always be a board exercise of the same form, in which students copied sentences with blanks and chose the correct word from several options. In other classes, certain forms of dittos or workbook sheets were used frequently, such as reading a sentence and then choosing one of three pictures that illustrate the meaning of that sentence. Thus, explicit explanations of assignments were not always given since the students had learned the usual procedures for certain forms.

In six of the eight classes, at least half of the seatwork assignments were given to the whole class. That is, all students, regardless of reading level, completed the same assignment.

Thus, the typical pattern revealed by these data shows classrooms where seatwork is a regular and unremarkable occurrence, where workbooks and associated dittos of familiar form are used to provide practice on reading skills, and where there are frequent occasions in which students can compare their progress with one another because of common assignments.

Students' Understanding of Why They Do Work:
Similarities across Students

After careful review of all qualitative data, the research team concluded that for most of our target students, both low and high achievers, the most salient aspect of doing their seatwork is simply to get it done.

We began to form this impression as we observed students' behavior while doing seatwork. The following are examples of behavior that, when occurring repeatedly for the same students, indicated to us that they were concerned with getting their work finished:

- Frequent questions to peers about "How far are you?", and frequent statements of "I'm almost done—just two more" or "I'm ahead of you!"
- Upon completing the last item on a page, immediately turning it in or moving on to the next page without any indication of checking or reviewing.
- Completion of work accompanied by expressions of relief (e.g., a long sigh and "There!" as student is stacking papers, or, as one student was overheard saying to himself, "There! I didn't understand it, but I got it done").

These behaviors by themselves do not necessarily mean that students are not also attending to the content-related purposes of the work. However, our "on-the-spot" interviews with the students support the behavioral observations.

Some students answered questions about "What are you learning?" in terms of broad skill areas: "I'm learning to read better" or "I'm learning how to write." We seldom received an answer that described specific skills being practiced or specific concepts being applied. This is in spite of the fact that most of the seatwork assignments for reading and math were designed to emphasize a particular skill. For example, one workbook page included five sentences that each included words ending in –ot (e.g., "Look out for the hot pot"). Students were to indicate a picture that illustrates the sentence (e.g., a boiling pot is chosen instead of a steaming pie or a frankfurter being roasted). When asked, "What are you learning about when you do this page?" a student responded, "How to read these sentences and draw circles around the right picture." There was no indication during this conversation that the student recognized the similarity among the sentences (i.e., all featured –ot words) or the specific content-related purpose of the page (i.e., to practice decoding words with –ot.) The few exceptions to this pattern occurred when short and long vowels were introduced. Here students said, "This page is about words with long a sounds." Perhaps the analysis of vowel sounds was enough of a novelty that students attended to that content when describing the page.

Taken altogether, the behavioral and student interview data suggested that while doing seatwork, these first-grade students perceive purpose in terms of "doing the work" and progressing through a book rather than understanding the specific content-related purposes of assignments. At this point, we are not saying that this is either desirable or undesirable, simply that this seems to be a prevalent pattern.

We can only speculate about reasons for this pattern of student response. Certainly the age and developmental level of the children should be taken into account, in that one would not expect first graders to give answers suggesting a grand scheme for analyzing reading skills or to have a firm set of concepts for thinking about their own learning processes.

Our observations of the teachers and their presentations of assignments have led us to consider an additional hypothesis. We think that students' perceptions of the purposes of seatwork may be related to the information that they receive from teachers about their work. Unfortunately we cannot test this hypothesis systematically with our present data because there is so little variance for either dependent or independent variables.

Teacher Communications about Seatwork: Similarities across Classes

The following characterized most instances of teacher communication about seatwork:

- Presentation or explanations of assignments seldom included statements about content-related purposes of the work (e.g., references to what will be learned or practiced and how that related to other learning).
- While students were working and teachers commented on their work, most comments concerned looking busy and finishing work rather than actual performance. Many of the teachers seemed to be monitoring student be-havior but not student understanding or success while completing the assignment. This is probably because teachers were usually busy with in-struction while other students did seatwork. Thus their communication about seatwork while it was being done was influenced by the teacher's immediate goals: to maintain a quiet working environment so that the teacher could concentrate on face-to-face instruction. This was appropriate in many cases (when students could gain from independent practice with-out constant monitoring), and we do not mean to imply otherwise. The point here is that the teacher's communications emphasized something other than understanding and accuracy while the work was in progress.
- Teachers very seldom focused on cognitive strategies when presenting seat-work assignments. For example, few statements were heard about ways of checking one's work for accuracy and meaningfulness, identifying areas of difficulty, or applying a general strategy to a particular type of task. In-stead, teacher explanations were usually procedural (e.g., "Read the sen-tence and circle the word that goes in the blank," with no reminders about how to select the appropriate word.)
- Most recorded instances of teacher feedback to seatwork included state-ments about correctness or neatness but seldom included questions or explanations of processes for figuring out the correct answer.

These patterns of teacher communication may have suggested to the students that seatwork is to be done as a routine part of the day, but little thought about it is necessary beyond the self-control needed to stay on task and finish one's work. Certainly the responses of the students reflected this perspective.

It is likely that for some assignments and some students, these kinds of com-munication are appropriate. If students are working on tasks of familiar form and have a good grasp of necessary cognitive strategies and are doing the assignment to increase speed and fluency, then it would be inefficient to dwell on explicit statements of purpose and strategies. However, students working on new task forms or students who are not at all fluent with a particular skill or concept might benefit from more specific content-related explanations, monitoring and feedback than was typically seen.

This suggestion is based on an analysis of the subgroup of students whose responses to seatwork often seemed not to contribute to their learning and under-standing. Having discussed what was the same about all teachers and students, we turn now to a discussion of the differences between students in their patterns of response.

Students Whose Responses to Seatwork Did Not Contribute to Increased Understanding

In reviewing the narrative records of all 30 students, the researchers were struck by the experiences of some of the low achievers. These students frequently did poorly on their assignments and were often observed to use strategies for deriving answers that allowed them to complete assignments without really understanding what they did (as was stated so explicitly by the child quoted at the beginning). Of special concern to us, especially after talking to the students about their work, was the lack of concern on their part about whether their work "made sense." Like all of the target students, they seemed to define their task in terms of finishing assignments, but because they frequently had difficulty reading and thinking at the level of the assignment, they were placed in a perplexing position: They had to complete the work, but they did not know how to do so in a completely meaningful way.

The students did not give up in frustration. Instead, they adapted to the environmental demands ("Finish your work") by developing and using a variety of strategies that helped them get finished. The major question that arises from these data is how these students' short-term adaptations and use of "getting finished" strategies may affect longer-term learning, especially learning of metacognitive skills such as comprehension monitoring and assessment of difficulty.

Some examples are provided below of students responding to seatwork in ways that did not further understanding. In each case, the student was working under two conditions. First, there was an emphasis on completing one's work on one's own, "keeping busy," and staying on task. Second, the assignment required skills and concepts that the child either lacked or did not understand well enough to use easily. We now believe that when these two conditions occur together, they lead to a pattern of responses that have undesirable long-term consequences.

Sally (a low-achieving target) is working on an assignment that requires her to copy sentences off the board, read them, and draw pictures to illustrate that she understands them (e.g., "The green car is coming down the road"). This is a familiar form of assignment in Sally's class, and all students are to work on it while the teacher meets reading groups. Sally copies a sentence correctly, looking at the board frequently, appearing to copy it letter by letter (rather than in words or phrases, as is usually done by higher achievers). When finished with a sentence, she looks at her neighbor's paper or asks a friend, "What do we draw here?" The friend answers, "A green car," and Sally draws it. When the observer asked Sally to read the sentences, she could not. However, she was able to complete the paper in this fashion and thus go to lunch and recess (a consequence of not finishing was to stay in the room when the class left for lunch).

Considering the demands of the task as Sally perceived them (i.e., get all sentences copied and some pictures drawn before lunch), her strategy is reasonable. She had mastered letter-by-letter copying and managed to produce an acceptable paper without ever reading, which she did poorly.

Ron (a low-achieving target), along with all other students in his class, is to spend 30 minutes of allotted seatwork time composing a story about "My Family." The teacher has written some words on the board that students might want to use in writing their stories, although she emphasizes that spelling "does not count." Ron writes the following story by himself:

You can be my brother.
You can be my puppy.
I like my pup.
I like my father.
I like my mother.
I am happy.

When the observer asked him to read his story to her, he hesitated on the word *my* (because his *y* was not clearly a *y* and he read it as a *t*). He did not attempt to read the words *brother, puppy, pup, father,* or *mother*; instead he stared at each of them for several seconds and then asked what they were. After they finished reading his story, the observer asked him how he knew to write the word *father* when he wrote it. He pointed to the board and said, "I got it off there."

Ron had used his understanding of sentence structure and functions of various words to create an acceptable product. It was later marked "good" by the teacher, but there was no other feedback given. However, his inability to read what he had written suggested to us that the act of writing the story may have been driven by the need to "get it done" rather than an interest in communicating his thoughts about his family. This is post hoc conjecture, of course, but the incident is consistent with other observations of Ron when he behaved in ways that kept the teacher "off his case" and minimized academic and other contacts with her. His work was frequently difficult for him, but he always got it finished, usually with some incorrect answers. Conversations with him frequently revealed a lack of concepts or skills that were presumably necessary for the work given to him.

Sean (a low-achieving male) is in a class where students do "individualized" work. This means that all students proceed through the same reading and math books, but they "move at their own pace," according to the teacher. The pace seemed to be determined by how long it took each student to get through a page and get the teacher's attention for checking rather than the amount of time spent in instruction. Sean was assigned a page from his reading workbook that emphasized words ending in *–ake* (e.g., cake, make, take). There were six sentences to read and six pictures to match to them. The observer asked Sean to tell her about the page while he was doing it. He readily agreed and began reading aloud. He read most of the *–ake* words as *cake*, and most of his reading did not make sense due to frequent miscalls. However, he did not seem disturbed by the lack of sense of the sentences, and he quickly drew lines to whatever picture he thought went with it. He proceeded through the six sentences, getting three correct despite his misreading, although these correct answers were apparently flukes. For example, the first correct sentence done simply matched the picture closest to the sentence. (On the next assignment, Sean was observed using a similar "proximity" principle to determine the correct choice: Draw the shortest possible line.) The last sentence was done correctly without Sean even attempting to read the sentence because, as he explained, "There's only one picture left, so that's the answer." Coincidentally, it was the right one. Throughout this session, Sean did not indicate that he was aware that he was making errors nor did he demonstrate any concern that what he read was nonsense. As soon as he drew the line between the last sentence and picture, he immediately turned to the next page of his workbook and continued in a similar fashion.

CONCLUSION

Such incidents have led us to hypothesize that one result of a combination of inappropriate (i.e., too difficult) assignments and an emphasis on finishing work may be that students come to define success on seatwork in terms of completion instead of understanding. This way of defining success may occur for all students, but is more likely to be detrimental to low students. The high achievers, because they were usually working at a higher level of success than were low achievers and thus were probably gaining more from the practice opportunities afforded by seatwork, may have come to expect their reading seatwork to make sense to them because it was more often assimilable (or at their "independent level"). If this pattern continues, it may help them develop adaptive learning-to-learn skills as they continue through school because when something does not make sense or seems confusing, it will be an unusual event. Therefore, it will be salient and likely to trigger action to reduce confusion, add necessary information, or both. This highlighting of unexpected misunderstanding may help further the development of metacognitive skills (which aid in information seeking to reduce confusion), even though formal classroom instruction seldom is focused on the development of such skills. Low achievers, whom we saw more often with assignments that were difficult for them, may be less likely to expect their work to "make sense." Because "sense" is not predictable, a lack of sense (i.e., recognizing that you do not understand) is not unusual. If something is not unusual, then it is not as likely to serve as a signal that something is wrong and needs resolution.

Other elements of classroom life are probably more predictable to low achievers than their assignments making sense. We think that the rewards and sanctions attached to finishing work and covering content are very predictable, at least in the classrooms we have observed. Given unpredictability about how easily assignments can be comprehended, it is not surprising that low achievers may focus their immediate goals while doing seatwork on the predictable elements, such as the need to "get it done" and move on. Over time, this approach may interfere with the development of metacognitive skills that allow students to become better guides of their own learning. Thus, higher achievers are more likely to learn more about how to learn from their assignments as they progress through school, contributing to a widening gap between higher and lower achievers over time. This phenomenon cannot be attributed entirely to the aptitude differences between high and low achievers (although those are influential).

The point here is that the history of a student's experiences with school tasks can influence expectations that assignments, text, activities, and so on can and should make sense, and these expectations in turn will influence a student's responses to instruction. While this has implications for instruction generally, it is particularly relevant to comprehension instruction. If reading is indeed a meaning-getting process, then instruction in comprehension must emphasize sense making. This study suggests that such sense making is not emphasized in classrooms where difficult seatwork comprises a significant amount of some students' instructional time in reading, and where finishing is emphasized as the immediate goal. Such an instructional environment minimizes, rather than expedites, sense making.

REFERENCES

Anderson, L. Short-term student responses to classroom instruction. *Elementary School Journal*, 1981, *82*, 97–108.

Anderson, L., Evertson, C., & Emmer, E. Dimensions of classroom management derived from recent research. *Journal of Curriculum Studies*, 1979.

Doyle, W. *Student mediating responses in teaching effectiveness*. Final Report, National Institute of Education Grant No. NIE-G-76-0099. Denton, Texas: Department of Education, North Texas State University, March 1980.

Emmer, E., & Evertson, C. *Effective management at the beginning of the school year in junior high classes*. R & D Rep. No. 6107. Austin: Research and Development Center for Teacher Education, The University of Texas at Austin, 1980.

Fisher, C., Berliner, D., Filby, N., Marliave, R., Cohen, L., Dishaw, M., & Moore, J. *Teaching and learning in elementary schools: A summary of the beginning teacher evaluation study*. San Francisco: Far West Laboratory for Educational Research and Development, 1978.

Good, T., & Beckerman, T. Time on task: A naturalistic study in sixth-grade classrooms. *Elementary School Journal*, 1978, *78*, 193–201.

8

The Environment of Instruction: The Forms and Functions of Writing in a Teacher-Developed Curriculum

Susan Florio and Christopher M. Clark
with
Janis L. Elmore, June Martin,
Rhoda Maxwell, and William Metheny

This chapter emphasizes the production rather than the comprehension side of literacy. Because writing instruction is not often based in standardized curricula such as the basal text employed in reading, it provides a contrast to the previous chapters. However, as reading and writing are two sides of the coin of meaning, it is hoped that a great deal of what is presented here will shed light on reading as well as writing, on students as readers as well as authors of written texts, and on classroom environments as they affect instruction.

There is a great deal that we do not know about literacy. In anthropology, debates are waged about the effects of the advent of writing on the intellectual traditions and history of a society (Goody and Watt 1977, Goody 1977). In psychology, much inquiry concerns the intellectual consequences of literacy in the life of the individual (Scribner and Cole 1981) and the cognitive processes thought to underlie the process of composition (Hayes and Flower 1980). On the practical side, social critics and educators struggle with questions of the appropriate environments, techniques, and goals for literacy instruction. For some, literacy is operationally defined as an array of technical skills requisite for performance in many occupations. For others, literacy is the key to other worlds—both within and outside oneself (Bettelheim 1967). For still others, literacy is a crucial form of "cultural capital" (Bourdieu 1977) without which social mobility is impossible.

Publication of this work is sponsored by the Institute for Research on Teaching, College of Education, Michigan State University. The Institute for Research on Teaching is funded primarily by the Program for Teaching and Instruction of the National Institute of Education, United States Department of Education. The opinions expressed in this publication do not necessarily reflect the position, policy, or endorsement of the National Institute of Education. (NIE Contract No. 400–81–0014 and NIE Grant No. 90840.)

Some go so far as to suggest that without literacy, effective critique of the conditions of one's life is difficult, and the means to change those conditions out of reach (Friere 1970, Giroux 1979). Clearly literacy is important, and we need to know a great deal more about it both as a cognitive process and as a social act that occurs in historical, political, and cultural context.

However we think of the effects of literacy on the individual and the community, there appears to be consensus among scholars and practitioners alike that writing is a cultural tool making possible a variety of expressive activities (Vygotsky 1978). In our society, schools are vested with great responsibility for teaching people to wield that cultural tool. There is much contemporary concern about the effectiveness with which schools impart literacy skills to students. Beyond these superficial observations, consensus and good information end. Apart from the manifest curricula for reading and language arts, relatively little is known about writing in either the school or nonschool lives of children (Hymes 1979), and the classroom is not well understood as an environment for literacy. The research reported in this chapter was undertaken to learn more about writing in the school lives of children and about the classroom as an environment for literacy.

THE STUDY

The two-year study from which this chapter derives was conceived in curiosity about the classroom as an environment for literacy. Thus it began not with an exclusive focus on the reading or language arts curriculum and instruction per se but by observing broadly the everyday life of the classroom. By means of extensive participant observation and long-term interchange with teacher and students, the researchers hoped to discover and describe the way that classroom participants create and make sense of their literate world.

Two assumptions guiding the study were that writing is an expressive option that is, like speech, acquired in use, and that in our society the classroom is a key site in which the young are exposed to literacy. For these reasons it was decided to examine not only the social context for written literacy that the classroom provides but also the perspectives of teachers and children on what writing is for and what it means to be literate. Thus the theoretical underpinnings and design of the research were interdisciplinary. In an effort to document the classroom as an environment for written literacy, perspectives and methods of ethnography, sociolinguistics, and cognitive psychology were combined and augmented with insights of the experienced teachers who participated in the research.

In the face of our relative ignorance about the classroom as an environment for written literacy, it was decided to adopt a phenomenological stance in the research. In phenomenology, our aim is to encounter the object of our curiosity in a state of wonder (Schutz 1976). We endeavor to put aside our presuppositions about what the reality of the situation might be and to discover its reality anew by immersion within it. In so doing, our aim is not to explain but to describe (Wittgenstein 1953/68).

In developing the descriptive model of the classroom under study, analytic categories were arrived at inductively. The researchers and informants sifted the naturalistic data for patterns of meaningful activity in writing. In addition, insights from previous research on writing and teaching and the experiences of participating teachers provided useful conceptual levers to interpret the data (Schatzman and Strauss 1973). Of focal importance was the grounding of inferences about written literacy in the everyday activities of teacher and students. Such inferences were tested by repeated observations. Competing explanations were sought and evidence from multiple data points was compared (Gorden 1975). The interdisciplinary and collaborative nature of the study enabled these activities. Eventually a descriptive model of writing in the classroom was derived. The model portrays the functions of writing in the classroom, the forms attendant to those functions, and the values implicit in those functions about writing and its purposes.

The classroom in question in this report was a combination second-third grade open-space classroom called Room 12. It was studied as a small community in its own right and as a social group within the wider communities of Conley School[1] and suburban East Eden, Michigan (Florio 1979). The teacher, Ms. Donovan, was a key informant in the study since it was she who planned most classroom activities and prepared the learning environment for students (Clark and Yinger 1980). Data collected in the study reflected the interdisciplinary nature of the research and were intended to yield a broad and rich documentation of writing in Room 12. Data collected included the following:

- Field notes of year-long participant observation
- Videotapes of selected classroom activities
- Weekly journals kept by the teacher reflecting her thoughts on teaching in general and on writing in particular
- Interviews with the teacher about the contents of videotapes and journal entries
- Student writings collected naturalistically
- Conversations with students about their writing

Details of the methods and findings of the larger study are available elsewhere (see Clark, Florio et al. 1982). This paper offers only a partial report of the findings of the study. It presents the descriptive model of the functions of writing in Room 12 that was derived by analysis of the many types of descriptive data collected. Following the discussion of the functions of writing in Room 12 are some thoughts on the nature of the writing curriculum and on this classroom as an environment for literacy.

THE FUNCTIONS OF WRITING IN ROOM 12

This study was instituted with an interest in the social situations in which students' written products arise and in which their beliefs and values about writing are shaped. To address questions of this nature, one needs to approach writing holistically, not as a series of discrete skills to be mastered but as a cultural tool in use. Viewed in this light, writing functions are the focus of inquiry. This focus on function stands in sharp contrast to other ways of studying language that have typically emphasized the study of language forms (Shuy 1981).

Table 8.1 summarizes the four broad purposes to which writing was put by Ms. Donovan and her students in their corner of Room 12. Life in that classroom was varied. As an open-space classroom, there was time and space for scheduled and impromptu lessons, group and individual activities, teacher-planned and student-choice times. Written communication in Ms. Donovan's class reflects this social and academic diversity. Each of the four functions of written literacy documented in this class arises out of particular intellectual and social needs and opportunities presented by the school and classroom. In addition, each function is constrained or enabled by the peculiar institutional norms of school and classroom.

Table 8.1 presents as a formal matrix what was in reality a series of dynamic, interactive occasions for writing (see Florio and Clark 1982 for a detailed discussion of these occasions for writing). The matrix was derived from analysis of the various descriptive data collected in Room 12 during the 1979–80 academic year. It was developed with Ms. Donovan's collaboration as the year progressed and was tested and elaborated with data from subsequent observations during the year. In developing it the researchers attempted to code exhaustively the many occasions for writing they had documented in Room 12.

Implicit in the matrix is the notion that classroom literacy resides not entirely in the production and comprehension of documents but in a complex of social and cognitive features of the writing task and the environment in which it occurs (Scollon and Scollon 1981). Among the features that constitute occasions for writing are a variety of social roles, expressive intentions, resources for communication, and fates that befall written products. The four general functions of writing can thus be distinguished from one another not only in terms of the documents produced within them but also in terms of the ways in which those occasions variously combine and manifest these social and cognitive distinctive features. Thus, an observer who works backward from documents of a social group (e.g., Ms. Donovan's class) to the social occasions in which they were produced finds that there may be many different social contexts within which different kinds of writing get done.

As the matrix demonstrates, writing in Room 12 is used to serve multiple purposes including, but not limited to, the demonstration of academic mastery. Writing occurs throughout the curriculum—in reading and language arts, but also in science, social studies, and the like. Beyond its appearance in the manifest curriculum, moreover, writing occurs and serves important purposes in the establishment, enactment, and regulation of the classroom life. Thus, writing appears to be vitally important in the establishment and maintenance of what Jackson has called the "hidden curriculum" as well as the more manifest curriculum of reading and language arts (Jackson 1968).

THE FOUR FUNCTIONS IN COMPARISON AND CONTRAST

Varying somewhat systematically with the sociocognitive purposes to which writing is put in Room 12 are the distinctive features presented in the matrix. These features reflect the truly local norms of life in Room 12 (Hymes 1976). They also reflect broader norms regarding the social roles, intentions, and outcomes that abide in much writing undertaken in institutional settings in general and in schools and classrooms in particular. The features that vary meaningfully from function to function in Room 12 have been identified to include the *initiator* of the occasion for writing, the *composer* of the written product, the person (s) who actually *write*

TABLE 8.1 The Functions of Writing in Room 12

Function Type	Sample Activity	Distinctive Features					
		Initiator	Composer	Writer/ Speaker	Audience	Format	Fate	Evaluation
Type I: Writing to participate in community	classroom rule setting	teacher	teacher & students	teacher	student	by teacher and students: drafted on chalkboard; printed in colored marker on large white paper	posted; referred to when rules are broken	no
Type II: Writing to know oneself and others	diaries	teacher	student	student	student	by teacher: written or printed on lined paper in student-made booklets	locked in teacher's file cabinet or kept in student desk; occasionally shared with teacher, other students, or family	no
Type III: Writing to occupy free time	letters and cards	student	student	student	other (parents, friends, family)	by student: printed or drawn on lined or construction paper	kept; may be given as gift to parents or friend	no
Type IV: Writing to demonstrate academic competence	science lab booklets	teacher	publisher	publisher & student(s)	teacher	by publisher: printed in commercial booklet	checked by teacher; filed for later use by student; pages sent home to parents by teacher	yes

(s) the document, the writing's intended *audience*, the *format* of the document (and the person(s) who plan that format), the ultimate *fate* that befalls the written document, and the presence or absence of formal *evaluation* of the writing.

The distinctive features of the four functions of writing are intimately bound up in the social contexts within which the writing is undertaken and the documents ultimately produced. Thus, to perform these functions of written literacy in school entails not only competence to manipulate written symbols but the negotiation and enactment of a variety of social roles and purposes within the context of school and classroom. To paraphrase linguistic philosopher John Searle, to make meaning, one must combine convention with intention (Searle 1969).

The important facets of writing in this classroom include some that appear regularly in the literature as generic parts of the composing process (e.g., composer, audience, format). Others reflect the unique context of the school and classroom. One would expect, for example, that *audience* would be a relevant feature for most or all writing. However, one would not expect that all writing would necessarily have as a distinctive feature the presence or absence of formal evaluation. In general, judgments about the effectiveness of writing are made informally and are based on the writer's ability to persuade or elicit the desired response from an audience. Similarly, in the case of the solitary writer in a private setting, it might not be relevant to distinguish the initiator from the composer or the writer in an occasion for writing. A diarist initiates her or his own writing, as does a housekeeper preparing a shopping list. This is not always the case in the classroom.

Finally, some of the distinctive features reflect the particular context of the elementary classroom. For example, in most adult literacy events it is unlikely that we would count a speaker as a writer. One would assume that at the least one would have to inscribe graphically to be considered engaged in writing. In the elementary classroom, however, as researchers such as Cook-Gumperz and Gumperz (1978) and Michaels (1980) have shown us, a child may gradually approach writing through the oral medium of discussion or sharing with others. Thus an event like Show and Tell may take on a distinctively literacy-related quality in a setting such as the elementary classroom.[2]

One peculiarity in the matrix reflecting the local norms of the elementary classroom social context is the breaking down of the graphic activity into three distinct roles—initiator, composer, and scribe. In Room 12, as in other classrooms, the teacher was the frequent initiator of writing activities. In fact, the matrix shows that in only one kind of writing is the student the initiator—writing to occupy free time. In an open-space classroom like Room 12 there is a great deal of free time to be structured by the student. Students often initiated writing projects during that time. But one could imagine classrooms organized differently in which the teacher would be the sole initiator of all written activity.

In general, in Room 12 the roles of initiator, composer, and scribe are not held by the same person. The matrix demonstrates that the teacher is usually the initiator of occasions for writing in which students are the composers. The students often have the opportunity collectively to compose a document while the teacher writes it down at the chalkboard or on white butcher paper. In such cases, the students undertake the composing activities typically related to writing including brainstorming for ideas, finding words to express one's intentions, placing punctuation, and proofreading and correcting. However, for the ease of group generation of a text (or because early in the year children lack sufficient manual skills to write privately), these interactive compositions are encoded by the teacher.[3]

Another distinction that applies uniquely to institutional settings is that of separation of the *formatting* role from the roles of *composer* or *encoder* in the occasion for writing. We have all had the experience of filling out forms—whether they be for income tax, unemployment, or mail orders. In so doing we are painfully aware of our subordinate status in the writing process. In order to communicate effectively we must capitulate to the thematic categories, technical language, and space limitations of the form. Although it can be argued that to communicate effectively under any circumstances we must submit to constraints including the orthography of the language, conventions of genre, and the like, the filling out of forms is an extreme case of the separation of the formatter role from the encoder role. It can be argued in such cases that the formatter and the person filling out the form at best collaborate in composing the completed document.

Viewed in this way, children in Room 12 are at least in part collaborators with publishers as fillers-out of forms. This is a role they identified for the researchers when asked to sort and describe their own biweekly writing folders. They uniformly separated forms such as worksheets and workbook pages into a separate catagory, calling it "work" and pointing out that it was special because it was in part "written by machine." Because of the nature of the open classroom organization and curriculum of Room 12, it is notable that such form filling was only one of four kinds of written enterprises observed. However, it is worthy of note as well that while other student written work may or may not have received formal or informal evaluation, the writing that students did in collaboration with publishers was always evaluated formally—hence, perhaps, the common categorization of it as "work" by the students and its similar labeling in the ordinary educational parlance. This writing was also the predominant type shared with parents.

As mentioned previously, the matrix reveals a great deal of what can be thought of as the "hidden curriculum" (Jackson 1968) for written literacy in Room 12. This hidden curriculum both shapes and is shaped by norms that govern appropriate behavior in school and values about what should be learned there. Writing continues to be unique among the basics in East Eden in that it lacks many explicit props or guidelines for curriculum and instruction. Other than a districtwide (and teacher-generated) set of loose guidelines called the Common Writings,[4] teachers are not required to specify their writing curriculum, nor are they typically supplied with prepackaged materials for writing instruction as they are in such areas as math, reading, science, and social studies.

Although four functions of writing appear in the classroom, they are not all claimed as part of the writing curriculum by the teacher. While our descriptive analysis documents that, contrary to critics, writing clearly does occur in the classroom and that a great range of kinds of writing is undertaken there, much of the writing documented in the matrix has a somewhat incidental quality.[5] The curricular hiddenness of many of the varied ways in which children are using writing as a cultural tool in Room 12 obscures some potentially rich opportunities to make explicit literacy-related aspects of an activity. It also obscures aspects of student competence from teacher purview and evaluation. Finally, the student has many opportunities to write, but those opportunities vary greatly in the degree to which they offer the student access to the whole expressive process—from initiation of an idea through the formatting, composing, and encoding of it.

Such differences in the complex of sociocognitive features of various occasions for writing may not only teach children different intellectual skills related to literacy (Scribner and Cole 1981) but may also impart different beliefs and values about literacy and its use. In this classroom children may see the association, for example, of form filling with work and performance evaluation. They also see that some writing is collaborative and public and related to the management of social relations. Students may learn that the written word can be a safe haven into which to retreat when, in a busy and crowded open space, they want some time to relax and be alone. They may see that writing is a bridge to others—through letters and gifts—and to one's inner world—through diaries. They may also learn, however, that such writing "doesn't count." These values and meanings about literacy and what is available to one as a literate member of a community are remarkable to learn, but they may go unremarked upon as part of the communicative ecology of the classroom. It can be argued that these values and local meanings deserve at least as much explicit attention as do the mechanical skills of production (Elsasser and John-Steiner 1977) and that their taken-for-granted quality needs to be confronted to expose tacit institutional norms about what literacy is and what it ought to be.

CONCLUSION

One way to characterize curriculum is, in Eggleston's (1977) words, as "a body of learning experiences responding to a societal view of knowledge that may not always be fully expressed or even fully accepted by teachers and students" (p. 20). It was not until this study was well under way that the researchers realized that to study the processes of teaching and learning writing in the classroom was, in fact, to study the writing curriculum. Thus it was a long time before the teachers and researchers in dialogue with one another discovered the curricula for writing embedded in everyday activities in the classroom.

Perhaps because writing instruction in Room 12, unlike instruction in reading, lacks a "received" and highly standardized system of objectives and materials, it is easy to assume that it lacks a curriculum. But as Eggleston's characterization indicates, curriculum may exist without full consensus about or full expression of the structure and contents of knowledge, the appropriate ways to impart knowledge, the persons to whom it should be taught, the means to evaluate such efforts, or the values underlying its instruction.

In large part we have found that this state of affairs characterized the writing curriculum in Room 12. The teaching and learning of writing was, first and foremost, largely unarticulated. Free of the commercial materials and precise district mandates that both supported and limited instruction in academic subjects such as reading, writing posed a problem and an opportunity for the teacher and students we observed.

It is possible that relative freedom from outside management of curriculum makes writing the last bastion of independent teacher decision making among school subjects. Potentially it is still an area in which teachers can make fundamental choices about the knowledge to impart, the ways to impart it, the nature of assessment, and the reasons for learning. But it is also possible for such lack of specification of the curriculum to be a source of problems. Teachers may enact writing instruction unreflectively—filling up the time with activities that merely recapitulate their own limited experience as former students of writing. Such an approach runs the risk of being inordinately bound up by the structure of authority abiding in school and classroom to the potential distortion of meaningful written communication. In addition, such an unregulated part of the course of study can suffer for lack of legitimacy. Thus we sometimes see writing slighted in a busy school day or passing unremarked upon as it is used throughout the day as a means to other academic ends.

The absence of curricular materials in writing has engendered a paradoxical situation with respect to writing instruction. On one hand, research on the teaching of writing portrays teachers engaging in some of their most creative and rich preactive and interactive planning precisely because they lack the curricular and managerial props and constraints that materials would provide (Clark and Elmore 1981). However, much of that creative instruction is invisible—to analysts, students, and teachers themselves. One source of invisibility is related to teacher decision making. Teachers often engage students in writing that is incidental to the completion of other academic tasks and in their efforts to complete those tasks, miss opportunities to draw student attention to the important aspects of the writing process they are using. Another source of the invisibility of writing instruction lies in the nature of classrooms as places in which to study and communicate with others. Writing is ubiquitous in classrooms, although explicit writing instruction may not be. Writing of papers and tests can become such a part of everyday life in classrooms that it goes unremarked upon by its users. Thus the powerful potential of writing in use in everyday school life may go unexploited.

The contrast between highly standardized systems of curricula (such as the basal text instruction which dominated the classrooms reported in Chapter 7) and curricula embedded in activities of the classroom (such as the writing instruction reported here) have two relevant implications.

First, writing becomes a strategic site for research on both curriculum and teaching. Writing is a school subject that potentially calls forth considerable professionalism in teachers. In creating the writing curriculum for and with their students, teachers may find themselves having to reflect upon their own experience as writers, the lives of their diverse students and the role of writing in them, the opportunities for becoming literate in their classrooms, the problems of standards in writing, and our societal definitions of and values about literacy.

Second, the findings from the study of writing provide insight into the nature of instruction in more standardized curricula. Reading comprehension is one example. There the curriculum is prescribed in detail in commercial materials and curriculum objectives. The constraints this places on instruction are different from the constraints on writing instruction and, as such, raise interesting questions about the contrast between comprehension instruction and writing instruction.

NOTES

1. Pseudonyms are used throughout this chapter.
2. Although not brought out in this matrix, the same could also apply to the rather fuzzy distinction that might be made between early drawing and early writing. Much as it is difficult to pinpoint precisely the beginnings of literacy in societies, in part because pictorial representation preceded and is so closely re-

lated to it (Goody and Watt 1977), so it is with early writing and the mingling of drawing and writing that often marks the written literacy of young children (Gardner 1980, Clay 1975, Ervin-Tripp and Mitchell-Kernan 1977).

3. It has been argued elsewhere that such interactive cognitive events may help to expand and extend the individual beyond the limits of what her or his production would be alone (Vygotsky 1978, Cole et al. 1979, Cazden 1979). In addition, they are particularly suited to literacy events of a public nature such as the generation of a code of classroom rules, the production of a class thank-you note to someone who has served the group, or the teaching of a whole group session.

4. The Common Writings are the only district mandates in East Eden that pertain to writing. They are a series of performance objectives for grades K-12 presented as "writing forms" that students at various grades must be able to produce. Mastery of the forms (usually five or six per grade) must be evidenced by one example that is placed in the student's cumulative record. These writing samples accompany the child through the grades as evidence of competence in writing. The teacher has considerable latitude in deciding when and how to elicit the samples.

5. Even when this incidental writing is noticed by the teacher, the problem of how to evaluate such work without discouraging student initiative and risk taking is one with which Ms. Donovan struggled. The way it was resolved, at least in part, was to assess formally only a small sample of student writing. Informal assessment, or the effect of written expression on the student's intended audience, was inevitable and available as well in the letters and stories written by students. But it is difficult for such informal assessment to enter into what Doyle (1978) called the "grade economy" of the classroom—to be capital in the classroom environment.

REFERENCES

Bettelheim, B. *The empty fortress.* New York: Free Press of Glencoe, 1967.

Bourdieu, P. Cultural reproduction and social reproduction. In J. Karabel & A. H. Halsey, *Power and ideology in education.* New York: Oxford University Press, 1977.

Cazden, C. B. *Peekaboo as an instructional model: Discourse development at home and at school.* Paper presented at the Child Language Forum, Stanford University, Stanford, Calif, April 1979.

Clark, C. M., & Elmore, J. L. *Transforming curriculum in mathematics, science, and writing: A case study of yearly planning.* Research Series No. 99. East Lansing: Institute for Research on Teaching, Michigan State University, 1981. (Originally presented at the American Educational Research Association annual meeting, Los Angeles, April 1981.)

Clark, C. M., & Florio, S., with Elmore, J. L., Martin, J., Maxwell, R. J., & Metheny, W. *Understanding writing in school: A descriptive study of writing and its instruction in two classrooms.* Final Report of the Written Literacy Study (Grant No. 90840) funded by the National Institute of Education, U.S. Department of Education. East Lansing: Institute for Research on Teaching, Michigan State University, 1981.

Clark, C. M., & Yinger, R. J. *The hidden world of teaching: Implications of research on teacher planning.* Research Series No. 77. East Lansing: Institute for Research on Teaching, Michigan State University, 1980.

Clay, M. M. *What did I write?* New Zealand: Heinemann Educational Books, 1975.

Cole, M., Hood, L., & McDermoot, R. *Ecological niche picking: Ecological invalidity as an axiom of experimental cognitive psychology.* La Jolla, Calif.: Laboratory for Comparative Human Cognition, 1979.

Cook-Gumperz, J., & Gumperz, J. From oral to written culture: The transition to literacy. In M. F. Whiteman (Ed.), *Variation in writing.* New York: Lawrence Erlbaum Associates, 1978.

Doyle, W. *Task structures and student roles in classrooms.* Paper presented at the American Educational Research Association annual meeting, Toronto, 1978.

Eggleston, J. *The sociology of the school curriculum.* London: Routledge and Kegan Paul, 1977.

Elsasser, N., & John-Steiner, V. An interactionist approach to advancing literacy. *Harvard Educational Review,* August 1977, *47,* 355–369.

Ervin-Tripp, S., & Mitchell-Kernan, D. *Child discourse.* New York: Academic Press, 1977.

Florio, S. The problem of dead letters: Social perspectives on the teaching of writing. *Elementary School Journal,* September 1979; *80* (1), 1–7.

Florio, S., & Clark, C. M. The functions of writing in an elementary classroom. *Research in the Teaching of English,* 1982, *16* (2), 115–130.

Friere, P. *Cultural action for freedom.* Monograph Series No. 1. Cambridge, Mass.: Harvard Educational Review and Center for the Study of Development and Social Change, 1970.

Gardner, H. *Artful scribbles.* Cambridge, Mass.: Harvard University Press, 1980.

Giroux, H. Mass culture and the rise of the new illiteracy: Implications for reading. *Interchange,* 1979–80, *10* (4), 89–98.

Goody, J. *The domestication of the savage mind.* Cambridge, England: Cambridge University Press, 1977.

Goody, J., & Watt, I. The consequences of literacy. In J. Karabel & A. H. Halsey, *Power and ideology in education.* New York: Oxford University Press, 1977.

Gorden, R. L. *Interviewing: Strategies, techniques, and tactics.* Homewood, Ill: Dorsey Press, 1975.

Hayes, J. R., & Flower, L. Identifying the organization of writing processes. In L. W. Gregg & E. R. Steinberg, *Cognitive processes in writing.* Hillsdale, N.J.: Erlbaum, 1980.

Hymes, D. Ethnographic monitoring. Presented at the symposium *Language development in a bilingual setting.* Pomona, Calif.: Multilingual/Multicultural Materials Development Center, California State Polytechnic University, March 1976.

Hymes, D. Language in education: Forward to fundamentals. In O. Garnica & M. King (Eds.), *Language, children and society.* Oxford: Pergamon Press, 1979.

Jackson, P. *Life in classrooms.* New York: Holt, Rinehart and Winston, 1968.

Michaels, S. *Sharing time: Oral preparation for literacy.* Paper presented at the Ethnography in Education Research Forum. University of Pennsylvania, March 1980.

Schatzman L., & Strauss, A. *Field research: Strategies for a natural sociology.* Englewood Cliffs, N.J.: Prentice-Hall, 1973.

Schutz, A. In Bernstein, R., *The restructuring of social and political theory*, 139. New York: Harcourt Brace Jovanovich 1976.

Scollon, R., & Scollon, S. *Narrative, literacy and face in interethnic communication.* Norwood, N.J.: Ablex Publishing Co., 1981.

Scribner, S., & Cole, M. *The psychology of literacy.* Cambridge, Mass.: Harvard University Press, 1981.

Searle, J. *Speech acts: An essay in the philosophy of language.* Cambridge, England: Cambridge University Press, 1969.

Shuy, R. *Relating research on oral language function to research on written discourse.* Paper presented at the American Educational Research Association annual meeting, Los Angeles, April 1981.

Vygotsky, L. L. *Mind in society: The development of higher psychological processes.* In M. Cole, V. John-Steiner, S. Scribner & E. Souberman (Eds.), Cambridge, Mass.: Harvard University Press, 1978.

Wittgenstein, L. *Philosophical investigations.* New York: Macmillan, 1953/1968.

9

Schools as a Context for Comprehension Instruction

Lawrence Lezotte

Suppose, through a miracle of modern technology, we could transfer the students, teacher, and physical classroom in one school to another school some distance away. Imagine further that we had carefully studied this classroom both prior to and after we had relocated it. The observed changes in either teacher or student behaviors could be attributed to school effect. By school effect, we mean those patterns and practices in the classroom that can be predicted to occur as a result of the school setting. If changes in particular behaviors, attitudes, and beliefs in one classroom were in conformity with attitudes, beliefs, and behaviors of other teachers or the administrative policies and practices in the school to which it was moved, then this would be further evidence of the presence and influence of the school effect.

Clearly we do not have the ability to manipulate classrooms to produce such clear alterations in the school context. Nevertheless, the hypothetical example illustrates what is meant by school effects.

BACKGROUND TO SCHOOL EFFECTS RESEARCH

Two general approaches have been used by researchers to isolate, describe, and estimate the magnitude of school effects. One is to conduct interviews, make observations, administer questionnaires, and the like for the purpose of isolating instructional patterns, practices, or student-teacher interactions that occur throughout the school. Patterns or practices shared by all teachers could be defined as schoolwide effects. Such studies have tended to focus on instructional processes that have been of general interest and have contributed to the school effects literature. Unfortunately, practitioners who read such process-oriented descriptions of school effects often persist in asking, "So what?" What difference does it make that the educational staff in a single school sees the educational world in similar ways and responds similarly?

More recently, a second methodological approach has been used to identify and describe school effects. This methodology has been most heavily associated with school effectiveness research. The goals of this second methodology are identical to the first and the nature of data collected is also similar. The difference is the anticipation of the "So what?" question by studying schools that are known to differ on measured student outcomes. Specifically the typical effective schools study examines pairs of schools. Usually the schools are in a single local school district and serve a similar student body composition (e.g., socioeconomic, racial, and ethnic mix). While the two schools serve similar students, they differ in student achievement outcomes. Typically, an effective schools study includes several sets of such pairs of schools. The major research question is this: What school factors are shared by the school with the higher-achievement outcomes but are not shared by the lower-achieving, less effective member of the pair?

During the 1970s, a number of effective schools research studies using this general methodology were reported in the literature. While most of the studies have examined the elementary school, some secondary level studies have also been reported. Because of the increasing interest in this growing body of research, additional studies can be anticipated in the next few years.

One of the earliest of these studies was George Weber's (1971) study, which examined schools notable for their measured reading achievement. A similar study focusing on reading achievement at the elementary level was also published by Hoover (1978).

Several other studies, examining more general student outcomes, include the works of Madden, Lawson, and Sweet (1976), Austin (1979), and Brookover et al. (1979). The best-known secondary-level effective school study is that of Rutter et al. (1979). The results of their study of 12 inner-city London high schools attracted a great deal of attention in the United States.

Several recent publications have attempted to synthesize these and other school effectiveness studies. Three such publications are Clark, Lotto, and McCarthy (1980), Edmonds (1979), and Mann and Laurence (1981). A review of any one of these synthesis articles will reinforce the view that the characteristics of these effective schools are remarkably similar across the individual studies.

Throughout the remainder of this chapter, reference will be made to either effective schools research generally or to our own work. When a general reference is made, it is meant to include our own work plus those referenced above. When the more narrow reference to our work is made, two particular studies are suggested. The first refers to the Brookover and Lezotte (1979) study of the characteristics of a set of elementary schools that have evidenced a pattern of improvement or decline in measured achievement over the preceding three years. The factors that seemed to be associated with improving or declining achievement test scores were discussed. The second study refers to that portion of the Edmonds (1979) work that focused on the descriptions of schools in Michigan and New York having the kind of achievement growth discussed in the following section of this chapter.

Effective schools research studies are increasing in number. The degree of agreement across the several independent studies suggests that any examination of classroom or teacher effects must also examine the school effects.

The remainder of this chapter (1) describes our definition of an effective school, (2) reviews the characteristics found in those effective schools, and (3) offers some working hypotheses as to what patterns might be anticipated regarding comprehension instruction. The major premises are these:

1. School effects, mediated through individual classroom systems, have a significant influence on student achievement.
2. The emerging effective schools research provides a framework for identifying which school-level variables are likely to have a direct effect on outcomes as reflected in assessed pupil performance.

These two premises are based on the belief that the individual school is a complex social system and that although instruction tends to occur in single classrooms, the interaction between the school's social system and the individual classrooms significantly influences the nature of instruction. While school outcomes can be defined in a variety of ways, this chapter illustrates how "comprehension instruction" may be influenced by school effects.

DEFINING THE EFFECTIVE SCHOOL

The first challenge faced by the effective schools researcher is to define an effective school so that we know one when we see it. The definition must be operational and must meet the usual specifications of clarity and reliability. The definition must also anticipate the fact that the purposes of schools are expected to differ from place to place and that therefore the definition must permit schools with a different focus to be able to qualify as effective for their purposes.

The U.S. government, nearly every one of the fifty states, and a large majority of local school districts have joined in proclaiming two universal goals for American public education. We are committed to providing every school-aged youngster with a quality education, *and* we are committed to providing an equal educational opportunity to all. Though very broad, these two public education policy goals provide the basic foundation for our definition of an effective school. The first standard for any definition of an effective school is that it must be responsive to these two policy statements simultaneously. An effective school must meet a quality and an *equality* standard simultaneously.

In our research, we have developed the following definition:

> An effective school is a school in which the proportion of students evidencing mastery of the intended curriculum from the highest socioeconomic group served by the school is matched by the proportion of students from the lowest socioeconomic group served by the school who also evidence mastery.

This definition is sensitive to the rights and obligations of local authorities to define the aims of education because it calls for them to define the intended curriculum. For our purposes, the intended curriculum is that statement of educational aims or goals set forth by the appropriate local educational authorities (e.g., Board of Education). Our definition is responsive to the quality issue because, to be effective, a high (90 percent plus) proportion of the students should be able to evidence minimum mastery of that intended curriculum. Finally, our definition seeks to ensure equality by stipulating that measured achievement should be unrelated to such factors as social class and family background.

In order to conduct an analysis of student achievement and determine whether the school is effective by the definition, three elements are needed. First, one needs student achievement scores for each student. Second, one needs a measure of socioeconomic status for each student. Finally, a locally specified standard of minimum mastery of the intended curriculum is needed. With these, we can make a judgment as to whether a school is effective or not.

The first two elements are the focus of many questions. The question most frequently asked centers on the heavy reliance on standardized tests. While it is true that we use these instruments as a practical matter, we do so because schools do not systematically record any other outcome measures. If you go back and carefully study the definition of effective schools, you will note that it does not restrict the measures to standardized tests. Other measures could and should be used, but few, if any, are typically available. As other measures are developed, we strongly advocate that they be incorporated into the process used to assess school effectiveness.

The second focuses on our indicators of socioeconomic status. In the course of the research, we have examined various indicators of socioeconomic status. The best single indicator was found to be the mother's educational level because it had high correlations with most other, more complex measures; was more readily available to a school staff; and possessed a degree of face validity. When schools do not have the mother's educational level recorded and feel it cannot be easily secured, we have suggested a less desirable alternative. Most schools have judged whether or not students are eligible for free or reduced lunch. Such designations can be used to determine socioeconomic status.

CHARACTERISTICS OF EFFECTIVE SCHOOLS

As previously mentioned, several studies of effective schools have been reported in the literature in the last ten years or so. While different researchers have used different definitions of effectiveness, the various studies share two features in common. First, such studies identify schools that already meet the definition of effectiveness. We know they exist. Once found, the characteristics of these effective schools are compared with similar but less effective schools. Second, effective schools studies all look at measured student achievement as the outcome on which to base a judgment about effectiveness. While the various research studies use somewhat different lists of characteristics, the degree of agreement is remarkable.

A particularly good summary of the research on effective schools was offered by Murnane (1981). His conclusions are as follows: (1) There is compelling evidence that schooling makes a difference in determining the cognitive skills of children; (2) the primary resources consistently related to student achievement are those closest to the learning setting, namely, teachers and students; and (3) those most proximate school resources (teachers and other students) will respond to changes in the institutional rules, customs, or contract provisions that determine the allocation of resources, some of which enhance student achievement while others diminish achievement.

Murnane's summary is comparable to the orientation presented in this chapter. The following section briefly describes those institutional rules, customs, patterns or practices that we have observed in effective schools. For purposes of this discussion, I have chosen to use the effective schools characteristics described by Shoemaker and Fraser in their synthesis of these studies (1981). After presenting each description, I comment briefly on the characteristics from the perspective of our research.

Safe and Orderly Environment

There is an orderly, purposeful atmosphere which is free from the threat of physical harm. The climate is not oppressive and is conducive to teaching and learning.

I would only underscore the importance of this characteristic. I would suggest that the "safe" aspect can be thought of as separate from the "orderly" aspect of the school. Our research would suggest that it would be difficult for teaching and learning to proceed if the teachers or the students felt physically at risk. The notion of purposeful and orderly environment is something that goes beyond safety. Many schools could be judged safe but could not be judged as projecting a sense of purposefulness, especially regarding teaching and learning.

Clear and Focused School Mission

There is a clearly articulated mission of the school through which the staff shares an understanding of and a commitment to instructional goals, priorities, assessment procedures, and accountability.

Effective schools have clearly developed a mission that is focused and clear for the teachers, students, and parents. This characteristic takes on added meaning when one realizes that effective schools have deliberately used their mission to state that they care more about some things than others. In contrast, less effective schools usually were found to take on more and more while scarce resources, such as time itself, remained fixed or became even scarcer. Similarly, effective schools possess a sense of common and shared purpose; schools that permit teachers to "do their own thing" often have a disjointed curriculum.

Instructional Leadership

The principal acts as instructional leader and effectively communicates the mission of the school to the staff, parents, and students. The principal understands and applies the characteristics of instructional effectiveness in the management of the instructional program.

If we accept the premise that the school is a complex social system driven toward the accomplishment of specified goals, then it follows that teachers expect certain leadership qualities and behaviors from the principal. In our work, we have attempted to classify leadership as proactive (goal setting), reactive (assessment and accountability), and interactive (supportive, informative, corrective). When principals see themselves as an integral part of the curricular program and when they spend time observing classrooms, they find these leadership qualities more comfortable, welcomed and helpful. When they do not perceive themselves to be instructional leaders, they tend to invest their time and energy in areas other than classrooms.

Climate of High Expectations

This is a climate of expectation in which the staff believes and demonstrates that all students can attain mastery of basic skills and that they (the staff) have the capability to help all students attain mastery.

Our research, while it does not permit us to order the characteristics as to their importance, suggests that the climate of expectations may be the most critical characteristic. If the staff believes that all students can learn, then they will not permit some to fail. On the other hand, if they believe that, for whatever reason, some students (usually the poor and minorities) cannot learn and proceed on this premise, the prediction tends to be realized. At a minimum, teachers should teach with the belief that all students can learn and that they (the teachers) have the capacity to teach all the students. We know that if anything less than 100 percent mastery is presumed, poor students are at most risk.

Frequent Monitoring of Student Progress

Student academic progress is measured frequently. Multiple assessment methods are used. The results of assessments are used to improve individual student performance and to improve the instructional program.

Three concepts embedded in this description deserve further comment and added emphasis. First, the personnel in effective schools appear more willing to accept the fact that the best way to evaluate student progress is to collect measures of pupil performance frequently. This point deserves emphasis because many of the less effective schools rely much more heavily on teacher judgment alone or on teacher judgment in combination with grades assigned to routine worksheets and the like. While useful, such measures alone do not suffice as curricular based assessments of skill mastery.

The second point of emphasis is that multiple methods of assessment are used. This serves two useful purposes. First, the various measures reinforce one another. Second, the various measures themselves provide useful lessons for the students, who come to have at least a working understanding of many measurement approaches.

Third, the feedback from the various measurements serve both as a source of information about each student and as valuable feedback regarding curriculum and instruction across students. The latter is particularly meaningful when teachers believe that achievement derives largely from instruction. If, in contrast, teachers believe that achievement derives from variables such as home and family background, they find little meaning in the examination of aggregated pupil performance data.

In summary, the approach to measuring student performance tells a lot about the effectiveness of the school. The most effective schools tend to measure progress frequently, to employ multiple methods, and to use the results.

Home-School Relations

Parents understand and support the basic mission of the school and are given the opportunity to play an important role in helping the school to achieve this mission.

In many ways, the role of parents in the effective schools turns out to be one of the more controversial findings. The controversy stems from the fact that some effective schools research carefully examined the parent dimension while others virtually ignored it. Therefore, some studies are silent on the issue while others are explicit. Our own work is nearly silent on the matter. Our reason is that we have observed both effective and less effective schools, and some schools in both groups have relatively high levels of parent involvement, and some in both groups have lower levels of involvement. We are unable to comment on this variable. Nevertheless, when making recommendations based on effective schools research as a whole, we are persuaded to advocate the following: Any school improvement program should provide for and aggressively pursue active parent participation, but no school ultimately depend on it. Parents should be involved; their lack of involvement, however, cannot be an excuse for inaction.

COMPREHENSIVE INSTRUCTION IN EFFECTIVE SCHOOLS

The first section of this chapter provides background on effective schools research and the second section characterizes the instructionally effective schools. The concluding section illustrates the major thesis of this paper: Comprehension instruction varies as a function of the presence or absence of certain school characteristics. Some school characteristics, such as safe and orderly environment, would not be limited in their effect to comprehension instruction. Clearly, the absence of safe or orderly environments has a generally depressing influence on achievement across the curriculum. But, since a perceived safe and orderly environment permits achievement to rise generally, one can expect comprehension to rise with it.

Three other characteristics have a more direct and immediate effect on comprehension instruction. For instance, a teacher's instructional planning will be significantly altered when the school's mission statement clearly emphasizes comprehension as a priority curricular goal. In contrast, schools that either do not state an explicit mission or state a mission in which comprehension is not emphasized tend not to alter a teacher's instructional planning relative to comprehension. When the mission characteristic is linked with frequent monitoring of pupil progress, even more positive growth in comprehension can be expected. The designation of comprehension as a priority area and the intention to frequently measure comprehension outcomes provides the teacher with an operational meaning for comprehension. Once such a meaning had been ascribed, the teacher plans lessons around this conceptualization.

The role of the principal is another characteristic that can be expected to directly effect comprehension instruction. When the principal is an instructional leader, he or she is much more closely involved in the ongoing instructional program. Frequent visits by the principal to classrooms to observe comprehension instruction and frequent discussions by teachers and principal regarding such issues as comprehension instruction influence teacher behavior. This leadership further sets the expectation that the teacher should be prepared to inform parents about comprehension instruction. This form of public discussion becomes part of the accountability process. By routinely engaging in such discussions, individual teachers reflect more on what they intend to do in comprehension and why.

Teacher expectations is a third area where instruction differs as a function of school characteristics. If the school believes that the failure of some segment of the student population to learn how to comprehend is essentially inevitable, teachers evaluate instruction differently than when the school presumes that all students can master basic comprehension tasks.

Other examples of the interaction between school characteristics and comprehension instruction will no doubt become obvious as this line of research continues. For the moment, the message is clear. There are school characteristics that are strongly associated with achievement generally; it is not unreasonable to assume that these characteristics will also be associated with comprehension instruction in particular.

CONCLUSION

Clearly there are many constraints on comprehension instruction. The teacher's thinking, described in Chapters 5 and 6, and the environment of the classroom, described in Chapters 7 and 8, are examples of constraints that shape what comprehension instruction ultimately becomes. The social context of the school is another. The message from school effects research is that comprehension instruction will reflect the social system of the school. If the school places high value on comprehension and focuses on it, greater achievement outcomes can be expected. If comprehension is less highly valued and less heavily emphasized by the school, achievement will be less impressive. Hence school characteristics must be considered when efforts are made to improve comprehension instruction.

REFERENCES

Austin, G. R. *An analysis of outlier or exemplary elementary schools and their distinguishing characteristics.* Unpublished manuscript, University of Maryland, Center for Educational Research and Development, March 1979.

Brookover, W. B., et al. *School social systems and student achievement: Schools can make a difference.* New York: Praeger, 1979.

Brookover, W. B., & Lezotte, L. W. *Changes in school characteristics coincident with changes in student achievement.* Occasional Paper No. 17. East Lansing: Michigan State University, Institute for Research on Teaching, 1979.

Clark, D. L., Lotto, L. S., & McCarthy, M. M. Secondary source study of exceptionality in urban elementary schools. In *Why do some urban schools succeed?* Bloomington, Ind.: Phi Delta Kappa, 1980. Pp. 143–225.

Edmonds, R. R. *A report on the research project, search for effective schools . . .* and *Certain of the designs for school improvement that are associated with the project, 1974–1981.* East Lansing: Michigan State University, September 1981.

Edmonds, R. R. Effective schools for the urban poor. In *Educational Leadership*, 1979, *37*, 15–27.

Hoover, M. R. Characteristics of black schools at grade level: A description. *The Reading Teacher*, 1978, *31*, 757–762.

Madden, J. V., Lawson, D. R. & Sweet, D. *School effectiveness study.* Unpublished manuscript, State of California Department of Education, 1976.

Mann, D., & Lawrence, J. Introduction. In *Impact on Instructional Improvement*, 1900, *16* (4), 5–10

Murnane, R. Interpreting evidence on school effectiveness. *Teachers College Record*, Fall 1981.

Rutter, M., et al. *Fifteen thousand hours: Secondary schools and their effects on children*. Cambridge, Mass: Harvard University Press, 1979.

Shoemaker, J., & Fraser, H. W. What principals can do: Some implications from studies of effective schooling. *Phi Delta Kappan*, November 1981.

Weber, G. *Inner city children can be taught to read: Four successful schools*. Occasional Paper No. 18 Washington, D.C.: Council for Basic Education, 1971.

Summary of Part II

Constraints on Instruction

Much in the previous five chapters is intriguing: Clark's notion of the teacher as a comprehender, Brophy's concern with better-prepared curriculum materials, the Florio and Clark assertion regarding the importance of writing as a research site for studying literacy, Anderson's suggested relation between student metacognition and future growth as a learner, and the Lezotte position regarding the school as a social system.

The theme that ties these chapters together is instructional constraints. Both Clark and Brophy, while citing the strides made in studying preactive and interactive teacher thinking, report that concerns for classroom management and activity flow limit teacher instructional thinking, that teachers strive to impose structure and predictability on their environment, and that even the most aware teachers deal with general lesson concerns rather than multiple alternatives or specific subject-matter components. Both Anderson and Florio and Clark, while reporting dramatically different research, establish the importance of the social context of the classroom in shaping the form and quality of instruction. In the case of Florio and Clark, it was an environment free from commercial instructional materials; in the case of Anderson, it was an environment in which teachers emphasized monitoring of behavior rather than understanding as a means for implementing a standard basal text approach to instruction. The classroom environment influenced instruction in both cases. Finally, Lezotte, while reviewing effective schools research, establish that the social context of schools affects instruction.

In short, instruction is not a static commodity. It cannot be treated as a one-dimensional abstraction or an isolated concept. Instead, instruction occurs as a complex and fluid response to a situation. To understand it, one must understand the context within which it occurs and the forces with which it interacts.

SELECTED BIBLIOGRAPHY, PART II

Au, K. H., & Mason, J. M. Social organization factors in learning to read: The balance of rights hypothesis. *Reading Research Quarterly*, 1981, *17* (1), 115–152.

Bossert, S. *Tasks and social relationships in classrooms.* Cambridge, England: Cambridge University Press, 1979.

Doyle, W. Classroom tasks and students' abilities. In P. Peterson & H. Walberg (eds.), *Research on teaching: Concepts, findings, and implications.* Berkeley: McCutchen Publishing, 1979.

Doyle, W. Research on classroom contexts. *Journal of Teacher Education*, 1981, *32* (6), 3–6.

Duffy, G. *Theory to practice: How it works in real classrooms.* Research Series No. 98. East Lansing: Institute for Research on Teaching, Michigan State University, 1981.

Edmonds, R. Effective schools for the urban poor. *Educational Leadership*, 1979, 15–24.

McDermott, R. P. Social relations as contexts for learning in school. *Harvard Educational Review*, 1977, *47* (2), 198–213.

Mehan, J. *Learning lessons: Social organizations in the classroom.* Cambridge, Mass.: Harvard University Press, 1979.

Metheny, W. *The influences of grade and pupil ability levels on teachers' conceptions of reading.* Research Series No. 69. East Lansing: Institute for Research on Teaching, Michigan State University, 1980.

Rist, R. *The urban school.* Cambridge, Mass.: MIT Press, 1973.

Shavelson, R., & Stern, P. Research on teacher's pedagogical thoughts, judgments, decisions and behavior. *Review of Educational Research*, 1981, *51* (4), 455–498.

PART III

Text and Comprehension Instruction

Reading is an interactive, constructive, and strategic process. Readers make sense of what they read by integrating text information with their own knowledge, by monitoring their understanding, and by using procedures for reinterpreting what they read. The quality of the text, of course, plays a critical role in their success at comprehension. This section examines various kinds of text found in classrooms and considers elements of text that can either aid or hinder students' understanding of written information. Ramifications for comprehension instruction are discussed.

The section opens with a chapter on general readability of texts. The validity of readability formulas and their effect on comprehension in all kinds of text are discussed with questions raised regarding the utility of readability criteria that make text frustrating to low-achieving readers because certain cohesive elements are omitted, yet boring to more successful readers because the style creates monotonous stories. Chapters 11 and 12 examine the content of basal materials. In Chapter 11 the content of basal selections is analyzed in terms of subject matter emphasized, the function described, and the ethos reflected. In Chapter 12 the content of student practice exercises found in workbooks that accompany school reading books (basal readers) is analyzed from the standpoint of instructional utility. The final two chapters in this section examine materials for content-area subjects taught in elementary school. Chapter 13 exemplifies problems with science materials and procedures as a result of student preconceptions of scientific concepts. In Chapter 14, using selections principally from students' social studies texts, the author demonstrates that the structure and content of a text can be either considerate or inconsiderate of readers' need for well-organized and complete information.

All the chapters in this section emphasize the close relation between text and instruction in comprehension. The central message is that the teaching of comprehension is hampered if the material students read, practice, and learn from is disorganized, disjointed, or unclear, or does not feature concepts that students require. Hence, making teachers aware of variation in text quality so that adaptations can be made while instructing students is the theme of this section.

10

Readability Formulas and Comprehension

Alice Davison

Readability formulas were first constructed in the 1920s as a means of estimating the level of reading difficulty in a written text. The basic idea was to match reading material with readers of the appropriate level of reading skill so that readers would not have to try to read materials that are too difficult for them to read and comprehend. There is an excellent survey of the history and development of readability formulas in Klare (1963), which traces them from the first lists of frequent words to the ones now in common use. The earlier formulas are interesting because they are more complex than the more modern ones. Their originators tried to isolate factors that they felt might cause or correlate with difficulties in comprehension. So the use of a formula would involve taking 100-word samples and finding averages for some or all of the following:

1. *Properties of sentences*
   a. sentence length in words or syllables
   b. the number of coordinate or subordinate sentences
   c. the number of prepositional phrases
   d. the number of pronouns and definite articles
   e. the number of personal references
2. *Properties of words*
   a. infrequent or frequent words (from word lists)
   b. unfamiliar or familiar words (from word lists)
   c. polysyllabic words or monosyllables
   d. percentage of Latin or Germanic roots
   e. abstract or concrete references

Scores were obtained by multiplying these values with some constant factors to yield either a grade level or a score on a scale roughly correlated with grade level.

Scores were compared with the number of correctly answered comprehension questions for the McCall-Crabbs Reading Passages (McCall and Crabbs 1925), and it was eventually found that the two factors best correlated with degree of success in comprehension questions were vocabulary complexity and sentence length (Gray and Leary 1935, Klare 1963). Bormuth (1966) uses cloze tests as the means of validating formula scores. The formulas that have been used most, and are in use today, are the familiar two-factor ones illustrated by the Dale/Chall formula, which uses a word list, and the Gunning formula, which uses syllable length of words:

Dale/Chall formula (*Dale and Chall 1948*):
Comprehension = .1579 (% words on Dale/Chall list of familiar words) + .0496 (words per sentence) + 3.6365

Gunning formula (*Gunning 1952*):
Readability index = .4 (mean sentence length) + % of words over 2 syllables

Concealed within these fairly simple formulas are several assumptions that need to be examined more closely.

For example, it is assumed or at least implicit in the use of formulas that it is sufficient to measure the factors that reflect difficulty rather than directly measure the factors that cause difficulty in reading. "It seems altogether probable that whether an idea is abstract or concrete, whether it is familiar or unfamiliar, are more important issues in determining difficulty than whether an idea is expressed in words of one or several syllables." The factors that may actually *cause* difficulty are precisely the ones that may vary, as different readers have different background knowledge and different motivations in reading. Texts also may differ, some being meant to inform readers in a straightforward ways, others having more complex purposes of entertaining, pleasing, or challenging the reader. These factors are also subjective, hard to quantify, and liable to some variation in the observer's judgment. "Why, then, have structural elements been given precedence...? The answer lies frankly in the fact that they lend themselves most readily to quantitative enumeration and statistical treatment."

This quotation and the preceding one were not written recently by some critic of formulas complaining of their widespread use and their insensitivity to different genres and purposes in reading. The quotations in fact they come from Gray and Leary (1935, pp. 6–7) and represent both sides of a debate that is still unresolved. Readability formulas are widely used, perhaps for the right reasons but often for the wrong ones, in spite of the fact that their originators and proponents have always hedged them around with reservations, intended vagueness, and special conditions on their legitimate uses.

For example, there are many genres, especially ones involving figurative uses of language or important technical terms that formulas do not apply to. The level of reading the formulas yield does not predict total success at that level; rather, it means that a certain percentage of readers at that level answer a certain percentage of questions correctly. In any case, there is some percentage of error, since the formula scores are not *perfectly* correlated with other measures. They are *highly* correlated by statistical standards (about .8) but not infallible. Finally, formulas measure difficulty indirectly so that they are not supposed to serve as guides in writing or rewriting. As everyone knows, correlation does not mean causality.

Nevertheless, the same attractions that objective factors have for measuring reading difficulty also work for writing, and *in the absence of other models* for measuring and reducing difficulty, it is an inescapable temptation to use formulas as guides. I give some examples of real instances of this and its consequences in a later section.

Readability formulas constitute a sort of crude model of reading comprehension—if they are a model of anything at all. They were invented over fifty years ago in an era when the disciplines of cognitive and educational psychology as well as linguistics were very different from what they are today. It would be surprising, perhaps, if the knowledge available then produced what we would call a sophisticated model today. Certainly there are some grains of truth to the idea that difficulty in reading would be connected in some way with vocabulary and sentence length. Few first graders read unabridged Dickens novels or the U.S. Tax Code (though one could argue that the subject-matter and background knowledge assumed are alone sufficient to make these works too difficult for first graders). But formulas imply that sentence length and vocabulary complexity together define difficulty, at least statistically, across all contexts, readers, and genres. Further, they imply that these two factors contribute in the same way at all levels, that sentence length is just as important for second-grade material as for college material. The only formula that does not rest on this assumption is the Fry formula. The score given by this formula is not a straight line, but a curve. At the lower end of the scale, first to third grade, sentence length has a much greater weight than it does at the upper end of the scale. The relation is reversed for the high school and college end, where average number of syllables in 100-word samples has more effect than sentence length. (The relation expressed in this graph is probably based on empirical results, but I do not know what these are; in any case, it would be important to see if the same relation holds in replications and for all kinds of readers and texts.)

The original formulas were devised for children's reading material, but there is also a need for carefully graded writing for adults—tax form instructions, for example—and the assumption seems to be that what measures the difficulty children may have, as unskilled readers, also measures, in the same way and just as precisely, what is difficult for adults. Again, there is undoubtedly some overlap, but adults have much more background knowledge than children and probably more skill in interpreting oral language. It is likely that there is some difference between children and adults, but empirical proof or disproof seems not to have been found, except in studies done by the military (Kern 1977; and Duffy and Kabance, in press). For children, it is often assumed that the sentence length variable is justified because long sentences are also complex sentences. But strings of coordinate clauses are much easier to process than intricately nested subordinate clauses (cf. Glazer 1974). There is a longstanding tradition also that subordinate clauses are harder to understand than single clauses, based in part on the undeniable fact that children aged 2–6 learn to produce subordinate clauses after they produce single-clause sentences. Are subordinate clauses in spoken language hard for preschool children in the same way as for older school-aged children who have mastered the constructions of spoken language and are learning to read? Again, no one seems to have asked the question (cf. discussion in Huggins and Adams 1980).

The real problem is that readability formulas, if models at all, are such crude models of reading difficulty that they cannot be used to find out anything not already known. Research in readability formulas seems to have been concerned with refining the coefficients used in the formulas or finding different and more convenient ways of counting items or different and more reliable validation. What is singularly lacking in even the modern readability formulas is the capacity to incorporate results from psychology, education, and linguistics, and to frame new questions and hypotheses that would be the subject of further investigation. There has been an enormous accumulation of knowledge about cognition, learning, and language in the last fifty years, but none of it has had any impact on readability formulas. I do not believe that this is accidental. There is no way that formulas of the modern kind could incorporate real causes of reading difficulty except in the way that the earliest formulas did, as a long list of variables.

Formulas provide no insight into what causes difficulty of reading, or why. In the next section, I give a demonstration of how formulas fail to diagnose the real cause of complexity and difficulty and then give some real instances of how simplification can be done well or badly.

DEFINING THE SOURCE OF DIFFICULTY

One of the greatest failings of readability formulas is that they do not define what makes a passage difficult to read. They reflect only the outside, statistically general features of difficulty, such as long sentences and unfamiliar vocabulary. So if they are used to find out if a passage is too difficult for a particular audience, the score assigned by formulas will not be of any use in revising a passage to make it less difficult for that particular audience, or for matching a passage to an audience prepared to deal with its difficult feature. While I think that this is a conclusion that no one would disagree with in public—it has been said even by judicious proponents of formulas such as Klare (1963)—undoubtedly there has been a lot of under-the-counter diagnosis done with readability formulas, simply because the notions of sentence length and vocabulary complexity are clear and simple and have some intuitive plausibility as aspects of difficulty.

Here I give three different examples of difficult passages that present obvious problems even for adult readers. I have chosen some extreme examples so that the adult reader can experience some of the bafflement that a young and unskilled reader might feel in the face of something too difficult, and because the formulas themselves do not define any upper limit—except for Fry. Each of the three has a different major cause of difficulty—vocabulary complexity, sentence length—as well as complexity of meaning, and other factors not measured by formulas. In each example it can be seen that formulas do not measure the real cause of difficulty, and for this reason, reversing the values measured by the formula will not make the passage easier to understand.

The first example consists of a single sentence 254 words long, taken more or less at random from the first book of Marcel Proust's *Remembrance of Things Past*, a work famous for its long and intricate sentences. The italics and the letters in parentheses are mine and will be explained shortly; the structure of the translation corresponds closely to the original.

> And in this way—(a) whereas an artist who had been reading memoirs of the seventeenth century, and wished to bring himself nearer to the great Louis, would consider that he was making progress in that direction when he constructed a pedigree that traced his own descent from some historic family, or (b) when he engaged in correspondence with one of the reigning Sovereigns of Europe, and (c) so would shut his eyes to the mistake he was making in seeking to establish similarity by an exact and therefore lifeless copy of mere

outward form—*a middle-aged lady in a small country town*, by doing no more than yield whole-hearted obedience to her own irresistible eccentricities, and to a spirit of mischief engendered by the utter idleness of her existence, *could see*, (d) without ever having given a thought to Louis XIV, *the most trivial occupations of her daily life*, her morning toilet, her luncheon, her afternoon nap, assume, (e) by virtue of their despotic singularity, *something of the interest* (f) that was to be found in what Saint-Simon used to call the "machinery" of life at Versailles; *and was able too to persuade herself that her silence, a shade of good humour or arrogance on her features would provide Françoise with matter for a mental commentary* (g) as tense with passion and terror, as did the silence, the good humour or the arrogance of the King when a courier, or even his greatest nobles had presented a petition to him, at the turning of an avenue, at Versailles. (pp. 150–51.)

Clearly this is a very long and complex sentence, though the vocabulary is not particularly difficult. According to the Fry formula, if this passage were divided normally into separate sentences, the reading difficulty score would be anywhere from third to ninth grade. The background knowledge the passage demands includes a little European history and some familiarity with tyrannical ladies in small towns, neither of which are very exotic subjects. But it is obvious that the intricate structure of parenthetical and subordinate clauses is both what makes the sentence long and also makes it hard to understand. It is also obvious, as I show below, that shortening this sentence or breaking it into unconnected pieces does not make it easier to understand because the structure is an essential device for expressing the writer's intentions.

The point of the sentence is an extended comparison of the life of a middle-aged provincial lady with the court of Louis XIV at Versailles. The "core" of the sentence about the lady is italicized and is framed and interwoven by a series of comparisons to the king and his court that I have labeled (a) to (g). So to simplify the sentence, the "inner" and "outer" parts of it would have to be carefully disentangled and somehow reconstituted as a comparison between corresponding parts. Otherwise, an unrelated sentence about the middle-aged provincial lady followed by a sentence about absolute monarchs and their courts might not make much sense. Alternatively, the connection would have to be inferred, part by part, by the reader. Finally, the original sentence has a rhythmic life of its own, so that every part of the comparison ends with a significant phrase, such as "at Versailles."

Not to belabor a point, the form of this intricate and complex sentence is not an accident, nor an indulgence in long-windedness. It is a feature of the sentence that must be perceived and interpreted by the reader for a full understanding of this particular sentence. It is an instance of a general feature of the style of the work. If such a sentence must be simplified, its meaning would have to be translated into shorter components with a considerable amount of stylistic expertise. The way to do this would not be indicated by a general measure of readability. As I said earlier, this is an extreme example, but it has the same features as some less exotic examples that I discuss later in which the structure of a sentence helps determine its correct interpretation.

The second example (Raynolds 1976) involves fairly normal sentence length combined with unfamiliar vocabulary.

To put these observations in context, it must be stressed that Agent-action units are neither sensory nor motor units, but both. They are a relationship between an agent, and action, and (usually) an environmental component. One of the most interesting things about skilled behavior from a linguistic point of view is that it already incorporates a structure in which motor representations interact with sensory representations to form externalizable sequences of behavior.

Of the 69 words in the quotation, 41 are ordinary English words used nontechnically. The rest are uncommon, abstract, or technical. A readability formula that measures either unfamiliarity via a word list or syllable length overall would probably diagnose the problem here as one of difficult vocabulary. If it had to be simplified, one of the first things to be changed would be the words used. But what substitutes are there for *motor units* and *sensory representations*? The concepts these phrases stand for could be paraphrased, at fairly great length, in simpler terms. But it is unlikely that the paraphrases would be much more intelligible than the originals to someone who lacked the conceptual background into which these ideas could be placed. That is, this passage is intelligible to people who think about certain issues of behavior and mental processes, and is not very intelligible to most of us who do not have a detailed knowledge of these issues. In other words, the conceptual background the passage requires as a context is what makes the passage hard, and the use of technical terms only reflects this fact. Therefore, changing the words is not going to make the passage conceptually simpler.

The last extreme example has all the foregoing features. The words are technical, the sentence in question is complex syntactically, and the issue has to do with a complex subject, the income-tax laws. The quote is taken from Form 1116 of the Internal Revenue Service. Readability formulas would say that the passage could be made more intelligible by simplifying the syntax, changing the words, and with a little more sophisticated view, adding some background information:

The credit must be computed using the overall limitation. Under the overall limitation, the credit is limited to that percentage of the total U.S. income tax against which the credit is allowed which taxable income from sources outside the U.S. (but not in excess of total taxable income) is of total taxable income.

But clearly these measures will not help a sentence like this one because the problem is that its meaning can be expressed very simply as a mathematical relation, but not as a sentence in English. It means something like this:

(a) tax credit on foreign income : (b) total U.S. tax : (c) foreign income : (d) total taxable income

Any successful revision must start from here and not from the quote, which can be chopped up and rearranged in any way one likes without getting much closer to resolving the basic problem of meaning. One of the chief problems is that the phrase "that percentage" appears to refer to either a certain quantity or one that has already been determined. But in actual fact, the value of "that percentage" is computed on the basis of the "incomes" mentioned last in the sentence. The main difficulty lies in forming the correct combination of four factors in the proportion in the formula above.

The reason for parading these somewhat grotesque examples is to show by analogy why readability formulas do not work and cannot work as diagnostic principles for simplifying difficult language. These examples are extreme, but they cannot exceed the boundaries of formulas because, except for the Fry formula, the formulas do not specify limits. The problems of style, of meaning in syntactic structure, of background knowledge and technical vocabulary are also to be found in materials that adults will not find particularly difficult but that are hard to read for children or unskilled adult readers. In the next section, I give an overview of various instances of simplification and the consequences of simplification motivated by readability formulas.

AN OVERVIEW OF THE CONSEQUENCES OF READABILITY FORMULAS IN REVISIONS

As everyone recognizes, exactly what goes into a text, and the ways that the components go together, are complex matters. In principle, any or all of these features can contribute to text difficulty. In fact, the complexity of the materials of a text, and the unknown ways in which these factors may combine, have helped add to the popularity of objective readability formulas that measure just two values. Given that it is sometimes necessary to make a text simpler to read, what should get changed? We have seen in the previous section that readability formulas are insensitive to the real causes of complexity in three samples of text. If they measure only factors that statistically *reflect* complexity but not necessarily the ones that *cause* complexity, they are not useful as diagnostics of difficulty. They do not define what needs to be altered to make a text simpler in some important way, that is, by removing the cause of difficulty.

By studying and comparing the original and simplified versions of texts, it is possible to see what was changed in the name of simplification. It is often possible to reconstruct the reasons that the writer probably had in making a particular change. In a study of revisions made in adaptations (Davison et al. 1980, Davison and Kantor 1981), a number of different changes were categorized and analyzed both for their probable motivation and for their success as simplifications. Some of the changes made were amply justified by problems in the text, and the revisions were often improvements, in our view, on the original. But many changes had no real justification in the text. Their motivation seems to have been to affect the overall score of the passage on readability formulas. And such changes often had unintended consequences, which means that the text is not any easier to understand and may even be harder to interpret correctly. All the following examples come from the Davison et al. (1980, 1981) study except where a difficult source is cited.

I start with a fairly innocuous example in which difficult words and the use of a name requiring extensive background knowledge have been paraphrased: (The corresponding parts are numbered.)

a. Original (*10 words, 21 syllables*):
   Hippocrates recommended milk to his patients as a *curative beverage.*
   1   3   4

b. *Adaptation* (*16 words, 20 syllables*):
   One of the most famous Greek doctors told his patients to *drink* milk *to*
                  1   4
   cure illness.
      3

The writer has used considerable sense in supplying the background information implied by the name *Hippocrates*. If readability formulas cover proper names at all, they do not say what to do with them if they are unfamiliar or polysyllabic. The writer's solution is a paraphrase giving information that is much longer than the original. The whole adapted sentence, which is a pretty fair approximation of the original, is longer than the original if you count words, though about the same if you count syllables, and there are formulas that count one or the other. Thus, depending on the formula, there is a possible contradiction between the implied need to simplify words—perhaps by paraphrase—and the implied need to shorten sentences.

Aside from just deleting parts of the text to shorten it overall, one of the most common changes made in adaptations is the shortening of overall average sentence length. This means that relatively long sentences are generally split into their component clauses, which become separate sentences, or may be deleted entirely. If the components are kept as separate sentences, what is necessarily missing from the new version is the connection that the components previously had. An example of this is the following:

a. *Original*:
   If given a chance before another fire comes, the tree will heal its own wounds by grow*ing* bark over the burned part.
b. *Adaptation*:
   If given a chance before another fire comes, the tree will heal its own wounds.   *It* will grow
         (and next)
         (how this comes about)
   bark over the burned part.

The original sentence is clear and unambiguous, but it is fairly long. It has two subordinate clauses in it, though these clauses are not unreasonable. The second subordinate clause is separated off in the adaptation, which means that it becomes a main clause, and loses the -*by* and -*ing* affix on the verb that connected it *and*, most important, expressed the meaning relation between it and the main clause. In the adaptation, this relation is not explicitly expressed, and so must be inferred. Given the right background knowledge, it is possible to infer the right connection. But there is another common inference, that successive sentences express successive and possibly unrelated events, which might well be made by a younger reader, without knowing much about the technicalities of trees. Furthermore, there would be no indication in the text that this interpretation is wrong. It would just be a case where the real connections of meaning are missed, and there is nothing unusual about texts, especially school textbooks, seeming disconnected and irrelevant to their youthful readers.

So this is an example of a change made to shorten sentence length that has the effect of making it more difficult for a younger reader to comprehend it correctly. The following example is an example of the opposite case, in which the adaptor has combined sentences to eliminate the need to infer the correct connections. In the adaptation, the sentence is both longer and easier to understand. As in the previous example, the necessary inferences are given in parentheses at the point in the text where they need to be made.

> a. *Original*:
>   We had water to drink *after that*. We set out basins and caught raindrops.
>   (because)   (consequently)
> b. *Adaptation*:
>   We set out basins *to* catch the raindrops *so that* we would have water to drink.

Here two sentences, of 6 and 7 words respectively, are combined into one sentence that is 16 words long, well above the desired average for a text at seventh- to eight-grade level according to formulas. But the addition of the explicit connectives *to* (purpose) and *so that* has made the sentence relations explicit and clear, where they would have to be inferred in the original. They were even harder to infer correctly in the original because of the order of the sentences, which does not follow the order of events referred to; the result comes before the means. The adapter, guided in this instance more by literary skill than readability formulas, has rearranged the clauses in the adaptation so that they go in the preferred order of temporal/causal relations.

In writing for less skilled readers, the usual justification for keeping sentences relatively short is that complex (and therefore long) sentences require too much short-term memory capacity for readers at lower levels of skill (cf. Richek 1976). In order to understand complex sentences, the reader has to keep a large amount of material in mind and go through fairly complicated cognitive routines to process the structure, assigning syntactic structures to the string of words, comprehending the words themselves and their relation to other words (cf. discussion of empirical studies in Huggins and Adams 1980). There is considerable evidence that a major unit of syntactic/semantic processing is the clause (cf. Bever 1970, Warner and Maratsos 1978, and Jarvella 1971). Many studies have been done on the processing load placed on a hearer or reader when it is necessary to relate something in the clause being processed in short-term memory with something already processed, and transferred into a semantic representation (Townshend and Bever 1978), on two-clause sequences (Tannenhaus and Seidenberg 1980), on pronouns and their antecedents, and so forth. But little experimental work has been done that measures the demands of making inferences on linguistic processing. An important exception is the study (Haviland and Clark 1974) on definite expressions such as *the beer*. If no discourse antecedent precedes it, the connection with the context has to be inferred, and the Haviland and Clark study shows that it takes longer to understand a sentence with a definite expression and no antecedent than it does if there is an antecedent. But inferences are of many kinds, some depending on linguistic elements like *the*, others on word meaning or sentence form, others on real-world knowledge in general and the particular content of the sentence. Since it is not *clear* what the demands of inferences are (and even *that* an inference needs to be made, since they are sometimes optional, and sometimes not indicated by any explicit feature of the sentence), it is often taken for granted that they can be made without additional effort.

As an example of a superficially "simple" text with a high, but hidden, inference load, consider the following excerpt:

1. Before   the Civil War the Negroes in the South were slaves.
   (and after?—if not, why?)   (but not the North?)
2. Many people in the North
        (so no slaves in the North?)
   thought this   was wrong and formed a party
   (slavery in the South?)   (consequently)
   (slavery in general?)   (next after that)
   to prevent the spread of slavery.
   (why not the existence of slavery everywhere?)

An adult reader with fairly full background knowledge about the Civil War can interpret this passage correctly by filling in a lot that is not made explicit. But someone without background knowledge and experience in making inferences would not derive the same interpretation, or even a coherent one. The antecedent of "this" is unclear—is it slavery in general, or wherever it was, or slavery in the South? The phrase "the spread of slavery" seems to contradict the mention of existing slavery. "Before" and the phrase "in the North" and "in the South" suggest contrasts that are not clear. The logical relation between the first and second clauses in the second sentence depends on the reader's ability to infer the correct relation, "consequently," if in fact the reader makes an inference at all. Hence the full comprehension of the passage, which is not very coherent, depends on a large hidden-inference load.

Successful adaptations take the inference load into account, at least to some extent. In the following example, the adaptor anticipated the need to make an inference:

a. *Original*:
   In Toronto, a *suburban* ice-skating rink was flooded with *250 surplus gallons* of it (=skim milk). Skaters found that it chipped less easily than frozen water.
b. *Adaptation*:
   An ice-skating rink was flooded with it. Skaters found that *when it froze* it chipped less easily than frozen water.

The adaption is longer than the original because the clause "when it froze" has been added, anticipating a false start on the part of the reader. The reader might be able to infer "retroactively" that the milk was frozen after reading to the end of the sentence, where "frozen water" is mentioned. Or with more background knowledge, the mention of skating rinks might suggest freezing, except for the unusualness of skim milk in such a context. If the added phrase were not there, the reader might not make the correct inference until the end of the sentence had been reached. The added information rules out an incorrect interpretation earlier rather than later. The added length in the sentence is compensated for by the deletion of "background" information in the first sentence, about location and quantity. Curiously, the word "surplus" is also deleted, probably because it is an uncommon word. But it gives the rationale for the otherwise unusual and potentially wasteful use of skim milk in a rink.

The splitting of clauses into separate sentences can affect how the whole discourse is perceived and lead the reader to a wrong interpretation of the overall theme of a paragraph. The example that follows came from a study by Anderson, Armbruster, and Kantor (1980) and was discovered by comparing the first and second editions of a sixth-grade science textbook:

> a. *First edition*:
> You probably saw lily pads, grass, reeds and water weeds *growing in the shallow water near the shore*. And maybe there were water striders gliding over the surface of the lake, *and* small fishes darting among the shadows of the lily pads. (Bendick and Gallant 1980)

The theme of this paragraph is the *visibility* of various things, which will be contrasted in later paragraphs with the *invisible* microorganisms in the pond. Certain changes were made in these sentences in the second edition, possibly because of reports that the first edition was too hard for some readers. The changes affecting this paragraph included splitting sentences into their component clauses. The reduced relative clause "growing in ... " is made a full sentence, with an explicit subject, "these plants":

> b. *Second edition*:
> You probably saw lily pads, grass, reeds and water weeds. *These plants grow in the shallow water near shore*. There may have been water striders gliding over the surface of the lake. Did you see small fishes darting in the shadows of the lily pads? (Ibid.)

This subject defines a new topic in the discourse, "these plants," in addition to the pond. Each successive sentence, including the two made from the deletion of "and," seems to focus on the *location* of some additional thing. The emphasis of the paragraph is now different from the first edition; it seems now to be "about" the places where things grow or live. This impression is not given in the first edition, where information about location is in a subordinate clause in the first sentence, and not very prominent in the second sentence, where two other kinds of pond creatures are introduced together into the discourse. The distortion of the paragraph theme is a direct consequence of splitting complex sentences into simpler sentences, which will affect the score assigned by readability formulas. Yet the misperception of the point of this paragraph will make it harder for the reader to see its relation to the discussion of microorganisms which comes later.

Another unintended bad effect of shortening sentences comes about when certain "redundant" clauses and adverbs (such as *clearly, apparently*) are deleted. These words or phrases indicate whether the assertion in the sentence is founded on fact or opinion, and whether the fact stated is supported by the speaker or writer's own beliefs. For example:

a. *Original*:
A railway freight agent has figured that it would require at least 40 modern flat cars to haul just the trunk alone.
b. *Adaptation*:
And at least forty freight cars would be needed to haul away just its trunk.

What is deleted is an indication of the source of the fact asserted here, about the size of a tree trunk. Since the author agrees with the fact, the deleted clause is redundant in a certain sense. But in the original version the inclusion of the source added extra credibility to the assertion, since the estimate of size is being made by an expert on freight. Without an indication of source, the assertion just comes directly from the author—who therefore seems all-knowing. One of the skills that must be acquired in learning to read at an adult level is the skill of evaluating the reliability of information on the basis of its source. If such information is systematically deleted because it does not seem to be very important, then younger readers are deprived of opportunities to learn and use this skill.

A more subtle effect of readability formulas on texts is a general degradation of style and individuality. So far I have not said much about vocabulary changes because the changes found in the study reported in Davison and Kantor (1981) did not have such profound effects on comprehension as deletions and alterations of sentence structure. But the systematic substitution of familiar words for less familiar words will mean that idiosyncratic words cannot be used, nor ones with particular stylistic connotations. For example, one of the texts studied in Davison and Kantor (1981) was a first-person narrative of the Dayton Flood of 1913, written the same year. It contained a certain number of archaic uses of words (*kettle* for *pot*, for example), and a number of words and structures that are more appropriate in spoken language than written language. In the parts used for the adaptation, all of these were removed, so that the sense of the era, and of an individual person speaking, were lost. Some of the interest a reader might feel in the story was lost also, as well as the property of an authentic "voice," which is more credible than an impersonal tone. Of course, these are the perceptions of an adult, and it is not clear how much effect style has on younger readers. But Green and Laff (1980) show that even first graders can recognize distinctive literary styles.

It is worth noting that a textbook that conforms to readability formulas may lose both good and poor readers. Because of vocabulary constraints and the need to shorten sentences, the style of the text will be dull and without variety. The background details, including information about particular things or striking examples, will be generally left out. So the good readers who can cope with the inferences needed to comprehend a textbook of this kind will find it boring, while the less-good readers will not be able to understand it very well because the text will be inexplicit and disconnected. If the textbook is found to be "too hard," then it may be revised by simplifying the vocabulary and sentence structure still further. The use of readability formulas as diagnostic guides to rewriting can easily be self-defeating if the *real* sources of difficulty are not identified and if the writer fails to anticipate the new sources of difficulty which may be created by the revisions of the old difficulties. Adherence to readability formulas does not guarantee a particular level of difficulty, and never has.

CONCLUSION

I have discussed the limitations and liabilities of the use of formulas from several points of view. First, from a theoretical point of view, readability formulas are of no use whatever as an explanatory measure and are completely useless in adding to the store of knowledge about reading. The reason is that readability formulas are not theories of how the human mind processes and interprets written language. At best they are very crude approximations of what *reflects* difficulties in processing and interpreting. As such, they cannot be the basis for framing hypotheses that can be tested, and they cannot be integrated with other disciplines, like psychology and linguistics, which are based on inquiry via hypothesis. Consequently it is impossible for a researcher in obstacles to reading comprehension to make use of what is known at present about learning, cognition, and language *and* make any meaningful claims about readability formulas.

Second, readability formulas fail to make diagnostic predictions that fit the intuitions of the normal reader about what the real source of difficulty might be in a text. The demonstration of the difficulties that an adult reader would have in reading and interpreting very difficult prose was supposed to illustrate this point. It was also intended as a demonstration of the inappropriateness of formulas for measuring *all* kinds of text and of giving accurate measures beyond a certain point. Yet there is no *inherent* property of any formula except graphlike formulas, such as Fry's, which specifies the cutoff points above which the formulas should not be expected to give results. And the difficult passages were also intended as demonstrations that if a text has a certain difficult feature, and if the text is to be preserved as intelligible, the procedures for rewriting are not necessarily standard ones. That is, the reviser must choose very carefully, and sometimes very ingeniously, the most appropriate ways of recasting the text.

Finally, I have shown a number of actual instances of adaptation in which changes were made in a text in order to make it easier to read. Some of these changes actually improved the text, by eliminating misleading features and making explicit the important relations within the sentence or text. These changes were made in accordance with the knowledge and training of skilled writers, not by following formulas. Other changes, which did seem to be motivated by formulas, altered sentence length or vocabulary but did *not* make the text easier. In many cases, they made the sentence less explicit and more open to misinterpretation. In some cases, also, the simplifications removed from the text some opportunities for the unskilled reader to encounter and practice on some of the features of normal written discourse, which must be mastered in the course of becoming a skilled reader (cf. MacGinitie, in press).

For some writers on readability, the usual remedy is to try again. The search goes on for new formulas, different numbers in the fourth decimal place of the coefficients, better ways of calculating number of syllables per hundred words, and so on. Another alternative is to take some of the other features of texts that have been shown experimentally to affect comprehension and to make those the variables in a formula-like procedure. Some of these are Botel, Dawkins, and Granowsky (1973), Endicott (1973), and von Glaserfeld (1970–71). These have some promise as models of one or two aspects of reading comprehension, but to the extent that they isolate a few variables, they share the defects of formulas in general for measuring the difficulty of all kinds of texts and readers, and of diagnosing difficulty and suggesting the appropriate remedy. An earlier study by Bormuth (1966) demonstrated that nearly all possible variables in texts were correlated with sentence length and vocabulary complexity as predictors of difficulty.

The approach I want to advocate is not so optimistic. I do not think that *any* new formula can be found that is more accurate and realistic than the current ones and that makes use of a small number of variables that interact in a standard way for all texts.[1] Instead, I want to propose that we confess our ignorance, which is virtually total, of what causes a text to be hard to process and understand. The originators of formulas in the 1920s in effect confessed their ignorance by measuring external factors that only *reflect* difficulty. They did not then have as good an opportunity as we have now to remedy our ignorance. The way this goal is to be achieved is in the construction of theoretically sound models of reading comprehension, by which the real variables can be isolated and their interactions discovered. Nothing further will be discovered about reading difficulty and the causes of obstacles to comprehension without disciplined experimentation, which is neither easy nor cheap. But the simpler and cheaper methods used in the last half century have not made us much wiser than before.

In the meantime, all that there is to lean upon is a number of commonsensical or empirically based guidelines for writers, such as Dawkins (1975), Kern (1977), Felker (1980), and Holland (1981), listing features of texts that *may* contribute to difficulty or facilitate comprehension in readers. The only way to know if they *do* is to use adequate testing procedures, in which the text being evaluated is read by a sample of the intended readers, who are tested in some way to see if the text is successful in communicating what it is meant to communicate. The alternatives to readability formulas are not obvious, but the small amount of progress made in the last fifty years is an eloquent argument for a new approach.

NOTES

1. One of the newer formulas is the FORCAST formula, which is used now by the military for assessing the reading difficulty of technical manuals used by military personnel of different ranks, training, and responsibility (Kern et al. 1977). It is interesting that in the guidelines for writers, the assessment of the reading level, using the formula, is explicitly dissociated from diagnosis of difficulty and choice of appropriate measures of correction. Furthermore, much attention is paid to directing the revision to its intended audience, matching the text to the specific pieces of background knowledge that can be assumed in the reader and the purposes for which the technical material will be used.

REFERENCES

Anderson, T. H., Armbruster, B. B., & Kantor, R. N. *How clearly written are children's textbooks? Or, of bladderworts and alfalfa.* Reading Education Report No. 16. Urbana: University of Illinois, Center for the Study of Reading, 1980. ERIC Document Reproduction Service No. ED 192 275.

Bendick, J., & Gallant, R. *Elementary Science 6*. Lexington, Mass.: Ginn & Co., 1980.

Bever, T. G. The cognitive basis for linguistic structure. In J. R. Hayes (Ed.), *Cognition and the development of language*. New York: John Wiley, 1970.

Bormuth, J. R. Readability: A new approach. *Reading Research Quarterly*, 1966, *1*, 79–132:

Botel, M. J., Dawkins, J., & Granowsky, A. A syntactic complexity formula. In W. H. MacGinitie (Ed.), *Assessment of problems in reading*. Newark, Del.: International Reading Association, 1973, 77–86.

Dale, E., & Chall, J. A formula for predicting readability. *Educational Research Bulletin*, 1948, *27*, 37–54.

Davison, A. Readability: Appraising text difficulty. In *Learning to read in American schools: Basal readers and content texts*. Hillsdale, N.J.: Erlbaum, in press.

Davison, A., & Kantor, R. N. On the failure of readability formulas to define readable texts: A case study from adaptations. *Reading Research Quarterly*, 1982, *17*, 187–209.

Davison, A., Kantor, R. N., Hannah, J., Hermon, G., Lutz, R., & Salzillo, R. *Limitations of readability formulas in guiding adaptations of texts*. Tech. Rep. No. 162. Urbana: University of Illinois, Center for the Study of Reading, 1980. ERIC Document Reproduction Service No. ED 184 090.

Dawkins, J. *Syntax and readability*. Newark, Del.: International Reading Association, 1975.

Duffy, T. M., & Kabance, P. Testing a readable writing approach to text revision. *Journal of Educational Psychology*, in press.

Felker, D. B. (Ed.), *Document design: A review of the relevant research*. Washington, D.C.: Document Design Project, American Institute for Research, 1980.

Fry, E. B. A readability formula that saves time. *Journal of Reading*, 1968, *11*, 513–516; 575–578.

Glazer, S.M. Is sentence length a valid measure of difficulty in readability formulas? *The Reading Teacher*, 1974, *27*, 464–68.

Green, G. M., & Laff, M. O. *Five-year-olds' recognition of authorship by literary style*. Tech. Rep. No. 181. Urbana: University of Illinois, Center for the Study of Reading, 1980. ERIC Document Reproduction Service No. ED 193 615.

Gray, W. S., & Leary, B. E. *What makes a book readable?* Chicago: University of Chicago Press, 1935.

Gunning, R. *The technique of clear writing*. New York: McGraw-Hill, 1952.

Haviland, S. E., & Clark, H. H. What's new? Acquiring information as a process in comprehension. *Journal of Verbal Learning and Verbal Behavior*, 1974, *13*, 512–521.

Holland, V. M. *Psycholinguistic alternatives to readability formulas*. Washington, D.C.: Document Design Project, American Institute for Research, 1981.

Huggins, A. W. F., & Adams, M. J. Syntactic aspects of reading comprehension. In R. J. Spiro, B. C. Bruce, & W. F. Brewer (Eds.), *Theoretical issues in reading comprehension*. Hillsdale, N. J.: Erlbaum, 1980.

Jarvella, R. Syntactic processing of connected speech. *Journal of Verbal Learning and Verbal Behavior*, 1971, *10*, 409–416.

Kern, R. P., Sticht, T. G., Welty, D., & Hauke, R. N. *Guidebook for the development of army training literature*. Alexandria, Va.: U.S. Army Research Institute for the Behavioral and Social Sciences, 1977.

Klare, G. R. *The measurement of readability*. Ames: Iowa State University Press, 1963.

McCall, W. A., & Crabbs, L. M. *Standard test lessons in reading*. New York: Teachers College Press, Columbia University, 1925.

MacGinities, W. H. Readability as a solution adds to the problem. In *Learning to read in American schools: Basal readers and content texts*. Hillsdale, N. J.: Erlbaum, in press.

Proust, M. *Swann's Way*. Translated by C. K. Scott-Moncrief. New York: Modern Library.

Reynolds, P. C. Language and skilled activity. In S. R. Harnad, H. D. Steklis, & J. Lancaster (Eds.), *Origins and evolution of language and speech, Annals of the New York Academic of Sciences*, 1976, *280*, 150–166.

Richek, M. A. The effect of sentence complexity on the reading comprehension of syntactic structures. *Journal of Educational Psychology*, 1976, *68*, 800–806.

Tanenhaus, M. K., & Seidenberg, M. S. *Discourse context and sentence perception*. Urbana: University of Illinois, Center for the Study of Reading, 1980.

Townshend, D. J., & Bever, T. G. Interclause relations and clausal processing. *Journal of Verbal Learning and Verbal Behavior*, 1978, *17*, 509–521.

Wanner, E., & Maratsos, M. An ATN approach to comprehension. In M. Halle, J. Bresnan, & G. Miller (Eds.), *Linguistic structure and psychological reality*. Cambridge, Mass.: MIT Press, 1978.

11

Content of Basal Text Selections: Implications for Comprehension Instruction

William H. Schmidt, Jacqueline Caul,
Joe L. Byers, and Margaret Buchmann

The teaching and assessment of reading comprehension is dependent upon a substantive context; the comprehension attained through reading is of the "something" found in written text. Reading and comprehension do not happen in the abstract; one always reads and comprehends some content. Although these statements are tautological in nature, they need to be made. The relationship of reading and comprehension skills to educational content must be stressed when we consider instruction in reading comprehension because the organization of the elementary school curriculum to some extent uncouples content and reading skills.

In the elementary school, reading is treated as a separate curricular area. Reading is demarcated from the rest of the curriculum, with textbooks, most often basal readers, of its own. As a consequence, reading comprehension tends to be taught as a skill separated from the reading comprehension necessary for the study of such areas as science, mathematics, art, and social studies.

This isolation of reading and reading comprehension from subjects in the curriculum has resulted in teachers turning to instructional *tools* for the substance

This work is sponsored in part by the Institute for Research on Teaching, College of Education, Michigan State University, East Lansing, Michigan. The Institute for Research on Teaching is funded primarily by the Program for Teaching and Instruction of the National Institute of Education, U.S. Department of Health, Education, and Welfare. The opinions expressed in this publication do not necessarily reflect the position, policy, or endorsement of the National Institute of Education. (Contract No. 400–76–0073.) The authors wish to acknowledge the thoughtful contributions of Annegret Harnischfeger and David Wiley to the development of the content taxonomy. We also acknowledge the assistance of other members of the Language Arts Project in the content coding of the basals and in the analysis of the data. Their assistance has been invaluable. We thank Laura Roehler, Patricia Cianciolo, David Soloman, Frank Jenkins, Linda Vavrus, Barbara Diamond, Susan Wildfong, Robert Hill, and Donna Hamilton.

of instruction in these areas. Goodlad (1976) noted that, in general, textbooks predominated as the medium of instruction in the elementary school. Duffy (1982), as well as Osborn and Shirey (1980), pointed out that this is also true for the area of reading; teachers typically rely on basal readers as the context in which to teach reading. In addition, observational and survey data suggest that teachers draw heavily on commercially prepared curricular materials in reading instruction (see Austin and Morrison 1963; Durkin 1978–79; Goodlad 1970).

The purpose of Part 3 of this book is to examine text. The prevalant text is the basal. We are interested in basal texts not from a skill point of view. Nor do we examine questions of consistency with any particular reading or developmental theory. We look at basal texts from the point of view of educational content. What is the educationally relevant content to which children are exposed as they are taught or attempt on their own to comprehend what they read in basals?

This is an important question in itself and gains added significance in view of the typical separation of reading and reader's comprehension instruction from the rest of the curriculum. It has curricular implications beyond the area of reading, since it addresses (1) the issues of content exposure in general and (2) potentially missed opportunities for content exposure in reading and reading comprehension instruction. These questions have achievement and resource implications. Time in school is limited, but the evidence suggests that time allocations to subjects have powerful consequences for learning. We have to keep in mind that language instruction, including reading, has been estimated to comprise 40 to 60 percent of the elementary school day (see, e.g., Roehler, Schmidt, and Buchmann 1979). Hence the potential and reality of content exposure during the "reading" part of the curriculum must not be overlooked as we think about opportunities to learn in elementary schools.

Basals, as the dominant instructional tool in reading, are of interest for reading comprehension goals as well. Bettelheim and Zelan (1981) report from their clinical studies that children could not remember what they had read in a basal story because it was meaningless to them. These young readers felt the basal selections did not deal with substantive issues, such as coping with life's more serious problems. Bettelheim and Zelan conclude that basal texts "have become emptier and emptier. . . . Since the texts have no meaning, the child is expected to learn skills without their being meaningfully applied. . . . Because this has happened children are not interested in learning to read" (p. 265). Where there seems nothing worth comprehending, interest in the activity of reading and in getting better at reading is liable to be stultified.

To explore the issue of educational content in basal readers, we analyzed 34 recent basals. They represent eight of the most commonly used series in American elementary education.

Three dimensions define and categorize educational content for purposes of analysis: subject matter, function, and ethos. These categories represent central aspects of educationally relevant knowledge that philosophers have characterized as "knowing that," "knowing how," and "knowing to," or as knowledge of facts, skills, and right action.

In this chapter we present the results of the content analysis. It is a profile of the educational content to which American students are exposed as their reading comprehension is developed through elementary school basals.

A TAXONOMY OF CONTENT

To describe the substantive context in which reading comprehension is taught and learned when basal selections are used, a definition of content together with a taxonomy to elucidate the distinctions embedded in the definition are needed. The three components that, taken together, operationalize the concept of educational content are subject matter, function, and ethos. In the analysis, each is itself variable in that it is characterized by a series of distinctions, including its own absence.

The components of content can be thought of as the dimensions of a three dimensional matrix. Each cell in the matrix is a content defined in terms of a level for each of three dimensions, including its absence. This implies that one cell in the matrix represents the absence of all three components of content. This might appear to be a null set, but represents the absence of educationally relevant content according to certain categories. In what follows, these will be clarified.

Subject-Matter Content

The subject-matter component covers theories, facts, and information that can be found in written text. The traditional building blocks of the elementary school curriculum are the levels of this factor. It includes language content, fine arts and crafts, physical education (sports and recreation), mathematics, music, science, philosophy, economics, psychology, and social studies. Social studies are subdivided as a content area by the subject matter of the social sciences (history, geography, anthropology) and the treatment of social themes. These themes concern enduring problems of individual and social life, such as growing up, taking responsibility (growth and development), and living with others (family, significant others, peers, and community). Knowledge in this dimension means "knowing that" something is true, something has happened, or something is conceptualized in certain ways.

Functional Content

This component is concerned with applied knowledge of a process nature. It answers to the question "how?" Basal selections, for example, that contain a detailed description of scientific processes of discovery and analysis would be coded under that category. But the fictional treatment of problem solving in the context of mysteries conveys process knowledge as well, and would be coded as functional content. Here it is through the model provided by the sleuth that the reader gains insight into how to go about finding out things. Levels of this content factor include reasoning/problem solving, moral reasoning, contemplation, creativity, feeling/catharsis, initiative/persistence, absurdity/paradox, humor in the use of language, and cunning/mother wit. Thus, functional content spans the variety of activities of the life of the mind and emotions that people have valued and passed on in texts. In their literary forms—poems, fables, stories, rhymes, and jingles—these texts present a variety of opportunities to describe and model these processes.

Ethos Content

The ethos component concerns virtue, that which we ought to do. In basals this content component is found especially in folk and fairy tales that indicate what people ought to strive for, or to avoid. The levels of this content factor are humility, patience/forbearance, courage, kindness/generosity, honesty, hope, and "other." Ethos content explains or demonstrates what people ought to do in order to live right; it presents the ethical knowledge of ordinary life with its time-tested virtues. As explained above, a category included for all three content components is "no content."

PROCEDURES

The Basals

Thirty-four basals were chosen to represent the second-, fourth-, and fifth-grade texts of eight major publishing companies. These companies dominate the market for basal texts in the American educational system. We chose second grade to have some representation at the lower elementary level, but concentrated at the upper elementary level (fourth and fifth grades) where reading comprehension is a major focus. We analyzed the most recent series available from the company at the time the study was conducted. In addition to the text (or texts, in the case of the second grade) for each of the three grade levels in that series, a fifth-grade literature basal was included from Harcourt Brace Jovanovich. This book is considered by the company as part of the series (they also have a fourth-grade literature basal that we did not analyze). The names of the texts and the publishing companies are as follows:

Houghton Mifflin (1979)
　　Sunburst　　(2nd)
　　Tapestry　　(2nd)
　　Medley　　(4th)
　　Keystone　　(5th)
Scott-Foresman (1978)
　　Hootenanny　　　　(2nd)
　　Daisy Days　　　　(2nd)
　　Flying Hoofs　　　(4th)
　　Fins & Tales　　　(5th)
Ginn (1979)
　　One to Grow On　　　　　(2nd)
　　The Dog Next Door　　　　(2nd)
　　A Lizard to Start With　　(4th)
　　Tell Me How the Sun Rose　(4th)
　　Measure Me, Sky　　　　　(5th)
Harcourt Brace Jovanovich (1979)
　　World of Surprises　　(2nd)
　　People and Places　　(2nd)
　　Building Bridges　　(4th)

> *Reaching Out*   (5th)
> *Changing Scenes*   (5th-Literature)

Harper & Row (1980)

> *Wings and Wishes*   (2nd)
> *Pets and Promises*   (2nd)
> *Dreams and Dragons*   (4th)
> *Moccasins and Marvels*   (5th)

Holt, Rinehart (1977)

> *People Need People*   (2nd)
> *The Way of the World*   (2nd)
> *Time to Wonder*   (4th)
> *Freedom's Ground*   (5th)

Laidlaw (1980)

> *Tricky Troll*   (2nd)
> *Wide-Eyed Detectives*   (2nd)
> *Reflections*   (4th)
> *Patterns*   (5th)

Open Court (1979)

> *A Flint Holds Fire*   (2nd)
> *From Sea to Sea*   (2nd)
> *Burning Bright*   (4th)
> *Spirit of the Wind*   (5th)

Coding Procedures

Each basal selection was analyzed separately on all three dimensions of educationally relevant content. The question asked by the coder relative to each component was whether there was sufficient detail—descriptive, explanatory, evocative, or processual—to code for the presence of this content category. The mere mention of a subject matter or appearance of a social theme did not warrant coding for that content. Nor did the fact that the selection was a fairy tale or a mystery story imply that ethos or functional content were coded as present. Detailed coding conventions were developed to regulate the behavior of the raters.

After some practice, determining whether there was sufficient detail to code for content in factually oriented basal selections was straightforward. In the case of fictional selections, content mostly concerned social or life themes. To be coded as content, there had to be enough *detail* to give the reader an opportunity to gain a conceptual and/or factual understanding of that aspect of coping with life. If in the rater's judgment there was no *conceptual undergirding* to the social or life theme, the selection was coded as having no subject-matter content.

In the functional content domain, educationally relevant processes were often modeled by a main character. Again, not all selections in which the protagonist (or author, if he or she assumed a point of view) solved a problem, was confronted with a moral dilemma, or contemplated some aspect of the world were coded under the category of functional content. Sufficient detail was necessary so that the reader could gain some cognitive understanding of what is involved in a particular way of human functioning.

For the ethos component, the key feature for determining the presence of content was that a virtue was rewarded or its opposite punished. The punishment or reward was meted out by someone with authority, and a character had to be in the selection with whom a child could identify. When all elements were present in sufficient detail, the selection was coded under ethos content. For all three dimensions, the aim was to determine whether a basal selection in itself would constitute an opportunity to learn substantive content. Selections could be coded as having content on more than one dimension.

The following literary forms were also determined: fantasy, historical fiction, realistic fiction, fairy or folk tales, science fiction, poetry, letters, journals, speeches, plays, songs, factual articles, advertisements, cartoon/jokes, and riddles/puzzles.

Interrater Reliability

A team of eight coders performed the content analyses. Each was trained and then coded a randomly selected pilot text. The eight basals used represented three different publishers and grade levels 2, 4, and 5. The pilot led to revisions of the taxonomy and coding rules. Following the pilot, 30 selections (ten from each of three basals randomly selected by grade level) were coded by all eight coders. Coders had 88 percent agreement on the subject-matter dimension, 84 percent agreement on the functional dimension, and 97 percent agreement on the ethos dimension, a high degree of interrater agreement.

Given the high agreement, only one rater coded each basal in the actual coding of the 34 basals for the study. However, to check for coder error, a sampling plan was developed based on the number of selections found in each book. Ten percent of the selections in each basal were coded by a second rater. If the two coders disagreed on the categorization of enough of the selections in this sample so as to cast doubt on the assumption that there was at least 90 percent interrater agreement over the entire book, the entire book was recoded by a panel of three coders. Probability tables were developed to aid in this decision process.

RESULTS

Selections

Subject-matter dimension. Of the 1,959 individual selections contained in the 34 basals, 360 different coding combinations, each representing a different content, characterized the range of differences on the subject-matter dimension.[1] An analysis of the number of selections coded as containing content under each of six major subject-matter designations illustrates the general areas most frequently addressed in elementary basals (see Table 11.1). Of the 1,959 selections, 828 (42.3 percent) were coded as having no subject-matter content, 20.3 percent of the selections had language skills content, 19.9 percent had social science content, and 11.9 percent had science content. Less than 6 percent of the total selections had content in any other major subject matter area, including art, physical education, philosophy, mathematics, and music.

Functional dimension. On the functional dimension (see Table 11.2) 1,389 (70.9 percent) of the selections had no functional content. The most frequently repre-

TABLE 11.1   Frequency of Content Categories on the Subject-Matter Dimension

Subject Matter	Number of Selections	Percentage of Total
No subject-matter content	828	42.3
Language skills	398	20.3
Fine arts and crafts	63	3.2
Physical education	30	1.5
Mathematics	8	.4
Music	8	.4
Science	234	11.9
Philosophy	1	.1
Social science	389	19.9
Economics	4	.2
Psychology	11	.6
History, geography, and anthropology (HGA)	175	8.9
Social themes	120	6.1
Both HGA and social themes	79	4.0
Total	1,959	100.0

sented functional content categories included initiative/persistence, 5.4 percent; contemplation, 4.5 percent; reasoning/problem solving, 4.0 percent; cunning/ mother wit, 3.7 percent. The remaining categories each accounted for 3 percent or less of the selections.

Ethos dimension. Selections having no ethos content equaled 1,719 (87.7 percent of the total). The ethos categories most frequently present in selections were kindness/generosity and courage, totaling 8.5 percent of the selections (see Table 11.3).

Literary form. The two literary forms most frequently used across selections were factual articles (38.6 percent) and stories (37.4 percent) which together

TABLE 11.2   Frequency of Content Categories on the Functional Dimension

Functional Content	Number of Selections	Percentage of Total
No functional content	1389	70.9
Reasoning/problem solving	79	4.0
Moral reasoning	59	3.0
Contemplation	81	4.1
Creativity	55	2.8
Feeling/catharsis	21	1.1
Initiative/persistence	105	5.4
Absurdity/paradox	53	2.7
Humor in use of language	44	2.2
Cunning/mother wit	73	3.7
Total	1,959	100.0

TABLE 11.3   Frequency of Content Categories on the Ethos Dimension

Ethos Content	Number of Selections	Percentage of Total
No ethos content	1719	87.7
Humility	20	1.0
Patience/forbearance	18	.9
Courage	77	3.9
Kindness/generosity	91	4.6
Honesty	16	.8
Hope	6	.3
Other	12	.6
Total	1,959	100.0

accounted for three fourths of all selections (see Table 11.4). The next most frequently used literary form was poetry (19.4 percent), with the remaining forms accounting for less than 5 percent of the selections. Among stories, the most often used form was realistic fiction (17.4 percent).

The literary form of a selection has an impact on the nature of its educational content. Seventy-two percent of the prose selections (including stories, factual articles, letters, journals, plays, and speeches) have subject-matter content, while only 10 percent of selections classified as poetry, rhymes, advertisements, cartoons, and riddles have such content. Most of the content present in prose selections deals with language skills (25 percent), science (15 percent), or social studies (25 percent).

Functional content is well represented in poetry selections (45 percent) but only modestly so in prose selections (26 percent). No major differences exist among the literary forms on the presence of ethos content.

TABLE 11.4   Frequency of Literary Forms

Literary Form	Number of Selections	Percentage of Total
Stories	733	37.4
Fantasy	123	6.3
Historical fiction	72	3.7
Realistic fiction	341	17.4
Fairy and folk tales	183	9.3
Science fiction	8	.4
Other stories	6	.3
Poetry, rhymes, and limericks	380	19.4
Letters	2	.1
Journals	5	.3
Plays	27	1.4
Songs	9	.5
Factual articles	757	38.6
Cartoons and jokes	9	.5
Riddles and puzzles	37	1.9
Total	1,959	100.0

TABLE 11.5 Grade-Level Differences in the Educational Content of Selections

Grade Level	Subject-Matter Content					Functional Content						Ethos Content							
	None	Language Skills	Science	Social Science & Philosophy	Other	None	Reasoning	Contemplation	Initiative	Cunning	Other	None	Humility	Patience	Courage	Kindness	Honesty	Hope	Other
2	52.1	18.4	10.9	13.7	4.9	85.7	2.8	1.1	3.5	2.7	4.2	92.7	.6	.6	1.1	3.8	.8	.4	0
4	38.1	21.2	12.5	21.5	6.7	59.8	5.9	4.6	6.1	3.6	20.0	86.9	1.6	1.1	4.6	3.6	.5	.3	1.3
5	34.7	21.7	12.6	25.9	5.1	65.1	3.6	7.0	6.7	5.0	12.6	83.2	.9	1.1	6.4	6.5	1.1	.2	.6

Grade level. Striking differences exist among grade levels in the use of literary form and in the presence of educational content. The number of selections without subject-matter content decreases for higher grade levels with a decrease of 17.4 percent from second grade (52.1 percent) to fifth grade (34.7 percent). This change seems to be related to an increase in selections containing social science/philosophy content (from 14 percent to 26 percent). The same pattern of decrease holds for both functional and ethos content, although for ethos content the decrease is not as great and although the decrease from second to fifth grade for functional content is similar, fourth grade has the smallest percentage (see Table 11.5).

At all grade levels, the literary form most frequently used was "factual article," ranging from 33.8 percent of the selections at grade 2 to 41.8 percent of the selections at grade 5. The second most frequently used literary form at the second-grade level was realistic fiction, and at the fourth- and fifth-grade levels poetry. Other grade-level changes were a drop in fantasy, and a corresponding increase in historical fiction.

Content defined at the cell level. The above discussion examines the marginals of the content taxonomy (i.e., the frequencies associated with the levels of each of the three components separately). The taxonomy is comprised of three dimensions which, taken together, define content as a cell in the matrix. Its specification, however, defines over 800 different cells or content areas even when ignoring various subclassifications.

To simplify the multidimensional complexity of our definition of content while capturing major content distinctions, we dichotomized each of the three dimensions into the presence or absence of content; this produced eight cells. The results are presented in Table 11.6.

The cell defined as the absence of educational content on all three dimensions is of particular importance to the teaching of reading comprehension using basal texts. The 405 selections coded in this cell represent about 21 percent of all selections in the 34 basals. This suggests the presence of a sizable number of selections whose use in teaching reading comprehension might be questioned from a curricular point of view.

The largest single cell — representing 44 percent of the selections — is defined by the presence of subject-matter content but without functional or ethos content. The presence of functional content only appeared in 15 percent (290) of the selections, and ethos content alone appeared in 4 percent (86) of the selections. Summing these single-content selections with the 405 that do not contain content on any of the three dimensions reveals that 86 percent (1,649) of the selections do not have content on more than one dimension. Only 12 percent have content on two dimensions, and 4 percent have content on all three dimensions.

Another way to examine the results of Table 11.6 is by the use of conditional statements. Of those selections coded as having subject-matter content, 20.8 percent also have functional content, and 7.1 percent have both functional content and ethos content. However, of those having subject-matter content, 76.5 percent have neither functional nor ethos content. Looking at only those selections with no subject-matter content, 49.2 percent also did not have functional or ethos content, 35.2 percent have functional content only, 10.4 percent have ethos content only, and 5.2 percent have both functional and ethos content.

TABLE 11.6   Frequency of Content Categories Defined by the Three Dimensions

Subject Matter	Ethos			
	Presence of content		Absence of content	
Presence of content				
Function:				
Presence of content	81	(4%)	156	(8%)
Absence of content	30	(2%)	868	(44%)
Absence of content				
Function:				
Presence of content	43	(2%)	290	(15%)
Absence of content	86	(4%)	405	(21%)
Total			1,959	(100%)

Basals

While the above analyses provide a profile of the total pool of selections available to elementary students through the 34 basals, further analysis permits the construction of a content profile for each of the basals separately. If the content profiles vary by basal, this has important implications for instruction in reading comprehension since a random sample of selections from the total pool would not be available to students in a classroom; teachers, at most, use several basals and frequently only one.

Subject-matter dimension.   The analysis points out salient differences among the 34 basals in terms of the presence of educational content. In one basal, for example (*Tell Me How the Sun Rose*), over 70 percent of the selections had no subject-matter content, while in another (*Building Bridges*), all the selections had subject-matter content; both were fourth-grade basals. For most basals, however, between 30 percent and 65 percent of the selections did not have subject-matter content.

Language skills represented the content for 70 percent of the selections in one basal while another had no such selections. Between 0 and 20 percent of the selections in basals had science content while between 0 and 50 percent had social studies content. These figures serve to illustrate that the content profiles of basals are not the same, at least with regard to subject-matter content.

Functional and ethos dimensions.   The picture is not that different for functional and ethos content. Between 0 and 26 percent of the selections in basals contained ethos content while the range for functional content was 63 percent (varying between 0 and 63 percent). Correspondingly large differences existed among basals on the percentage of selections having a particular kind of functional or ethos content.

Grade level.   A grade-level analysis of the differences in percentages of selections in basals with no subject-matter content indicated a range of 35.6 percent (highest = 64.6 percent) at the second-grade level, of 71.2 percent (highest = 71.2 percent) at the fourth-grade level, and of 63.5 percent (highest = 64.6 percent) at the fifth-grade level.

The ranges in percentages of selections with no functional content was 40.2 percent (highest = 97.9 percent) at the second-grade level, 63.3 percent (highest = 100.0 percent) at the fourth-grade level, and 57.9 percent (highest = 93.3 percent) at the fifth-grade level. On the ethos dimension, the ranges were 10.2 percent (highest = 100.0 percent) at the second-grade level, 25.7 percent (highest = 100.0 percent) at the fourth-grade level, and 35.4 percent (highest = 100.0 percent) at the fifth-grade level.

A comparison of selected basals.   A detailed analysis and profiling of the educational content of each of the 34 basals is beyond the scope of this paper; for a catalogue describing the content found in the 34 basals, see Caul and Byers (1982). To illustrate the basal-level analysis, we provide a brief content profile of several basals. Profiles of the two fourth-grade basals, *Building Bridges*, published by Harcourt Brace Jovanovich, and *Dreams and Dragons*, published by Harper & Row, present striking differences. Almost 99 percent of the selections in *Building Bridges* are coded as factual articles, contrasting sharply with 35 percent in *Dreams and Dragons*. On the other hand, roughly 34 percent of the selections in *Dreams and Dragons* are without content, while all the selections in *Building Bridges* were judged to have some content. This was primarily language skills content (64 percent).

The functional and ethos dimensions also reflect content differences between these two readers. Over 50 percent of the selections in *Dreams and Dragons* were coded as having some functional content, while *no* functional content was coded for selections in the other reader. A much smaller difference in the readers is evident on the extent to which their selections reflect ethos content. Neither reader shows a substantial level of ethos content in its selections, but *Building Bridges* has *no* ethos content in any of its selections.

Using content profiles, teachers can make informed basal choices. If, for example, a heavy emphasis on language skills is desired, the basal choice seems to be *Building Bridges*. If a basal is desired that can increase science or social studies knowledge, *Dreams and Dragons* would be a better selection.

Basals can also be compared on literary form. For example, the three basals with the highest percentage of selections coded as realistic fiction are *The Dog Next Door* (47.8 percent) and *One to Grow on* (37.3 percent), second-grade basals by Ginn; and *Tricky Troll* (38.5 percent), a second-grade basal by Laidlaw. The three basals containing the lowest percentage of realistic fiction selections are *Building Bridges* (0.0 percent), a fourth-grade basal, and *Reaching Out* (2.2 percent), a fifth-grade basal by Harcourt Brace Jovanovich; and *A Flint Holds Fire* (6.3 percent), a second-grade basal by Open Court. In contrast, over 90 percent of the selections in both *Building Bridges* and *Reaching Out* are coded as factual articles.

If we continue to look at these two basals on the subject-matter dimension, we find that 70 percent of the selections in *Reaching Out* and 63.8 percent of the selection in *Building Bridges* contain language skills content. This content focus is quite different from the content emphasis of *From Sea to Sea*, a second-grade basal by Open Court, in which 46.7 percent of the selections have social studies content; or *Patterns*, a fifth-grade basal by Laidlaw, in which 20.5 percent of the selections have science content.

A basal-level analysis also reveals marked differences in the amount of content along the functional dimension. *Building Bridges* does not have any selections with content on the functional dimension. The two basals having the highest percentage of selections with content on the functional dimension are *Measure Me, Sky*, a fifth-grade basal by Ginn (64.6 percent); and *Burning Bright*, a fourth-grade basal by Open Court (63.3 percent). Within this dimension, 18.8 percent of the selections in *Measure Me, Sky* model contemplation, and 10.4 percent model initiative/persistence. Of the selections in *Burning Bright*, 15.6 percent model creativity and 13.3 percent model moral reasoning. Thus, again, basals are greatly different even on the "knowing how" dimension.

Slightly less than half the basals (16 out of 34) were coded as having no content or almost no content (less than 10 percent of the selections) on the ethos dimension. That is, they did not contain information on how to live right and do right by others. The basal containing the highest percentage of selections with ethos content is Ginn's fifth-grade basal, *Measure Me, Sky*. In this basal, 12.5 percent of the selections model courage and 10.4 percent model kindness/generosity.

Basal Series

The final section examines differences in educational content among basal series. Many districts adopt a single series for their reading program. In such districts, basals are used to teach reading and reading comprehension across all elementary grades, having an impact on all students in the district. Over time, the use of a basal series also has a cumulative effect on educational content exposure for individuals as they progress through the grades. Hence, differences in the content profiles of basal series have important implications for reading comprehension instruction.

Subject-matter dimension. There are remarkable differences among publishers in the number of selections having content on the subject-matter dimension: 72.2 percent of the selections in the Harcourt Brace Jovanovich series[2] have subject-matter content, compared to 39.7 percent of the selections in the Ginn series (see Table 11.7).

The type of subject-matter content included in the series also shifts dramatically from publisher to publisher. Looking at each subject matter, the publishing companies with the largest percentage of selections in each area are:

> Language skills content—Harcourt Brace Jovanovich (41.2 %)
> Arts and crafts, physical education, and music—Harper & Row (4.8%)
> Mathematics—Laidlaw (1.5%)
> Science—Laidlaw (15.6%)
> Social science and philosophy—Laidlaw (28.9%)

Notice, however, that the Laidlaw series has substantially fewer selections. As a result, other series will have more selections on mathematics (Ginn), science (Harcourt Brace Jovanovich) and social science (Open Court), even though Laidlaw has the largest percentage of selections on each subject matter.

TABLE 11.7 Subject-Matter Content of Basal Series

Subject-Matter Content	Houghton Mifflin	Scott-Foresman	Ginn	Harcourt Brace Jovanovich	Harper & Row	Holt, Rinehart	Laidlaw	Open Court
None	97 (43.9)[1][a]	98 (33.4)	140 (60.3)	85 (27.3)	78 (36.4)	105 (43.4)	68 (50.4)	153 (49.2)
Language skills	34 (15.3)	112 (38.2)	20 (8.6)	128 (41.2)	48 (22.5)	25 (10.4)	1 (.7)	30 (9.6)
Fine arts and crafts	6 (2.7)	8 (2.7)	3 (1.3)	14 (4.5)	11 (5.1)	12 (5.0)	2 (1.5)	7 (2.3)
Physical education	4 (1.8)	3 (1.0)	1 (.4)	7 (2.3)	7 (3.3)	2 (.8)	2 (1.5)	4 (1.3)
Mathematics	1 (.5)	0 (0)	3 (1.3)	0 (0)	1 (.5)	1 (.4)	2 (1.5)	0 (0)
Music	1 (.5)	1 (.3)	0 (0)	2 (.6)	0 (0)	2 (.8)	0 (0)	2 (.6)
Science	23 (10.4)	35 (11.9)	25 (10.8)	39 (12.5)	25 (11.7)	31 (12.8)	21 (15.6)	35 (11.3)
Social science[b] and philosophy	55 (24.9)	36 (12.3)	40 (17.2)	36 (11.6)	44 (20.6)	64 (26.4)	39 (28.9)	80 (25.7)

[a] The figures included in parentheses are the percentages of the total selections in a basal series.
[b] See Table 11.1 for the content areas inlcuded in social science.

TABLE 11.8 Functional Content of Basal Series

Functional Content	Houghton Mifflin	Scott-Foresman	Ginn	Harcourt Brace Jovanovich	Harper & Row	Holt, Rinehart	Laidlaw	Open Court
None	153 (69.2)	239 (81.6)	146 (62.9)	268 (86.2)	147 (68.7)	151 (62.4)	80 (59.3)	205 (65.9)
Reasoning/problem solving and cunning/mother wit	13 (5.9)	18 (6.1)	19 (8.2)	11 (3.5)	29 (13.6)	15 (6.2)	26 (19.3)	21 (6.8)
Moral reasoning	8 (3.6)	4 (1.4)	6 (2.6)	0 (0)	10 (4.7)	12 (5.0)	1 (.7)	18 (5.8)
Contemplation	9 (4.1)	4 (1.4)	19 (8.2)	12 (3.9)	9 (4.2)	10 (4.1)	7 (5.2)	11 (3.5)
Creativity	1 (.5)	2 (.7)	11 (4.7)	1 (.3)	2 (.9)	19 (7.9)	3 (2.2)	16 (5.1)
Feeling/catharsis	2 (.9)	2 (.7)	3 (1.3)	3 (1.0)	2 (.9)	3 (1.2)	0 (0)	6 (1.9)
Initiative/persistence	20 (9.0)	15 (5.1)	17 (7.3)	3 (1.0)	8 (3.7)	15 (6.2)	12 (8.9)	15 (4.8)
Absurdity/paradox and humor in use of lang.	15 (6.8)	9 (3.1)	11 (4.7)	13 (4.2)	7 (3.3)	17 (7.0)	6 (4.4)	19 (6.1)

Functional dimension.   Across publishers, Laidlaw had the highest percentage of its selections coded for functional content (40.7 percent), in contrast to Harcourt Brace Jovanovich, which had the lowest percentage (13.8 percent). The results in Table 11.8 also show in what way basal series vary on the type of functional content included in the selections. Houghton Mifflin, for example, emphasizes initiative/persistence; Harper & Row and Laidlaw emphasize reasoning/problem solving and cunning/mother wit, while Holt, Rinehart and Winston emphasizes creativity.

Ethos dimension.   The series also varied somewhat in their use of the ethos dimension with no series having more than about 20 percent ethos content but one series with only 3.5 percent of selections with any ethos content (see Table 11.9).

The two literary forms most often used across publishing companies are factual articles and realistic fiction with Ginn and Laidlaw having the highest percentage in the realistic fiction category. In all other series, factual articles dominate as a literary form.

The percentage of selections coded as having no educational content *on all three dimensions* varied from 16.1 percent of the selections in the Harcourt Brace Jovanovich series to 26.7 percent of the selections in the Houghton Mifflin series.

SUMMARY

This content analysis of elementary basals shows that the choice of a basal is not only a decision with implications for reading comprehension but for other areas of the curriculum as well. Many articles, poems, and stories in these texts expose students to content dealing with (1) subjects such as art and science, (2) enduring social themes, (3) applied knowledge of processes of human functioning, and (4) living and acting rightly. But many basal selections contain no opportunities to learn any or all of these dimensions from text.

In fact, across texts, only 4 percent of all selections have content on the three dimensions of subject matter, function, and ethos. Of those selections that present educational opportunities for subject-matter learning, three quarters have nothing else to offer to the young reader. That is, they present facts and information but no applied knowledge about processes of human functioning or modeling of time-tested virtues.

If we compare basal readers, we find that some model processes of human functioning in more than half their selections, while others contain no educational content of this kind. There are readers relatively high on subject-matter content, but the particular subject focus varies greatly (e.g., language skills vs. science). Slightly less than half the texts (16 out of 34) for elementary school children contain essentially no ethos content (less than 10 percent of the selections). But there is a basal in which one out of three selections concerns questions of living and acting rightly.

In text, content and form have some inherent relations. Given the differences in educational content, it is not surprising that some basals, at the same grade level, stress poetic selections or realistic fiction as a form. But the range of variation is surprising. Some readers have half their selections coded as poetry, others

TABLE 11.9 Ethos Content of Basal Series

Ethos Content	Houghton Mifflin	Scott-Foresman	Ginn	Harcourt Brace Jovanovich	Harper & Row	Holt, Rinehart	Laidlaw	Open Court
None	187 (84.6)	274 (93.5)	190 (81.9)	300 (96.5)	189 (88.3)	207 (85.5)	110 (81.5)	262 (84.2)
Humility	2 (.9)	1 (.3)	6 (2.6)	0 (0)	2 (.9)	5 (2.1)	0 (0)	4 (1.3)
Patience/forbearance	5 (2.3)	2 (.7)	2 (.9)	0 (0)	0 (0)	1 (.4)	1 (.7)	7 (2.3)
Courage	13 (5.9)	6 (2.0)	11 (4.7)	4 (1.3)	17 (7.9)	7 (2.9)	7 (5.2)	12 (3.9)
Kindness/generosity	12 (5.4)	8 (2.7)	13 (5.6)	3 (1.0)	4 (1.9)	18 (7.4)	13 (9.6)	20 (6.4)
Honesty	2 (.9)	0 (0)	3 (1.3)	2 (.6)	1 (.5)	1 (.4)	3 (2.2)	4 (1.3)
Hope	0 (0)	0 (0)	3 (1.3)	0 (0)	0 (0)	1 (.4)	0 (0)	2 (.6)
Other	0 (0)	2 (.7)	4 (1.7)	2 (.6)	1 (.5)	2 (.8)	1 (.7)	0 (0)

none at all. The same is true for realistic fiction, half or none makes a whole lot of difference from an educational point of view.

When we consider publishers, we find that they focus on different subjects in their series. Some stress language skills in about 40 percent of their selections; others have skill content of this kind in under 10 percent of their selections contained in a basal. Interestingly, the amount of science content in basal texts is fairly stable across series from different publishers (10.4 to 15.6 percent). But social science/philosophy content ranges from roughly 10 to 30 percent in different basal series.

We have to face the fact that basals are different. They imply commitments to different forms of knowing, and they favor one subject in the elementary school curriculum over another. Basal texts give or do not give children some understanding of right living; they address the mind *or* the emotions in detailing modes of human functioning.

Asking the question of reading comprehension in the context of basal series centrally means, What are children taught to comprehend? What are content characteristics of texts in our classrooms from the point of view of educational knowledge, knowledge that is valued and regarded as worth passing on? We must ask, furthermore, whether the content that can be inferred from basal readers makes sense. What is the picture of young readers—their capacities and quest for knowing—and our curricular goals that emerge from the study of typical texts in elementary schools? This content analysis is a solid basis for answering such educational questions.

For reasons as disparate as motivation for reading and learning, limits on time and resources, and educational goals associated with comprehending different forms of knowledge, we cannot afford to leave the tacit curriculum of American basals unexamined. Basals matter; we have to look seriously at the educational opportunities they do or do not offer and the implications they have for teaching children to comprehend.

NOTES

1. The ten-digit subject-matter code, for example, can distinguish between a selection with science content and a selection with social studies content. In addition, it can subdivide science into general science, biology, physics/chemistry, and technology. The biological sciences can be further characterized as human, animal, plant, ecology, and so on. This detailed coding of the subject-matter content of each selection can provide a manageable cataloging system for teachers to aid them in the choice of selections.

2. Each publisher typically has more than one basal series. We analyzed only the one referred to by the dates given previously. For convenience in this section we refer to the basal series by publishers' names only.

REFERENCES

Austin, M., & Morrison, C. *The first r*. New York: Macmillian, 1963.

Bettelheim, B., & Zelan, K. *On learning to read*. New York: Alfred A. Knopf, 1982.

Duffy, G. Commentary: Response to Borko., Shivelson, and Stern: There's more to instructional decision-making in reading than the "empty classroom." *Reading Research Quarterly*, 1982, *17*, 295–300.

Durkin, D. What classroom observation reveals about reading comprehension instruction. *Reading Research Quarterly*, 1978–79, *14*, 481–533.

Goodlad, J. *Behind the classroom door*. Worthington, Ohio: Charles Jones, 1970.

Goodlad, J. I. *Facing the future: Issues in education and schooling*. New York: McGraw-Hill, 1976.

Osborn, J., & Shirley, L. *Do teachers really use manuals?* Paper presented at a preconvention conference in reading comprehension. Urbana, Ill.: Center for the Study of Reading, University of Illinois at Urbana, May 1980.

Roehler, L., Schmidt, W., & Buchmann, M. *How do teachers spend their language arts time?* Research Series No. 66. East Lansing: Institute for Research on Teaching; Michigan State University, December 1979.

12

Workbooks That Accompany Basal Reading Programs

Jean Osborn

Basal reading programs, which so predominate in reading periods in elementary school classrooms, have three major components: (1) A teacher's guide provides procedures for the teacher to use to teach reading; (2) a reader contains the narratives, expository passages, and poetry the students read; and (3) the workbooks, skill books, and ditto masters contain tasks the students work on independently. This is not to say there is nothing else available for users of basal programs; most basal programs have supplementary materials including flip charts, games, word cards, film strips, and audio cassettes. Nevertheless, the primary instructional units of a basal reading program are the teacher's guide, the reader, and workbook materials.

The focus of this paper is on the workbook materials. In an earlier paper (Osborn 1982), 20 guidelines were presented for consideration by publishers designing workbooks and teachers evaluating workbooks. These guidelines suggest that the vocabulary and concept of workbooks tasks should relate to the rest of the lesson; the art appearing in workbook tasks should be clear; and the layout of pages, instructions to students, and instructional design of the tasks should be unambiguous. (A copy of the guidelines appears at the end of this paper.)

In this paper the application of some of these guidelines is illustrated by examining workbook tasks from lessons of a widely used basal reading series. To assess how (and if) workbook tasks change from one edition to the next, one set of workbook tasks from the 1976 edition and one set of workbook tasks from the 1982 edition of the same series are contrasted. Tasks from each edition are from approximately the same lesson in the level of a program designed for use in the second half of the second grade. The stories in the new edition have been changed. Lessons in both editions are organized similarly: The teacher introduces some of the vocabulary the students will read in the story and does some comprehension preparation for the story; the students read the story; the teacher asks questions both during and after the students read the story. After the story has been read, the teacher is given instructions for the teaching of further vocabulary, decoding, study, and comprehension activities. All these after-story activities have related workbook tasks. The workbook pages to be used with the lesson are indicated in the teacher's guide. Two workbooks accompany each edition of this series.

In the older edition there are four workbook tasks in one workbook (workbook A) and five workbook tasks in the other (workbook B). (See Figure 12.1–12.9). Each task presents one or more of the problems for which the guidelines were written.

The first guideline suggests that "a sufficient proportion of workbook tasks should be relevant to the instruction that is going on in the rest of the unit or lesson." Although each of the tasks in the figures relates in some way to the rest of the lesson, the question has to be asked about sufficiency. For example, does all the important new vocabulary in the story appear again for the students to apply in a workbook context? Of the 46 words that appear for the first time in the story for this lesson, less than half are target words in the two tasks (task 1 in workbook A, and task 1 in workbook B) that concentrate on vocabulary. If sufficiency were a greater concern of workbook designers, some of the other tasks, for example the decoding tasks, could be written to incorporate some of this lesson's new vocabulary. Such a concept of workbook design would also prompt the use of vocabulary from previous stories in a variety of workbook tasks. Such a practice would make both sufficiency *and* relevance much more evident in workbooks that accompany basal readers.

The guideline concerning sufficiency and relevance can also be applied to the two sequencing tasks in this lesson. Sequencing is a comprehension skill the teacher is instructed to teach as a part of the lesson. In the teacher's guide the teacher is told to review sequencing of story events and then have the students do a workbook task (task 2 in workbook A). Students are to number (so as to put into correct order) the randomly arranged sentences that describe events in the story they have just read. The students can refer to their readers for help if they need it.

Workbook tasks that so directly relate to what the students have just read are not found in all basal series; this series is to be applauded for designing this kind of task. But the question of sufficiency should still be asked. There is an additional sequencing task in workbook B. In task 2 in workbook B, students must sequence two sets of related events, one from 1 to 5 and then the other from 6 to 10. Recall that the task in workbook A used events from the story the students read. The task in workbook B requires the application of sequencing to groups of sentences unrelated to anything the students have read. Students who have trouble with the story-related task probably need more tasks of the same type, based on other stories they have read. But there are no more sequencing tasks in either workbook during this lesson, nor for the rest of this level of the program. Thus, although these are *relevant* tasks for this lesson, there is probably not a *sufficient* number of tasks across lessons to give students who need to practice sequencing events an adequate opportunity to do so.

One complaint about workbook tasks is that they are either too easy or too hard—too easy for the student who can already do the task and makes no errors, and too hard for the student who has trouble with the task and makes a lot of errors. A guideline that reflects a part of this complaint is guideline 9: "Workbook tasks should contain enough content so that there is a chance a student doing the task will *learn* something and not simply be *exposed* to something." The sequencing tasks can be used as a basis for discussing this guideline. Students who have a good sense of sequence in a story and of the words that signal sequence will probably find this task easy and maybe even boring. Students who do not

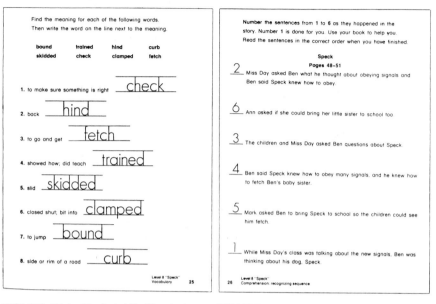

Find the meaning for each of the following words.
Then write the word on the line next to the meaning.

| bound | trained | hind | curb |
| skidded | check | clamped | fetch |

1. to make sure something is right   **check**

2. back   **hind**

3. to go and get   **fetch**

4. showed how; did teach   **trained**

5. slid   **skidded**

6. closed shut; bit into   **clamped**

7. to jump   **bound**

8. side or rim of a road   **curb**

Level 8 "Speck"
Vocabulary   25

FIGURE 12.1   Task 1, Workbook A, 1976 Edition.

Number the sentences from 1 to 6 as they happened in the story. Number 1 is done for you. Use your book to help you.
Read the sentences in the correct order when you have finished.

Speck
Pages 48-51

__2__ Miss Day asked Ben what he thought about obeying signals and Ben said Speck knew how to obey.

__6__ Ann asked if she could bring her little sister to school too.

__3__ The children and Miss Day asked Ben questions about Speck.

__4__ Ben said Speck knew how to obey many signals, and he knew how to fetch Ben's baby sister.

__5__ Mark asked Ben to bring Speck to school so the children could see him fetch.

__1__ While Miss Day's class was talking about the new signals, Ben was thinking about his dog, Speck.

Level 8 "Speck"
26   Comprehension: recognizing sequence

FIGURE 12.2   Task 2, Workbook A, 1976 Edition.

Write the letters **sp** in each blank to make a word.
Read the words. Then write the word that completes each sentence.

sp ace   **sp** eak   **sp** ell

sp ot   **sp** ort   **sp** oon

1. Would you **speak** a little more softly?

2. The boy dropped his **spoon**

3. The rocket could not be seen far off in **space**.

4. The ink I dropped left a **spot** on my dress.

5. Can you **spell** all these words?

6. The **sport** I like best is baseball.

Level 8 "Speck"
Decoding: /sp/sp (spell)   27

FIGURE 12.3   Task 3, Workbook A, 1976 Edition.

Draw a line under the word that completes each sentence.
Then find the underlined word in the puzzle and circle it there. The first one is done for you.

1. The king's boat was lifting   __drifting__ down the river.

2. He saw an old man on a __raft__   gift who needed help.

3. The man had cut his __shift__   left leg.

4. The king pulled the raft to land and drifted   __lifted__ off the man.

5. He put the man on the sift   __soft__ grass.

6. The old man wanted the king to have a fine __gift__   draft for helping him.

```
e s d r i f t i n g p a
l o p p t u r a f t s o
a n l e f t c l i n d a
s o f t i s u s a n e
f t i n l i f t e d p h
g e r u t h r m g i f t
```

Level 8 "Speck"
28   Decoding: r h ft (gift)

FIGURE 12.4   Task 4, Workbook A, 1976 Edition.

MATCH THE PICTURE AND THE WORD

Read the words. Draw a line from each picture to the word that tells about it

question   Spaniel   crosswalk   signals

Choose from the list below the word that means about the same as the part
that is underlined in each sentence. Write the letter for the word on the line.

a. obeys	d. fetch	g. master
b. screaming	e. clamped	h. interrupted
c. special	f. highway	i. train

1. When I tell my dog what to do, he <u>does it</u>. He _____.

2. The girl was <u>yelling loudly</u>. She was _____ .

3. Jim <u>started to talk</u> while his mother and teacher were still talking.

   He _____ them.

4. She was trying to <u>teach</u> her dog. She was trying to _____ her dog.

5. The dog <u>fastened</u> his teeth into my coat.

   He _____ his teeth into it.

6. I told my dog to <u>bring</u> the paper. I told my dog to _____ the paper.

Vocabulary: Word meaning   17

FIGURE 12.5   Task 1, Workbook B, 1976 Edition.

have this skill will have an enormous amount of trouble (probably with the first
task and certainly with the second) and will most likely make a lot of errors.
Unfortunately for these students, these are the only sequencing tasks to appear in
this level of the program. For students who have a lot to learn about sequencing
events, these two tasks provide *exposure* but not the amount of practice that will
result in *learning*.

Guideline 2 states that "another portion of workbook tasks should provide
for a systematic and cumulative review of what has already been taught." In this
lesson the teacher is to conduct two decoding activities: The sound-symbol correspondence /sp/*sp* is introduced and the /ft/*ft* correspondence is reviewed. The students practice using the same correspondences in three workbook tasks, but they
do not see these correspondences in any workbook tasks for the rest of this level
of the program. Although workbooks seem the ideal place for a systematic review
of skills and concepts that are important to "keep alive," the workbooks of this
series (and of the other series examined) are notable for their *lack* of review tasks.

Guideline 15 is about instructional design. It states: "The instructional design

What's the Right Order?

These sentences make a story when they are in the right order. Number them in the correct order. The first set is to be numbered from **1** to **5** and the second set from **6** to **10**.

____ She ate breakfast and dashed out.

_1_ Jean was up and dressed by 8 o'clock.

____ As she hurried down the street, she thought about the big boat race.

____ They were all painted bright and cheery colors.

____ All the children were racing the boats they had made.

____ When the signal was given, they all pushed their boats.

____ Everyone was jumping around and screaming.

____ As she had hoped, Jean's boat came in first.

_6_ Just before the race started, everyone checked their boats.

____ Jean was so happy as she pulled her boat from the water.

18   Comprehension: Inferring sequence of events

FIGURE 12.6   Task 2, Workbook B, 1976 Edition.

of individual tasks and of task sequences should be carefully planned." Task sequences are not discussed in this paper (other than to say that there is not a flow of tasks that develop from simple to complex in any of the basal workbooks examined), but the design of individual tasks is discussed. Although there has been no research that has produced agreed-upon rules of "ideal" task design, it seems reasonable to say that tasks should be designed so that they are do-able, so that they provide practice on an important or particularly difficult aspect of reading, and so that the purpose of the task is evident to students doing the task. A task should also be designed so that its intent is achieved when the students do the task.

Task 3 in workbook A has as its intent that students will practice the /sp/sp correspondence. The task design probably achieves that goal. Students write *sp* in front of word parts to make words and then write those words in the blanks in sentences. The students see how /sp/sp works to make words and then how those words are used in sentences. Task 4 in workbook A intends to review the /ft/ft correspondence. The students underline one of two words to make a sentence and

Words That Begin Alike

The word that will finish each sentence begins with the letters **sp** and ends like the word at the right of the sentence. Write the word on the line.

1. Buy a _____ of thread.   **cool**

2. The rocket will reach outer _____   **face**

3. Mike liked to _____ to his teacher.   **beak**

4. Father's car has a new _____ tire.   **care**

Choose the right word for each sentence. Draw a box around it.

1. Mother did not want to ...... Bobby.   **spun**   **spank**

2. Ben ...... all his money for candy.   **spoke**   **spent**

3. Can you ...... the new words in the story?   **spell**   **spike**

4. The fairy ...... gold thread.   **spun**   **spool**

5. Amy's ...... was very good.   **spool**   **speech**

6. Juan has a ...... hat he likes to wear.   **special**   **spell**

7. The clean floor didn't have a ...... of dirt. **speck**   **spun**

8. June ...... to everyone as she came in.   **spark**   **spoke**

9. The parking ...... is too small for the truck. **space**   **spill**

Decoding: /sp/**sp** as in **spell**   **19**

FIGURE 12.7   Task 3, Workbook B, 1976 Edition.

then circle the same words in a puzzle. Although all of the "choice" words have the *ft* combination in them, it is likely that students doing the task operate from context alone and pay little, or more likely *no*, attention to the *ft* combination in the words they select. The task is not a bad task; the point is that it probably does not achieve its stated intent—that of providing directed practice for the /ft/*ft* correspondence.

Task 1 in workbook B is a basis for a discussion of two other guidelines. Guideline 17 reads: "The art that appears on workbook pages must be consistent with the prose of the task." Pictures are to be matched with words in this task. The large and colorful question mark to be matched with the word *question* is unlikely to cause much trouble for most students. But it is likely that the words *crosswalk* and *signals* are going to be connected to the wrong picture by a lot of students. Crosswalks and signals are so intertwined in most students' experience that it would seem better to have a picture with both a crosswalk *and* a signal and to have students draw lines to the appropriate spots in the one picture. The vocabulary of this task is that used in the lesson story. The fourth picture is of a dog.

Using the Contents Page

Read the Contents page below. Then answer each question.

Unit 2 **VERY SPECIAL FRIENDS**

Speck	**48**
Roady Roadrunner and Yoshi	**57**
Aquí Está Mi Nieta	**63**
The Mystery of the Suitcase	**70**
Fun for Maria CYNTHIA STONE RICHMOND	**78**
• Take the Right Road	**84**
• Think of a New Ending	**85**

1. Who wrote "Fun for Maria"?

2. On what page does "Aquí Está Mi Nieta" begin?

3. On what page could you find a story about a suitcase?

4. Which story begins on page 57?

5. What is the name of Unit 2?

6. On what page can you read about a dog named Speck?

7. On what page can you read about Maria?

20   Study Skills: Locating information on the Contents page

FIGURE 12.8   Task 4, Workbook B, 1976 Edition.

This picture is to be matched to the word *Spaniel*. The problem would be for a student who did not catch the one reference to the kind of dog in the story. Finally, there is also a dog (a spaniel?) in the crosswalk picture; surely this is a source of confusion for some students.

A more serious problem occurs in the second half of this task. Guideline 14 states that student responses should be the closest possible to reading and writing. The task requires students to copy letters designating words in blanks. A much stronger task would have the student write words in blanks. Correct answers could then be confirmed by reading, for example: "He *clamped* his teeth in it" instead of "He ___*e.*___ his teeth into it."

Guideline 7 reads: "Instructions to students should be clear, unambiguous, and easy to follow: brevity is a virtue." Some of the instructions in this lesson adhere to that guideline, but some have problems. For example, the instruction in task 1 of workbook A: "Find the meaning for each of the following words. Then write the word on the line next to the meaning." This seems clear and concise, given the context of the task. In contrast, two of the instructions in workbook B

DO YOU KNOW THESE PLACES?

Look at the picture. Read the question and check the answers.

Which ones can be true of the high desert?

____ very little water or rain
____ roads running through it
____ plants that have thorns
____ sandy beaches
____ tall, leafy trees
____ many lakes and ponds
____ rattlesnakes that hide under
        rocks and bushes

Which things could be true about the seashore?

____ piles of seaweed
____ rocks and small stones
____ tall trees
____ swimsuits and beach balls
____ things drifting in from the sea
____ the dry earth

Which of these could be true of the very high mountains?

____ very few green plants
____ gardens with flowers
____ rocky paths
____ a little stream rushing down
____ snow on high peaks
____ bears eating nuts
____ beach balls and large umbrellas
____ steep slopes

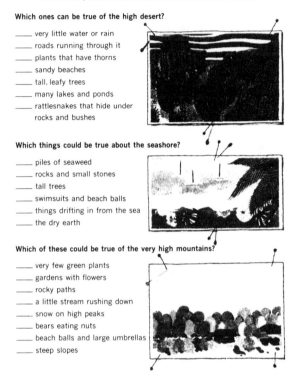

FIGURE 12.9   Task 5, Workbook B, 1976 Edition.

are probably confusing and unclear, at least for some students. These two sets of instructions seem unclear as directions for the tasks they are attached to; they also seem capable of causing confusion as students move from one task to another. Whereas the instruction for task 1 in workbook B has the students writing letters that stand for words in blanks in sentences, the instruction for task 3 in workbook B asks students to *begin* a word with some letters, end the word "like the word at the right of a sentence," and write the new word on a line in the sentence. This complex set of instructions also requires the children to drop the first letter of each of the words to the right before copying the word in the blank. In the second part of this task, students are to choose the correct word for each sentence and then draw a box around the correct word. Three such different instructions in the same lesson about similar tasks probably leads to confusion for many children and especially for those whom practice with words is especially important.

In addition, the second part of task 3 in workbook B violates guideline 14: "Student response model should be the closest possible to reading and writing." Even after the students complete an item in the task, a sentence still reads, for example: "Mother did not want to _____ Bobby." The word *spank*, if correctly identified, is boxed and off to the right and is not a part of the meaning of the sentence. If the word *spun* is boxed, a student does not have the opportunity to see if it makes sense in the sentence.

Task 4 in workbook B is about using a contents page. If the "closest possible to reading and writing" guideline were observed, the task would either begin or end by having the students answer some questions about the contents of the actual book they are using, rather than with only the excerpt from that book's content that appears on the workbook page. Such a change would be simple for the workbook designer to make.

Before we compare the tasks in this edition with the newer edition of this program, let's discuss one final task. Task 5 in workbook B is from the next lesson and is presented to illustrate guideline 5, "the vocabulary and concept level of workbook tasks should relate to that of the rest of the program and to the students using the program," and guideline 17, "the art that appears on workbook pages must be consistent with the prose of the task."

In task 5 the locations *high desert, seashore,* and *very high mountains* have not appeared in any of the stories the students have read in the reader. So only students who know these locations are going to have a chance at performing this task successfully. Even for these students the conflict between what a student knows about these locations and what that student sees in these very stylized pictures is surely going to lead to error. For example, the dry earth and tall trees are both supposed to be wrong answers to the "seashore" item. There is a leaf from what could be a rather tall tree in the picture and the sand looks like a patch of dry earth. Similarly, there are mountain resorts with gardens with flowers and lakes that have beach balls and large umbrellas. The vocabulary and the art conspire to make this task one that is likely to cause a lot of student errors. It would be hard to predict which students would make the most errors—those who *do not* read well or those who *do* read well.

What changes have been made in the most recent edition of this program? There are six tasks in workbook A and three tasks in workbook B in the 1982 edition. (see Figure 12.10, then Figure 12.18) None of the tasks are pickups from the previous edition; all are new tasks for new stories.

Tasks 1 and 2 of workbook A are labeled "vocabulary." Task 1 requires students to use all but two of the new words presented in the lesson; some of the new words are used several times in these two tasks. In these 1982 edition vocabulary tasks, the students mark the *words* that fit into a sentence. In other tasks in this workbook, the students circle the correct word or write the correct word in a blank to complete a sentence. The writing of a letter that stands for a word response has been completely dropped. Thus the guideline of designing tasks that are closest to reading is more nearly satisfied in the 1982 edition of this program.

The directions for task 2 in workbook A, a vocabulary task labeled "classification," direct students to cross out the one word that does not belong in each row. For the most part, the words that appear in the rows are words that have appeared in previous stories. Guideline 2 says that a portion of tasks should provide for a systematic review of what has already been taught. This task functions as a review task; however, rows 2, 5, and 9 contain words that have not been read in any of the previous stories. Given the conceptual difficulty of this task for some students, it is hazardous to include words that they may not be able to read (or know the meaning of).

The guideline about exposure (guideline 9) can also be applied to this clas-

```
 _____
(                                                 30  )
    Name _____
```

Read each sentence. Then fill in the circle next to
the word that goes into each sentence.

---

1. _____ ducks swam in the water.
   ○ Boots   ○ Baby   ○ Bugs

2. Nicky uses _____ to catch fish.
   ○ worms   ○ boots   ○ socks

3. The _____ is ten miles long.
   ○ tadpole   ○ river   ○ radio

4. Jenny and Dan saw a _____ at the zoo.
   ○ honk   ○ lion   ○ yawn

5. The _____ walked out of the water.
   ○ alligator   ○ birthday   ○ airplane

6. Mel _____ the cake into the house.
   ○ hugged   ○ surprised   ○ carried

7. We will eat lunch at _____.
   ○ bugs   ○ noon   ○ lion

8. Lin _____ the gifts under the bed.
   ○ hid   ○ woke   ○ asked

9. Ann found some _____ under the rock.
   ○ bugs   ○ squeaks   ○ parties

VOCABULARY: word identification in context

FIGURE 12.10   Task 1, Workbook A, 1982 Edition.

sification task. Students who make a lot of errors on this task will not get enough practice on this important logical skill. There is only one more classification task in the latest edition of workbook A (none in the 1982 workbook B), and that task appears 47 pages later. Students who make errors on this task and whose teacher tries to help them by repeating an instruction in the teacher's guide will probably be further confused because the instruction to the teacher says that this task will "provide practice in classifying words according to function." By no means are all of these groups examples of classification according to *function*. The group in row 1 are members of a larger class, *animals*. The group in row 2 are noises made by animals (and ambiguously, also by cars, stairs at night, and annoyed grandmothers). The group in row 5 are coverings of animals. Of the ten groups, only row 2 classifies words according to function. Guideline 11 reads, "workbook tasks must not present wrong information nor perpetuate misrules." If, when presenting this task, a teacher talks to the students about classifying words according to function (or what things do), a misrule will certainly be perpetuated.

Finding the main idea is probably the most frequently appearing comprehension skill in teacher's guides and workbooks of all basal reading programs. Task 3 in 1982's workbook A is a typical main idea task. Whether or not identifying one

```
 ┌─────────────────────────────────────────────────────┐
 (                                                31    )
  \  Name                                              /
```

Mark an X through the word that does not belong
in each row.

---

1. lion   bear   alligator   kitchen

2. honk   squeak   apple   cluck

3. bugs   worms   rhymes   tadpoles

4. bus   egg   bread   cheese

5. hair   fur   fuzz   apple

6. bike   tree   truck   car

7. Ben   Mel   toy   Tom

8. grass   kitten   puppy   chick

9. bat   pink   ball   mitt

10. Kate   Joan   Jeff   Ana

VOCABULARY: vocabulary development
(classification)

FIGURE 12.11   Task 2, Workbook A, 1982 Edition.

sentence as the main idea sentence out of a set of three sentences has any relevance to the real-life act of identifying, summarizing, and putting together the
main ideas in a story or expository passage is a discussion that is beyond the scope
of this paper. Nevertheless, in real life a reader is not often presented with three
sentences and asked to choose one sentence in order to determine a main idea.
Guideline 14 says that student response modes should be the closest possible to
reading and writing. A task that required students to write out main idea
sentences of connected paragraphs they have read would be a more realistic
assessment of a student's ability to determine the main ideas of paragraphs and
passages.

The three remaining tasks in the 1982 edition of workbook A are labeled as
decoding tasks. The supposition is that each provides practice with an aspect of
decoding that the teacher is directed to review with the students before assigning
the workbook pages. However, both the procedures described in the teacher's
guide and the workbook tasks rely solely on the context of the sentences and the
meanings of the words. So instead of being decoding tasks, these three tasks are
vocabulary-in-context tasks. If the designers of this workbook wanted tasks that
would give students the opportunity to practice consciously, for example, the de-

Name

Read the story. Then fill in the circle next to the sentence that best tells what the story is about.

Some animals move quickly. Some move slowly. A cow hardly ever runs. A fox is almost always running. Some birds fly quickly past you. Some seem to float in the air above you.

1. ○ A fox is almost always running.
   ○ Animals move at different speeds.
   ○ Birds fly quickly past you.

Plant roots grow well in soil that has worms. Worms dig through soil. They move the soil as they dig. Their paths in the soil make little tubes. Air can get through these tubes. Water can, too. Plants need air and water.

2. ○ Worms are bad for soil.
   ○ Worms move the soil as they dig.
   ○ Worms make soil better for plants.

Todd and Jane want to surprise their class. They get some paper and pens. Jane and Todd start to write. Then the surprise is ready. The surprise is a class newspaper! The newspaper is called "The Room 7 News."

3. ○ Todd and Jane make a class newspaper.
   ○ Todd and Jane start to write.
   ○ Todd and Jane get some paper and pens.

COMPREHENSION: main idea

FIGURE 12.12   Task 3, Workbook A, 1982 Edition.

coding skill that labels task 6 (dropped *e* before endings), they could try something like the following:

○ Cross out the final *e*, and add *est* to make a new word.
   Write the new word on the line. Read the sentence.
   1. strange
      Fred had the _____ pets.
   2. nice
      His cat is his_____ pet.
○ Cross out the final *e*, and add *ed* to make a new word.
   Write the new word on the line. Read the sentence.
   3. hike
      Yesterday we_____ in the mountains.
   4. save
      Sara _____ bottle caps.

This task provides the opportunity for students to cross out a final *e*, add an ending, and see how the new word fits in a sentence. Task 4 (*y* changed to *i* before

33

Name

Read each sentence. Then fill in the circle next to
the word that goes into each sentence.

1. You can eat soup with a _____.
   ○ spoon   ○ spies   ○ fries

2. I hope you will feel _____ tomorrow.
   ○ lumpier   ○ happier   ○ hurries

3. That room is the _____ it has ever been!
   ○ messiest   ○ furriest   ○ mightier

4. I have lived in two big _____
   ○ skies   ○ flies   ○ cities

5. Today my hair feels _____ than it did yesterday.
   ○ fluffier   ○ happier   ○ flies

6. The baby _____ at this time every day.
   ○ crows   ○ fries   ○ cries

7. Dan and I _____ the dishes.
   ○ dresses   ○ pried   ○ dried

8. I know a _____ story than that one.
   ○ furriest   ○ funnier   ○ sleepier

9. The baby deer had the _____ legs I ever saw.
   ○ scariest   ○ wobbliest   ○ wilder

DECODING: y changed to i before endings

FIGURE 12.13   Task 4, Workbook A, 1982 Edition.

endings) could be done in a similar manner. Such tasks would more likely make students aware of what happens when letters are dropped from words and endings are added, and would adhere to the guideline about the planning of instructional design.

Task 5 in the 1982 edition of workbook A is not a decoding task and probably should not be converted to one. But the concern with the task, even as it is written, is with vocabulary. Guideline 5 recommends that the vocabulary of a task relate to the rest of the program. Of the 23 different medial consonant with *-le* words the student is supposed to read to get the nine correct answers, only three have appeared in stories the students have read. The teacher's guide directs the teacher to use only one of these 23 words (and three additional words that have not appeared before) as preparation for this task. So, for most students, most of the words they must choose from have not been read in stories and will not be read again (at least in this level of this program). Thus the vocabulary in this task does not relate to the rest of that program, and in no way does the task really achieve its stated decoding goal.

Although the tasks in the 1982 edition of workbook A still have significant problems, some do attempt to relate to the rest of the program. The tasks are

34

Name

Read each sentence. Then fill in the circle next to
the word that goes into each sentence.

1. Sometimes Pat plays that she is _____ of a huge boat.
   ○ scatter   ○ skipper   ○ slipper

2. A _____ is just a little rain.
   ○ drizzle   ○ letter   ○ scatter

3. A _____ can help you reach something up high.
   ○ chatter   ○ shutter   ○ ladder

4. You can get clean in a _____ bath.
   ○ whittle   ○ bubble   ○ dipper

5. I have a _____ in my tool box.
   ○ scatter   ○ fiddle   ○ hammer

6. Sometimes I like to _____ a snack.
   ○ chatter   ○ nibble   ○ fiddle

7. Fried eggs _____ in the pan.
   ○ drizzle   ○ zipper   ○ sizzle

8. He likes to eat bread and _____.
   ○ chatter   ○ butter   ○ better

9. Ken put a _____ on his dog's mouth.
   ○ puzzle   ○ muzzle   ○ buzzer

DECODING: doubled medial consonant with -le,
-er

FIGURE 12.14   Task 5, Workbook A, 1982 Edition.

characterized (as was true of the earlier edition) by a certain clearness of purpose
and businesslike layouts. There are no frills, and perhaps the developers worry
because the tasks are not much "fun."

Two of the three tasks in the 1982 edition of workbook B were probably
designed to be more fun, but these two tasks have major problems and conceiv-
ably are not fun at all for students who have trouble doing them. Most of the
words in task 1 of workbook B are words from previous stories and have perhaps
been used in previous workbook tasks, but there are still some concerns: Animals
typically found in zoos have not been read about in a recent story nor in a previous workbook task. So the workbook designer is relying on the students' prior
knowledge. Some of the phrases, notably *a fishing reel*, *a leaping line*, and *a rag
rug*, have words in them that do not appear in the vocabulary list of this level of
the program (this list includes words taught in previous levels). Students who are
a little uncertain of what you would see at a zoo might have even more trouble
with the concepts of *a leaping line* and a *shell under cover*. But even those who
have visited a zoo might have trouble deciding between *a rag rug* and *a big bug*.
To successfully perform this task, a student would have to be a good reader and a
good guesser; having made several trips to a zoo would also be a great help. Such

35

Name

Read each sentence. Then fill in the circle next to
the word that goes into each sentence.

1. Fred had the _____ pets.
   ○ soonest   ○ nearest   ○ strangest

2. The people are _____ because they are happy.
   ○ smelled   ○ smiling   ○ timing

3. Yesterday we _____ in the mountains.
   ○ hugged   ○ hiked   ○ helping

4. Sal _____ for animals by the river.
   ○ locks   ○ liked   ○ looked

5. Fred was _____ than Jan to the fence.
   ○ closer   ○ braver   ○ cleanest

6. Elizabeth found that _____ for a pet is not easy.
   ○ caned   ○ caring   ○ cracking

7. The kitchen is a good place for _____ food.
   ○ storming   ○ stepped   ○ storing

8. Dave liked _____ the ball with the bat.
   ○ hitting   ○ hated   ○ hiding

9. Sara _____ bottle caps.
   ○ saved   ○ sawed   ○ sanding

DECODING: dropped e before endings

FIGURE 12.15   Task 6, Workbook A, 1982 Edition.

a student probably does not need to do this task. The students who need practice
in identifying words in context deserve to practice with words and contexts they
are more likely to recognize. The guideline about the vocabulary and concept
level of workbook tasks relating to the rest of the program has not been observed
by the developers of this task.

Task 2 in the 1982 edition of workbook B is a critic's dream. The layout is
wasteful of space and does not combine attractiveness with utility (guideline 8).
The art and prose of at least three of the items is bound to cause confusion (guideline 17). For example, how many students know that the ball is made of rubber?
How many students know that a violin can be called a fiddle? How many students
will determine that it is the water drip coming out of the faucet that they are
supposed to look at?

Most of the words used do not relate to the vocabulary of the rest of the
program (guideline 5), and will not be read again—except perhaps in other workbook tasks with double medial consonant words. And although more guidelines
could be cited, guideline 18 probably best summarizes what is wrong with this
task: "Cute, nonfunctional, space- and time-consuming tasks should be avoided."

In contrast, task 3 of the latest edition of workbook 3 is much more direct.

Circle each answer.

What would you see at the zoo. . .

a big airplane **or** a big alligator?

a baby monkey **or** a fishing reel?

a sleeping lion **or** a leaping line?

a seal on a rock **or** a shell under cover?

a worm in the dirt **or** a dish at work?

a rag rug **or** a big bug?

a man in the moon **or** a bear at noon?

Vocabulary: word identification in context **31**

FIGURE 12.16   Task 1, Workbook B, 1982 Edition.

Students read an informational paragraph about an octopus and write out answers to questions. This task satisfies many of the guidelines. For example, the instructions to the students are clear (guideline 7). The student response modes are close to reading and writing (guideline 14). The layout of the page combines attractiveness with utility (guideline 8), and there is ample room for the students to write their answers. A suggestion: The last time the students read about an octopus was in the previous level of the program. A picture of an octopus on this page would be helpful for a lot of students and make the page a good example of guideline 17: "The art that appears on workbook pages must be consistent with the prose of the task."

A final example from the 1982 edition of workbook A (task 7; see Figure 12.19) will complete the discussion of workbook tasks. This page comes much later in the book, but is included because it is an example of a very effectively designed workbook task. This vocabulary task will probably be valuable for most of the students who do it. The directions are clear, the items are well written, the choices require the student to consider the meaning of the phrase in the item and the related words that are the possible answers. This is only one example of one

MATCH-UPS

Draw a line from each picture to the right word.

rubber   rug

high   hammer

kite   kettle

slipper   slid

cattle   can

drip   dipper

glimmer   grass

feel   fiddle

32   Decoding: doubled medial consonant with -*er* and -*le*

FIGURE 12.17   Task 2, Workbook B, 1982 Edition.

kind of task, but it is a model of the kind of task that has a good chance of contributing to the reading skill of students.

Workbook tasks we have discussed that have pictures in the lessons do not by any means represent the worst of what a close examination of a number of different basal workbooks has revealed, nor do they show any great improvement from one edition to the next but they do provide the basis for a discussion of the need for improved workbooks. Before that discussion begins, an often asked question should be addressed: "Are workbooks really important?"

The importance of workbooks is attested to by classroom observations done in a study of elementary school classrooms using basal materials (Mason and Osborn 1982). That teachers treat workbook tasks as *more* than busywork activities and as a functional part of a basal reading package was evidenced by the amount of time the 40 teachers in the study spent on workbook activities.

Workbooks were a regular feature of instruction in every one of the third- and fourth-grade classrooms observed. In most classrooms students spent as much or more time with their workbooks as they did with their teachers. This is not to say that students spend all of the reading period with either their teachers

THE OCTOPUS

Read the paragraph. Then answer the questions.

The Octopus

The octopus is a sea animal that has a soft body. Its body has no bones and no outside shell. The octopus also has eight arms called tentacles. The octopus has large, shiny eyes and a strong, hard jaw.

The octopus lives in the sea among rocks. It hides all day and comes out at night to hunt for food.

The octopus uses its tentacles to catch its food. It catches clams, crabs, mussels, and other shellfish. It uses its jaw to break apart the shell and cut up the food.

1. How many arms does an octopus have? _____

2. Where do octopuses live? _____

   _____

3. How does an octopus catch food? _____

   _____

4. What does an octopus eat? _____

   _____

5. What does the octopus do with its jaw? _____

   _____

Literature: nonfiction (informational paragraph)   **33**

FIGURE 12.18   Task 3, Workbook B, 1982 Edition.

or their workbooks; they spent time reading in their readers and occasionally with other materials. Sometimes they did not do much of anything. But no matter what kind of classroom organization, self-contained or cross-class grouping, workbooks were used about the same amount of time. In self-contained classrooms, work-books have an obvious management function: The teacher can teach one small group of students with undivided attention only when the other students are doing something that engages them, and doing what the teacher considers a worthwhile activity. In the cross-class grouped classrooms, a teacher taught only one group at a time; even in these one-group classrooms, work in workbooks formed a sizable part of the reading lesson. Thus it was evident in these 40 classrooms that the teachers organized reading periods to include time for students to work in work-books even when there was not a management need to do so. The teachers seemed to regard work in workbooks as an essential component of their reading programs.

Another study, of first-grade classrooms, estimates that students spent 40 to 60 percent of an average reading lesson doing seatwork (Anderson et al. 1982). The researchers found that of the students observed, about 70 percent seemed to

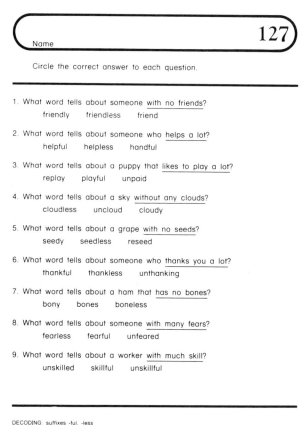

DECODING: suffixes -ful, -less

FIGURE 12.19   Task 7, Workbook A, 1982 Edition.

be performing satisfactorily on seatwork and "seemed to learn the things the assignments are designed to reinforce." A focus of the study is on the differing strategies used by this group and the students who were not doing well. The researchers suggest that teachers monitor the lower-performing students as they do their seatwork, rather than wait until the work is completed.

Although many reading educators warn against the use of workbooks, the overwhelming evidence is that teachers use them a great deal. A careful interviewing of a large group of teachers might reveal some of the reasons why work in workbooks takes up such a large segment of instructional time during reading periods. In the absence of such data, several conjectures can be made to explain the widespread use of workbooks:. Workbook tasks can provide practice on the most difficult or confusing parts of the instruction of a lesson; workbook tasks can review what has already been taught, integrate what *has* been taught into what *is* being taught, and permit students to apply what they have been taught in new and varying settings. In addition, in the context of what happens in reading instruction in classrooms, workbook tasks have some properties that are unique:

1. Workbooks provide the teacher with what is often the only clear and uncompromised feedback about what each student can do. No such unequivocal

feedback about student performance is available to a teacher during other parts of a reading period. Typically, a teacher working with a group of students will ask one student to read a passage or to answer some questions. If that student's response is acceptable, the teacher will move to another student. The teacher must assume that the students who are not responding are able to read that passage and answer those questions. In contrast, workbook activities require students to work independently. Student performance in workbooks gives a teacher information about the performance of each student on all parts of a task. This knowledge permits the teacher to make decisions about whether additional instruction is needed for students or whether students can skip ahead.

2. From this point it follows that workbook tasks can be diagnostic and prescriptive tools that not only give the teacher information about each student but also allow the teacher to provide individualized instruction for each student. Workbooks can be and usually are an essential component of individualized instruction plans.

3. Workbooks keep students busy while the teacher teaches other students. Although this aspect of workbooks is easy to ridicule by calling workbook pages "busywork," the critic should not be too quick to criticize. Most teachers find teaching reading to students in small groups preferable, especially in the primary grades, and most teachers do not feel comfortable doing this (and indeed do not have the quiet in the classroom essential to teaching small groups) unless students *not* being instructed are doing something their teachers believe is contributing to their learning.

4. Workbook activities train students to work independently. In most classrooms, students work at workbook tasks independently. It is likely that several years of this kind of activity does help prepare students to work on their own. What is important, of course, is that the work provided in the workbooks is possible to do independently, worth spending time on, and leads to the task demands of the more complex independent work that students will face in junior high and high school.

If it is acknowledged that workbooks play an important role in reading instruction in elementary classrooms, and if it is also acknowledged that a good proportion of workbook tasks are at best imperfect and not very efficient (and at worst, misleading and confusing), then some obvious questions are: "Should workbooks be improved?" and "Can workbooks be improved?" The answer to the first question must be yes because workbooks are relied upon so heavily in the teaching of reading. The answer to the second question could be a resounding yes if three groups of people took it upon themselves to pay some concerted attention to the workbook situation. These three groups are (1) educational researchers involved with classroom practice and curriculum design, (2) publishers of basal reading programs, and (3) teachers using the workbooks associated with basal reading programs. Some suggestions for each group follow.

Educational researchers. The developers of workbooks do not have a solid, sophisticated body of research from which to operate when they create workbooks. Researchers have done little to study the relationship of the content of workbooks to that of teacher's guides and student readers and the effects of that relationship. Almost nothing has been written about the instructional design, instruction giving, or quality of activities in workbooks. The existence of such information would be invaluable for the developers of workbook tasks. Even more basically, there is almost no research that can make statements about the relevance of workbook activities to the acquisition of reading skill. There seems a lot more about the use and design of workbooks that we do not know than we *do* know. Researchers interested in how children learn to read, the kinds of materials and activities that facilitate reading acquisition, and the design of programs are urged to carry out research that publishers can apply to the development of workbook tasks.

Publishers of basal materials. Most of the workbooks associated with basal readers have the appearance of materials written separately from the rest of the program. Some give the impression of being afterthoughts completed at the last minute. Therefore, the first suggestion to publishers is that at the start of planning for a new edition of a program, a *lot* of planning time be devoted for developing strategies for the integration of the workbook tasks with the rest of the program. Mechanisms should be developed that will permit people who write workbook tasks to work regularly with other members of the writing team.

What integration with the main program that exists at present is at a surface level; what is being suggested is a much deeper level of integration. For example:

1. New vocabulary from the stories being read, and from stories previously read, should be used in a variety of tasks and in a variety of contexts, not only in tasks about the story. Recent work on vocabulary (Beck 1982) emphasizes how many times and in how many different contexts vocabulary needs to be presented for students to acquire new vocabulary. Workbook tasks are an idea medium for the application of this research.
2. The main reading should be emphasized and program content and skills maintained. Since students spend a good part of the reading period reading a story or expository passage in the reader, it seems only sensible that the major proportion of workbook tasks should be based on this reading. Questions in workbook tasks that ask about the salient features of stories (plot, settings, characterizations) and about the important aspects of expository passages seem of more value than questions about short paragraphs unrelated to any other reading the students do. The application of the comprehension and decoding skills to the main reading done in the lesson would seem to make the teaching (and use) of these skills much more functional and meaningful. Therefore, the recommendation is that essentially all workbook tasks relate to the current lesson, review aspects of previous lessons, or provide for the application of vocabulary skills and information in new but related contexts.

Workbooks are the ideal place for the maintenance of the information that students read in their readers. In any given program, students read a lot of different stories and encounter a variety of vocabulary, sentence structures, and content. Some workbook tasks designed for the maintenance of this body of information would provide students with a strong base of useful knowledge.

Workbook tasks that are integrated with the entire program, that capitalize on the main reading, and that maintain what is being taught would eliminate the one page-one, one-skill compartmentalization that now exists in essentially all workbooks. Such changes would make workbooks a valuable adjunct to the rest of the reading program.

The second major suggestion to publishers is that materials be carefully tried out before being published. Small-scale intensive tryout procedures are essential to the development of workbook tasks. A simple and feasible tryout procedure is to place tryout versions of a workbook in two to four classrooms. Teachers must agree to being observed as they present the tasks, and students must agree to being observed as they do the tasks. The tryout team should observe in the classrooms as often as possible, and they should collect all the students' papers. By analyzing what teachers say as they present tasks, and by observing students as they do the tasks (such as listening to the questions they ask about what they are supposed to be doing), workbook developers can get some information about the effectiveness of tasks. By looking at the workbook pages and tallying all the errors, workbook designers can identify weak tasks and either eliminate or remedy them. Such tryout procedures would improve workbooks enormously.

Teachers.   The advice to teachers is for the most part obvious. Workbook tasks should be evaluated carefully before being assigned to students. Teachers should *not* operate from a position of faith in the printed word, but from a position of skepticism. Some tasks should be abandoned because they are confusing, not important, or nonproductive consumers of time. On the other hand, tasks that are difficult but valuable should be run off so that they can be repeated. Some particularly effective tasks can be adopted by the teacher to permit students to practice further examples or instances of what is being taught. Teachers should become aware of which tasks require additional instructions, which pictures require clarification, and which tasks most students can do independently. Teachers should also realize how counterproductive it is for students to spend a long time working on tasks on which they make many errors. Such tasks, if worthwhile, should be done when teachers have time to monitor students as they do the tasks.

In addition, teachers should make their observations about unsatisfactory workbooks and unsatisfactory tasks known to publishers of basal series. Publishers will change as the demands of their markets encourage them to change. Information from teachers to publishers *will* affect the quality of workbooks.

Finally, it is important that educational researchers, publishers, and teachers keep hard-to-teach students at the forefront of their thinking. Students who are the hardest to teach probably spend the most time with workbook tasks because they work slowly, make lots of mistakes, and have to spend extra time correcting their errors, or because they are given extra tasks as remedial help (actually often for all three reasons). These are the students who need the most practice. These are the students who need consistency from task to task and clear and unambiguous directions. The relevance of the workbook tasks to the rest of what they are learning needs to be evident. These students need more help in learning vocabulary and the chance to integrate and apply what they are learning. These are the students workbook designers should be continuously aware of as they design workbook tasks. *All* students need the best that educational researchers, program developers, and teachers can offer, but for hard-to-teach students the best can make the difference between the satisfactory achievement and unsatisfactory achievement of reading skill.

GUIDELINES FOR WORKBOOK TASKS

1. A sufficient proportion of workbook tasks should be relevant to the instruction that is going on in the rest of the unit or lesson.
2. Another portion of workbook tasks should provide for a systematic and cumulative review of what has already been taught.
3. Workbooks should reflect the most important (and workbook-appropriate) aspects of what is being taught in the reading program. Less important aspects should remain in the teacher's guide as voluntary activities.
4. Workbooks should contain, in a form that is readily accessible to students and teachers, extra tasks for students who need extra practice.
5. The vocabulary and concept level of workbook tasks should relate to that of the rest of the program and to the students using the program.
6. The language used in workbook tasks must be consistent with that used in the rest of the lesson and in the rest of the workbook.
7. Instructions to students should be clear, unambiguous, and easy to follow; brevity is a virtue.
8. The layout of pages should combine attractiveness with utility.
9. Workbook tasks should contain enough content so that there is a chance a student doing the task will *learn* something and not simply be *exposed* to something.
10. Tasks that require students to make discriminations must be preceded by a sufficient number of tasks that provide practice on components of the discriminations.
11. The content of workbook tasks must be accurate and precise; workbook tasks must not present wrong information nor perpetuate misrules.
12. At least some workbook tasks should be fun and have an obvious payoff to them.
13. Most student response modes should be consistent from task to task.
14. Student response modes should be the closest possible to reading and writing.
15. The instructional design of individual tasks and of task sequences should be carefully planned.
16. Workbooks should contain a finite number of task types and forms.
17. The art that appears on workbook pages must be consistent with the prose of the task.
18. Cute, nonfunctional, space- and time-consuming tasks should be avoided.
19. When appropriate, tasks should be accompanied by brief explanations of purpose for both teachers and students.
20. English-major humor should be avoided.

REFERENCES

Anderson, L. M. *Student responses to seatwork: Implications for the study of students' cognitive processing*. Research Series No. 102. East Lansing: IRT Publications, Michigan State University, 1982.

Clymer, T., et al., How it is nowadays. Skilpak and Studybook in *Reading 720*. Lexington, Mass.: Ginn, 1976.

Clymer, T., & Venezky, R. L. Give me a clue. Skillpak and Studybook in *Ginn Reading Program*. Lexington, Mass.: Ginn, 1982.

Mason, J., & Osborn, J. *When do children begin "reading to learn?" A survey of classroom reading instruction practices in grades two through five.* Tech. Rep. No. 261. Urbana: University of Illinois, Center for the Study of Reading, September 1982.

Osborn, J. The purposes, uses and contents of workbooks and some guidelines for teachers and publishers. In R. C. Anderson, J. Osborn, & R. J. Tierney (Eds.), *Learning to read in American schools: Basal readers and content texts*. Hillsdale, N.J.: Erlbaum, 1982.

13

Children's Preconceptions and Content-Area Textbooks

Charles W. Anderson
Edward L. Smith

In this chapter we report results from a two-year study of science teaching in fifth-grade classrooms. We begin by considering children's comprehension of a passage from a science text. We attribute the children's difficulties to the existence of preconceptions or schemata that prevent them from interpreting the passage correctly. We then describe how children's preconceptions often affect their understanding not only of textbooks but of science instruction in general. Finally, we discuss materials we have developed that have helped teachers make science concepts more comprehensible to their students.

Comprehension of a Science Textbook Passage

Have you ever thrown a rubber ball at something? If you have, you know that when the ball hits most things, it bounces off them. Like a rubber ball, light bounces off most things it hits.

When light travels to something opaque, all the light does not stop. Some of this light bounces off. When light travels to something translucent or transparent, all the light does not pass through. Some of this light bounces off. When light bounces off things and travels to your eyes, you are able to see. (p. 154)

The above passage comes from Laidlaw's *Exploring Science*, a popular fifth-grade science text (Blecha, Gega, and Green 1979). Since 1979, we have collected test data on more than 200 fifth-grade students who have read the above passage. Our data indicate that, under normal conditions, less than one fourth of the students who read the passage actually understood it.

Publication of this work is sponsored by the Institute for Research on Teaching, College of Education, Michigan State University. The Institute for Research on Teaching is funded primarily by the Program for Teaching and Instruction of the National Institute of Education, United States Department of Education. The opinions expressed in this publication do not necessarily reflect the position, policy, or endorsement of the National Institute of Education. (NIE contract No. 400-81-0014 and NIE Grant No. 90840.)

We believe that children's difficulties with the textbook passage quoted above can best be understood from the perspective of schema theory. Rather than simply decode the meaning of a written passage, a reader must actively interpret the passage by using schemata. The schemata available to a reader depend on his or her prior experience and understanding of the world. We have found that most fifth-grade students have a schema for how vision occurs that is very different from the one implicit in the textbook passage.

Scientifically trained adults understand that the statement "I see the book" is not literally true. Rather, we see *light* that has bounced off of the book to our eyes. Our pretest data indicate that this understanding was shared by only about 5 percent of the fifth-grade students in our study. Most of the other students understood vision as an act of direct perception. They believed that we see the object itself rather than light reflected from the object. In their view, light provides a *condition* necessary for seeing to take place: Light makes objects bright or visible. The passage from *Exploring Science* makes sense only if it is interpreted with the adult schema. The children's schema renders it incomprehensible.

We refer to the children's unscientific ideas about the world as *preconceptions*. A rapidly growing body of research indicates that people of all ages have preconceptions that affect their understanding of many scientific and mathematical concepts (Davis 1981; Larkin, McDermott, Simon, and Simon 1980; Nussbaum and Novak 1976; Shayer and Wylam 1981). Furthermore, preconceptions are often difficult to detect because they are quite compatible with our common, everyday language. Thus the role that student preconceptions play in determining how they understand science instruction and science textbooks is often hidden by their use of apparently normal and acceptable language. For instance, students may say that "light has to shine on objects for you to see them" without understanding the role of reflected light in vision.

Thus the textbook passage quoted above was not understood by most students because the authors depended on a schema for vision that the students did not understand. What could be done to make the passage more comprehensible to the students? It might be possible to rewrite the passage so that it no longer depends on the scientific schema for vision. We do not regard this as a satisfactory solution because the scientific schema for vision is correct, and the children's preconceptions are wrong. It would be preferable to make the passage comprehensible by changing the *students* so that they have a scientific understanding of how we see.

One solution might be to rewrite the text so that it would induce conceptual change in the students. However, simply making the passage clearer would probably be insufficient. We believe that most fifth-grade students lack sufficient self-monitoring ability and sensitivity to dissonance between their own belief systems and the content of the written text. Text material designed to directly attack specific preconceptions might be more effective. However, we believe that many students will abandon strongly held preconceptions only in response to experiences that have a more immediate and powerful impact than reading the textbook. Thus, comprehension of information in textbooks depends on instruction rather than exclusively on characteristics of the written text.

We have focused on a specific example of what we believe to be a very general problem: Successful learning in science and other subjects is often prevented by a failure to bring about conceptual change. Students must abandon preconceptions and replace them with more adequate scientific conceptions. Such changes are among the most important of learning outcomes. The scientific schemata are not only essential for comprehending information in the text; they are the basis for all further learning about science and for dealing with problems that the students will encounter in the adult world.

STUDYING CONCEPTUAL CHANGE IN CLASSROOMS: RESEARCH METHODS

In our study, we have tried to define the characteristics of teaching that successfully induces conceptual change in students. Our choice of research methods has been guided by our belief that the process of conceptual change can be understood only through detailed knowledge of specific instructional episodes. We have focused on teaching at the fifth-grade level, and we have focused on units from two very different science programs.

The first unit is the one from which the sample textbook passage was taken: the "light" unit from the *Exploring Science* textbook series. We also focused on a series of activities on plants and photosynthesis from *Communities*, the fifth-grade life science unit in a revised version of the Science Curriculum Improvement Study (abbreviated SCIIS; Knott, Lawson, Karplus, Thier, and Montgomery 1978). SCIIS is an activity-based program; students learn by conducting a series of investigations and recording data in student manuals. There is no textbook.

Our study began with a careful analysis of the two units we had chosen to focus on. This analysis produced a detailed description of the intended conceptual learning outcomes for each unit, stated as a list of propositions. Examples of propositions from our analysis of the "light" unit include "Light travels in a straight line" and "Light bounces off most things that it hits."[1]

This list of propositions was then used to construct pretests and posttests for each unit. The analysis of the two units also produced a detailed description of the sequence of activities that would take place if the teacher followed the teacher's guide literally. This procedural description served as the basis for our observations of classroom instruction.

We studied the teaching of the two units by conducting case studies. Each case study focused on a single teacher, teaching either the light unit or the plant unit to his or her regular students. A case study consisted of (1) pretests and posttests administered to the students, (2) observations that produced detailed narrative records of some or all of the lessons taught during the course of the unit, and (3) interviews with the teacher and observations of teacher planning.

During the first year of the project, we observed nine teachers teaching the plant unit and five teachers teaching the light unit. We tried to observe these teachers naturalistically. That is, we did not attempt to advise the teachers or otherwise affect the way they taught.

During the second year of the project, we tried to modify the programs so that the teachers could more successfully induce conceptual change in their students. Six teachers used these modified materials to teach the light unit, and four teachers taught the plant unit.

YEAR 1 RESULTS: TEACHING METHODS THAT DO NOT WORK

None of the 14 teachers we observed during the first year of the program was particularly successful in inducing conceptual change in his or her students. We therefore spent the first year of the study observing teachers who employed a variety of unsuccessful teaching methods and trying to understand why these teachers failed.

Two of the most interesting failures will be discussed. We consider these cases interesting because by any reasonable assessment, Ms. Rosal and Ms. Howe (not their real names) were excellent teachers, and they were using widely recommended instructional methods. The failure of these teachers and their methods has led us to conclude that there are serious difficulties with both the materials and the methods generally used to teach science in our schools.

Ms. Rosal: The Failure of Didactic Teaching

We observed Ms. Rosal as she taught the "Light" unit from the *Exploring Science*.[2] Ms. Rosal was a very skillful and apparently successful practitioner of didactic science teaching. She viewed the textbook as a source of facts and information to be presented to the students. She tried to present these facts in a clear and logical manner, and she enriched her presentations with a variety of activities that made her classes fun and interesting for her students. Both Ms. Rosal and her students enjoyed the light unit and were pleased with its apparent success. However, Ms. Rosal never became aware of her students' preconceptions, and most of her students never understood the scientific conception of how we see.

The conceptual change problem. Ms. Rosal's students had several important preconceptions or schemata which interfered with their understanding of *Exploring Science*. The first of these preconceptions is discussed above. All but one of her students believed that we see by perceiving objects directly, rather than by detecting light reflected off those objects.

A second preconception concerns the nature of color and the mechanism of color vision. Ms. Rosal's fifth graders (and many adults) believed that *objects* have colors. They believed that white light, which they perceived as "clear" or "colorless," brightens the objects and thus reveals their colors to our eyes. In contrast, the textbook devotes an entire chapter to developing a scientific conception of color vision, in which (1) white light contains all the colors of the spectrum, (2) pigments in objects absorb some of the colors in white light and reflect other colors, and (3) we see the color of the *light* that is reflected to our eyes.

Neither the textbook nor the teacher's guide mentions the existence of the students' preconceptions of how we see or of color vision. Our interpretation is that the authors of the textbook did not suspect the existence of these preconceptions.

Ms. Rosal's planning. Ms. Rosal planned her teaching very carefully. In contrast with many teachers (Smith and Sendelback 1982), Ms. Rosal's primary emphasis in planning was *not* on management of student activities.[3] She began her planning for the unit by thinking about the content she would teach. She read the background information, main concepts and objectives, and other content information provided for the teacher in the teacher's guide. She tried to make sure that she understood the material well enough to share it with her students.

Ms. Rosal also devoted a good deal of planning time to thinking of ways to make science fun, interesting, and meaningful to her students. For each chapter, she thought of a "sparking activity," a demonstration designed to stimulate student interest. She made use of a variety of books and other outside resources, and she thought of ways to connect the light unit to other subjects that the class had studied during the course of the year. For instance, she associated a discussion of translucent objects with an earlier social studies unit in which students had made windows from oil paper as had the pioneers.

Ms. Rosal also attended to essential procedural details in her planning. She made sure that materials were ready ahead of time, classroom management strategies were worked out, and so on.

Even though Ms. Rosal was a thorough and careful planner, she did not suspect that her students might have preconceptions that would keep them from learning, and so she did not plan for those preconceptions or their effects. Even though Ms. Rosal was teaching this unit for the first time, a substantial portion of her unit planning was completed before the beginning of the first lesson and thus before she had any information about her students' understanding of light. She assumed that the textbook presented information in a manner that was appropriate for her students. To quote her: "Well, somebody must have known something when they wrote the text. Laidlaw is an old, established textbook company, and if they include something in a text it must be pretty well written."[4] Thus, Ms. Rosal began teaching unprepared for her students' preconceptions, and unaware that some parts of the text would be very difficult for her students to understand.

Ms. Rosal's teaching. Perhaps the most striking characteristic of Ms. Rosal's teaching was its lively and interesting nature. Her students did much more than just read the textbook. They observed prisms and spectra, bouncing balls and bouncing light beams, color wheels, transparent, translucent, and opaque objects, and optical illusions. Ms. Rosal was entertaining and humorous; her students enjoyed the unit and told her so.

Ms. Rosal also maintained clear expectations for her students' learning and behavior. Students in her class worked hard. They were expected to read the text, write definitions of vocabulary words, perform experiments, answer written questions, draw pictures of the eye parts, participate in class discussions, and take a unit test. Ms. Rosal was an effective and demanding instructional manager as well as an entertaining teacher.

Yet, at the end of the light unit, only seven of the 20 students in Ms. Rosal's class understood that we "see objects" by detecting reflected light. Two students were aware that we see colors because objects reflect colored light to our eyes. Why was such a skillful teacher so unsuccessful in communicating these basic ideas to her students?

A closer examination of the classroom observational data makes it clear why Ms. Rosal's students were not more successful. Ms. Rosal's lessons were rarely *about* how we see or how we see colors. Rather, she talked about how light travels, how light bounces off objects, how light interacts with transparent, translucent, and opaque objects, and so on. Thus, her students' exposure to the scientific conception of how we see was much more limited than might be expected. In this respect, Ms. Rosal was following the *Exploring Science* text, which emphasized many other points more strongly than the description of how we see.

Our judgment is that both Ms. Rosal and the text were in error in presenting so many "facts about light" without emphasizing the scientific conception of how we see. The scientific conception seems simple and obvious to someone who already possesses it. Its significance was made clear, however, when we observed the attempts of students with the preconception described above to make sense of scientific information about light. Without the scientific schema, the facts were misinterpreted, ignored, or learned in isolation as "school learning" having little to do with the real world.

The students' difficulties can also be attributed in part to Ms. Rosal's failure to give them clear feedback indicating that their preconceptions were wrong. She did sometimes have opportunities to give students such feedback. For instance, the following statements were made during three separate lessons by students trying to explain images in mirrors:

> *T:* What is an image?
> *S:* It's a picture of you in the mirror or something like that. If you look in a mirror, it will reflect or show your image. (2-27-81)
> *T:* Why can you see yourself better in a mirror than in a pie pan?
> *S:* Because a mirror is really smooth and it's made out of glass and it's easy to see yourself, and a pie pan has all the designs on it. (3-2-81).
> *T:* We talked, about mirrors, right? Why do we see things in mirrors?
> *S:* Because one of those pieces of things we had did something to our eye.
> *T:* What helps us see in a mirror?
> *S:* Your eyes and just the sun. (review lesson, 3-23-81)

These exchanges and others like them reflect a continuing tendency of the students to explain visual phenomena without reference to reflected light or the scientific schema for vision. They probably would have benefited if Ms. Rosal had told them what was wrong with their answers and contrasted those answers with more adequate explanations.

Ms. Rosal did not do this. Although she mentioned reflected light after each of the above statements, she never gave any direct indication that she saw anything wrong with the student's answers. Neither did she ask the students to elaborate on or explain their answers. The net result was that students in her class heard a variety of explanations for many phenomena without a clear indication of which ones were correct and which ones were incomplete or inadequate.

Although the effects of Ms. Rosal's behavior were unfortunate, the reasons for it are understandable. Students' answers during class discussions are rarely exactly what the teacher anticipates, and no teacher has time during class to ponder the nuances of every student utterance. For Ms. Rosal, who had no knowledge of her students' preconceptions, the students' answers undoubtedly sounded reasonable enough. In fact, we became aware of the significance of the students' statements only in retrospect, after we understood the nature of their preconceptions.

Ms. Rosal's failure to give her students clear feedback was also partly attributable to gaps in her own understanding of light. Although she understood the scientific conception of vision, she sometimes had difficulty applying that conception to special situations, such as those where light interacts with mirrors, lenses, or water. Although the textbook devotes nine pages to such situations, neither the text nor the teacher's guide provides adequate answers to many of the questions that came up in Ms. Rosal's classroom.

Summary of Ms. Rosal's case. Ms. Rosal was typical of teachers we observed using textbooks in that she viewed her primary function as one of presenting information in a logical and interesting manner. The *Exploring Science* textbook and teacher's guide encouraged this viewpoint. Ms. Rosal conducted lively and well-managed lessons, which her students obviously enjoyed. However, she never became aware of her students' preconceptions about vision or color. Most of her students ended the unit without comprehending the scientific conceptions presented in the text.

We believe that Ms. Rosal failed to change her students' conceptions primarily because her didactic orientation toward teaching affected her planning and teaching behavior. She planned much of her unit without having or seeking any information concerning her students' prior understanding of light and vision. She did not emphasize concepts, which we consider to be of crucial importance. Finally, she was unable to interpret statements from her students that revealed their commitment to preconceptions about light and seeing. We believe that problems like Ms. Rosal's are inevitable whenever teachers or textbook authors try to present information without being aware of the schemata that students will use in interpreting that information.

Ms. Howe: The Failure of Discovery Teaching

Many science educators would not be particularly surprised or concerned about Ms. Rosal's failure. The didactic teaching method that she used, although favored by most of the teachers we observed, has not been popular among science educators. Instead, many science educators have advocated an "inquiry" or "discovery" approach to science teaching. They have argued that science education would be more effective if, instead of being told about the theories of other people, children were allowed to develop their own theories through direct experience with concrete materials. We have chosen Ms. Howe as an example of a teacher who tried to use this approach in her teaching.

Ms. Howe was one of seven teachers we observed teaching *Communities* (Knott et al. 1978), the fifth-grade life science unit of the Rand McNally SCIIS program. SCIIS is an activity-based program in which students perform a series of investigations rather than read a textbook. The major components of the program are the teacher's guide, a kit containing equipment and supplies, and student manuals with questions and pages for recording data and answers to questions.

The *Communities* unit is designed to introduce students to the groups of organisms that interact in biological communities: producers, consumers, and decomposers. Our study focused on Chapters 3 through 6 in Part I: "Producers." The major ideas to be developed in these chapters are (1) that green plants use food stored in the seed to begin to grow, and (2) that after this food is used up they must have light in order to make their food (through the process of photosynthesis) and survive.

A key experiment in this unit is one in which the students grow grass seed in the light and in the dark. The grass begins to grow in both conditions. However, the grass in the dark eventually dies, while that in the light continues to grow. The usefulness of the major ideas presented above in explaining these results is obvious: All the grass seeds begin to grow by using their stored food, but only the grass in the light can make its own food after the stored food is used up. In fact, Ms. Howe expected her students to develop the main ideas after they had observed results of this experiment.

The conceptual change problem. In fact, our tests indicate that the conceptions developed by most students were quite different from the main ideas presented above. Most students began the unit believing that plants need both light and food in order to grow and be healthy. Most students, however, believed that "food for plants" was either water or fertilizer ("plant food")—things that plants take in from the soil. They believed that plants needed light "to grow," "to stay green," or "to be healthy," but no student in the class associated plants' need for light with food production.

Thus, the grass-growing experiment, like the textbook passage about light, could be interpreted by using two different schemata. The naive schema is that food must be taken in by plants from their environment. The scientific schema assumes that plants can make their own food through the process of photosynthesis.

Given their commitment to the naive schema, the students' interpretation of the experimental results is understandable. Many students were surprised to see that the grass in the dark began to grow at all. This led them to doubt their initial conviction that plants needed light. Eventually, though, as they saw the plants in the dark grow spindly and yellow, then fall over and wilt, most students became convinced that plants needed light in order to live. None of these results, however, materially affected most students' beliefs about *food* for plants. They remained convinced that food was something that the plants take in from the soil. Thus they saw no connection between experiments involving light and the question of where plants get their food.

Ms. Howe's planning and teaching. Ms. Howe was like Ms. Rosal in a number of respects. She was an experienced and successful teacher and a good classroom manager who had good rapport with her students. Like Ms. Rosal, she was very concerned about her students learning. She was also like Ms. Rosal in that at the beginning of the unit she was unaware of her students' preconceptions or their likely effects on learning.

Ms. Howe's teaching differed from Ms. Rosal's in that, rather than present facts and information to her students, she tried to make sure that her students conducted the experiments correctly, observed the results carefully and accurately, and discussed those results and their implications. In this respect she was highly successful. Her students became sensitive to very subtle differences between plants growing in the light and plants growing in the dark and discussed them intelligently in class.

Ms.Howe also differed from Ms. Rosal in that she often demanded that her students explain or clarify their beliefs, and she often confronted them when their theories did not adequately explain all the observational evidence.

Seeing how successful her students were in performing experiments and making and discussing their observations, Ms. Howe expected them to develop the idea that the grass plants were dying because they had no light to make their food. No matter how carefully she went over the experimental results with her students, however, they never "came up with" the idea of photosynthesis. In fact, it became increasingly apparent to Ms. Howe that most of her students still believed that plants got their food from the soil.

Her initial response was to hold additional class discussions that emphasized results incompatible with the students' beliefs. For example, she focused on evidence from an earlier experiment that plants could survive even without soil. Even these discussions did not enable her students to produce the idea of photosynthesis.

Eventually, Ms. Howe decided that her students would not develop the concept of photosynthesis. She then launched a "media blitz," exposing her students to films and filmstrips about photosynthesis and drilling the students on their contents. Even this media blitz was only partially successful in altering her students' ideas about food for plants. Most of her students continued to believe that food was something that the plants take in. Those students who accommodated the new information about photosynthesis tended to do so by believing that light was a "kind of food" that plants take in rather than an input to the process by which plants make their food.

Discussion of Ms. Howe's case. Ms. Howe's implicit definition of comprehension was more like our own than that of any other teacher in the study. She could not be satisfied that her students understood the grass experiment until they could use scientific schemata to explain the results. Thus she became aware of her students' conceptual difficulties and tried to address them. In doing so, she eventually reverted to a relatively didactic teaching style, like Ms. Rosal's. Like Ms. Rosal, she was only partially successful in helping her students to undergo conceptual change.

Ms. Howe's difficulties may have been due partly to a misinterpretation of the SCIIS teacher's guide. The teacher's guide calls for the teacher to "invent," which in SCIIS terminology means to present and explain, the concept of photosynthesis. The students are to use the concept to explain the results of the grass experiment only *after* photosynthesis has been "invented" by the teacher.

We did not encounter a single teacher in our study who understood "invention" as intended by the SCIIS developers. The message implicit in the title of the SCIS training film *Don't Tell Me, I'll Find Out* seems much more powerful for these teachers than a few paragraphs buried in the introductory section of the teacher's guide.

Nevertheless, we feel that Ms. Howe's case carries a clear message for advocates of inquiry teaching: Students conducting hands-on experiments are likely to use their own naive schemata to interpret the results. Thus, they will not necessarily develop scientific schemata as a result of their experiences.

YEAR 2 RESULTS: BRINGING ABOUT CONCEPTUAL CHANGE

If neither didactic nor inquiry approaches to teaching help most students to develop scientific conceptions, then what alternatives are left? This was the challenge we faced as we tried to develop an intervention for the second year of the study. In studying the first-year results, we became convinced that although Ms. Rosal, Ms. Howe, and the other teachers who participated in the first year of our study were different in many ways, they were alike in that, while teaching, they did not explicitly contrast their students' preconceptions with scientific conceptions. They failed to create what Rowe (1978) calls a condition of *conceptual conflict* in their students.

We therefore attempted to design materials that would help teachers create and resolve conceptual conflict in their students. Those materials and the rationale behind them are described below, and preliminary results from our second-year data are presented.

Developing Modified Teaching Materials

The different nature of the two science programs caused us to approach development of the new materials in different ways. We believe that Ms. Rosal and the other teachers using the *Exploring Science* text were using it more or less as intended by its developers. However, since the writers of the text were apparently unaware of common student preconceptions, the program was inadequate for bringing about conceptual change. We addressed this problem by developing additional materials to be used as supplements to the text: a set of 13 overhead transparencies and a teacher's guide to accompany them. A sample page from the teacher's guide[5] is illustrated in Figure 13.1.

Each of the transparencies consists of two layers. The bottom layer describes a situation and asks a question about that situation. After the students have discussed their own answers to the question, the teacher can flip down the second layer, which provides a "scientific" answer based on information from the textbook. The commentary in the teacher's guide contrasts the common student answers with the textbook answer, clarifying the nature of the conceptual change that the students should undergo.

The development of a treatment for the SCIIS program presented a different problem. We became convinced upon close observation that the SCIIS teaching strategy had been designed to deal with precisely the preconceptions we found most commonly among the students. However, that teaching strategy was described so poorly in the teacher's guide that neither Ms. Howe nor any of the other SCIIS teachers completely understood or implemented it. We therefore reorganized and rewrote three chapters of the *Communities* teacher's guide so that the teaching strategy and its rationale would be more clearly communicated. The first page of the chapter with the grass-growing experiment from the new teacher's guide[6] is presented as Figure 13.2.

In both teacher's guides we attempted to do three things:

1. We tried to describe the most common and most important student preconceptions.
2. We tried to describe conceptual goals or objectives by contrasting those common preconceptions with more acceptable scientific conceptions.
3. We tried to describe a teaching strategy which would bring about conceptual conflict and lead (hopefully) to conceptual change on the part of the students.

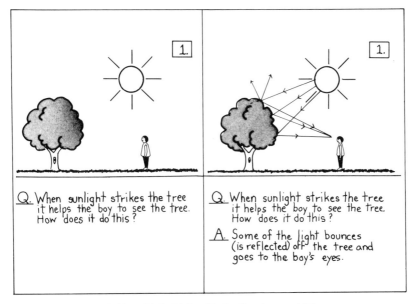

1. How Light Helps Us to See (page 145)

Common student answers. Many of your students will probably give answers like these to the question:

"The sun shines on the tree."

"The light makes it brighter."

"You can't see in the dark."

Although these answers are not wrong, we find that children who give answers like those above often do not understand the role that *reflected light* plays in seeing. They tend to believe that we see objects directly rather than detecting light that is reflected from objects. They also commonly think of light as a condition (like warmth), rather than as a form of energy that travels through space.

Textbook answer. The arrows on the transparency make it possible for you to follow the path that light takes to the boy's eyes. Notice that the boy does not see the object directly. Instead he sees the light that is *reflected* from the tree and reaches his eyes.

FIGURE 13.1   Sample Page from *Light* Teacher's Guide.

Most science teacher's guides available today provide little besides suggested teaching strategies. Preconceptions are virtually never discussed, and presentations of goals or objectives are usually inadequate for either guiding teaching behavior or justifying the recommended strategies.

In developing the revised materials, we tried to remain faithful to the different philosophies of teaching embodied in the two programs. The light transparencies, like the *Exploring Science* text, are didactic in nature. Students are encouraged to express their ideas primarily as a prelude to being told that they are wrong. The scientific concepts are presented as correct and justified on the basis of authority rather than evidence. Students are expected to change their thinking

DO PLANTS NEED LIGHT TO GROW?

MATERIALS

FOR EACH CHILD:
Student manual pages
4 and 5

FOR EACH TEAM OF 2
CHILDREN:
crayons (1 green,
1 yellow)*
1 label
1 planter cup
1 ruler
FOR THE CLASS:
wax pencil
100-watt light bulb[+]
soil[+]
light source
2 trays
6 water sprinklers
1 package grass
seeds
adhesive dots (4
green, 4 yellow)
1 large cardboard box

*Provided by Teacher
[+]Sand and Soil Box

SYNOPSIS

Students grow grass in the light and in the dark. They see that grass growing in the dark eventually dies, and the concept of photosynthesis is introduced to explain this: without light, the grass plants cannot make food, and they starve to death.
Suggested time: 2 to 3 weeks

ADVANCE PREPARATION

Set up centers for the distribution of seeds, soil, water sprinklers, labels, rulers, and cups.
Set up the light source (see Figure 5.1).

WHAT YOUR STUDENTS WILL KNOW

By the time they have finished Chapter 4, your students should be using the terms "Embryo" and "Cotyledon" correctly and confidently. Most of them probably will also believe correctly that the embryo is the part of the seed that grows, and that the role of the cotyledon is to provide food for the growing embryo. However, you can still expect that many of your students will hold the following misconceptions:

1. Many students believe that light is necessary for sprouting as well as continued growth. However, because the sprouting seed gets its food from the cotyledon, plants can begin growing even in the dark.

2. Most of your students will be aware that "plants need light to grow." Many will not realize, however, that plants will die without light. In fact, the plants starve to death after their stored food is used up. Their only source of food is the process of photosynthesis, which depends on light.

3. Most of your students will probably identify the soil as a source of "food for plants." In fact, all that plants get from the soil is water and some minerals. The "stuff" that supplies energy for the maintenance of life processes and "building blocks" for growth—what we would normally call food—is made by the plants through the processes of photosynthesis. The use of the term "plant food" for fertilizer tends to reinforce the children's misconceptions. In fact fertilizer supplies a plant only with minerals. It is not a "food" in the normal sense of the word.

LEARNING FROM THIS CHAPTER

As they do the activities in this chapter, the students will observe a number of events that are hard to explain if they believe in the misconceptions described above. They will see grass seed sprout and begin to grow in the dark, then gradually wither and die as the food stored in the cotyledon runs out. In a discussion at the end of these activities, you will introduce the term photosynthesis, then help the students to see how photosynthesis can explain their observations better than the idea that plants get their food from the soil.

FIGURE 13.2   Sample Page from SCIS Revised Teacher's Guide.

to conform with the scientific conceptions as presented in the text and on the transparencies. They are not encouraged to challenge the scientific ideas or to develop their own theories.

In the SCIIS program, on the other hand, authority does not lie primarily in the teacher or in a textbook but in the available experimental evidence. Students are encouraged to develop their own theories and use them to predict the results of the experiments they perform. They then compare their predictions with the actual results. Conceptual change is expected to occur when the students see that the experimental results are predicted better by the scientific theory than by their own theories.

Although the SCIIS approach seems to be more in accord with historical and philosophical ideas about the development of scientific concepts, we are not convinced that this approach is more effective for inducing conceptual change. As a practical matter, the results of experiments in which ten-year-old children are growing their own plants are often ambiguous, so students may never actually make observations that lead them to question their preconceptions. Even "correct" experimental results may not have an immediate and powerful enough impact to cause students to abandon strongly held preconceptions.

Preliminary Results

Although data analysis is just beginning for the second year of the project, we can discuss some of our impressions. We believe that the revised materials did in fact affect both teachers' thinking and their classroom behavior. We also believe that these changes in teacher behavior led to enhanced student learning.

Virtually every teacher who participated in the second year of the study told us that the revised materials helped them clarify their understanding of what they should be teaching, and why. Many teachers also commented that they had learned about light or photosynthesis from the materials. The effects of this improved understanding were observable in their classroom behavior, even when they were not using the materials that we had prepared.

Our impressions from second-year classroom observations include the following. We are beginning work on formal data analyses designed to test these impressions.

1. Teachers were much more likely to require students to relate empirical observations (such as plant growth or the appearance of objects through frosted glass) to theoretical constructs (such as photosynthesis or light rays). Thus, their emphasis in hands-on experiences shifted from doing them correctly or making them fun to the learning and application of specific scientific concepts.
2. Most teachers were much more successful in giving feedback to students. They were more likely to request clarification or explanation of ambiguous statements (e.g., "You said that the boy couldn't see the car because the wall was in the way. *What* was it in the way of?") They were also more likely to contradict incorrect statements or to explain which of several suggested answers to a question they thought was best and why.

TABLE 13.1   Percentage of Students Understanding Two Key Concepts in Ms. Rosal's Class

Concept	Year 1	Year 2
Our eyes detect reflected light (rather than detect objects directly)	35	81
We see the colors of *light* reflected from objects (rather than the colors of objects themselves)	10	33

Our preliminary test data indicate that student learning was also enhanced. For example, Table 13.1 contrasts posttest results from the first and second year for two key concepts in Ms. Rosal's class. During the second year, most of the children in Ms. Rosal's class achieved a basic understanding of how we see. A substantial minority also mastered the much more difficult concepts associated with color vision. These results were achieved in spite of the fact that Ms. Rosal considered the second-year class to be less academically talented and harder to manage than her first-year class. Preliminary data from other *Exploring Science* classrooms indicate similar results: Student learning was enhanced to a degree that was both statistically and educationally significant. No data are yet available for the SCIIS classrooms.

CONCLUSION

Children's comprehension of science instruction is often affected by their prior beliefs or preconceptions—ideas about the world that are at variance with accepted scientific thinking.

In this chapter we have discussed fifth-grade children's preconceptions of two scientific topics, vision and photosynthesis, and described how those preconceptions affected their understanding of science instruction. We have found that many children are quite strongly committed to their preconceptions; these children often learn very little, even from science instruction that is by most standards very good. We have, however, experienced considerable success with teaching materials designed to make children aware of the specific differences between their preconceptions and the scientific conceptions.

Changing children's conceptions about science is a difficult and demanding process for any teacher. We have found it very gratifying to see how willing our teachers were to accept the challenge posed by our new materials, even if those materials required substantial changes in their thinking and teaching methods. We believe that through our materials we have helped these teachers achieve a higher level of professional performance—a level that was more rewarding to the teachers and more productive of student learning. Improved materials and training that prepares teachers for student preconceptions could make that higher level of professional performance the norm rather than a rarely achieved ideal.

NOTES

1. Lucille, Slinger, Charles W., Anderson and Edward L. Smith. *One view of fifth-grade text-based science instruction.* Paper presented at the annual meeting of the National Association for Research in Science Teaching, Fontana, Wis. 1982.

2. For a more detailed version of their case study, see Gerald, Duffy; and Lonnie McIntyre. *A qualitative analysis of how various primary grade teachers employ the structured learning. Component of the direct instruction model when teaching reading.* Research Series No. 80. East Lansing: Institute for Research Teaching, Michigan State University, June 1980.

3. Walter Doyle. Learning the classroom environment: An ecological. analysis. North Texas State University, 1977.

4. Slenger, Anderson, and Smith, note 1.

5. Charles W. Anderson, and Edward L. Smith. *Transparencies on light: Teacher's manual.* East Lansing: Elementary Science Project, Institute for Research on Teaching, Michigan State University, 1982.

6. Edward L., Smith, Glenn D., Berkheimer, and Charles W. Anderson. *SCIS revised teacher's guide.* East Lansing: Elementary Science Project, Institute for Research on Teaching, Michigan State University, 1982.

REFERENCES

Blecha, M. K., Gega, P. C., & Green, M. *Exploring science,* Green book. 2nd edition. River Forest, Ill.: Laidlaw, 1979.

Danis, R. B. The postulation of certain specific, explicit, commonly-shared frames. *Journal of Mathematical Behavior,* 1981, *3* (1), 167–201.

Knott, R., Lawson, C. A., Karplus, R., Thier, H. D., & Montgomery, M. *SCIIS Communities: Teacher's guide.* Chicago: Rand McNally, 1978.

Larkin, J. H., McDermott, J., Simon, D. P., & Simon, H. A. Models of competence in solving physics problems. *Cognitive Science,* 1980, *4* (4), 317–345.

Nussbaum, J., & Novak, J. D. An assessment of childrens' conceptions of the earth using structured interviews. *Science Education,* 1976, *60,* 535–550.

Rowe, M. B. *Teaching science as continuous inquiry: A basic.* 2nd. edition. New York: McGraw-Hill, 1978.

Shayer, M., & Wylam, H. The development of the concepts of heat and temperature in 10–13 year olds. *Journal of Research in Science Teaching,* 1981, *18* (5), 419–435.

Smith, E. L., & Sendelbach, N. B. The programme, the plans, and the activities of the classroom: The demands of activity-based science. In J. Olson (Ed.), *Innovation in the science curriculum: Classroom knowledge and curriculum change.* London: Croom-Helm, 1982.

14

The Problem of "Inconsiderate Text"

Bonnie B. Armbruster

The textbook is a cornerstone of American education. During a decade of class-room observations, John Goodlad (1976) discovered that "the textbook pre-dominated throughout as the medium of instruction, except in kindergarten. With each advance in grade level, dependence on the textbook increased . . ." (p. 14). A study in Texas (EPIE 1974) concluded that students spend 75 percent of their classroom time and 90 percent of their homework time using textbooks and re-lated materials. Given the pervasive influence of textbooks, few people would argue with the following premises: (1) Textbooks should promote understanding and learning, and (2) textbooks should promote learning *important* information. From research on learning from written materials, or text, we know some of the characteristics of text that affect these learning outcomes. The purpose of this chapter is threefold: (1) to present results of research on characteristics of text that affect learning from text and learning *important* information from text, (2) to illustrate these text characteristics with excerpts from actual content area text-books, and (3) to suggest some implications of text factors related to learning for practitioners. A little background in reading theory is prerequisite to an under-standing of research on the role of text in learning.

A BRIEF INTRODUCTION TO A THEORY OF READING

A popular theory of reading is *schema theory*. According to schema theory, a reader's schema, or organized knowledge of the world, provides much of the basis for comprehending, learning, and remembering information in text. Comprehen-sion occurs when the reader activates or constructs a schema that explains events and objects described in a text. As readers first begin to read, they search for a

Portions of this chapter were presented in 1982 at Research Foundations for a Literate America, a conference organized by the Center for the Study of Reading and sponsored by the Hegeier Institute, the Johnson Foundation, the Exxon Education Foundation, the Uni-versity of Illinois Educational Fund, the Monsanto Fund, and the National Institute of Education.

schema to account for the information in the text, and on the basis of the schema, they construct a partial model of the meaning of the text. The model then provides a framework for continuing the search through the text. The model is progressively refined and constrained as the reader gathers more information from the text. Reading comprehension thus involves the progressive focusing and refinement of a complete, plausible, and coherent model of the meaning of the text.

Schema theory underscores the importance of the reader's existing knowledge to text comprehension. Indeed, dozens of experiments have verified the role of background knowledge in understanding and recalling information from text. What the reader brings to the text, however, is not the only factor that affects learning from text. Characteristics of the text itself, by influencing the reader's ability to construct a coherent model of the text's meaning, also affect learning outcomes. The next section discusses some characteristics of text that affect learning outcomes. These characteristics are illustrated with excerpts from actual textbooks.

CHARACTERISTICS OF THE TEXT THAT AFFECT COMPREHENSION AND LEARNING

The most important text characteristic for comprehension and learning is *textual coherence*. The more coherent the text, the more likely the reader will be able to construct a coherent cognitive model of the information in the text. Texts cohere both globally and locally (Armbruster and Anderson 1981, Cirilo 1981). *Global coherence* is achieved by text characteristics that facilitate the integration of high-level, important ideas across the entire section, chapter, or book. *Local coherence* is achieved by several kinds of simple links or ties that connect ideas together within and between sentences.

Global Coherence

Global coherence is achieved by the overall structure or organization of the text. Unfortunately, structure is rather difficult to define. Generally, structure refers to the system of arrangement of ideas in a text and the nature of the relationships connecting the ideas. A few basic text structures appear to capture fundamental patterns of human thought. These structures have been identified by rhetoricians, linguists, and psychologists. The most common structures are these:

1. *Simple-listing*—a listing of items or ideas where the order of presentation of the items is not significant
2. *Comparison/contrast*—a description of similarities and differences between two or more things
3. *Temporal sequence*—a sequential relationship between ideas or events considered in terms of the passage of time
4. *Cause/effect*—an interaction between at least two ideas or events, one considered a cause or reason and the other an effect or result
5. *Problem/solution*—similar to the cause/effect pattern in that two factors interact, one citing a problem and the other a solution to that problem

Another approach to defining text structures has been to identify structures that are somewhat more specialized, that is, appropriate for particular content or text genres (e.g., narratives, newspaper articles, or expository text). A generic structure for *narrative* text has been defined by two so-called story grammars. Story grammars specify the relationship among the story elements (e.g., goals, actions, and outcomes) that underlie narrative accounts. Another specialized text structure is used to describe *systems*. A description of a system (such as the circulatory system of the human body or the exhaust system of an automobile) typically includes information on the function of the system in the larger entity of which it is a part, the components of the system and their individual functions, and the operation of the system. Specialized structures for content-area text are just beginning to be identified (Dansereau, in press; Lunzer, Davies, and Greene 1980).

What research evidence is there that structure makes a difference to a reader who must learn from a text? Perhaps the most decisive evidence comes from the research on story grammars. The consistent result of this research is that memory for stories is superior when the content is organized according to a well-known story grammar (e.g., Mandler and Johnson 1977; Kintsch, Mandel, and Kozminsky 1977; Mandler 1978; Stein 1976; Thorndyke 1977). When the structure of a story is altered by displacing or deleting story parts, readers not only say the stories are less understandable but they also do not remember the stories as well (Thorndyke 1977).

Other evidence for the importance of structure comes from the research of Bonnie Meyer and her colleagues using informative, "textbooklike" prose. Meyer and Freedle[1] showed that changing the structure, while leaving the content the same, affected memory for text. That is, the same ideas could be remembered better when expressed in one type of structure than another. A study by Meyer, Brandt, and Bluth (1978) found that ninth graders who identified the structure of well-organized text and used this structure as the basis of their own recall of the content of the text could remember more from a passage than those who did not use the author's structure. In another study, ninth graders who were taught to identify and use the author's structure dramatically improved their memory for text (Bartlett 1978).

Other research has shown that learning can be affected by how clearly the structure is indicated in the text. Information about structure can be provided in two ways. One way is through "signaling." Meyer (1979) has defined signaling as information in the text that emphasizes certain ideas in the content or points out aspects of the structure. Types of signaling that authors use include (1) explicit statements of the structure or organization; (2) previews or introductory statements, including titles; (3) summary statements; (4) pointer words and phrases such as "an important point is . . ."; and (5) textual cues such as underlining, italics, and boldface. Some research evidence suggests that average students remember more from text that includes signaling devices (see Meyer 1979).

Another means of providing information about structure is through the repeated, consistent use of a particular structure. For example, readers reading a series of stories will remember more of the ideas in later-presented stories if the later stories have the same structure as earlier-presented stories (Thorndyke 1977). Presumably, the reader learns the structure in early presentations of text and comes to expect that ideas in later presentations will be organized in the same way.

This research indicates that text structure *does* have an important effect on learning. If readers know to use the author's structure as a tool in building a coherent model of the text, the following seems to be true: The better organized the text and the more apparent the structure to the reader, the higher the probability that the reader will learn from reading.

In addition to structure, another important contributor to global coherence is *content*. (Actually, content and structure are so related that content might be considered an aspect of structure, as is the content of a story in a story grammar.) One area of research indicates that learning and memory are improved when people are given information clarifying the significance of facts that might otherwise seem arbitrary (Bransford and Johnson 1973; Bransford, Stein, Shelton, and Owings 1980; Dooling and Mullet 1973). Consider the following simple example from Bransford et al. (1980). College students who read sentences such as "The tall man bought the crackers. The bald man read the newspaper. The old man purchased the paint" tend to perform poorly on questions such as, "Which man bought the crackers?" The students rate such sentences as comprehensible, but they have difficulty remembering the sentences, probably because the relationship between each type of man and the actions performed seems arbitrary. Their recall improves dramatically for sentences such as "The tall man bought the crackers that were on the top shelf. The bald man read the newspaper to look for a hat sale. The funny man bought the ring that squirted water." The elaborations clarify the significance of the relationship between each type of man and the action he performs.

The effect of significance-imparting information also holds for longer text. Drawing once again on the research with story grammars, we know that information about a character's goal and events that lead up to a goal has a significant effect on comprehension and memory for narratives (Kintsch and vanDijk 1978, Rumelhart 1977, Thorndyke 1977). Presumably, knowledge of the goal and the events leading up to a goal helps readers understand the significance of a character's actions and the consequences of those actions, and thus aids the reader's effort to build a coherent model of a text. Bransford (in press) has suggested that the reciprocal relationship between structure and function provides the reader with information relative to the significance of the context. For example, readers are better able to understand the significance of differences in the structure of veins and arteries if they know the different functions that veins and arteries perform. In sum, the content an author chooses to include can influence the global coherence of the text. In particular, global coherence is greater when the author establishes a meaningful context for facts that are presented in the text.

Structure in Textbooks. Since structure is a characteristic of extensive prose, it cannot readily be illustrated using short text excerpts. As mentioned, however, authors use signaling devices to indicate the structure of text. Therefore, one index of the structure of the text is the author's use of signaling. One kind of signaling device used universally in textbooks is titles and subtitles. A glance at a table of contents or outline of chapter titles and subtitles can be very revealing. For example, compare these chapter outlines from two different American history textbooks.

Textbook 1[2]	*Textbook 2*[3]
What Were the Problems of the New Government?	Growing Cities, Growing Industries
	Early Cities
A. The Basic Problem	More Cities Grow
B. Economic Troubles	Industrial Growth and Immigration
1. An Empty Treasury	Americans All
2. Economic Depression	Labor Unions
3. The Money Problem	Jane Addams
C. Conflicts Among the States	Americans Prosper
D. Unfriendly Foreign Countries	Cities Today
E. Calling the Constitutional Convention	Industrial and Technical Progress
	Progress Through Inventions
	Technology

The chapter outline from Textbook 1 suggests a better, clearer structure than the chapter outline from Textbook 2. The Textbook 1 chapter outline has an overall structure of "simple-listing"; it is easy to predict that each subtopic will probably be cast in a "cause/effect" or "problem/solution" structure. On the other hand, it is difficult to find any logical structure for the topics from Textbook 2.

Another signaling device is the introduction to a unit or chapter. Some introductions give the reader a good overview of the content and structure of the ideas to follow. Introductions from three social studies textbooks follow.

> Do you remember that, in Unit 2, we said that part of our nation's heritage was change? A terribly important change began in 1776, with the Declaration of Independence. Before that, the people of America were colonists under the rule of England. But after that, they were citizens of an independent country. This unit will tell you about the causes of the Revolution, the war itself, and the early years of the United States.[4]

Here's the beginning of another good introduction, in which the reader is nicely set up for a compare/contrast structure.

> In this chapter, we are going to look at how people in the 13 English colonies lived in the middle of the 1700's. Ways of life differed from colony to colony in 1750. Black slaves in Maryland lived differently from white merchants in Massachusetts. German-speaking farmers in Pennsylvania lived very differently from large land owners living in Virginia.
> Yet there were ways many people in the colonies were alike. ...[5]

Now read the following chapter introduction:

> People worked hard to rebuild and unify America after the Civil War. It was time to move ahead. In 1790 the first census (sen'səs) of the United States was taken. A census is an official count of people. Every 10 years a census is taken in the United States. In 1790 there were 4 million Americans. Most of them were living in small settlements or on farms. Today the United States has more than 220 million people. Most of these people live and work in or near cities.[6]

This introduction is terribly confusing. The first two sentences lead the reader to believe that the chapter will discuss the post-Civil War years, the Reconstruction perhaps. The third sentence changes the topic *and* the time frame. The reader is left wondering what the chapter will be about, not to mention what its structure will be.

Another form of signaling is topic sentences that alert the reader to the organization of upcoming text. The following is a good example of a useful topic sentence as well as the use of markers in the text to reinforce the indicated structure.

> There were five main areas of change related to nationalism. Four of these were *domestic* changes. One involved foreign policy.
> 1. There was a decline in political party struggles. . . .
> 2. The national government gained more power through legislation . . .
> 3. The national government was also strengthened by the decisions of the Supreme Court. . . .
> 4. The population of the United States began to move west. . . .
> 5. In foreign policy, the United States began to assert itself as a power in the Western Hemisphere. . . .

In sum, signaling devices provide some information about structure in textbooks. Titles and subtitles, introductions, and topic sentences can be particularly revealing about the relative degree of structure in the text.

Another aspect of global coherence is the content itself—the inclusion of information that clarifies the significance of facts. For example, in history textbooks, information about motivations and goals can clarify the significance of events. The following textbook excerpt about the building of the first transcontinental railroad does not include information about motivations and goals.

> Many Americans wanted a railroad that would connect the East to the West. In 1862, Congress passed a law to build the first transcontinental rail line. The Central Pacific and Union Pacific railroad companies were formed to do the work. Find these railroads on the map on page 251.
> The Central Pacific's line headed east from Sacramento, California. Workers laid track through the Sierra Nevada, which are high mountains. The workers built trestles and hauled dirt to make a level roadbed. They hunted for passes through the mountains. They blasted tunnels through solid rock. Once across the mountains, they worked in the heat of the deserts.
> The Union Pacific's line headed west from Omaha, Nebraska. Its workers faced attacks by Indians who knew that the railroads would bring millions of white people to their lands. The builders also had trouble with herds of buffalo tearing up tracks. The Union Pacific hired hunters to kill the buffalo. Armed guards fought the Indians.
> On both lines, the rail companies began running trains as soon as a section of track was laid. Now settlers could go west by train.
> On May 10, 1869, the two lines met at Promontory, Utah. A golden spike was hammered to hold the last rail in place. A worker described what happened:
> When they came to drive the last spike, Governor Stanford, president of the Central Pacific, took the hammer. The first time he struck he missed the spike and hit the rail.
> What a howl went up! Irish, Chinese, Mexicans, and everybody yelled with delight. "He missed it. Yee." The engineers blew the whistles and rang their bells. Then Stanford tried it again and tapped the spike. The tap was

reported by telegraph in all the offices east and west. It set bells to ringing in hundreds of towns and cities.[8]

This text presents a colorful, interesting, detailed description of an event; however, the text includes nothing about the *significance* of the event: Why was the railroad built in the first place? What important changes did it precipitate?

The following excerpt does a better job of establishing the significance of building railroads by answering the question "Why were railroads needed?"

To make a profit from their land, farmers had to send their crops to market. To work their land, they needed tools from city factories. As factories grew to supply the nation's wants, the factories consumed more and more raw materials—iron, wood, and cotton. To keep the whole process going, the vast nation, spread across a continent, needed transportation. The nation was already served by its broad rivers, its many canals, and roadways. But there had to be easier, speedier ways.[9]

Because readers are told the motivation for building railroads, it is likely they will learn more about the building of the transcontinental railroad.

The following excerpt on cities of the Middle Atlantic states is another example of text lacking global coherence because the author was not included information clarifying the significance of the facts.

The capital of Pennsylvania is Harrisburg. A large number of people there work for the government. Many others work in clothing and shoe factories. Steel is also an important industry, as it is in Pittsburgh.

New Jersey's capital is Trenton. It has many factories. Making electrical goods, metal products, machinery, and rubber products are leading industries. Trenton is also a printing and publishing center. About one-third of the people there work for the government.

Newark is New Jersey's largest city. It is the third largest insurance center in the United States and a major banking center. Newark has many factories. The chief industries make electrical equipment, metal products, and processed foods. Newark is a leading New Jersey port and air cargo center.

Wilmington is Delaware's largest city. It is one of our country's largest chemical and petrochemical centers. A petrochemical is made from petroleum or natural gas. Wilmington's factories make automobiles, steel, plastics, dyes, textiles, and rubber and leather products. Dover, the capital of Delaware, is in a rich farming region. Its chief industries are canning, airplane repairing, and rubber products.[10]

The text is really nothing more than a list of facts that could only be "learned" by rote memorization. Information about the relationships among location, natural resources, and economy would help readers understand the significance of the facts and thus improve their chances of truly learning something important about cities of the Middle Atlantic states.

In the next section of the chapter, we turn to another aspect of text that influences comprehension and learning—local coherence.

Local Coherence

Local coherence functions like a "a linguistic mortar to connect ideas in the text together" (Tierney and Mosenthal 1980). Local coherence is achieved by means of several kinds of cohesive ties—linguistic forms that help carry meaning across phrase, clause, and sentence boundaries. Examples of common cohesive ties are *pronoun reference*, or the use of a pronoun to refer to a previously mentioned noun ("The doctor will be back shortly. He's with a patient now"); *substitution*, or replacement of a word or words for a previously mentioned noun phrase, verb phrase, or clause ("My pen is out of ink. I need a new *one*"); *conjunctions* or *connectives* ("I'd give you a hand, *but* I'm busy"). A rather large body of research has established the importance of cohesive ties in understanding and remembering text.

One area of research has demonstrated that repeated references that help to carry meaning across sentence boundaries can decrease reading time and increase recall of text as an integrated unit (de Villiers 1974; Kintsch, Kozminsky, Streby, McKoon, and Keenan 1975; Miller and Kintsch 1980; Haviland and Clark 1974; Manelis and Yekovich 1976). As an example (Manelis and Yekovich 1976), people can read faster and remember better sentences such as "Arnold lunged at Norman. Norman called the doctor. The doctor arrived" than the sentences "Arnold lunged. Norman called. The doctor arrived." Even though the first sentence set is longer, cohesive referential ties render it easier to learn and remember than the second sentence set.

Another area of research has indicated that children prefer to read, are able to read faster, and have better memory for sentences connected by explicit conjunctions, particularly causal connectives, than sentences in which the conjunction is left to be inferred (Katz and Brent 1968, Marshall and Glock 1978–79, Pearson 1974–75). For example, in the study by Pearson (1974–75), third and fourth graders were asked which of several sentences they would prefer to use in answering a "Why" question. They selected sentences such as "Because John was lazy, he slept all day" over sentences such as "John was lazy. He slept all day." The children also recalled sentences with an explicit conjunction better than sentences in which the connective was left implicit. Thus, sentences with explicit conjunctions produced better comprehension and recall even though the added conjunction increased the grammatical complexity of the sentence.

The explanation for the consistent finding that more cohesive text is read faster and remembered better goes something like the following: Readers try to find a coherent model or interpretation of the text. When an incohesive text makes this difficult, readers spend extra time and cognitive energy to remediate the incohesiveness. The reread the text to search for the link, or they search through their memories to retrieve the connection, or they make an inference about a possible relationship. With this extra effort, mature readers may be able to form a coherent interpretation of the text. Children have less chance for successfully reading such text. They are less likely to know that rereading text and searching memory are appropriate "fix-up" strategies (Armbruster, Echols, and Brown 1982). Children are also less likely than adults to be able to infer connections when coherence breaks down, simply because they have less linguistic and world knowledge to draw upon. Thus, local coherence in the form of strong, explicit cohesive ties is particularly important in textbooks for children.

One index of local coherence is the explicit statement of relationships among ideas, particularly causal relationships. The following paragraph is an excerpt from a sixth-grade textbook. Many of the connectives indicating relationships are missing and left to be referred.

In the evening, the light fades. Photosynthesis slows down. The amount of carbon dioxide in the air space builds up again. This buildup of carbon dioxide makes the guard cells relax. The openings are closed.[11]

The paragraph below is a more coherent version of the same content; local coherence is improved because the relationships are more explicit.

What happens to these processes in the evening? The fading light of evening causes photosynthesis to slow down. Respiration, however, does not depend on light and thus continues to produce carbon dioxide. The carbon dioxide in the air spaces builds up again, which makes the guard cells relax. The relaxing of the guard cells closes the leaf openings. Consequently, the leaf openings close in the evenings as photosynthesis slows down.

Here is another pair of examples; the second is more coherent than the first.

Many of the farmers who moved in from New England were independent farmers. Land cost about a dollar an acre. Most men could afford to set up their own farms. Livestock farming was quite common on the frontier. Hogs could be fed in the forests. The cost of raising hogs was low.[12]

Most of the farmers who moved in from New England were independent farmers. Being an independent farmer means that the farmer can afford to own his own farm. Around 1815, most men could afford to own their own farms because lands was cheap—it cost only about a dollar an acre. Many of these independent farms were livestock farms. For example, many frontier farmers raised hogs. Hog farming was common because hogs were inexpensive to keep. The cost of raising hogs was low because the farmer did not have to buy special feed for the hogs. The hogs did not need special feed because they could eat plants that grew in the surrounding forests.

The order of presentation of events in a text is another index of local coherence. The order of presentation should generally proceed from the first event to the final events, especially in textbooks for younger children. Young readers can become confused if the order of events in the textbook does not match the order of actual occurrence. For older readers, the temporal sequence may not be so critical. However, for most students, it would seem that the text should remain consistent and not skip around in time. Text that changes the order of events in time may send the reader on a wild goose chase; the reader may be unwilling to put forth the effort to figure out the temporal or logical order that underpins the order of presentation in the text.

In the following paragraph from a textbook, the order of events is not consistent. The sentences are numbered so that commentary is easier to follow.

[1]Adult female alligators make large cone-shaped nests from mud and compost. [2]The female lays from 15 to 100 eggs with leathery shells in the nest and then covers it. [3]The heat from both the sun and the decaying compost keeps the eggs warm. [4]The eggs hatch in about nine weeks. [5]Unlike other reptiles that hatch from eggs, baby alligators make sounds while they are still in the shell. [6]The mother than bites off the nest so the baby alligators can get out. [7]When first hatched, baby alligators are about 15 to 25 cm long.[13]

Note the many shifts in the temporal sequence. The first four sentences are fine; they present the order of events from earliest to latest. The fifth sentence reverts back to when the baby alligators were still in the shell. The time frame for the sixth sentence is unclear, because readers don't know when the alligators leave the nest. The final sentence returns to when the baby alligators were first hatched.

Another index of local coherence is clarity of references. The following excerpt illustrates a confusing use of pronoun reference—the pronoun "they." Does "they" refer to "the people from the North" or "the Bronze Age people"?

> The people from the North learned from the Bronze Age people. They were skilled workers and traders. They made fine tools and jewelry from metals. They traded their beautiful cloth and pottery to peoples around the Mediterranean. They kept records of their trade on clay tablets.[14]

This section has reviewed research that establishes the importance of textual coherence—structure and cohesion—in texts. The more coherent the text itself, the more coherent the cognitive model the reader is likely to construct of that text. Textual coherence is particularly important for children, who may not have sufficient linguistic experience and background knowledge to infer the content and relationships absent in incoherent text. This section also presented some excerpts of textbook prose that illustrate aspects of textual coherence. In the next section we look at characteristics of text that affect students' ability to learn *important* information from text.

CHARACTERISTICS OF TEXT THAT AFFECT TYPE OF INFORMATION LEARNED

One obvious determinant of the type of information that will be learned from text is the type of information *included* in the text. While the research evidence on this point is slim, a series of studies by Reder and Anderson (1980) is pertinent. In these experiments, college students read one of two versions of an introductory chapter from a college textbook. They read either the original version or a summary version one fifth the length of the original. When tested, students who had read the summary version were better able to recognize important facts and learn new, related material than students who had read the full version. Reder and Anderson (1980) concluded that helping students focus attention in contrast to having them shift attention between main points and details is an effective way to aid learning. Although the evidence is not conclusive, it suggests that including excessive details in text distracts students from learning important information.

Another determinant of what is learned from text is the kinds of questions students are asked about the material they are reading. Numerous studies have demonstrated that students tend to study and learn information they expect to be tested on (see Anderson and Armbruster 1980). Questions typically appear at the end of sections or chapters. One line of research examined the effect on learning of questions that are inserted periodically in the text. These studies have shown that questions inserted in the text have a striking focusing effect on studying behaviors and learning outcomes. Students tend to spend more time studying text relevant to the inserted questions and they tend to perform better on posttest items testing the type of information tapped by the inserted questions (Reynolds, Standiford, and Anderson 1979). The implication of this research is that questions asked of students should reflect the kind of information we want them to study and learn. If we want them to study and learn important information, we should ask them important questions.

Textbooks vary in the relative emphasis given to "important" and "unimportant" points, or "main ideas" and "details." To illustrate the variation in emphasis, let's compare excerpts from two fifth-grade textbooks, each about 450 pages long, on the topic "Washington, D.C." In the first excerpt, information on Washington, D.C., appears in a section entitled "We have a national government." The first five subsections, 14 paragraphs of prose, discuss the Constitution and the three branches of government. The last three subsections, also 14 paragraphs, describe Washington, D.C. (A map of the city and five pictures also accompany the text on Washington, D.C.) Here are three paragraphs from the text on Washington, D.C.:

> Washington, D.C., is located on the winding Potomac River. As its center is the Capitol Building. Its white dome rises 300 feet (90 m) above the round center of the building. On each side is a large wing. In the right wing an entrance leads to the chamber where the Senate meets. The entrance in the left wing leads to the chamber where the Representatives gather. There are 540 rooms in the Capitol. These rooms include committee rooms, offices, and rooms where visitors can watch Congress at work.
>
> Look at the map of Washington. Notice how the Capitol faces a long mall. This green, park-like mall leads to the tall Washington Monument. It is 555 feet (170 m) high. It is covered with white marble that is 7 inches (18 cm) thick. The inside of the monument is hollow. It has an elevator to carry visitors to the top.
>
> ... The White House has 132 rooms. Five of these are open to the public. Special dinners and receptions are held in them. The State Dining Room can hold as many as 140 people for dinner. The Blue Room is where the President greets guests. The walls of the Green Room are covered with light green silk. The room is used as a sitting room. So is the Red Room. The largest room in the White House is the East Room. It is 79 feet (24 m) long and 37 feet (11 m) wide.[15]

In a section that purports to be on the vast topic of the national government, more space is devoted to the White House than to the legislative branch of government, and more detail is provided about the Capitol Building than the job of the President.

A less intense treatment of Washington, D.C., appears in the following excerpt:

> Washington, D.C., is our nation's capital. The most important business of the city is conducted in the Senate, the House of Representatives, the President's office, and in many other buildings where people work for our government.
>
> Our nation's capital is built on the Potomac River in the District of Columbia. This location was approved by George Washington, and the land was donated to our nation by the state of Maryland.[16]

The kinds of questions that appear at the ends of chapters and in unit tests also influence whether important information will be learned from textbooks. Ideally there should be a balance between "main idea" questions about the most important information and questions about facts, details, and supporting information. I recently completed a small-scale survey of questions asked in four textbook units, one unit from each of four fifth-grade social studies textbooks. I counted the total number of questions asked about the text in these units and then the number of questions that asked for information found in no more than five contiguous sentences of text. These questions asked for information such as names, dates, places, definitions, and lists of facts; I will thus call them "detail" questions. The total number of questions included in these four units ranged from 40 to 66. The percent of "detail" questions ranged from 44 to 88 percent, with an average of 70 percent. Two of the four textbooks contained unit tests. The unit test of one textbook contained 82 percent "detail" questions and the unit test of the other textbook contained 100 percent "detail" questions. In these textbooks at least, the detail questions far outweigh the main idea questions; the questions may be shaping students to attend to details at the expense of main ideas.

So far, this chapter has presented research evidence about characteristics of text that influence comprehension and learning in general and the learning of important information in particular. Excerpts from actual textbooks illustrated text that violated these research-based principles of effective learning. I call such text "inconsiderate text" after Kantor (1977). I cannot accurately estimate what proportion of the prose in textbooks is inconsiderate. However, my investigation of textbooks over the past three years has convinced me that during their elementary school years, children read many pages of inconsiderate text from poorly written textbooks. The next section presents some implications for practitioners of the existence of inconsiderate text.

IMPLICATIONS FOR PRACTITIONERS

Knowledge of text characteristics that influence learning outcomes could have an impact on comprehension instruction in two major way: (1) by helping textbook adoption committees make more informed decisions about selecting textbooks, and (2) by suggesting the need for teachers to help students learn from inconsiderate text.

Textbook adoptions are often made without consideration of text characteristics that influence learning. Decisions about which textbook to adopt are often made on the basis of "content coverage," aesthetic appeal (i.e., number of color illustrations and format), apparent ease of using the teacher's manuals, and other aspects of the textbook unrelated to the text itself.

Usually, the only "assessment" of the text itself has been done by the publisher in the form of assurances that the textbook has a given "readability" level as determined by readability formulas. These formulas yield an index that supposedly makes it possible to match the reading demands of textbooks with the reading capabilities of the reader. Two of the better known readability formulas, Dale-Chall (1948) and Fry (1977), use measures of word difficulty and sentence length to determine the appropriate reading level of the text. Readability formulas do *not* measure the kinds of text variables discussed in this chapter.

I believe that wiser decisions about textbook selections could be made if adoption committees also considered the text itself. Ideally, candidate textbooks should be "tried out" on a representative sample of students. A measure of the relative ease of learning from the candidate textbooks would be student performance on criterion tests reflecting curriculum objectives. Limitations of time and resources usually preclude this method of textbook evaluation. An alternative procedure is to evaluate samples of text from the candidate textbooks with respect to the characteristics of text known to influence learning outcomes. It is important for the evaluator to remember that as mature, competent readers who are experts in the content area, they may judge text to be considerate that their younger, less skilled, novice students would find inconsiderate. Therefore, it is important for adoption committee members to try to assume the perspective (e.g., age and prior knowledge) of the student who will be reading the textbook.

The short-term effect of following the proposed procedure would be better textbooks for the immediate target audience; the long-term effect would be better textbooks in general. By rejecting the more inconsiderate textbooks, adoption committees would be sending the message to publishers that they will not tolerate inconsiderate textbooks. Since publishers respond to market pressures, the result is likely to be production of more considerate textbooks in the future.

Until textbooks change, students still have to deal with inconsiderate text. The second major way that knowledge of text characteristics can have an impact is by suggesting to teachers the need to help students learn from inconsiderate text. One way teachers deal with textbooks that students find difficult to read is to put the books back on the shelf and resort to telling students the content. While this strategy may accomplish the immediate curriculum objectives, the long-term result is that students will not learn how to read and learn from content-area textbooks. Instead, teachers need to be encouraged and helped to teach students to read textbooks, including inconsiderate textbooks. By knowing text characteristics that influence learning, teachers at least know what aspects of the text may be causing learning difficulties. Teachers may thus help students overcome these problems, for example, by suggesting an appropriate structure, by clarifying an unclear referent, or by encouraging students to make reasonable inferences about missing connectives.

CONCLUSION

This chapter has presented evidence that many characteristics of text have an important influence on *how much* and *what* students will learn from reading a textbook. There is strong evidence that students will understand and learn more from text that is coherent. Coherent text has a clear overall structure that establishes the significance of the ideas presented and has tight cohesive ties that bind the ideas together. Students will learn more important information from a textbook that emphasizes main ideas and asks questions about important understandings. "Inconsiderate" text, text that is neither conducive to learning in general nor to the learning of important information, was illustrated by several excerpts from actual content-area textbooks. Finally, the chapter highlighted two practical implications of work on factors of text related to learning. One implication is the need for textbook adoption committees to give serious consideration to factors of coherence and importance when evaluating and selecting textbooks. A second implication is the need for teachers to be aware of the problems of inconsiderate text in order to help students cope with such materials.

NOTES

1. B. J. F. Meyer and R. O. Freedle. *Effects of discourse type on recall.* Unpublished manuscript, Arizona State University, Tempe, Ariz., 1979.

2. S. Schwartz and J. R. O'Connor. *Exploring our nation's history, Vol. 1, The developing years.* New York: Globe Book, 1971.

3. A. Y. King, I. Dennis, and F. Potter. *The United States and the other Americans.* New York: Macmillan, 1982.

4. H. H. Gross, D. W. Follett, R. E. Gabler, W. L. Burton, and B. F. Ahlschwede. *Exploring our world: The Americas.* Chicago: Follett, 1980. P. 173.

5. S. Klein. *Our country's history.* New York: Scholastic Book Services, 1981. P. 117.

6. King, Dennis, and Potter. *The United States and the other Americas.* P. 126.

7. J. Abramowitz. *American History.* 5th edition. Chicago: Follett, 1979. P. 231.

8. R. M. Berg. *Scott, Foresman social studies (Grade 5).* Glenview, Ill.: Scott, Foresman, 1979.

9. D. J. Boorstin and B. M. Kelley. *A history of the United States.* Lexington, Mass.: Ginn, 1981. P. 344.

10. King, Dennis, and Potter. *The United States and the other Americas.* P. 184.

11. J. Bendick and R. Gallant. *Elementary Science 6.* Lexington, Mass.: Ginn, 1980. P. 71.

12. L. Senesh. *The American way of life.* Chicago: Science Research Associates, 1973. P. 149.

13. C. F. Berger, G. D. Berkheimer, L. E. Lewis, Jr., and H. J. Neuberger. *Houghton Mifflin Science (6).* Boston: Houghton Mifflin, 1979. P. 55.

14. G. S. Dawson. *Our world.* Lexington, Mass.: Ginn, 1979. P. 29.

15. G. S. Brown. *The country.* Lexington, Mass.: Ginn, 1982. PP. 246–248.

16. Gross et al. *Exploring our world: The Americas.* P. 168.

REFERENCES

Anderson, T. H., & Armbruster, B. B. *Studying.* Tech. Rep. No. 155. Urbana: University of Illinois, Center for the Study of Reading, January 1980.

Armbruster, B. B., & Anderson, T. H. *Content-area textbooks* Reading Ed. Rep. No. 23. Urbana: University of Illinois, Center for the Study of Reading, July 1981.

Armbruster, B. B., Echols, C., & Brown, A. L. The role of metacognition in reading to learn: A developmental perspective. *Volta Review*, 1982, *84* (5), 45–56.

Bartlett, B. J. *Top-level structure as an organizational strategy for recall of classroom text.* Unpublished doctoral dissertation, Arizona State University, 1978.

Bransford, J. D. Schema activation and schema acquisition: Comments on Richard C. Anderson's remarks. In R. C. Anderson, J. Osborn, & R. J. Tierney (Eds.), *Learning to read in American schools: Basal readers and content texts.* Hillsdale, N.J.: Erlbaum, in press.

Bransford, J. R., & Johnson, M. K. Considerations of some problems of comprehension. In W. Chase (Ed.), *Visual information processing.* New York: Academic Press, 1973.

Bransford, J. D., Stein, B. S., Shelton, T. S., & Owings, R. Cognition and adaptation: The importance of learning to learn. In J. Harvey (Ed.), *Cognition, social behavior and the environment*. Hillsdale, N.J.: Erlbaum, 1980.

Cirilo, R. K. Referential coherence and text structure in story comprehension. *Journal of Verbal Learning and Verbal Behavior*, 1981, *20*, 358–367.

Dansereau, D. F. Learning strategy research. In J. Segal, S. Chipman, & R. Glaser (Eds.), *Thinking and learning skills: Relating instruction to basic research*, vol. 1. Hillsdale, N.J.: Erlbaum, in press.

de Villiers, P. A. Imagery and theme in recall of connected discourse. *Journal of Experimental Psychology*, 1974, *103*, 263–268.

Dooling, D. J., & Mullet, R. L. Locus of thematic effects in retention of prose. *Journal of Experimental Psychology*, 1973, *97*, 404–406.

EPIE Institute: *Fits and misfits: What you should know about your child's learning materials*. Columbia, Md.: National Committee for Citizens in Education, 1974.

Goodlad, J. I. *Facing the future: Issues in education and schooling*. New York: McGraw-Hill, 1976.

Haviland, S. E., & Clark, H. H. What's new? Acquiring new information as a process in comprehension. *Journal of Verbal Learning and Verbal Behavior*, 1974, *13*, 512–521.

Kantor, R. N. Anomoly, inconsiderateness, and linguistic competence. In D. M. Lance & D. E. Gulstad (Eds.), *Proceedings of the 1977 Mid-America Linguistics Conference*. Columbia, Mo.: University of Missouri, 1977.

Katz, E., & Brent, S. Understanding connections. *Journal of Verbal Learning and Verbal Behavior*, 1968, *1*, 501–509.

Kintsch, W., Kozminsky, E., Streby, W. J., McKoon, G., & Keenan, J. M. Comprehension and recall of text as a function of content variables. *Journal of Verbal Learning and Verbal Behavior*, 1975, *14*, 196–214.

Kintsch, W., Mandel, T. S., & Kozminsky, E. Summarizing scrambled stories. *Memory and Cognition*, 1977, *5*, 547–552.

Kintsch, W., & van Dijk, T. Toward a model of text comprehension and production. *Psychological Review*, 1978, *85*, 363–394.

Lunzer, E., Davies, F., & Greene, T. *Reading for learning in science*. Schools Council Project Report. Nottingham, England: University of Nottingham, School of Education, 1980.

Mandler, J. M. A code in the node: The use of a story schema in retrieval. *Discourse Processes*, 1978, *1*, 14–35.

Mandler, J. M., & Johnson, N. S. Remembrance of things parsed: Story structure and recall. *Cognitive Psychology*, 1977, *9*, 111–151.

Manelis, L., & Yekovich, F. R. Repetitions of propositional arguments in sentences. *Journal of Verbal Learning and Verbal Behavior*, 1976, *15*, 301–312.

Marshall, N., & Glock, M. D. Comprehension of connected discourse: A study into the relationship between the structure of text and information recalled. *Reading Research Quarterly*, 1978–79, *16*, 10–56.

Meyer, B. J. Organizational patterns in prose and their use in reading. In M. L. Kamil & A. J. Moe (Eds.), *Reading research: Studies and applications*. Twenty-eighth Yearbook of the National Reading Conference, 1979, 109–117.

Meyer, B. J. F., Brandt, D. M., & Bluth, G. J. *Use of author's schema: Key to ninth graders' comprehension.* Paper presented at the meeting of the American Educational Research Association, Toronto, March 1978.

Miller, J. R., & Kintsch, W. Readability and recall of short prose passages: A theoretical analysis. *Journal of Experimental Psychology: Human Learning and Memory*, 1980, *6*, 335–354.

Pearson, P. D. The effects of grammatical complexity on children's comprehension, recall, and conception of certain semantic relations. *Reading Research Quarterly*, 1974–75, *10*, 155–192.

Reder, L. M., & Anderson, J. R. A comparison of texts and their summaries: Memorial consequences. *Journal of Verbal Learning and Verbal Behavior*, 1980, *19*, 121–134.

Reynolds, R. E., Standiford, S. N., & Anderson, R. C. Distribution of reading time when questions are asked about a restricted category of text information. *Journal of Educational Psychology*, 1979, *71*, 183–190.

Rumelhart, D. E. Understanding and summarizing brief stories. In D. LaBerge & J. Samuels (Eds.), *Basic processes in reading: Perception and Comprehension.* Hillsdale, N.J.: Erlbaum, 1977.

Stein, N. L. *The effects of increasing temporal disorganization on children's recall of stories.* Paper presented at the Psychonomic Society Meetings, St. Louis, November 1976.

Thorndyke, P. W. Cognitive structures in comprehension and memory of narrative discourse. *Cognitive Psychology*, 1977, *9*, 77–110.

Tierney, R. J., & Mosenthal, J. *Discourse comprehension and production: Analyzing text structure and cohesion.* Tech. Rep. No. 152. Urbana: University of Illinois, Center for the study of Reading, January 1980.

Summary of Part III

Text and Comprehension Instruction

The way texts are prepared can either help or hinder students' comprehension and, ultimately, the teacher's responsibility for providing comprehension instruction. Davison illustrated how the demand for texts written according to formula has inadvertently created texts that are frustrating or boring. Schmidt et al. looked at the content of basal texts and found that large numbers of selections were content neutral—they contained little substantive content. Similarly, Osborn looked at the instructional content of workbooks and found little of value. The examination of content-area textbooks also yielded disconcerting findings. Anderson and Smith found that text materials failed to override the scientific misconceptions held by students, while Armbruster found that structures in text can hinder comprehension.

On the surface, these may sound like negative findings. In fact, they are positive in that they establish specific characteristics that make for readable text. With such knowledge, teachers are in a position to improve comprehension instruction in two ways: (1) by using the characteristics of readable text to select for students reading material that expedites the task of learning how to comprehend and, (2) by adjusting instruction to compensate for inadequacies in text when these are present.

SELECTED BIBLIOGRAPHY, PART III

Aaronson, D., & Scarborough, H. S. Performance theories for sentence coding: Some quantitative models. *Journal of Verbal Learning and Verbal Behavior*, 1977, *16*, 277–303.

Allen, F. G. Analyze the "what" before you write the "how to." *Industrial Education*, 1974, *63*, 34–36.

Anderson, R. C. Reynolds, R. E. Schallert, D. L., & Goetz, E. T. Frameworks for comprehending discourse. *American Educational Research Journal*, 1977, *14*, 367–382.

Anderson, R. C., Spiro, R. J., & Anderson, M. C. Schemata as scaffolding for the representation of information in connected discourse. *American Educational Research Journal*, 1978, *15*, 433–440.

Anderson, R. C., Spiro, R. J., & Montague, W. E. (Eds.). *Schooling and the acquisition of knowledge*. Hillsdale, N.J.: Erlbaum, 1977.

Anderson, T. H., Armbruster, B. B., & Kantor, R. N. *How clearly written are children's textbooks? Or, of bladderworts and alfa*. Reading Education Report No. 16. Urbana: University of Illinois, Center for the Study of Reading, August 1980.

Beauchamp, W. A preliminary experimental study of the technique in the mastery of subject-matter in elementary physical science. *Supplementary Educational Monographs*, 1923, *24*.

Beck, I., McKeown, M., McCaslin, E., & Burkes, A. *Instructional dimensions that may affect reading comprehension: Examples from two commercial reading programs*. Pittsburgh: University of Pittsburgh, Learning Research and Development Center, 1979.

Blom, G. E., Waite, R. R., & Zimet, S. G. A motivational content analysis of children's primers. In H. Levin & J. P. Williams (Eds.), *Basic studies on reading*. New York: Basic Books, 1970.

Chall, J. An analysis of textbooks in relation to declining SAT scores. Appendix to *On further examination: Report of the advisory panel on the Scholastic Aptitude Test score decline*. Princeton, N.J.: College Entrance Examination Board, 1977.

Davison, A., Kantor, R. N., Hannah, J., Hermon, G., Lutz, R., & Salzillo, R. *Limitations of readability formulas in guiding adaptation of texts*. Tech. Rep. No. 162. Urbana: University of Illinois, Center for the Study of Reading, March 1980. ERIC Document Reproduction Service No. ED 184 090.

Goetz, E. T., & Armbruster, B. B. Psychological correlates of text structure. In R. J. Spiro, B. C. Bruce, & W. F. Brewer (Eds.), *Theoretical issues in reading comprehension*. Hillsdale, N.J.: Erlbaum, 1980.

Kieras, D. E. Good and bad structure in simple paragraphs: Effects on apparent theme, reading time, and recall. *Journal of Verbal Learning and Verbal Behavior*, 1978, *17*, 13–28.

Kintsch, W., & Greene, E. The role of culture-specific schematic in the comprehension and recall of stories. *Discourse Processes*, 1978, *1*, 1–13.

Kintsch, W., Kozminsky, E., Streby, W. J., McKoon, G., & Keenan, J. M. Comprehension and recall of text as a function of content variables. *Journal of Verbal Learning and Verbal Behavior*, 1975, *14*, 196–214.

Klare, G. R. *The measurement of readability*. Ames: Iowa State University Press, 1963.

Lakoff, R. If's, and's, and but's about conjunctions. In C. J. Fillmore & D. T. Langendoen (Eds.), *Studies in linguistic semantics*. New York: Holt, Rinehart and Winston, 1971.

Langacker, R. W. On pronominalization and the chain of command. In D. A. Reibel & S. A. Schane (Eds.), *Modern studies in English*. Englewood Cliffs, N.J.: Prentice-Hall, 1969. PP. 160–186.

Lesgold, A. M. Pronominalization: A device for unifying sentences in memory. *Journal of Verbal Learning and Verbal Behavior*, 1972, *11*, 316–323.

Levin, H., & Kaplan, E. L. Grammatical structure and reading. In H. Levin &

J. P. Williams (Eds.), *Basic studies on reading*. New York: Basic Books, 1970.

Mandler, J. M., & Johnson, N. S. Remembrance of things parsed: Story structure and recall. *Cognitive Psychology*, 1977, *9*, 111–151.

Manelis, L., & Yekovich, F. R. Repetitions of propositional arguments in sentences. *Journal of Verbal Learning and Verbal Behavior*, 1976, *15*, 301–312.

Newport, E., & Bellugi, U. Linguistic expression of category levels in a visual-gestural language: A flower is a flower is a flower. In E. Rosch & B. B. Lloyd (Eds.), *Cognition and organization*. Hillsdale, N.J.: Erlbaum, 1978.

Nezworski, T., Stein, N. L., & Trabasso, T. *Story structure versus content effects on children's recall and evaluative inferences*. Tech. Rep. No. 129. Urbana: University of Illinois, Center for the Study of Reading, June 1979. ERIC Document Reproduction Service No. ED 172 187.

Nolen, P. S. Reading nonstandard materials: A study of grades two and four. *Child Development*, 1972, *43*, 1092–1097.

Olson, D. From utterance to text: The bias of language in speech and writing. *Harvard Educational Review*, 1977, *47*.

Pearson, P. D. The effects of grammatical complexity on children's comprehension, recall, and conception of certain semantic relations. *Reading Research Quarterly*, 1974–75, *10*, 155–192.

Pikulsky, J. J., & Jones, M. B. Writing directions children can read. *Reading Teacher*, 1977, *30*, 598–602.

Propp, V. I. *Morphology of the folk-tale*. Austin: University of Texas Press, 1958.

Reynolds, R. E., & Anderson, R. C. *Influences of questions on the allocation of attention during reading*. Tech. Rep. No. 183. Urbana: University of Illinois, Center for the Study of Reading, October 1980.

Robertson, J. E. Pupil understanding of connectives in reading. *Reading Research Quarterly*, 1968, *3*, 387–417.

Rubin, A. D. A theoretical taxonomy of the differences between oral and written language. In R. J. Spiro, B. C. Bruce, & W. F. Brewer (Eds.), *Theoretical issues in reading comprehension*. Hillsdale, N.J.: Erlbaum, 1980.

Ruddell, R. B. The effect of the similarity of oral and written patterns of language structure on reading comprehension. *Elementary English*, 1965, *42*, 403–410.

Schallert, D. L. The role of illustration in reading comprehension. In R. J. Spiro, B. C. Bruce, & W. F. Brewer (Eds.), *Theoretical issues in reading comprehension*. Hillsdale, N.J.: Erlbaum, 1980.

Schallert, D. L., Kleiman, G. M., & Rubin, A. D. *Analysis of differences between oral and written language*. Tech. Rep. No. 29. Urbana: University of Illinois, Center for the Study of Reading, April 1977.

Schmidt, E. L. *What makes reading difficult: The complexity of structures*. Paper presented at the annual meeting of the National Reading Conference, New Orleans, 1977.

Shimmerlik, S. M. Organization theory and memory for prose: A review of the literature. *Review of Educational Research*, 1978, *48*, 103–120.

Showell, R. Reading instructions. *Reading*, 1978, *12*, 30–38.

PART IV

Comprehension Instruction as Verbal Communication

Parts 2 and 3 focused on important instructional considerations. In Part 2, comprehension instruction was viewed from the perspective of constraints posed by teacher thinking, classroom environment, and school context. In Part 3, comprehension instruction was viewed from the perspective of the text students are expected to comprehend and the way features of text may expedite or impede comprehension.

This section goes beyond the previous two. It assumes that, regardless of constraints, text, or both, comprehension instruction ultimately involves teachers communicating to students about how to comprehend. The five chapters in this section all focus on the nature of this verbal communication.

While all five chapters focus on what teachers say during comprehension instruction, and even seem to agree that such verbal instruction should be explicit, there are nevertheless two decidedly distinct positions presented. The first three chapters (by Pearson, by Raphael and Gavelak, and by Palincsar) argue that the teacher's verbal communication during comprehension instruction should focus on strategies that reflect how comprehension occurs but does not specify the processes themselves. Hence, Pearson (Chapter 15) argues for strategic techniques that help students understand the demands of reading tasks and whether these are being understood; Raphael and Gavelek (Chapter 16) argue for the value of questioning as a strategy for generating comprehension; and Palinosar (Chapter 17) argues for putting students in the role of the teacher as a strategy for enhancing comprehension. Each chapter shows how the respective strategy helps improve comprehension. These three chapters are a contrast to the last two, which emphasize explicit explanations of the processes of comprehension (Chapter 18) and the content of the text (Chapter 19) and raise questions about how the teacher's verbal communication during comprehension instruction can be focused on information about the comprehension process itself, such as the goals for the lesson, error responses of students, and organization of newly acquired concepts.

15

Direct Explicit Teaching of Reading Comprehension

P. David Pearson

The time has come to begin a vigorous program of research that directly addresses the issue of how we can improve the reading comprehension abilities of students in our schools. Our knowledge of basic processes in reading and instructional processes in classrooms, while not complete, is sufficient to allow us to begin to apply knowledge about comprehension *and* instruction to issues of reading comprehension instruction.

In this chapter I summarize briefly important conclusions from research on basic cognitive processes involved in reading comprehension. I then do the same for research on classroom instruction. Next, I discuss what we have learned about how reading comprehension *is taught* (or is *not* taught) in today's schools. After that, I discuss the few experimental studies conducted in which experimenters have tried to intervene in the ecology of the school in order to improve students' reading comprehension. Finally, I speculate about promising directions that such research might take.

BASIC COGNITIVE PROCESSES IN READING COMPREHENSION

The first thing to note about the cognitively oriented research of the 1970s is that it was not directed so much toward reading comprehension as it was toward understanding how information of any sort, including information represented by graphic symbols on a page, is stored and processed. In other words, the research has been as much about attention, encoding, inference, memory storage, and retrieval as it has been about reading comprehension. This is as it should be. It would be counterintuitive and counterproductive to focus exclusively on reading comprehension, as if separate mechanisms and separate processes were necessary for

The research reported herein was supported in part by the National Institute of Education under Contract No. US-NIE-C-400-76-0116. Resources in the form of graduate assistantships were also provided by Ginn and Company, Lexington, Massachusetts. Some of the same findings are scheduled to be reported, in more elaborate form, in a forthcoming monograph for the International Reading Association, *Promoting Reading Comprehension*, ed. J. Flood.

processing print as opposed to auditory or other visual information. A unified theory of cognitive processing seems a more reasonable possibility than does a set of separate theories.

The most basic conclusion of this research is that reading, especially reading comprehension, is a complex interactive process (Rumelhart 1977, Stanovich 1980), one in which a reader varies his or her focus along a continuum from primarily text-based processing (concentration on getting the author's message straight) to primarily reader-based processing (concentration on predicting what the author's message will likely be). This variation in focus is determined by a number of intertwined factors: reader purpose (What do I have to do with this information once I've read it?), familiarity (How much do I already know about the topic addressed in the text?), interest and motivation (How much do I care about learning this subject?), and discourse type and complexity (How much do I already know about the conventions involved in this particular mode of discourse?).

A second conclusion to be drawn from basic research in cognition is that both *content* and *process* factors are implicated in reading comprehension. Content factors are the knowledge structures that determine how well we understand and integrate a particular text. There are two kinds. The first refers to the information itself, the data we use to form thoughts about what we read. To put it simply, the more we know about the topic addressed in the text, the greater the likelihood we will understand, integrate, and remember the information contained in the text. Such a likelihood has indeed been verified in a number of studies (e.g., Anderson, Reynolds, Schallert, and Goetz 1977; Pearson, Hansen, and Gordon 1979). The second type of content is knowledge about the text structure or text genre in which the topical content is embedded. The work on story structures (e.g., Neilsen 1977; Omanson, in press; Stein and Glenn 1979; Thorndyke 1977) and typical rhetorical structures found in expository writing (e.g., Meyer 1977; Meyer, Brandt, and Bluth 1980) indicates that familiarity with structure influences comprehension. Neilsen (1977), for example, found that even when topical information (as defined by the characters and activities) was controlled, subjects were better able to recall and recognize information presented in a causally organized structure than they were information presented in a mere sequentially organized structure. Several studies (e.g., Stein and Glenn 1979, Mandler 1978, Thorndyke 1977) have indicated that violations in what might be labeled *canonical story form* result in a decrement in recall of information. The point, in terms of content, is that both topical and structural content have identifiable influences on comprehension.

Process factors are comparable to what are called control procedures in computer processing. They refer to *how* data are processed instead of *what* data are processed. To discuss them in a paragraph separate from content factors may seem to imply that I think they are separate from and independent of content factors. To the contrary, I know of no data base that would allow us to determine the independence of content (data) and process (control) factors. Process factors may be but different facets of the same amalgam under consideration when content factors are discussed. The kinds of procedures I have in mind are attention, encoding, inference, retrieval, as well as executive monitoring of these procedures (what some people refer to as metacognitive processing—knowledge about the procedures or how they are "proceeding").

That these processes undergo developmental improvement seems intuitively obvious. In fact, empirical researchers have indicated such a trend for processes like inference (Paris and Lindauer 1976, Paris and Upton 1976), encoding of information into memory (Pichert and Anderson 1977), retrieval of information from memory (Pichert 1979), and metacognitive monitoring (Baker and Brown, in press). What is not clear in most of these studies is the factor or factors to which this growth should be attributed—a sheer developmental increase in cognitive capacity, an increase in subjects' world knowledge, instructional history (i.e., schooling), or a growing awareness that the processes are available and ought to be used.

For example, regarding inference, Paris and Lindauer (1976) seem to argue for an awareness of strategy availability, while Trabasso (1981) argues for knowledge changes. Chi (1978) presents evidence favoring a growth in world knowledge as a major determinant of retrieval from memory. Alternatively, recent studies by Hansen (1981) and Gordon (1980) suggest that inference performance increases with direct instruction, practice, or both.

The point that can be made to conclude this section is that both content factors (as defined by topical world knowledge and knowledge about textual organization) and process factors (as represented by attention, encoding, inference, retrieval, and executive monitoring) have been shown to influence comprehension.

CLASSROOM INSTRUCTION RESEARCH

In the past decade, researchers have spent a great deal of time in classrooms, observing what goes on in that environment. The general paradigm for the research is based upon the assumption that observation techniques will allow us to identify management, material, design, and verbal interaction patterns that discriminate between successful and unsuccessful classrooms and schools. This is typically accomplished by identifying in advance successful and unsuccessful schools, teachers, or classrooms. Then the researcher conducts controlled (preplanned, systematic, and theoretically determined) or uncontrolled observation (observing as much of the ecology as possible without predetermined scales or protocols) and examines the observational data, looking for factors that discriminate between successful and unsuccessful sites.

The research conducted under the auspices of the California Beginning Teacher Evaluation Study (Fisher et al. 1978), by Brophy and Evertson (1976), and reviewed by Rosenshine (1979, 1980) and Rosenshine and Berliner (1978) all represent variations on this theme.

Summarizing these and other studies, we get the following scenario. First, the greater the proportion of time students spend on a task, the better their performance on the task. Academic engaged time, to use Rosenshine and Berliner's (1978) term, is a reasonable predictor of reading achievement gain, ranging in magnitude from correlations of .30 to .59 (e.g., Fisher et al. 1978, Samuels and Turnure 1974, Stallings and Kaskowitz 1974).

A separate variable, related to engaged time, is "content covered" or "content measured." This, too, tends to be positively related to achievement and/or achievement gain (Anderson, Evertson, and Brophy 1979; Barr 1973–74; Brown

1978; Good, Grouws, and Beckerman 1979; Harris and Serwer 1966). This relationship seems to hold across a wide range of content: number of books read, number of words taught, number of basal levels completed, or number of computerized modules mastered.

Third, error rate seems to add a significant amount of power in predicting achievement above and beyond engagement and content covered. The California Beginning Teacher Evaluation Study (Fisher et al. 1978) examined the additional predictive power of error rate over simple engagement and time allocated for reading. They found that error rate increased the correlation with reading achievement in seven of ten predictions. Interestingly, the data suggest that lower error rates (about 80–90 percent correct) are successful with low achievers, whereas somewhat higher error rates (about 70 percent correct) are more effective with high achievers. These data derive from a variety of settings for teacher-student interactions (words correct, answers to questions correct, etc.).

Fourth, group instruction, particularly small group instruction, is consistently associated with positive gains in achievement, while individualized instruction is associated with negative or negligible gains (Fisher et al. 1978; Kean, Summers, Ranietz, and Farber 1979; Soar 1973; Stallings and Kaskowitz 1974). Granted, neither is as effective as one-to-one instruction (Smith and Glass 1980); however, assuming a normal student-teacher ratio (15: 1 to 30: 1), group instruction appears more effective than individualized seatwork-oriented instruction. Note, however, that grouping is confounded with task engagement; for example, in the BTES study (Fisher et al. 1978), engagement rates averaged 84 percent in group situations and about 70 percent in individualized situations, while conscious nonattendance to task averaged 16 percent when students worked alone versus 5 percent when students worked in groups.

Emerging from these findings is the conclusion that well-organized, systematic instruction has some beneficial effects. One is tempted to conjure up a picture of a hardhearted taskmaster of a teacher drilling students mercilessly on boring skills, using choral recitation as a major response mode. Such is not the case. Studies that have examined qualitative and affective variables in successful and unsuccessful classrooms tend to have difficulty discriminating between classrooms on these sorts of variables. In fact, most studies have found very little in the way of direct student criticism or harshness to students (e.g., Anderson, Evertson, and Brophy 1979), and such teacher behavior either correlated negatively with achievement (Soar 1973, Soloman and Kendall 1976, Stallings et al. 1979) or was positively related to achievement only when the criticism specified desirable alternative behaviors. Remember that these same studies found positive relationships between the four previously reviewed variables and achievement; thus it must be the case that this cluster of teacher strategies does not lead to cold or harsh teacher-student interactions.

CURRENT PRACTICES IN TEACHING READING COMPREHENSION

Typical of the research surveying current practices for *teaching* reading comprehension is a study by Durkin (1978–79). She observed 17,997 minutes of instruction in both reading and social studies classes. She developed a scheme for classifying teacher behaviors. Comprehension instruction was limited to activities in which the teachers conducted lessons in which they discussed/interacted with students about *how one goes about doing comprehension tasks*—finding main ideas, paraphrasing, determining sequence, and so forth. Comprehension assessment was represented by teachers quizzing students about stories they had read (and focusing on right answers). Comprehension assignment consisted of mentioning to students how they were to go about completing a workbook, ditto, or other written assignment. There were many other categories, but these are most relevant for our purposes.

Of the total 17,997 minutes of observation, Durkin found that less than 1 percent was devoted to activities that met one of her definitions of instruction. What were teachers doing in the classes she observed? First, they were giving many assignments for students to do on their own without teacher supervision. Second, they were asking students many questions about stories they read and were focusing on getting the right answer. Third, they answered a fair number of individual questions about assignments. What was going on in the name of comprehension instruction? Put simply, assignment giving and question asking. The prevailing wisdom concerning comprehension instruction seems to be that if students get enough exposure to a skill or kind of question, they will eventually improve at it. While such a position may be consistent with the engaged-time-on-task argument derived from Rosenshine and Stevens' (in press) review, it is not consistent with arguments emanating from the direct instruction or grouping findings. Furthermore, simply on common-sense grounds there is something suspicious about a position whose implicit rationale is that if children have trouble with X, what they need is to practice X more often. Such a position probably works fine for students who can perform the task at a moderate error rate; however, for students who hover near chance level on the task, the additional practice may only reinforce their already misguided strategies. In other words, what Durkin found in our schools in the name of comprehension instruction may be a practice that promotes a "the rich get richer and the poor get poorer" syndrome.

In a sequel to her classroom observation study, Durkin (1981) examined the teachers' editions of five currently popular basal reading programs, looking for instances of comprehension instruction defined in terms comparable to the criteria used in her earlier study (Durkin 1978–79). While the sheer incidence of comprehension instruction was higher than in her previous study, the general pattern of a dominant reliance on assessment and mentioning was replicated.

Durkin's two studies, taken together, reveal a picture of virtually no direct instruction in comprehension. Instead, teachers seem to spend most of their classroom discussion time asking students questions about stories they have read and giving assignments. Regarding comprehension skills—such as main idea, sequence, cause-effect, fact-opinion—manuals provide little guidance concerning how the skills ought to be presented to students; teachers apparently provide little guidance to students about how they ought to solve problems and/or answer questions exemplifying these skills. The prevailing wisdom is to provide massive doses of unguided practice. Nor is there much evidence, either in manuals or classrooms, that much goes on in the name of substantive feedback that would allow students to evaluate how well they were performing a task or, more important, what inappropriate strategies they might be adopting. The student who is not doing well on a particular comprehension skill seems to have little help to look forward to, save additional opportunities to improve performance on his or her own through practice.

RESEARCH ON COMPREHENSION INSTRUCTION

Durkin's two studies tend to engender an atmosphere of pessimism. Perhaps they should. They have probably provided the reading profession a definite service, for they prompt the question, What is the alternative to practice and assessment? As an antidote to that pessimism, let me turn to a review of a few recent studies that have evaluated the effects of direct explicit attempts to help students develop heuristic strategies (if not rules) for dealing with a range of comprehension tasks typically required in schools.

These studies share a set of features. First, all are derived directly from basic research on the reading process; that is, they represent attempts to bridge the gap from basic research to a real instructional issue. Second, all have evaluated the efficacy of their instructional treatments by using transfer tasks; they have asked the question, What happens to student performance when instructional crutches are removed? Third, all have obtained positive results; they have shown that intervention at issue elicits positive gains in some aspect of comprehension. Fourth, all have attended, at least in some way, to the question of control processes. They have included, directly or by implication, techniques that allow students to monitor for themselves whether or not they understand task demands or know when they are performing the task appropriately.

In the first study, Hansen (1981) was interested in ameliorating children's ability and predisposition to draw inferences. Beginning with the observation that children were best at answering the kinds of questions teachers ask most often (i.e., literal recall of story details), she wondered whether this observation represented a robust developmental trend, an accident of children's instructional history (i.e., they have more practice at literal questions), or a fact about the world (literal question are inherently easier than inferential questions).

She devised three instructional treatments. In the first, a business-as-usual approach, average second-grade students were given a traditional diet of questions accompanying their basal reader stories—about 80 percent literal to 20 percent inferential questions. In the second, a practice-only treatment, literal questions were removed from these children's basal reader lives altogether; they received only inferential questions. In the third, students received the traditional question diet but were confronted lesson after lesson with prereading strategy designed to help them process new (text) information in light of existing (head) knowledge structures. Prior to each story, they were asked to predict what they would do and what the story protagonist would do when confronting either two or three critical situations (actual situations from the story to be read). They then read the story to compare their predictions with what actually occurred (à la Directed Reading-Thinking Activity). In addition, they were provided with a visual model of comprehension as a process of relating the new to the known.

Four kinds of dependent measures were analyzed, using pretest story understanding tasks (answering literal and inferential probes) as a covariate in a multivariate analysis of covariance. On the first measure, literal and inferential probes from the last five stories in which the instruction was embedded, both the practice-only and the strategy training group outperformed the traditional group on both literal and inferential probes. In addition, where differences existed between the two experimental groups, they favored the strategy training group. The data suggest that a set for inferential processing induces a levels-of-processing effect that generalizes to both inference and literal tasks, at least in the local environment of the stories in which the instruction was embedded.

On the second measure, literal and inferential probes from totally new and unaided stories, the two inference-oriented groups exceeded the traditional group only on inference probes for the familiar transfer story. These data suggest that whatever heuristic developed could not overcome the strong influence that prior knowledge has on inference performance (i.e., no differences on the inference probes for the topically unfamiliar selection).

On the third measure, free recall of a totally new story, there were absolutely no differences, arguing for a transfer-of-identical-elements phenomenon. In short, since the students never practiced free recall, their ratio of intrusions (inferences) to text reproductions was not influenced.

On the fourth measure, a posttest-only standardized reading test, there was a treatment by subtest interaction. On the vocabulary subtest, there were no reliable differences among groups, strengthening the argument that there were no pre- or postexperimental general verbal ability differences among the groups. On the comprehension subtest, however, there were strong differences favoring both experimental groups over the traditional group. At first blush this may seem surprising, since standardized tests are typically insensitive to specific instructional treatments. However, the standardized test used was the Stanford Achievement Test, which has a modified cloze (fill-in-the-blank) response format. Such a format, if it does anything, places a premium on inferences to prior knowledge; how else would anyone determine the best fit for the cloze blank? Hence, the transfer is not so surprising.

The primary conclusion one can draw from these data is that inference ability, even for young students, is amenable to direct training and monitoring; however, the local and task-alike transfer effects are more impressive than the broad transfer effects.

Gordon (1980) extended, at least in part, the inference training hypothesis to older children (grade 4). Over a period of eight weeks, she contrasted the effects of an even more explicitly trained inference group with a placebo control group that received fun language experience and immersion activities and a second experimental group whose instruction focused on activating and fine tuning preexisting content schemata (the topics addressed in the stories) and structure schemata (helping students develop an abstract framework for what is entailed in a story) before and after reading.

Five dependent measures were used: (1) comprehension of literal and inferential probes summed over the eight stories in which the instruction was embedded, (2) comprehension of literal and inferential probes on transfer stories read immediately following the eight-week experiment, (3) same as (2) but delayed two weeks, (4) a standardized comprehension test measure, and (5) free recall protocols from the last story read in the training period.

While the results are not so dramatic as in the Hansen (1981) study, the patterns of significant results are consistent. There were no significant differences between groups on the standardized test or on the immediate comprehension test, again suggesting that broad transfer is difficult to obtain. However, there were statistically reliable differences favoring the inference training group on inference items derived from the instructional stories. Also, high-achieving but not low-achieving students in that group did better than other groups on the inference items on the delayed posttest. The most remarkable differences favored the content and structure schemata activation group on the free recall protocols; their scores were often two or three standard deviations above the inference group and the placebo control group, particularly on recall measures which were sensitive to the development and use of a story schema. Apparently these students developed an abstract story "map," which served them well in encoding and retrieving information structurally important in a story schema. As with the Hansen and Pearson study, one is more impressed with the local than the broad transfer effects. Also, one is struck by the specificity of the transfer that does occur; the principle of transfer of identical elements (the greater the similarity between training and transfer tasks, the greater the likelihood of transfer) suggests itself. One is tempted also to invoke Rosenshine's engaged-time-on-task principle in explaining these data.

Hansen and Pearson (in press) have followed up earlier inference training research with modified techniques and different populations. In earlier research, Hansen (1981) contrasted a strategy approach with a practice-only approach and a business-as-usual control condition. In the follow-up, Hansen and Pearson combined strategy and practice into a single treatment to be contrasted with the conventional approach. They also trained four teachers to administer the treatments instead of teaching the classes themselves, as had been done earlier. Finally, they used good and poor fourth-grade readers instead of average second-grade students.

The combined approach proved not to be advantageous for good readers in comparison to the control group; however, it proved remarkably effective for the poor readers. Experimental poor readers exceeded their control counterparts on inference measures taken from the materials in which the instruction was embedded, as well as on measures from three transfer passages for which no instruction was offered. In fact, when all students read and answered questions from a common transfer passage, poor experimental students reading at a 3.1 level scored as well as good control students reading at a 6.2 level. From these data, and the data from the earlier study, they concluded that younger and poorer readers benefit from conscious explicit attempts to alter comprehension strategies; older good readers, on the other hand, seem not to benefit, perhaps because they are capable of developing adequate strategies on their own.

Raphael (1980) cast the inference training paradigm directly in a more general approach to question-answering. Over four 45-minute sessions she trained average fourth-, sixth-, eighth-grade students (also low, average, and high sixth-grade students) to monitor their allocation of resources (information in the text versus knowledge stored in memory) in generating answers to questions that invited textually explicit comprehension (deriving an answer from the same text sentence from which the question was generated), textually implicit comprehension (deriving an answer from a text sentence different from the one from which the question was derived), or scriptally implicit comprehension (deriving an answer from one's store of prior knowledge). She modified this scheme, taken from Pearson and Johnson (1978), for students by labeling the three response types *right there, think and search*, and *on my own*, respectively.

Using a model → guided practice → independent practice → direct feedback instructional design, she guided the students to apply the strategy to increasingly larger text segments (one paragraph to a 600-word passage) with an increasingly larger number of questions per lesson and increasingly fewer feedback prompts from the instructor. In the strategy, students read the relevant text and the question, generated an answer, and then decided which of the three strategies they had used to generate the answer.

In the transfer test, students read entirely new passages on their own, answered questions, and decided on the strategy they thought they had used to generate the answer. The performance of the training group was contrasted not with an untreated control but with a control group that received a 20-minute orientation to the response classification task. Four dependent measures were analyzed: (1) hits (Did the student give his response strategy the same category rating as the experimenter thought was the most readily invited strategy given the particular question and text—in other words, did the student judge himself to do what the experimenter thought most students would do?), (2) matches (Irrespective of response quality, did the student actually do what she said she did?), (3) appropriate responses (Did the student give a response that, either because of direct selection from the target position or through a chain of logical and/or pragmatic reasoning from the target proposition, could be scored correct given a complex set of scoring protocols that allowed for considerable deviation from the expected response?), and (4) correct hit matches (given that student achieved of hit [Did what the experimenter expected] and a match [Did what she said she did] what was the probability that she got the item correct?).

On all these response measures, reliable differences were found favoring the training group over the orientation group; that is, trained students got better at discriminating task demands of different kinds of questions, evaluating their own behavior, and giving quality responses. Moreover, on the conditional measure, which requires discrimination *and* evaluation *and* response quality, training/orientation differences were magnified even further. Apparently students changed both their response strategies and their response monitoring strategies. Raphael concluded that they had developed both new comprehension and comprehension monitoring strategies that gave them more control over a traditional but pervasive question-answering task.

Working with low-ability community college students, Day (1980) contrasted approaches to training students to write summaries for prose passages. The treatments differed systematically from one another in terms of how rules for writing summaries were integrated with self-management strategies designed to help students monitor their own progress in summary writing. Treatment 1 consisted of self-management alone (a fairly traditional self-checking procedure to determine whether the summary conveyed the information the student intended to convey). Treatment 2 was rules alone; that is, subjects were trained to use van Dijk and Kintsch's (1978) five rules for summarizing narratives: delete redundancy, delete irrelevancies, subordinate subtopics, select topic sentences, create topic sentences. Treatment 3 simply put Treatment 1 and 2 together in sequence. First do one; then, the other. Treatment 4 *integrated* the rules and self-management strategies into a single coherent routine. One might say that the four treatments varied along a continuum of integration of explicit training and explicit monitoring devices. A model → feedback → practice instructional design was used.

The dependent measure was the proportion of time students used each of the five summarization rules (number of actual uses/number of potential opportunities to use). Day found that from pretest to posttest there was a ceiling effect on the two deletion rules; that is, almost all students could already apply them. On the subordination rule, all but Treatment 1 (self-management alone) students made significant gains, with the greatest gains accruing to the integrated group (Treatment 4). On the selection rule again Treatments 2, 3, and 4 exhibited greater gain than did Treatment 1; however, there were no reliable differences among Treatments 2–4. Also, average-ability students gained more than low-ability students. On the creation rule, a pattern similar to that found for subordination emerged: The greatest gains accrued to the integrated group (Treatment 4). Furthermore, posttest performance indicated that while pre-post gains were similar across rules, absolute performance levels were conditioned by rule complexity: Rule 3 > Rule 4 > Rule 5.

Day's data suggest that with different tasks and with slower students, ". . . explicit training in strategies for accomplishing a task coupled with routines to oversee the successful application of those strategies is clearly the best approach" (p. 15).

This summary provided by Day could well serve as a summary for all the studies reviewed in this section. All point to the direction of making clear what the task requirements are, providing heuristic guidelines for task completion, allowing substantial massed practice alone with substantive feedback, and insuring some provision for self-monitoring. The data are encouraging. It looks as though we can teach comprehension skills after all.

CONCLUSION

The above examples of research clearly reveal my own biases about what instruction in comprehension ought to be. It should focus on explicit attempts to help students develop independent strategies for coping with the kinds of comprehension problems they are asked to solve in their lives in schools. As a general model for how we might proceed, let me offer a set of guidelines paraphrased from Brown, Campione, and Day (1981):

1. The trained skill must be instructionally relevant.
2. Training should proceed from simple to complex.
3. An analysis of training and transfer tasks should provide evidence of where breakdowns occur.
4. There should be explicit instruction concerning when and how to use the strategies.
5. Feedback should be given during class discussions and for independent work.
6. A variety of passages (or other materials) should be used in order to facilitate transfer to new situations.
7. Self-checking procedures should be used as an inherent part of operationalizing the training strategy.

I think the justification exists for placing more emphasis on direct explicit teaching, interactive discussions, substantive feedback, and control and self-monitoring strategies. I hope that as we accumulate additional evidence supporting the efficacy of these techniques, particularly in natural classroom environments, we will return to the model of teacher as teacher and go beyond the model of teacher as assessor and mentioner that is so dominant in the findings of Durkin.

REFERENCES

Anderson, R. C., Reynolds, R. E., Schallert, D. L., & Goetz, E. T. Frameworks for comprehending discourse. *American Educational Research Journal*, 1977, *14*, 367–382.

Anderson, R., Evertson, C., & Brophy, J. An experimental study of effective teaching in first grade reading groups. *Elementary School Journal*, March 1979, 193–222.

Baker, L., & Brown, A. Comprehension monitoring and critical reading. In J. Flood (Ed.), *Comprehension and cognitive processes*. Newark, Del.: International Reading Association, in press.

Barr, R. Instructional pace differences and their effect on reading acquisition. *Reading Research Quarterly*, 1973–74, *9*, 526–554.

Becker, W. C. Teaching reading and language to the disadvantaged—What we have learned from field research. *Harvard Educational Review*, 1977, *47*, 518–543.

Brown, A. L. Knowing when, where, and how to remember: A problem of metacognition. In R. Glasser (Ed.), *Advances in instructional psychology*. Hillsdale, N.J.: Erlbaum, 1978.

Brown, A. L., Campione, J. C., & Day, J. Learning to learn: On training students to learn from texts. *Educational Researcher*, 1981, *10*, 14–24.

Brophy, J., & Evertson, C. *Learning from teaching: A developmental perspective*. Boston: Allyn & Bacon, 1976.

Chi, M. T. H. Knowledge structures and development. In R. S. Siegler (Ed.), *Children's thinking: What develops?* Hillsdale, N.J.: Erlbaum, 1978.

Day, J. D. *Training summarization skills: A comparison of teaching methods*. Unpublished doctoral dissertation, University of Illinois, 1980.

Durkin, D. What classroom observations reveal about reading comprehension instruction. *Reading Research Quarterly*, 1978–79, *14*, 481–533.

Durkin, D. Reading comprehension instruction in five basal reading series. *Reading Research Quarterly*, 1981, *16*, 515–544.

Dijk, T. A. van, & Kintsch, W. Cognitive psychology and discourse. In W. U. Dressler (Ed.), *Trends in text linguistics*. New York: DeGruyter, 1978.

Fisher, C., Berliner, D., Filby, N., Marliave, R., Cohen, L., Dishaw, M., & Moore, W. Teaching behaviors, academic learning time and student achievement: An overview. In C. Denham & A. Lieberman (Eds.), *Time to learn*. Washington, D.C.: National Institute of Education, May 1978.

Good, T., Grouws, D. A., & Beckerman, T. M. Curriculum pacing: Some empirical data in mathematics. *Journal of Curriculum Studies*, 1979, *11*, 263–281.

Gordon, C. J. *The effects of instruction in metacomprehension and inferencing on children's comprehension abilities.* Unpublished doctoral dissertation, University of Minnesota, 1980.

Hansen, J. The effects of inference training and practice on young children's comprehension. *Reading Research Quarterly*, 1981, *16*, 391–417.

Hansen, J., & Pearson, P. D. *an instructional study: Improving the inferential comprehension of good and poor fourth-grade readers* Tech. Rep. Urbana: University of Illinois, Center for the Study of Reading, in press.

Harris, A. J., & Serwer, B. L. The craft project: Instructional time. *Reading Research Quarterly*, 1966, *2* (1), 27–68.

House, E. R., Glass, G. V., McLean, L. D., & Walker, D. F. No simple answer: Critique of the follow-through evaluation. *Harvard Educational Review*, 1978, *48*, 128–160.

Kean, M., Summers, A., Ranietz, M., & Farber, I. *What works in reading.* Philadelphia: School District of Philadelphia, 1979.

Mandler, J. M. A code in the node: The use of a story schema in retrieval. *Discourse Processes*, 1978, *1*, 14–35.

Meyer, B. J. F. What is remembered from prose: A function of passage structure. In R. O. Freedle (Ed.), *Discourse production and comprehension*, vol. 1. Norwood, N.J.: Ablex, 1977.

Meyer, B. J. F., Brandt, D. M., & Bluth, G. J. Use of top level structure in text: Key for reading comprehension. *Reading Research Quarterly*, 1980, *16*, 72–103.

Neilsen, A. *The role of macrostructures and relational markers in comprehending familiar and unfamiliar written discourse.* Unpublished doctoral dissertation, University of Minnesota, 1977.

Omanson, R. C. An analysis of narratives: Identifying central, supportive and distracting content. *Discourse Processes*, in press.

Stallings, J. A., Needles, M., & Staybrook, N. *How to change the process of teaching basic reading skills in secondary schools.* Menlo Park, Calif.: Stanford Research Institute International, 1979.

Stanovich, K. D. Toward an interactive-compensatory model of individual differences in the development of reading fluency. *Reading Research Quarterly*, 1980, *16*, 32–71.

Stein, N., & Glenn, C. G. An analysis of story comprehension in elementary school children. In R. Freedle (Ed.), *New directions in discourse processing.* Norwood, N.J.: Ablex, 1979.

Thorndyke, P. W. Cognitive structures in comprehension and memory of narrative discourse. *Cognitive Psychology*, 1977, *9*, 77–110.

Trabasso, T. On the making and assessment of inferences during reading. In J. T. Guthrie (Ed.), *Reading comprehension and education.* Newark, Del.: International Reading Association, 1981.

16

Question-Related Activities and Their Relationship to Reading Comprehension: Some Instructional Implications

Taffy E. Raphael
James R. Gavelek

There is no doubt about the pervasiveness of questions in classroom settings, particularly regarding textual materials. Questions often follow stories in basal readers and are used in basal workbooks and content-area texts to "improve" prose comprehension or to assess what students have learned from text. In fact, the primary means for determining student's reading comprehension ability is through the use of question-answering tasks following short paragraphs on standardized tests (e.g., Stanford Achievement Test, Metropolitan Achievement Test). Moreover, in keeping with the increased emphasis placed upon the active role of the learner, there has been a growing interest in the use of students' question asking as a means for facilitating comprehension. Thus, questions can be thought of as an inducement to comprehension as well as being a means for assessing comprehension.

Despite the apparent importance of question-related behaviors to successful classroom performance, relatively little research exists in this area, and the literature that does can be characterized as being of a patchwork rather than unified nature. There are studies of how questions inserted in text influence comprehension, of the kinds of questions teachers generate in classroom settings, of the ability of students to generate questions, as well as studies of students' concepts of questions and their sensitivity to sources of information for responses to questions. Notably absent is a general framework in which to examine children's development of question-related skills or a theory of questioning related to comprehension.

We believe that a framework that delineates the major areas of importance in question-related activities would do much in the way of both synthesizing existing literature and directing future research. Question-related activities may vary greatly depending upon the source of the question and the reason for which the question has been asked. Thus, for the purposes of this chapter, we are defining these activities as being either other-generated (teacher- or text-provided questions designed to elicit answers from readers) or student-generated (questions designed to monitor understanding and seek clarification or to extend cognitive activity during reading).

This chapter is divided into three major sections. First, we consider the assumed relationship between question-related activities and reading comprehension. Second, we review a selective but representative sample of research concerned with question-related activities. Third, we present a conceptual framework of questioning and attempt to suggest some of the more important research questions that have yet to be answered.

WHY WORRY ABOUT QUESTIONS?

Both oral and written questions play a major role in styles of teaching and students' learning. One need spend only a few minutes in a classroom setting, be it in elementary, high school, or college, to realize that much of a teacher's time is spent asking questions, while much of a student's interaction with teachers involves responding to these questions or, at times, generating questions. However, mere prevalence does not dictate utility. There are several reasons for recognizing prose-related questioning activities as an important aspect of reading comprehension. The first involves the notion that they serve to focus the students' attention on important concepts and details in the text they are to read (Anderson and Biddle 1975, Frase 1968). These questions would include those asked by teachers prior to the students' reading of the text or the questions inserted in text that require students to respond as they read.

A second reason is that they may induce a review of the information presented in a passage and thus facilitate understanding or comprehension of that text (Watts and Anderson 1971, Frase 1968). These questions could be inserted in text after the information to which they refer, at the end of chapters in content-area texts, or at the end of basal stories, or they could be found in workbook pages related to a particular basal or textbook passage. They also can be generated by teachers during discussions to enhance students' understanding of and memory for important concepts and details included within the text.

A third use for text-related questions derives from work with learner-generated questions. If readers are generating questions concerning the text they are reading, the activity may enhance their integration of the textual information with that of their knowledge base, thus improving comprehension. In other words, these are the questioning activities designed to promote more effective reading comprehension specific to a given passage.

The fourth use for questions derives largely from research in children's comprehension monitoring. Research has suggested that students may be unaware of inconsistencies (Markman 1979) and anomalies (Winograd and Johnston 1982) in text. If students can be induced to ask questions related to the consistency of the information being presented and related to their ability to follow or comprehend the text, the reader's comprehension should be enhanced. That is, if students could be taught to monitor their level of comprehension, and could be led to recognize when "fix-up strategies" may be necessary, their reading comprehension abilities may improve as a result of more effective self-monitoring skills.

In addition to questions as effective tools for instruction, another factor involves the reality that questions are the primary source of assessment of students' reading comprehension. Students' ability to respond appropriately to questions often labels them as successful or unsuccessful learners. Scores on reading comprehension tests often are the basis for determining admittance to special programs, to reading group placement, to college-bound versus vocational tracks in high schools. With so much emphasis on these scores, it becomes imperative to provide students with specific strategies for responding to those questions they so often must face.

RESEARCH IN QUESTION-RELATED ACTIVITIES

Questioning research that is focused on educational practice can be contained within three general categories: (1) the natural ecology of questions, (2) other-generated questions, and (3) student-generated questions.

The Natural Ecology of Questions

Studies on the ecology of questions tend to be primarily descriptive in nature, concerning the incidence and kinds of questions teachers ask, kinds of questions used in testing, and students' concepts about questions.

Teachers' questioning activity has been an area of research for the past few decades. Guszak (1967) examined the questions teachers asked during reading lessons and found a preponderance of text-based, literal questions. More recently, Chou-Hare and Pulliam (1980) asked teachers to write questions with corresponding appropriate answers that they would be likely to use in a basal reading lesson. These questions were then analyzed according to the source of information (text or knowledge base) the reader must use to respond appropriately to the question. They further divided questions with text-based answers into those with the answer explicitly stated in the text or those that required the integration of textual information (see Pearson and Johnson 1978). As in the Guszak study, the dominant question type was that which required response information from the text, though this included information explicitly stated as well as implied. While teachers may be aware of different kinds of questions, their question-asking activities demonstrate lack of variety in questions posed to the students and lack of challenge to the students in the form of knowledge-based or inferential questions. There are a number of possible reasons for this, from cognitive constraints on the teacher to group size or time limitations. Chou-Hare (1982) extended her work in concepts about questions by examining the questions provided for discussion in the manuals of basal reading series. She examined the comprehension questions in two meaning-based and two linguistic/phonic-based basal series and found that publishers matched their philosophy of reading instruction with the kinds of questions they provided. That is, the series whose early emphasis was on decoding used more literal text-based questions in the early grades, while the series whose emphasis was more meaning oriented primarily used questions that required the integration of the print with the reader's background knowledge.

Another area that uses questions extensively is standardized tests. Questions are a major part of most tests designed to identify the level of ability of students in areas from reading and math to social studies and science. Crowell, Au, and Blake (in press) propose that a well-constructed test series should show increasing proportions of inferential questions as the grade level rises for the following reason: Children who are learning to read may have to focus much of their attention on decoding the symbols, leaving little attention for complex inferencing behavior; older children, whose decoding skills are more automatic, should be able to exhibit higher levels of comprehension. These differences should be reflected in the questions asked at each test level. To test these predictions they examined the reading comprehension sections of three major standardized achievement tests. They found that few tests reflected this developmental view in the construction of test questions. Instead of a gradual shift in the ratio of inferential to literal questions, there was a high proportion of literal, factual questions at all grades.

Children's concepts of questions have been examined by both Au (1981) and Wonnacott and Raphael (1982). Au's research involved case studies of one low-, one average-, and one high-ability third-grade reader conducting a reading lesson with a first-grade student. She videotaped the students in the tutoring situation, instructing the third grader to help the first grader in any way that might be useful as they "taught" them a story. She found distinct differences in their use of questions. The high-ability student asked the largest number of questions, a mix of inferential and literal questions designed to probe the first grader's understanding of the story. The average-ability student asked fewer questions in general, and the questions were narrower in range and largely concerned the sequence of events in the story. The low-ability student, who had the text read to him, asked no questions. During a follow-up interview, he indicated an awareness that his teacher asked questions, but it either had not occurred to him to do so, or he was unable to formulate questions himself.

A research question that follows from Au's work is exactly what children's concepts of questions are like, why some children ask questions or at least recognize their importance when others do not. Wonnacott and Raphael (1982) observed and interviewed low- and high-ability students from third and sixth grades. The observation data were collected while students read passages and responded to postreading comprehension questions. The amount of time spent in responding, the number of pages consulted, the amount of time spent in reading the question, and the consulting of target information were observed. Then each student was interviewed as to his or her understanding of what makes one a successful question answerer, why questions are asked of them, and what they do when responding to questions. Preliminary analyses suggest that differences in both behaviors and self-reports about questioning activities are found between skilled and less skilled question answerers. Successful question answerers are able to perceive the varying task demands of questions and enlist appropriate strategies for responding to those demands. They appear to have a strong sense of the relationship between means (strategies for accessing information) and ends (the accurate response to a question) in that they recognize how questions can best be answered. Their activity when responding to the questions is generally purposeful and more efficient in terms of the number of pages consulted. Their strategies appear to be more routinized with monitoring activities, such as rereading the question and the written response. The less skilled students tend to be more random in their selection of strategies. That is, they seem to feel that their behavior has little to do with the end result of locating an appropriate answer, or they seem oblivious to the fact that previous question-answering behaviors were unsuccessful. They do not seem confident of their scanning abilities and thus spend inordinately large amounts of time rereading passages. Alternatively, they may impulsively write their responses without checking for their relevance to the question. One of their criteria for a correct answer appears to be that some of the words that appear in the answer were also in the question. In terms of the students' perceived purpose of questioning activities, the less skilled question answerers view the activity as a school task designed to ensure that an assignment is completed or that attention is being paid. The more skilled question answerers view the activity as a means for promoting comprehension and assisting them in remembering important points.

In summary, these studies suggest both the pervasiveness of question-related activities in school settings and the preponderance of text-based questions asked by teachers. In addition, there exist individual differences across students' ability and age groups in their skills in both asking and responding to questions. These studies have been essentially descriptive in nature. We next consider studies that have been primarily experimental or intervention in their orientation, focusing specifically on other-generated questions.

Other-Generated Questions

The category of other-generated questions includes any question not generated by the students themselves. This can include questions in texts, workbooks, tests, and so on, as well as those generated by the teacher. There are two basic divisions we will make in discussing the research in this area. The first involves the research in adjunct questions, while the second concerns teaching or modeling the different sources of information available for responding to questions. We recognize that, to some extent, this division is arbitrary and serves organizational needs rather than signaling theoretical differences.

Adjunct questions. Questions inserted in text are often termed adjunct questions. Considerable research has attempted to document the effects of these questions on reading comprehension. The research is typically conducted by giving students passages with accompanying questions. The passages are usually divided into paragraphs either preceded or followed by questions related to the information in that paragraph, and variables examined include the number of questions, the position of the questions, the kind of information required for responding to the question, and the frequency of the questions. Students' performances on a posttest that includes questions seen during their reading as well as new questions typically serve to measure the effects.

Two explanations of the role adjunct questions play in reading comprehension have been suggested. The first is that the questions direct the students' attention to specific information in the text or to specific kinds of information. Another explanation is that the questions serve to review information read, thus assisting students in more deeply or more frequently processing the prose (Anderson and Biddle 1975, Watts and Anderson, 1971). The findings of this research suggest that when questions are placed before the related text information they serve to focus readers' attention on specific text details at the cost of incidental learning. If they occur following the related text information, they create the need for review of the entire text and focus attention on similar information in the following sections (Reynolds, Standiford, and Anderson 1978). Finally, the effectiveness of inserted questions appears to differ by developmental and ability levels of students. Rickards and Denner (1979) examined students' performances when using adjunct questions, underlining, or a combination of the two and found that, unlike adults, the insertion of these questions reduced students' performance levels. In contrast, Reynolds and Magleby (1981) and Rickards and Hatcher (1978) found that questions were facilitative for the children but that the effectiveness varied across ability levels and kinds of inserted questions. This research suggests that examining adult behavior is not sufficient in developing texts appropriate for children, and provides information for both teachers and publishers in using questions as a means for promoting comprehension during the reading process.

Sensitizing students to sources of information. An area of research directly related to reading comprehension instruction involves sensitizing students to the sources of information available for responding to other-generated questions. Comprehension instruction that directly teaches these informational sources makes students aware of question-answer relationships QAR (Raphael and Pearson 1982, Raphael and Wonnacott 1981).

One can draw a relationship between postreading comprehension questions and the sources of information used to respond to these questions. These sources can be broadly categorized as being either based in the text or in the readers' background knowledge. This text-based/knowledge-based relationship has been classified by Pearson and Johnson (1978) into three distinct categories: text explicit, text implicit, and script implicit. A text-explicit QAR is one in which an answer is explicitly stated in the text. Often, words used to create a question and those for the appropriate response are located within a single sentence. A text-implicit QAR is one in which the reader must draw a text-based inference, integrating information across sentences, paragraphs, or pages. In such cases, all the information for responding to a question is provided by the text but the reader must integrate the information appropriately. Finally, a script-implicit QAR is one in which the reader must respond to a question with information from his or her knowledge base. The answer is related to the topic discussed in the text, but it is not stated in that text.

The importance of these three categories of questions is its emphasis on the interaction of the print, the question, and the reader's knowledge base. Often, question taxonomies have identified questions in isolation (e.g., Barrett 1976, Sanders 1966) without considering the sources of information to which these questions refer.

It is our contention that teaching students about this three-way relationship may help them answer the questions they face, and may motivate teachers to ask questions of different types. A line of research conducted by the first author and a number of colleagues examines this hypothesis. This research has been conducted in three stages: a demonstration study, a training study, and an instructional study.

The demonstration study (Raphael, Winograd, and Pearson 1980), designed to describe a particular phenomenon (e.g., question answering) suggested that students were sensitive to QARs and that this sensitivity influenced the responses given. The more able readers seem to be more adept at invoking appropriate strategies for locating accurate answers to questions.

The training study attempted to enhance students' question-anwering performances by teaching them specific strategies (Raphael, in press) for locating information for responding to the questions. Four lessons were developed to be used on four consecutive days. In the first lesson, question answering in general was discussed, and the three QARs were introduced to provide a conceptual framework. Students were gradually led to understand the procedures and tasks that would be practiced with increasingly more difficult texts throughout the week. During this first session students read very brief passages with corresponding questions. Through these materials the three QARs were easily depicted as being (1) within a single sentence, (2) requiring information across two or more sentences, and (3) requiring information from the readers' knowledge base. Immediate feedback was provided on both the selection of the category and the quality of the response. In the succeeding lessons, application of the three QAR strategies was practiced under increasingly difficult situations (harder to read text, more questions to be answered, and more independent work required of the student). Following this week of instruction, the students were compared to a control group that had only received definitions of QARs. Comparisons were drawn on both their ability to answer questions and their ability to identify QARs represented by each question-answer dyad.

The major analysis focused on the quality of students' responses to questions. Little differences were expected between the high-ability readers in either the QAR treatment group or the control groups since they were probably already good question answerers as indicated by their scores on standardized and informal tests, tests that often consist of question-answering tasks. This is precisely what was found for text-explicit and text-implicit questions. However, the high-ability students in the training group were more successful than the control-group students in answering script implicit questions. As one student complained after the training and testing sessions were complete, "I wish someone had told me of QARs a long time ago. I had a lot of information in my head but didn't know I was supposed to use it!" It is possible that the students of higher ability possess enough background knowledge to accurately respond to the script implicit questions, but do not do so. Such a "production deficiency" may be the result of a heavy emphasis on text-based information, perhaps unwittingly modeled for them by their teachers.

For the average- and low-ability students, a slightly different picture emerged. Regarding text-based questions, students at each ability level in the training group performed at a level equal to that of the next highest group of control students. That is, the trained low-ability students were as successful as the average untrained students, while the average trained students were as successful as the high-ability untrained students. Both average- and low-ability students in the trained group, however, showed only minor improvement over their untrained counterparts on the script implicit questions. A possible explanation is that the students of average and low abilities are at a disadvantage in that they may have less background knowledge than higher-achieving students. Therefore, even if they understand the need to go to their background knowledge to retrieve information for the question's response, the information may not be accessible or available. As one of the students claimed, "I went to my head but there's nothing there!" One implication of this finding is that the training is not sufficient for those students who are lacking in background knowledge and that to be more effective, additional background is necessary.

The instructional study (Raphael and Wonnacott 1981) was designed to determine the feasibility of implementing the QAR program in real classrooms. The two primary concerns were the level of inservice training necessary before teachers could be expected to use the QAR program in their classrooms and how well the QAR training would work in nonexperimental testing situations. Four groups of teachers participated in the study. One group was provided with an inservice about QARs in which instruction in the use of QARs was modeled and all materials were provided. These teachers were observed throughout the initial week of training, with feedback provided to them in a group at the end of each of their lessons. Following the first week of instruction, they were observed during weekly maintenance lessons in which passages with six questions, two from each QAR category, were used for instruction. A second group of teachers received an inservice much like the first group but with no materials provided. Instead, an emphasis was placed on creating QAR instructional materials from those that occur in their classroom. These teachers conducted QAR instruction during the same period as the first group, but the actual lesson format and time period were left to their discretion. A third group of teachers was given all passages and questions provided to the first group, but received no inservice. A fourth group of teachers received no instructions prior to testing.

All students were tested twice. The first testing session was conducted by their classroom teachers after the instructional period. Students were given a passage with 18 questions, evenly and randomly distributed among the three QAR categories. The children were not told that these were part of the QAR program. Teachers asked them to read the passage and respond to the questions, indicating that the passage was an introduction into a unit about dinosaurs. The second testing session was conducted by the researchers two days later, again using passages followed by questions.

The results indicated that there were no differences in the children's responses to questions in the first two groups. Overall, both training groups performed at a higher level than did either the third or the fourth groups. We found no differences among high-ability students regardless of treatment, but there was a greater disparity between the average trained and untrained students, and a still larger difference between trained and untrained students of low ability. In fact, classroom training in QARs appeared to make average- and low-ability students look much like high-ability students in their ability to answer questions.

Three conclusions may be drawn from these data. First is that training is effective whether the teachers conducting the lessons use the materials provided by the experimenter or materials constructed independently. Second, the training appears to transfer to situations in which the QAR prompting is not present and in which no reference is made to strategy use. Finally, training effects will vary as a function of the students' reading ability, with effects gradually increasing as one moves from high to average to low ability readers.

The above research compliments that conducted by Hansen (Hansen 1981, Hansen and Pearson 1982) and Au (1979). These researchers have used techniques with elementary school children to sensitize them to the importance of background knowledge in understanding stories. Au (1979) has worked with underprivileged students of Hawaiian ancestry using a technique called ETR—

experience, text, and relationship—that relates the students' experiences or background knowledge to texts using pre and post comprehension questions. During the experience (E) phase, the teacher asks questions designed to elicit students' personal experiences relevant to the topic of the text to be read. Then the teacher has the students read a portion of the text silently. Next, in the text (T) phase of the lesson, details of the portion read are discussed. Finally, during the relationship (R) phase, the teacher draws a relationship between the students' own experiences and the text they have read, as well as having them predict future directions the story may take based upon their background knowledge and expectations. The students who have participated in this program show dramatic gains in reading skills when compared to similar students in more traditional classrooms.

Hansen (1981) and Hansen and Pearson (1982) used Inference Training with second- and fourth-grade students (also see Chapter 15, this volume). This training involved the teacher's identification of three important concepts in a story, then creating two questions per concept. The first question asks students to identify something from their background knowledge that is related to the story concept. The second asks a parallel question about an instance in the story. For example, a concept may be that recycling involves changing something that is no longer useful into something that is useful. The prior knowledge question could be: "Can you think of any time that you had something that you almost threw away, but made it into something you can use? Describe what you did." The question relating that to the story may be: "In our story today, an old newspaper is thrown away but someone finds it and changes it into something useful. What do you think he made it into?" This is repeated for two other concepts. A discussion about why it is important to think about background knowledge is also conducted. Following the prequestions and reading of the story, a discussion consisting of script-implicit questions is conducted. After ten weeks of basal story lessons such as these, younger and low-ability students in the training group performed at a higher level in responding to literal and inferential questions than did those in a control group. These studies of other-generated questions suggest that students' reading comprehension can be enhanced by sensitizing them to the importance of their knowledge base as a source of information related to text-based information. This facilitation takes place largely through the teacher's modeling of appropriate questioning sequences and explicitly stating how this sequence is important for improving comprehension.

In summary, research in other-generated questions has concerned noninstructional research that involves, first, the demonstration of the utility of questions and how the position of such questions in text effects particular kinds of comprehension and, second, instructional studies concerned with sensitizing students to sources of information for better understanding the text they read and for more appropriately responding to questions following their readings. The first emphasizes the need to provide high quality and easily comprehendible text while the second emphasizes the importance of providing students with as many means for accessing information relevant to the text as possible.

Student-Generated Questions

The research in student-generated questions is broad, including studies of modeling self-instructions during reading (e.g., Meichenbaum and Asarnow 1979;

Palincsar, this volume), instructing students in question-generation relative to their knowledge of story grammars (e.g., Singer and Donlan 1982), generation of questions after locating main ideas (e.g., Andre and Anderson 1978–79), and factors that influence the generation of questions (e.g., Miyake and Norman 1979). Much of this literature stems from or has influenced research in metacomprehension, the readers' awareness of and control over the reading process. This literature has used questioning as an indication of readers' level of understanding of the text. The assumption is that if a question generated during reading cannot be adequately answered, readers who are using the questions to successfully monitor their understanding will employ self-correcting strategies such as asking for clarification or further information. In this section, we categorize these studies into investigations of reflective and prospective questions.

Reflective questions are those that involve self-questioning about one's understanding of passage sections already read. These questions would be content independent to the extent that the same questions could be asked of any passage (e.g., Does this make sense? Who are the main characters? What are the main events? Do I understand how this all fits together?). For example, Meichenbaum and Asarnow (1979) describe a self-instructional training program that involves the modeling of reflective questions during reading as an example of cognitive-behavioral modification. They have successfully taught children to carry out an internal dialogue about a passage being read. The dialogue consists of reminders to ask themselves who the main characters are, what the important details are, how the characters feel, and why they feel this way. As a result, they improved the students' reading comprehension relative to two different control groups.

Similarly, Andre and Anderson (1978–79) and Wong and Jones (in press) taught students to determine the main idea and then create a general question relative to it. This is reflective to the extent that the questions are still general (e.g., What is the main idea?) and designed to encourage students to reflect on the purpose of the passage. Andre and Anderson used a population of secondary students, while Wong and Jones worked with learning-disabled middle-school students. In both cases, they found that self-questioning techniques were effective provided instruction was given in both main idea location and question generation.

Prospective questions, in contrast, are more content specific in nature. These are generally of a predictive nature, whereby students are asking what events are likely to occur given the current status of characters and events in the text. For example, Singer and Donlan (1982) taught high school students a problem-solving schema for generating questions specific to a story. The researchers identified aspects of stories (e.g., characters, goals, obstacles) based on research in story grammars. Corresponding to each aspect they developed a general question (e.g., What is the main character trying to accomplish?). They taught the students how to identify aspects of stories and which general questions corresponded to each aspect. Then they explained how to convert the general questions into story specific ones. Results of the study indicated that this questioning technique was effective in enhancing recall of students who had been through the training program.

Palincsar (this volume) also has conducted research testing a prospective type of self-questioning. Based on Manzo's reciprocal questioning procedure, she modeled for students appropriate types of content specific questions, alternating asking them questions and having them ask her questions specific to a text. Again, this type of self-questioning resulted in enhanced student performance.

Miyake and Norman (1979) studied college students question generation on an easy and a difficult task, defined in terms of the amount of background knowledge the students possessed. Half of the groups received pretraining to heighten their knowledge of word processors, while the other half received none. On the easy task, the manual was written such that people with no computer experience could learn. On the hard task, understanding the manual required some background with computers. When both groups were given an easy task, those with less background asked more questions. But when faced with the more difficult task, the experts asked the most and the best questions. Research such as this is important if educators are to not only develop effective questioning techniques but to know when the techniques would effect most gain.

We have indicated why an understanding of children's comprehension-related questioning activities is important. We have also presented a selective but representative review of studies concerned with a description of questions in school-related settings and children's understanding of the concept of questioning. Finally, we have reviewed studies designed to promote more effective comprehension through the use of both other- and student-generated questions. Missing throughout our presentation has been a conceptual framework or model within which to interpret extant findings concerned with questioning and to call attention to issues, both theoretical and applied, that need further investigation.

TOWARD A CONCEPTUAL FRAMEWORK FOR UNDERSTANDING THE DEVELOPMENT OF QUESTIONING

As suggested earlier, there is no comprehensive conceptual framework for interpreting the development of question-related activities in children. In this section, we suggest several working assumptions that we believe need to be considered in developing such a model.

First, we assume that, like other cognitive processes, questioning-related activities are both acquired and used in a social context. Here we have been influenced heavily by the work of Vygotsky (1978) and Luria (1959) and more recently by Bruner (1971) and Wertsch (1979). All these theorists share the belief that cognitive processes (e.g., questioning) are first acquired by children interpsychologically or under the direction of another (e.g., a parent or teacher). This "scaffolding" provided by an adult is likely to be a protracted process. Through repeated interactions with an adult, the child comes to make use of a cognitive process intrapsychologically. That is, the child can initiate and make use of the cognitive process(es) without any external support.

A second and related assumption draws heavily upon systems theory and has been influenced by the work of Brofenbrenner (1979). The social contexts within which a child's cognitive activity develops are themselves nested within a network of more inclusive levels. Thus the questioning activity that takes place within a teacher-child dyad is apt to be transformed markedly when embedded within an entire class of students. More specifically, within a dyad a teacher may be able to ask integrative questions, which requires the use of students' background knowledge as well as text-based information. In an entire class of students the teacher's goal may be transformed into maintaining the general level of activity, and he or she may be able to make use only of literal questions that call for obvious and readily available answers.

A third working assumption concerns the relative specificity of cognitive skills. Even though the child's use of a cognitive strategy (e.g., question asking) may come to occur somewhat independently of other individuals, its applicability is still apt to be tied to the particular context or contexts in which it was acquired. In other words, there is no such thing as "pure process," but rather processes in context (Rogoff 1982). The breadth or narrowness of a given process is a matter of considerable theoretical and practical import. With respect to instruction in comprehension, the goals of instruction may range from the relatively modest goal of facilitating comprehension within a particular content domain, to teaching metacomprehension skills (e.g. self-generated questions) that enable students to control their own comprehension, to the most ambitious (and perhaps most unrealistic) goal that the cognitive and metacognitive skills associated with comprehension generalize across a broad band of content domains. Thus, the same individuals who are able to ask many high-quality questions of a domain in which they have expertise may be muted in their question-asking activities in a domain in which they are relative novices (Miyake and Norman 1979).

Finally, we believe that the processes associated with questioning (i.e. both question answering and asking) may be profitably analyzed into a sequence of subcomponents or stages. We next describe the five components of the questioning process and suggest directions for future research.

Formulating the Questions

Consistent with a distinction made earlier, questions can originate with an external source (i.e., the teacher) or from the students themselves. Questions that derive from an external source presumably call children's attention to that which is important. And yet, as was suggested earlier, children may not respond to adjunct questions in the same manner as adults.

We discuss question answering and asking together because we believe they are related. However, a relationship between those processes has yet to be demonstrated. This issue has implications for both basic as well as instructional research. Are individuals who have been asked and had to answer questions better question askers themselves? One cannot presuppose that student-generated questions are necessarily always effective in promoting comprehension. Indeed, whether (and under what conditions) students are able to ask questions of text to promote comprehension is a major issue with respect to student-generated questions. What sort of self-generated questions are most facilitative of comprehension? What conditions even give rise to children's need to ask questions (of others or themselves) with respect to a given segment of text? As Miyake and Norman suggest, "To ask a question, one must know enough to know what is not known." What role does children's background knowledge play in both the quantity and quality of questions they ask for a given text? Brown (1975) has suggested that children are universal novices. This implies the need to delineate circumstances in which students should not be expected to seek clarifying information and where it would be appropriate for the teacher to model this behavior for them.

Understanding the Question

In the case of other-generated questions, the question is provided for the students. They in turn determine whether they understand it. If they do not understand, they may seek clarification from its source. Bruner (1966) has suggested that when asking children questions, one cannot assume that the question they answer is the same as that intended by the questioner. To know whether or not one understands a question asked by another is comprehension monitoring in its simplest form. In contrast, students who have generated questions are usually presumed to understand them. Whether this assumption is warranted has yet to be determined empirically.

Remembering the Question

Given that a question has been posed (either by another or oneself) and understood, it still must be remembered. The importance of this component may vary from trivial for easily stated, literal questions to significant in those cases where questions are so long as to require that the learner paraphrase to remember the gist. Remembering the question is particularly important for young children or readers naive in background knowledge since they often must hold the question in mind for a lengthy period of time while searching for an answer. This could be an additional cause for a reader's answering a question that has not been asked. If recall of a question itself is cognitively demanding, then constraints imposed on the student, such as whether look-backs are permitted and how long they have to determine the answer, become important. Again, the interactive nature of questions and tasks has yet to be extensively studied.

Identifying and Retrieving the Answer to the Question

Given that students have understood and remembered a question, they must then determine the source(s) of information for that question. Logically, such a source may reside externally (i.e., in text or as a part of another's background knowledge), internally (i.e., as a part of one's own background knowledge), or in some combination of external and internal sources. Sensitizing students to the relationship between questions and their sources of information has proven valuable in enhancing their performance on comprehension questions (Raphael, in press). Still to be studied are the kinds of questions that are most effective in promoting understanding of various materials and in various learning situations.

Decision Criteria for Answering Questions

A final stage in the answering of a question involves students' assessment as to whether they have adequately determined the correct answer(s). The decision criteria by which one judges the worth of one's answer is especially important. Further investigations concerned with memory monitoring, such as those on the "feeling of knowing" (e.g., Hart 1965, 1966; Gavelek and Raphael 1981), may suggest how these decision criteria develop. It would also seem critical that students be able to recognize when they cannot answer a question. Such a condition may exist when the source(s) for a given question are unavailable to the student *or* when the question itself is unanswerable. The determination of an unanswerable question may, of course, occur during the second stage concerned with understanding the question. Finally, research examining individual differences in these decision criteria would seem especially important because students are likely to vary in the standards they set for themselves. Extreme cases may range from students who search interminably for the "perfect" answer to impulsive students satisfied with only a part of the answer or with the first answer that comes to mind.

CONCLUSION

We believe that questioning activities are important for those concerned with reading comprehension instruction. Questioning activities have the potential for generating both comprehension and metacomprehension of textual materials and have ramifications for comprehension in nontext situations (e.g., computer interactions, listening activities). It is too simplistic, however, to assume that because children are often asked questions, comprehension is automatically promoted or that students become skilled question askers themselves. Therefore, we have attempted to outline our current level of knowledge about students' questioning skills and to delineate a possible conceptual framework for guiding future questions.

In addition to the more basic questions about questioning we have raised, there are implications for those whose primary responsibilities are teaching children. First, it is important for teachers to recognize the complexity of questioning in general. More specifically, it is necessary to realize the many meanings of the statement "I don't understand," which children often state in learning situations. Is it that they do not understand the question? the topic? the strategy they should use to answer the question? Do they understand the question but not how to respond to it due to a lack of background knowledge? Second, teachers use questions in several aspects of their teaching. It is useful to recognize the utility of different questions to provide the most effective teaching possible. That is, teachers need to recognize whether the instructional situation would be facilitated by asking questions prior to or after reading, whether to have students answer other-generated questions or whether they should generate questions of their own. Finally, it is important to recognize both the advantages and disadvantages in relying on standardized tests for information about students' progress in reading. Tests may vary in their consistency between the kinds of questions they ask and the cognitive progression of reading skills. In summary, while there is much about questioning that has yet to be studied, much of what has been learned is of direct relevance to classroom teachers.

REFERENCES

Anderson, R. C., & Biddle, W. B. On asking people questions about what they do when they are reading. In G. Bower (Ed.), *Psychology of learning and motivation*, vol. 9. New York: Academic Press, 1975.

Andre, M. D. A., & Anderson, T. H. The development of a self-questioning study technique. *Reading Research Quarterly*, 1978–79, *14*, 605–623.

Au, K. H. Using the experience-text-relationship method with minority children. *The Reading Teacher*, 1979, *32*, 677–679.

Au, K. H. *What children know about reading comprehension: Developing question-asking skills.* Paper presented at the International Reading Association, St. Louis, April 1981.

Barrett, T. C. Taxonomy of reading comprehension. In R. Smith & T. C. Barrett (Eds.), *Teaching reading in the middle grades.* Reading, Mass.: Addison-Wesley, 1976.

Bronfenbrenner, U. *The ecology of human development.* Cambridge, Mass.: Harvard University Press, 1979.

Brown, A. L. The development of memory: Knowing, knowing about knowing, knowing how to know. In H. W. Reese (Ed.), *Advances in child development and behavior*, Vol. 10. New York: Academic Press, 1975.

Brown, A. L., Campione, J. C., & Day, J. D. Learning to learn: On training students to learn from texts. *Educational Researcher*, 1981, *10*, 14–21.

Bruner, J. S. *The relevance of education.* New York: Norton, 1971.

Bruner, J. S. *Toward a theory of instruction.* New York: Norton, 1971.

Chou-Hare, V., & Pulliam, C. A. Teacher questioning: A verification and an extension. *Journal of Reading Behavior*, 1979, *12*, 69–72.

Chou-Hare, V. Beginning reading theory and comprehension questions in teachers' manuals. *The Reading Teacher*, 1982, *35*, 918–923.

Crowell, D., Au, K. H., & Blake, J. Reading comprehension questions: Differences among standardized tests. *Journal of Reading*, in press.

Frase, L. T. Some unpredicted effects of different questions upon learning from connected discourse. *Journal of Educational Psychology*, 1968, *59*, 197–201.

Gavelek, J. R., & Raphael, T. E. *The relationship between one's feeling of knowing and performance on comprehension questions.* Paper presented at the National Reading Conference, Dallas, Texas, 1981.

Guszak, F. J. Teacher questioning and reading. *The Reading Teacher*, 1967, *21*, 227–234.

Hansen, J. The effects of inference training and practice on young children's comprehension. *Reading Research Quarterly*, 1981, *16*, 391–417.

Hansen, J., & Pearson, P. D. *An instructional study: Improving the inferential comprehension of good and poor fourth-grade readers.* Tech. Rep. No. 235. Urbana, Ill.: Center for the Study of Reading, University of Illinois, March 1982.

Hart, J. T. Memory and the feeling of knowing experience. *Journal of Educational Psychology*, 1965, *56*, 208–216.

Hart, J. T. Methodological note on feeling of knowing experiments. *Journal of Educational Psychology*, 1966, *57*, 347–349.

Luria, A. R. The directive function of speech in development and dissolution. *Word*, 1959, *15*, 341–352.

Manzo, A. V. *Improving reading comprehension through reciprocal questioning.* Doctoral dissertation, Syracuse University, 1970. *Dissertation Abstracts International*, 1970, *30*, 5344A. University Microfilms No. 70–10, 364.

Markman, E. M. Realizing that you don't understand: Elementary school children's awareness of inconsistencies. *Child Development*, 1979, *50*, 643–655.

Michenbaum, D., & Asarnow, J. Cognitive-behavioral modification and meta-cognitive development: Implication for the classroom. In P. C. Kendall &

S. D. Hollon (Eds.), *Cognitive-Behavioral Interventions: Theory, Research, and Procedures.* New York: Academic Press, 1979.

Miyake, N., & Normal, D. A. To ask a question one must know enough to know what is not known. *Journal of Verbal Learning and Verbal Behavior*, 1979, *18*, 351–364.

Pearson, P. D., & Johnson, D. D. *Teaching reading comprehension*, New York: Holt, Rinehart, and Winston, 1978.

Pearson, P. D., Hansen, J., & Gordon, C. The effect of background knowledge on young children's comprehension of explicit & implicit information. *Journal of Reading Behavior*, 1979, *9*, 201–210.

Palincsar, A. M. Chapter 17, this volume.

Raphael, T. E. Teaching children question-answering strategies. *Reading Teacher*, in press.

Raphael, T. E., Winograd, P., & Pearson, P. D. Strategies children use when answering questions. In M. L. Kamil & A. J. Moe (Eds.), *Perspectives on reading research and instruction*. Washington, D. C.: National Reading Conference, December 1980.

Raphael, T. E., & Pearson, P. D. *The effect of metacognitive awareness training on children's question answering behavior*. Tech. Rep. No. 238. Urbana, Ill.: Center for the Study of Reading, University of Illinois, March 1982.

Raphael, T. E., & Wonnacott, C. A. *Metacognitive training in question-answering strategies: Implementation in a 4th grade developmental reading program.* Paper presentation at the National Reading Conference, Dallas, Texas, 1981. (ERIC Document Reproduction Service No. ED212 999).

Reynolds, R. E., & Magleby, L. B. *Developmental effects of question position and question type on children's learning of prose material.* Paper presentation at the National Reading Conference, Dallas, Texas, 1981.

Reynolds, R. E., Standiford, S. N., & Anderson, R. C. *Distribution of reading time when questions are asked about a restricted category of text information.* Tech. Rep. No. 83. Urbana, Ill.: Center for the Study of Reading, University of Illinois, April 1981.

Rickards, J. P., & Denner, P. R. Depressive effects of underlining and adjunct questions on children's recall of text. *Instructional Science*, 1979, *8*, 81–90.

Rickards, J. P., & Hatcher, C. W. Interspersed meaningful learning questions as semantic cues for poor comprehenders. *Reading Research Quarterly*, 1978, *13*, 539–553.

Rogoff, B. Integrating context and cognitive development. In M. E. Lamb & A. L. Brown (Eds.), *Advances in Developmental Psychology* (vol. 2). Hillsdale, N.J.: Lawrence Erlbaum Associates, 1982.

Sanders, N. *Classroom questions: What kinds?* New York: Harper & Row, 1966.

Singer, H., & Donlan, D. Active comprehension: Problem-solving schema with question generation for comprehension of complex short stories. *Reading Research Quarterly*, 1982, *17*, 166–186.

Watts, G. H., & Anderson, R. C. Effects of three types of inserted questions on learning from prose. *Journal of Educational Psychology*, 1971, *62*, 387–394.

Wertsch, J. V. From social interaction to higher psycholological processes: A clarification and application of Vygotsky's theory. *Human Development*, 1979, *22*, 1–22.

Winograd, P., & Johnston, P. Comprehension monitoring and the error detection paradigm. *Journal of Reading Behavior*, 1982, *14*, 61–76.

Wonnacott, C. A., & Raphael, T. E. *Question-answering: An investigation of comprehension monitoring.* Paper presented at National Reading Conference, Clearwater, Florida, December 1982.

Wong, B. Y. L., & Jones, W. *Increasing metacomprehension in learning-disabled and normally-achieving students through self-questioning training.* Unpublished manuscript, Simon Fraser University, 1982.

17

The Quest for Meaning from Expository Text: A Teacher-Guided Journey

Annemarie Sullivan Palincsar

A burgeoning interest in the distinction between the cognitive and metacognitive aspects of reading has focused attention on activating the inactive reader. While the cognitive aspects of reading refer to the actual knowledge or understanding of the material read, metacognition, as defined by Brown (1979), refers to (1) the learner's awareness of his (or her) cognitive resources and the compatability between himself and the demands of the reading situation; as well as (2) the self-regulation mechanisms, or control, used by the active reader in his efforts to understand what is read. These two facets of metacognition are naturally closely related. What the reader knows about the task of reading will certainly influence how he or she sets about controlling reading activities. A disturbing picture emerging from the classroom observational research suggests that the instruction of comprehension monitoring and comprehension fostering activities is currently receiving little attention (Bartlett 1979, Duffy and Roehler 1982, Durkin 1979). This appears to be the case particularly with "poor readers." The classroom teacher, striving for fluent decoding, may unwittingly reinforce the poor comprehender's notion that reading is "figuring out words" and not that reading is "figuring out meaning."

There are at least two steps prerequisite to bridging the gap between current teaching practices and those that appear more efficacious in the instruction of reading comprehension. The first is to supply further evidence that indeed there are strategies that enhance reading comprehension. The second is to identify in-

The research reported in this article represents a portion of the author's dissertation study funded by US PHS Grant HD–06864 from the National Institute of Child Health and Human Development. I would like to express sincere appreciation to the members of my dissertation committee for their valued recommendations and support: Colleen Blankenship, Ann Brown, Laura Jordan, Steve Lilly, and David Pearson. In addition, I wish to acknowledge the unflagging cooperation and skillful instruction of the teachers who participated in Study 3: Denise Canavit, Terry Kirbach, Sharon Poynter, and Nancy Richardson.

structional techniques, readily accessible to the classroom teacher, that will facilitate the teaching of these comprehension monitoring/fostering activities.

The research reported in this chapter was designed to investigate reading strategies by measuring effects of students' use of metacognitive techniques. The research investigated the effects of teaching poor comprehenders four activities: question generating, summarizing, predicting, and clarifying. The activities were instructed using a procedure referred to as reciprocal teaching in which students received explicit instruction, modeling, and corrective feedback regarding the four comprehension monitoring/fostering activities. Because the pilot study, as well as the study reported here, are formally described as investigations in other manuscripts (Brown and Palincsar 1982; Palincsar and Brown, in press), this chapter provides information about implementing a program of comprehension instruction in a school setting and on implications for educators.

THE SELECTION OF COMPREHENSION
MONITORING/FOSTERING ACTIVITIES

Four monitoring/fostering activities were selected. The first was self-questioning. The value of self-questioning to enhance reading comprehension has been investigated and documented previously by researchers such as André and Anderson (1978), Frase and Schwartz (1975), Manzo (1968), and Wong and Jones (1981). The focus here was to give students extensive modeling about how to ask questions followed by practice generating main idea questions about the text. Questions regarding detail that were generally discouraged included the following: "how many" (e.g., "My question is how many vertebrates do snake backbones have?"), "how long" (e.g., "How long did camels walk in the desert?"), fill-in-the-blank (e.g., "The western corral is only a blank and a blank blank long. Can anyone fill in the blanks?"), and information lifted directly from the text rather than paraphrased (e.g., "What can the spot of light from the sun cut through?"). In contrast, main idea questions such as the following were modeled and received praise: "The water in the ocean is not fit for drinking. How can the sun make the water fresh?" (following a paragraph on solar distillation).

The second instructional activity, summarization, has received less empirical attention (however, see Brown and Day, in press; Day 1980). Summarization was included to provide students an opportunity to monitor their own understanding of the text by learning to extract and integrate the gist of the material read. To illustrate, a student who, after receiving practice in summarizing, read a paragraph comparing the characteristics and habits of two principal kinds of camels, was able to demonstrate understanding of the text, saying, "It tells us about the two kinds of camels, what they are like, and where they live."

Collins and Smith (in press) have advocated that in addition to making interpretations about what is currently happening in the text, students should be taught to make predictions or hypotheses about what will occur in the text. Predicting constitutes the third component of this comprehension monitoring/fostering program. The predictions students made were of two kinds: text-based and content-based. To illustrate, a student reading the passage heading "How snakes catch their prey" made the following text-based prediction: "My prediction is they will now talk about different things about snakes, what they eat and stuff like that."

The teacher prompted a content-based prediction with the question, "O.K. What do you think they eat?" and the student predicted "animals." As another example, after reading the heading "Adaptations to Desert Living" the student made a text-based prediction when she suggested that the next segment would tell them "how camels can live in the desert." A content-based prediction was made when another student said, "Here they will tell us about the camel's humps and all the water that is stored up in them." Through the process of predicting, students establish for themselves a purpose for reading—to confirm or disprove their own hypotheses.

The failure of poor comprehenders to engage in spontaneous critical evaluation of text has been well documented (Markman 1977, 1979; Harris, Kruithof, Terwogt, and Visser 1981). For this reason, the explicit instruction of clarification was the final component of this training package. Critical evaluation of text is an activity that has to be practiced in moderation since it is not constructive to instruct students to be suspicious of each line. Our approach to this task was first to stimulate discussion among the students as to why text is sometimes unclear. Students readily thought of such factors as "hard words." Teacher input was required to add unclear referents, disorganized text, and unfamiliarity of content. Following this discussion, the teachers shared with students, at least two times daily, points in the passage that they felt required clarification or points where they, the teachers, reread, looked back in the text, or sought some other means of bringing meaning to the text. In addition to this daily modeling, teachers elicited clarifications by reminding students to "be looking for points that need clearing up," and prompting, "Does anyone have any clearing up to do?" Some of the students' responses to this inquiry included the following statements: "I don't see how they can say 'heat lightning occurs on hot summer days.' How could you see it?" "The word meter throws me off in this sentence." "Boy, this paragraph sure is a mess. It's all over the place." "I have one. What do they mean by 'far away dreams'?"

THE RECIPROCAL TEACHING PROCEDURE

The primary instructional technique employed to teach the four monitoring/focusing activities was an interactive dialogue through which the teacher explicitly modeled the four activities previously described. The students followed the teacher's example by engaging in the same activities, and the teacher prompted and shaped the students' participation through the use of corrective feedback.

Support for this instructional procedure is found in several sources. Two instructional components that appear to be predictive of academic achievement are engaged time and teacher monitoring. Engaged time refers to the proportion of the allocated time for an instructional activity in which the student is on task or engaged (Rosenshine and Berliner 1978). Teacher monitoring implies teacher-pupil interactions in which the teacher mediates the learning experience and evaluates progress (Anderson, Evertson, and Brophy 1979). This technique was designed to maximize both engaged time and teacher monitoring.

Empirical support for explicit comprehension instruction is found in a number of studies (Au 1980; Bird 1980; Brown, Campione, and Day 1981; Day 1980). In addition, others who have written extensively about strategy training have recommended that "one of the most potent methods of communicating learning strategies is modeling" (Dansereau 1980, p. 14). "Comprehension results from a dynamic cognitive process and not from the rigid application of a set of predetermined skills ... the comprehension process must be taught actively to demonstrate its usefulness to increasing understanding" (Harker 1973, p. 379).

There were several steps included in the introduction of the reciprocal teaching procedure, including a group discussion of why we sometimes experience difficulty understanding what we read. This was followed by instruction regarding the four activities the students would learn. For example, the students were instructed in the Brown and Day (in press) summarization rules: to identify topic sentences or make them up if they could not be found in the text, to name lists with appropriate labels, to delete from their summaries information that was unimportant or repeated. The students were instructed that these activities would help them keep their attention on what they were reading as well as help them make sure they understood what they read. Finally, discussion was held regarding the various classes (e.g., social studies and science) and school-related tasks (e.g., studying for tests and preparing book reports) with which these activities would be helpful.

The procedure by which the four activities would be learned was then described. Students were told that everyone in the group would take turns being teacher during the reading session. It was explained that whoever assumed the role of teacher was responsible for asking the group an important question, summarizing, predicting what might be discussed next in the passage, and sharing anything that he or she found unclear or confusing. The teacher was to call on someone to answer his or her question and was responsible for telling the student whether or not the answer was correct. In turn, the students who were not teaching that particular segment of the passage were to comment on the teacher's question(s) and statements and feel free to contribute to that segment.

This introductory information was reviewed for several days when the intervention was initiated. The following general procedure then occurred each day:

1. The students were given an expository passage about 1,500 words in length.
2. If the passage was new to the group, the adult teacher called the students' attention to the title and asked for predictions based on the title. If the passage was familiar to the students, the teacher asked the students to recall and state the topic of the passage as well as the important points already covered in the passage.
3. The teacher assigned a segment of the passage to be read (usually a paragraph) and either told the students that she would be the teacher (especially for the initial days of training) or assigned a teacher for the first segment.
4. The group read the assigned segment silently.
5. The teacher for that segment proceeded first to ask a question, then summarize, and offer a prediction and clarification when appropriate.
6. The adult teacher provided the guidance necessary for the student teacher to complete the preceding activities through a variety of techniques: prompting, "What question did you think a teacher might ask?"; instruction, "Remember a summary is a shortened version, it doesn't include a lot of detail"; modifying the activity, "If you're having a hard

time thinking of a question, why don't you summarize first?" and by soliciting the help of other students, "Who can help us out with this one?"

7. The remaining members of the group were invited to comment on or supplement that segment.

8. The adult teacher provided praise and feedback specific to the student teacher's participation; "You asked that question well, it was very clear what information you wanted," "Excellent prediction, let's see if you're right," "That was interesting information. It was information that I would call detail in the passage. Can you tell us the most important information in that paragraph?" After this feedback, adult teachers modeled any activity they felt continued to need improvement: "A question I would have asked would be ... ," "I would summarize by saying ...," "Did anyone else find this statement unclear?"

EVALUATING RECIPROCAL TEACHING OF COMPREHENSION MONITORING ACTIVITIES

Three studies have been conducted using the reciprocal teaching procedure. The first (Palincsar and Brown, in press) compared reciprocal teaching with a more traditional reading activity in which students who made errors answering comprehension questions were to refer back to the text to correct their errors. The results suggested that while both conditions resulted in greater accuracy with comprehension questions, reciprocal teaching resulted in the best performance and maintenance of performance. Encouraged by these results, a second and third study were undertaken in which only reciprocal teaching was investigated. In the first two studies, the investigator functioned as the adult teacher, met the students individually (Study 1) or in pairs (Study 2), on a resource room basis where the students participated in the studies in lieu of attending reading class. In Study 3, in contrast, the adult teachers were classroom or remedial reading teachers who met the students in groups that ranged in size from four to seven and the study was conducted during regular reading periods. Because it is anticipated that most educators would be interested primarily in Study 3, that one is emphasized here. However, it should be noted that the student selection procedures, research design, materials, and pattern of results were similar in all three studies.

Students

Four groups of junior high students participated in Study 3. They all attended rural schools with residential populations not exceeding 8,000 within 20 miles of a middle-sized midwestern city. There were 21 students, seven females and 14 males. Standardized tests administered by each school district prior to the initiation of the study (including the SRA [level 2] Diagnostic Reading Test, Iowa Test of Basic Skills, and California Achievement Test, Level V) indicated that comprehension scores averaged two years below grade and ranged from 5 years to .5 years below grade level. Two of the groups were instructed by Title I Remedial Reading Teachers, while two were instructed by classroom teachers working with "low track" language arts students. To ascertain whether the students met the criterion established for participating in the study, they were administered an informal screening device. The criteria were focused on identifying a discrepancy between decoding skills and comprehension ability. Specifically, students were to read a 450-word passage written at seventh-grade level, according to the Fry Readability formula, at a rate of at least 80 wpm (words per minute) correct with two or fewer error words per minute. These are the rates suggested by Lovett and Hansen (1976) as predictive of the probable instructional reading level of students. In addition, the students were to demonstrate comprehension difficulty by answering no more than 50 percent of the accompanying comprehension questions correctly. The passage used in the screening was piloted with a group of 13 seventh graders identified as good readers. The mean comprehension score attained by this group was 80.4 percent. The participants in Study 3 averaged 35 percent accuracy with comprehension questions, a 104 wpm oral reading rate, and a 1.5 wpm oral reading incorrect rate.

Materials

The passages used to facilitate the training sessions were drawn from a variety of reading series: *Reading Unlimited*, Scott Foresman (1976); *Keys to Reading*, The Economy Company (1980); *Adventures for Readers*, Harcourt Brace Jovanovich (1979); *Reading 720*, Ginn and Company (1976); *Corrective Reading Decoding*, Science Research Associates (1978); and *Serendipity*, Houghton Mifflin (1974). All passages were expository, averaged 1,500 words in length, and represented a range of topics including poisonous snakes, solar energy, the Inca civilization, lightning, and carnivorous plants. Passages were selected after determining that they were of a seventh-grade readability according to the Fry formula. The 13 passages were sequenced so that the first three lent themselves more readily to determining the main idea and extracting questions (i.e., the paragraphs were relatively short and there was frequent use of topic headings).

In addition to the training passage used each day of intervention, there was also an assessment passage completed daily and independently by each student. The assessment passages, ranging in length from 400 to 475 words, were also expository at a seventh-grade readability level and were taken from the same reading programs as the training material. Ten comprehension questions were constructed for each assessment passage using the Pearson and Johnson (1978) taxonomy, which defines the question's relationship to the text and the strategy to be implemented in answering the question. If the question is stated and integrated in the text, the question is considered to be text explicit. A text-implicit question has an answer stated but not in any one place in the text, forcing the reader to integrate information across sentences, paragraphs, or pages. Finally, a script-implicit question is one for which no answer is found in the text. The question is based on the topic of the text but requires the reader to answer the question by drawing upon information in his fund of knowledge. Each set of comprehension questions was composed of four text-explicit, four text-implicit, and two script-implicit questions.

Design

A multiple baseline design across groups (Hirsen and Barlowe 1976) was used to assess the effectiveness of reciprocal teaching. All students experienced the fol-

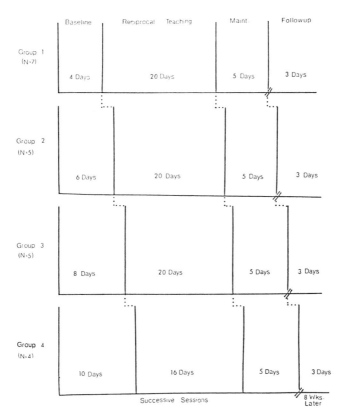

FIGURE 17.1

lowing four conditions: baseline, intervention, maintenance, and follow-up. The design is presented in Figure 17.1.

Procedures

After it was determined which teachers and students would participate in the study, three training sessions were scheduled with each teacher. In the first session, the investigator explained the rationale and development of the reciprocal teaching procedure being investigated. The investigator shared the general design and objectives of the study, showed a videotape of the investigator working with a group of students in a reciprocal teaching session, and assisted the teachers in resolving concerns of a management nature (e.g., grading, scheduling, homework).

In the second session, the teacher and investigator practiced, in isolation, the activities teachers would be modeling using a variety of the training materials. In addition, the investigator role-played situations that might be anticipated, such as a student who is unable to generate a question or a student who summarizes by reiterating the paragraph in detail.

In the final session, the teacher and investigator met with a group of seventh-grade students who were not participants in the study and practiced the reciprocal teaching with these youngsters. The investigator modeled how the procedure should be introduced to the students, modeled the four activities, and the process of corrective feedback. The teachers then assumed responsibility for the group, and as the practice session transpired, teacher and investigator discussed the proceedings with one another.

Procedural reliability checks which were conducted each week of intervention provided the opportunity to discuss and resolve difficulties experienced with the reciprocal teaching procedure.

Experimental Conditions

Baseline. During each day of baseline, the students were given an assessment passage that they were asked to read silently and carefully so that they could answer comprehension questions when they were finished reading. The students were also told to ask for assistance with any word(s) they could not read or understand. (There were very few requests for assistance.) Upon completing the passage, the passage was collected, and the students were given the accompanying comprehension questions to answer in writing. A graph indicating the percentage of comprehension questions answered correctly each day was maintained for each student and shared with the students each day of baseline. The total numbers of baseline days ranged from four to ten, as illustrated in Figure 17.1.

Intervention. During the intervention phase, the reciprocal teaching procedure was introduced and conducted as previously described in this chapter. After proceeding through the training passage in the manner described for a period of 25 to 30 minutes, the training passages were collected and the assessment procedure began as described under *Baseline*. The intervention was scheduled to occur for a maximum of 20 days. Groups 1, 2, and 3 had 20 days of training while Group 4 had 16. During the intervention phase, students were shown their graphs on a weekly basis.

Maintenance. The maintenance phase began immediately after the last day of intervention. Maintenance occurred for five consecutive school days and was conducted in the same manner as baseline.

Follow-up. Eight weeks after the maintenance probes, follow-up probes occurred for three consecutive school days and were conducted in a manner identical to that described for baseline. Students received daily knowledge of results.

RESULTS

Five research questions were posed in this study, each with its accompanying dependent measures. Because these have been delineated elsewhere (Palincsar and Brown), only the principal dependent measure, accuracy responding to comprehension questions as measured by the daily assessment passage, is reported here.

The reader is referred to Figure 17.2 as the following question is addressed. Did the students' ability to answer comprehension questions increase as a result of the reciprocal teaching procedure and were these increases maintained over time?

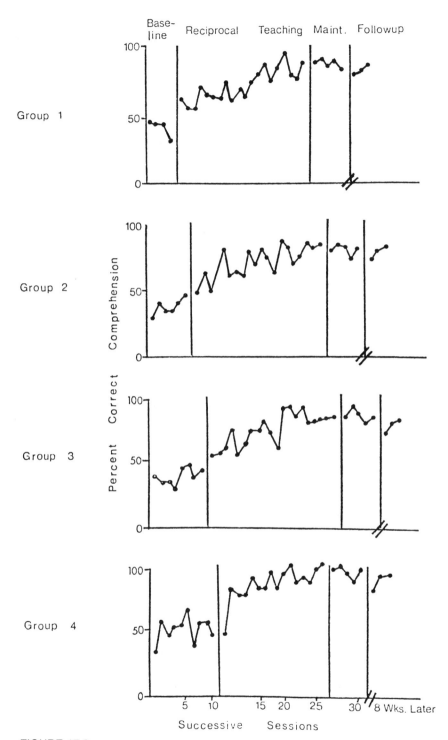

FIGURE 17.2

The data indicate that the students in Study 3 were typically achieving 40 percent accuracy on comprehension questions during baseline (B). With the introduction of the reciprocal teaching intervention, their accuracy increased steadily, if gradually, until all groups were consistently scoring above 70 percent by the fifteenth day of intervention. The students continued to demonstrate gains during maintenance (M) and a slight decrement in performance during follow-up (F).

These observations were confirmed by the following planned comparisons. Mean accuracy on comprehension questions was significantly greater during intervention than during baseline, $F(1,80) = 482.31, p < .0001$. There was a significant difference between mean performance during the first and second half of intervention, $F(1,80) = 76.71, p < .0001$. Students continued to gain in accuracy during the second half of intervention. There was also a significant difference between maintenance and the second half of treatment, $F(1,80) = 5.72, p < .02$. Students' mean performance was better during maintenance than during the second half of the intervention phase. A significant difference was discerned between maintenance and follow-up. Mean performance was higher for those probes that occurred immediately following training than for those that occurred eight weeks following intervention, $F(1,80) = 7.61, p < .01$. However, mean performance during follow-up was significantly greater than mean performance during baseline, $F(1,80) = 534.97, p < .0001$.

Other results of interest to educators will be mentioned in brief. At the conclusion of the study, the students experienced greater success implementing summarization rules, particularly in their awareness of main idea information and ability to extract and invent topic sentences. The students also made significant gains in their ability to identify material about which teachers ask questions and to construct clear and complete questions. In addition, the students were significantly more accurate detecting lines in passages that were anomalous to the titles of the passages.

DISCUSSION AND RECOMMENDATIONS FOR IMPLEMENTING THE RECIPROCAL TEACHING

Procedure

Results for the effects of reciprocal teaching of comprehension-monitoring/fostering activities are encouraging. They suggest that using a structured teaching procedure easily incorporated into a small group reading lesson, students' reading behaviors can be dramatically modified. Consistent effects were typically obtained by the twelfth to fifteenth day of training. Furthermore, students demonstrated the change on assessment passages that were independent of the training material. Finally, the effects of reciprocal teaching were durable, suggesting that students had assimilated these strategies into their reading routines and continued to exercise them without prompting. These are important observations in view of how little direction has traditionally been offered teachers regarding comprehension instruction (Durkin 1981).

Transcripts of the instructional dialogue that occurred during the intervention days, as well as teacher reports, indicated that the reciprocal teaching procedure provided an excellent opportunity to diagnose the difficulty(ies) students encountered in understanding text. Many of the errors students made were very informative. To illustrate, after reading a paragraph about the hibernation habits of snakes in which the following sentence appeared, "When it is too cold, the snakes become inactive or estivate," one student asked, "What do snakes do when it gets cold?" A student responded, "They become inactive." The student teacher rejoined, "Yes, and what else do they do?" A third student suggested, "They estivate," to which the teacher replied, "Correct." It became apparent that the student teacher and possibly the second respondent did not understand the "or" construction in that particular sentence.

In addition to diagnostic possibilities, the procedure provided opportunities for extending instruction. For example, teachers elicited discussion about parts of speech used in the text and, in the course of the dialogue, integrated the content with information the students had learned previously or were being exposed to in other classes.

Students, when asked to evaluate the procedures anonymously, spoke positively of their experience with it, particularly mentioning the opportunity to assume the role of teacher. In addition, the majority of students ranked the value of the four activities by assigning greatest value to summarizing, followed by self-questioning, then clarifying, and finally predicting what the author would discuss next.

CONCLUSION

To encourage practitioners to implement the reciprocal teaching procedure, the following guidelines are offered:

1. To determine that the student's reading difficulty is correctly identified as a comprehension problem and to ensure that the student is placed in reading material appropriate to his or her decoding ability, the teacher is advised to use the same screening procedure adopted in this investigation. Such a procedure takes into account the student's correct reading rate, incorrect reading rate, and level of comprehension, as well as the readability of the curricular material. A complete description of how this assessment procedure is executed and applied to curricular materials currently in use in the classroom is provided by Blankenship and Lilly (1981).

2. Teachers expressed apprehension about their ability to model the comprehension-monitoring activities. Initially, it was difficult for teachers to make overt the means by which they processed text using the suggested strategies. Practitioners should be assured that after a week of experience with the procedure, teachers reported feeling both more comfortable and competent with the procedure. Before attempting the procedure with their students, teachers may want to practice the activities using the materials they will use with their students.

3. Teachers also expressed skepticism with regard to their students' ability to engage in the procedure. Introducing the procedure with passages that are well organized (e.g., make frequent uses of headings and are logically arranged) facilitates acquisition of the activities, which can then be applied to text that is not as "considerate" (see Armbruster in this volume). In addition, during the initial days of introducing the procedure, the adult teacher should frequently model the activities and select the more capable students to provide further models.

4. To ensure minimal amounts of practice with each of the activities, it may be helpful for teachers to maintain a daily checklist of the strategies being used and the minimal number of times per session the strategy is modeled or prompted. Students could even maintain individual checklists that would indicate their contributions to the group.

5. Certain students experienced some difficulty mastering the activities, particularly question asking. Modeling and corrective feedback can be very powerful techniques in teaching and refining these skills. To illustrate the nature of the difficulty experienced by one student and the acquisition of question asking over time, portions of the dialogue between student 6 (Study 1), a minority student whose Slosson indicated an IQ of 70, and the investigator are presented:

Day 1:
S: What is found in the southeastern snakes, also the copperhead, rattlesnakes, vipers—they have. I'm not doing this right.
T: All right. Do you want to know about the pit vipers?
S: Yeah.
T: What would be a good question about the pit vipers that starts with the word "why"?
S: No response
T: How about, "Why are the snakes called pit vipers?"
S: Why do they want to know that they called pit vipers?
T: Try it again.
S: Why do they, pit vipers in a pit?
T: How about, "Why do they call the snakes pit vipers?"
S: Why do they call the snakes pit vipers?
T: There you go. Good for you.

Day 4:
S: No question.
T: What's this paragraph about?
S: Spinner's mate. How do Spinner's mate . . .
T: That's good. Keep going.
S: How do Spinner's mate is much smaller than . . . how am I going to say that?
T: Take your time with it. You want to ask a question about Spinner's mate and what he does beginning with the word "how."
S: How do they spend most of his time sitting?
T: You're very close. The question would be, "How does Spinner's mate spend most of his time?" Now you ask it.
S: How does Spinner's mate spend most of his time?

Day 7:
S: How does the pressure from below push the mass of hot rock against the opening? Is that it?
T: Not quite. Start your question with "What happens when?"
S: What happens when the pressure from below pushes the mass of hot rock against the opening?
T: Good for you. Good job.

Day 11:
S: What is the most interesting of the insect-eating plants and where do the plants live at?

T: Two excellent questions! They are both clear and important questions. Ask us one at a time now.

Day 15:
S: Why do scientists come to the south pole to study?
T: Excellent question. That is what this paragraph is all about.

On a number of occasions when students indicated that they could not find a question, asking the student to summarize first often triggered a good question.

6. Frequent measures of performance on comprehension measures are important to ascertain that the intervention is working successfully. If the intervention is not working for particular students, teachers can become more attentive to those students' participation in the training sessions, perhaps assigning them more opportunities to assume the role of teacher.

7. It is as important to share progress with the students as it is to evaluate progress. This not only communicates to the students that the activities they are learning pay off but also serves to maintain student interest in the instructional activity. Students in the current investigation were very pleased with their graphs, and it is certainly conceivable that students could maintain their own graphs. The teachers involved in this investigation indicated that in addition to sharing assessment results, they would continue to tape record the training sessions and would periodically share the recordings to demonstrate progress.

8. For those teachers who are interested in the teaching of comprehension-monitoring/fostering activities but do not meet students on a small group basis or are content teachers rather than reading teachers, several useful ideas were proposed by the teachers participating in the study. One of the teachers plans to introduce the reciprocal teaching procedure to a group of 20 students by dividing the class into four instructional groups and assigning a student trained in the procedure to each group, thereby implementing a peer tutoring situation. A second teacher intends to incorporate the technique when addressing appropriate study skills and preparing the class for history tests.

REFERENCES

Anderson, L., Evertson, C., & Brophy, J. An experimental study of effective teaching in first grade reading groups. *Elementary School Journal*, 1979, *79*, 193–222.

André, M. D. A., & Anderson, T. H. The development and evaluation of a self-questioning study technique. *Reading Research Quarterly*, 1978–79, *14*, 605–623.

Au, Kathryn Hu-pu. Comprehension-oriented reading lessons. *Educational Perspectives*, 1981, *20* (1).

Bartlett, E. J. Curriculum, concepts of literacy and social class. In L. B. Resnick & P. A. Weaver (Eds.), *Theory and practice of early reading*, vol. 2. Hillsdale, N.J.: Erlbaum, 1979.

Bird, M. *Reading comprehension strategies: A direct teaching approach*. Unpublished doctoral dissertation, University of Toronto, 1980.

Blankenship, C., & Lilly, M. S. *Mainstreaming students with learning and be-*

havior problems: Techniques for the classroom teacher. New York: Holt, Rinehart and Winston, 1981.

Brown, A. L. *Reflections on metacognition: Discussants' comments.* Paper presented at the Society for Research in Child Development, San Francisco, March 1979.

Brown, A. L., Campione, J. C., & Day, J. D. Learning to learn: On training students to learn from texts. *Educational Researcher*, 1981, *10* (2), 14–21.

Brown, A. L., & Day, J. D. *The development of rules for summarizing text.* Unpublished manuscript, University of Illinois, 1980.

Collins, A., & Smith, E. E. Teaching the process of reading comprehension. In P. K. Detterman & R. J. Sternberg (Eds.), *How and how much can intelligence be increased?* Norwood, N.J.: Albex, in press.

Dansereau, D. F. *Learning strategy research.* Paper presented at NIE-LRDC Conference on Thinking and Learning Skills, University of Pittsburgh, October 8–12, 1980.

Day, J. D. *Training summarization skills: A comparison of teaching methods.* Unpublished doctoral dissertation, University of Illinois, 1980.

Duffy, C., Lanier, J., & Roehler, L. *On the need to consider instructional implications.* Essay prepared in response to a Conference on Reading Expository Material, November 1980.

Durkin, D. Reading comprehension instruction in five basal reading series. *Reading Research Quarterly*, 1981, *16*, 515–544.

Durkin, D. What classroom observations reveal about reading comprehension. *Reading Research Quarterly*, 1979, *14*, 581–533.

Frase, L. T., & Schwartz, B. J. The effect of question production and answering on prose recall. *Journal of Educational Psychology*, 1975, *62*, 628–635.

Guszak, F. K. Relationship between teacher practice and knowledge of reading theory in selected classes. Project Report No. 5–437. Washington, D.C.: U.S. Department of Health, Education, and Welfare, 1966. ERIC Reproduction Service No. ED 001 0191.

Harker, W. J. Teaching comprehension: A task analysis approach. *Journal of Reading*, 1973, *16* (5), 379–382.

Harris, P. L., Kruithof, A., Terwogt, M. M., & Visser, T. Children's detection and awareness of textual anomaly. *Journal of Experimental Child Psychology*, 1981, *31*, 212–230.

Lovitt, T. C., & Hansen, C. L. Round one—Placing the child in the right reader. *Journal of Learning Disabilities*, 1976, *6*, 347–353.

Manzo, A. V. *Improving reading comprehension through reciprocal questioning.* Unpublished doctoral dissertation, University of Syracuse, 1969.

Markman, E. M. Realizing that you don't understand: A preliminary investigation. *Child Development*, 1977, *48*, 986–992.

Markman, E. M. Realizing that you don't understand: Elementary school children's awareness of inconsistencies. *Child Development*, 1979, *50* (3), 643–655.

Rosenshine, B., & Berliner, D. Academic engaged time. *British Journal of Teacher Education*, 1978, *4*, 3–16.

Wong, B., & Jones, W. *Increasing metacomprehension in L. D. normally-achieving students through self-questioning training.* Unpublished manuscript, Simon Fraser University, 1981.

18

Direct Explanation of Comprehension Processes

Laura R. Roehler
Gerald G. Duffy

This chapter focuses on how teachers explain the processes of reading. We submit that teachers must go beyond the currently prevalent practice of moving children through the story selections and workbook exercises prescribed in basal textbooks. Instead, they must explain to students, especially the slower ones, how to consciously employ strategies that good readers apparently learn without assistance. Hence, direct explanation calls for making explicit the implicit principles and algorithms which govern successful comprehension, rather than merely providing practice opportunities and corrective feedback to errors. Our research attempts to determine whether such explanation of the processes of reading results in better reading performance and more self-reported understanding of the strategies used by readers.

BACKGROUND

The concept of direct explanation should not be confused with the currently popular term "direct instruction." As we have pointed out elsewhere (Roehler and Duffy 1981), direct instruction emphasizes instructional time and student opportunity to learn. As such, it is little more than efficient management of material, activities, and pupils. While efficient management is an important prerequisite to effective instruction, it is not enough. As Brophy (in press) has said, " ... we need a renewed emphasis on the role of the teacher as an instructor, and not merely as an instructional manager."

This work is sponsored in part by the Institute for Research on Teaching, College of Education, Michigan State University. The Institute for Research on Teaching is funded primarily by the Program for Teaching and Instruction of the National Institute of Education, United States Department of Education. The opinions expressed in this publication do not necessarily reflect the position, policy, or endorsement of the National Institute of Education. (Contract No. 400–81–0014.)

The research reported here focuses on the teacher as an instructor. Specifically, it examines the teacher's role in explaining reading processes to students. This view of comprehension instruction is distinct from other views of how to teach comprehension in four ways.

First, our concept of direct explanation focuses on the skills that represent the processes used to comprehend. In contrast to researchers such as Beck (Beck, Omanson, and McKeown 1982) and projects such as the Kamehameha Early Education Program (Tharp 1982) in which the focus of instruction is on the interpretation of the story content, our emphasis is on the mental processing involved in comprehension skills and how competent readers do such processing in interpreting stories. As such, we agree with Collins and Smith:[1]

> We do not argue that reading curricula should not stress interpretation. We argue only that a reading curricula should also try to teach how to construct interpretations. . . . If we do not teach these skills, then the better students will develop them on their own, and the worse readers will find reading very frustrating. (p. 28)

Second, teacher explanations of the processes are designed to be metacognitive, not mechanistic. They make students aware of the purpose of the skill and how successful readers use it to activate, monitor, regulate, and make sense out of text, creating in students an awareness and a conscious realization of the function and utility of reading skills[2] and the linkages between these processes and the activities of reading. Gibson (1974) summarizes by pointing to the importance of:

> . . . ability to be aware of one's own cognitive processes, from the segmentation of the phonetic stream all the way up to the understanding of the strategies of learning and problem-solving. There seems to be a consciousness raising that goes along with many aspects of cognitive development and it turns out, I think, to be associated with attaining mature reading skill. (p. 681)

Third, direct explanation assumes that instruction is more than placing pupils in conducive environments in the expectation that they will indirectly invent the necessary strategies for themselves. Instead, it is based on the belief that a proactive rather than an indirect approach has the greatest potential for success, especially with low-ability students. By proactive, we mean that teachers exhibit these characteristics: (1) They are consciously aware of the function and utility of the skills they are teaching and the linkages between these processes and "real reading" of text; (2) they analyze the skill to be learned in order to identify the salient features of the mental processing required to do the skill; and (3) they take an active role in teaching students how to do the mental processing.

Fourth, direct explanation is based on the belief that a teacher's "active role" puts a premium on what teachers say during instruction. Past research on comprehension instruction has examined the *tasks* students are asked to perform. We examine what teachers *say* to students about the process of doing the task, because student outcomes depend not only on what they do but on what the teacher says to them about what they do. While students mediate the teacher's instructional talk and restructure it in terms of prior knowledge, the extent and quality of this restructuring is influenced by what teachers say and the clarity with which they sat it. Hence, we agree with Mosanthal (in press) who says that "reading researchers tend to assume that comprehension is constrained only by text variables and/or by reader prior knowledge variables. They overlook the fact that comprehension can be constrained also by the organization of the teacher's lessons."

Finally, direct explanation assumes that, in addition to verbal statements, the teacher's active instructional role includes the uses of assistance devices. Such assistance may take the form of advance organizers, thinking aloud, careful sequencing, highlighting of salient features, attention cues, analogies, and graphic illustrations that integrate concepts or create linkages between skills and reading tasks. In presenting such assistance, the teacher acts as the student's ally by making the learning of the skill as clear as possible, and by emphasizing salient features so that divergent restructuring of the explanation by students will be minimal.

In sum, the instructional concept discussed in this chapter is distinct from other views of instruction. It goes beyond the "opportunity to learn" perspective presented by direct instruction advocates and is distinct from what is typically recommended in reading education because of its emphasis on skills rather than story content, on developing in students a conscious awareness of how to use skills, on proactive teacher behavior, on teacher talk, and on devices of instructional assistance.

THE RESEARCH

Our understanding of direct explanation of reading comprehension has developed as a result of conducting two descriptive studies. The first was an examination of two teachers, both of whom were characterized as direct instruction teachers. It was hypothesized that there would be qualitative differences that distinguished the two teachers and that these differences would in turn provide useful instructional insights beyond opportunity to learn. The second study was based on the first. Using the instructional insights gleaned from the first study, the explanation behavior of three teachers was studied as a means for determining whether there was a relationship between the explicitness of teacher explanation and student achievement and awareness.

The First Study

Two direct-instruction teachers were examined to discover if there were qualitative differences in their direct instruction of reading. Teacher A was a regular second-grade teacher in a school; Teacher B was a professor and researcher who took over the reading and language arts instruction in Teacher A's classroom every morning for six weeks. Both teachers were judged to be direct-instruction teachers.[3]

Three sets of data were collected for each teacher. These included field observations on both teachers, self-analysis data on both teachers, and interview data on both teachers. To analyze the data, two researchers independently analyzed the data, noting critical moments. They then went back and again read through the data to verify those critical moments. Notes were then compared, and the critical moments were cooperatively agreed upon. Analysis of these critical moments revealed that the two teachers were similar in their instruction in some ways but that they were different in other important ways.

They were similar in three ways: They both were concerned professionals, they both were efficient and generated large amounts of time on task for their students, and their procedures for grouping were similar.

As concerned professionals, both teachers were dedicated and diligent in their performance of duties. Both exhibited a strong academic emphasis in the areas of reading and language arts, both were humanistic in their understanding of the emotional needs of children, both spent hours in preparation, both were gentle in their interactions with the students in the classroom, and both consciously sought to seek positive student self-images by avoiding situations that erode confidence.

In terms of efficiency and time on task, both teachers were cognizant of the need for a well-managed and monitored classroom environment. Consequently, both developed careful routines that minimized confusion and wasted motion, and both insisted on a businesslike atmosphere in the classroom.

Finally, in terms of their grouping, both teachers believed in ability grouping for reading instruction. Both teachers varied the order in which groups were met, with the low group being called first at times and the high group being called first at other times. Both teachers focused on comprehension in the high groups and decoding in the low groups.

The teachers were different in four ways: the amount of talk found at the beginning of the lesson as opposed to the end of the lesson, the content of the talk patterns, the internal flow of the lesson, and the connection of one lesson to other lessons.

The talk pattern of Teacher A was reactive; students had to err before instruction occurred. The following is typical of the instruction she generally used. In one lesson, the students had not done well on a worksheet previously assigned as seatwork. Since they had not done well, Teacher A brought the group back up for another lesson. Her instructional talk in this lesson focused on procedural concerns or requests to do the whole task. There was no evidence of the teacher's explaining the mental processing needed to do the task. There also was no progression from large amounts of teacher talk to relatively small amounts of teacher talk as one might expect if teacher explanation were provided early with students assuming more and more responsibility as the lesson progressed. In terms of the internal flow of the lesson, each item on the worksheet was an entity in itself, with little connection between them. Directions were given, the students took turns reading the possible choices, then the teacher asked for a response that required doing the whole task. This process was repeated through the second and third items, In addition, there was little external connection between this lesson and what preceded it or followed it. The only relationship between this lesson and the previous lesson was that the students had failed the task the first time and there was no relationship to future lessons whatsoever. When it was over, it was over.

In contrast, consider a main idea lesson taught by Teacher B. The content of Teacher B's talk patterns reflected an explanation of what one needs to do to find the main idea of a paragraph. Information was initially presented about (1) what the mental process was, (2) how to use the salient features of the skill, and (3) why the mental process is useful in connected text. After this direct explanation of what was to be learned, why it was important, and how to do it, Teacher B moved to a turn-taking model where he checked the students' restructuring of the skill and modified or reinforced that restructuring. Finally, when the students demonstrated that they understood, practice was provided. The content of the teacher talk went beyond procedural explanations and focused on the mental processing used to determine main idea. The talk patterns moved from high amounts of teacher talk to low amounts of teacher talk as the lesson progressed. Internal flow was evident because an explanation was provided first, then students responded with the teacher verifying or altering students' restructuring of the skills and, finally, practice was provided. External connection to other lessons was evident because this lesson was embedded in a larger unit in which main idea was used in a variety of reading and writing tasks across several days.

At the end of this study, we concluded that "direct instruction" was an inadequate term. Both teachers met the criteria for direct instruction by generating considerable opportunity to learn, but it was clear that Teacher B was engaging in a different brand of instruction than Teacher A.

The feature that seemed to distinguish Teacher B from Teacher A was his use of explanations. Such explanation had several characteristics. First, it represented a redesign of the typical basal lesson format, with the skill being taught before the story was read rather than afterward. Second, it was proactive in that the teacher assumed the responsibility for verbally explaining the skill rather than engaging in reactive turn taking in which the emphasis is on having students answer questions about the skill with a minimum of instructional teacher talk. Third, there was an internal flow in the lesson, a logical progression from explanation to practice. Finally there was an external connection from one lesson to another; skills that were taught were systematically applied in basal text stories read after the skill lesson.

Consequently, we concluded that explanation might be an important element of effective reading instruction and began planning the second study.

The Second Study

At the conclusion of the first study we were convinced that "direct instruction" was an inadequate term because it did not account for the qualitative differences we had noted in our two teachers. We felt that if we could teach teachers to use explanation in the manner of Teacher B in the first study, we would be able to show better pupil reading outcomes.

Consequently, the second study[4] was based on the hypothesis that, given equality of opportunity to learn, instructional effectiveness depends upon teacher communication of explicit explanations designed to help students become consciously aware of the mental processing employed by successful readers. Two research questions were asked:

1. Is there a relationship between the explicitness of a teacher's explanation in reading and low-group students' achievement and awareness of what has been taught?
2. What are the components of explicit explanation?

Verbal explanation was one step in a four-step sequence of instruction. First, the teacher has to organize the class to ensure high engagement rates and pupil involvement; second, once the children are attending, the teacher provides the explanation; third, once the children have a conceptual understanding of what is being taught, practice is provided; and fourth, the teacher ensures that students apply what was learned in basal stories or other reading situations following the skill lesson. It was our hypothesis that low-group pupils in particular will become better readers if teachers first explain to them the mental processing involved in using skills and then offer practice in workbooks or basal text selections. We would be able to determine such improvement both by measuring pupils' conscious awareness of what they were learning in reading and by measuring their achievement growth.

It must be noted here that our concept of teacher explanation does not mean that children are expected to learn everything as presented. Children will restructure information provided to them, and as a result, teacher explanation must also be made in reaction to this restructuring. Similarly, explanation is not conceptually limited to a deductive format, although inductive explanations appear to be more difficult for teachers.

Design and analysis. The study was an intervention one, with three second-grade teachers studied. Three additional teachers from the same building acted as control teachers. The teachers were selected on the recommendation of school administrators, using as a guide an expressed preference for teachers who were already competent classroom managers, thereby ensuring equality of opportunity to learn.

The study involved an eight-week cycle. To determine initial comprehension achievement levels, the low groups in the intervention and control classrooms were given the Passage Comprehension subtest of the Woodcock Reading Mastery Test, Form A. The observations started during the second week. We observed only the intervention teacher during low-group instruction. We conducted one observation a week for six weeks. For the first observation, we specified that the teachers should follow their normal instructional routine, using their basal textbooks as they regularly did.

For all observed lessons, the researchers audiotaped the lesson and collected timed field notes. Following each lesson, a brief teacher interview was conducted in which the researcher asked the teacher what the objective was what the desired outcome was, how the lesson went, and how it would be changed if there was an opportunity to teach it again. Then four children from the low group were taken one at a time to a quiet place for interviewing. Each child was asked three questions: What were you learning to do today? How do you do that? and Why is it important? Following each observation, the researchers audiotaped the timed field notes and their additional reactions and comments.

Several days later, the researchers intervened with the teachers, usually before or after school. Teachers were shown how to modify the basic turn-taking model of the basal and teach reading more explicitly by emphasizing what was to be learned, why it was important to learn it, the mental processing needed, the use of modeling to externalize the internal mental processing involved, and the use of highlighting. After each intervention, the researchers audiotaped their impressions of the intervention. Several days later, the researchers returned to the classroom and observed another lesson, collecting the same data for both teacher and students.

The cycle of observing and interviewing the low-group lesson and then intervening with the teacher before the next lesson was followed for a total of six weeks. At the end of the sixth lesson, a final measure consisting of Form B of the Passage Comprehension subtest of the Woodcock Reading Mastery Test was administered to the low groups of both the intervention and control classroom. The students in the control classrooms received only the initial and final measures of reading achievement.

The audiotapes of lessons were typed into transcript form, as were the pupil and teacher interviews. The researchers developed conventions for rating the explicitness of the teachers' explanation and the students' awareness of what was taught. The teachers were rated on the knowledge presented during the lesson about the mental processing and on the means used to explain the mental processing. Within the knowledge section, all teachers were rated on (1) their talk about what the mental process was, (2) their talk about why the mental processing was useful, (3) their talk about the salient features of the task and how one uses these salient features to do the mental processing, (4) their talk regarding the sequence for approaching and fulfilling the mental processing, and (5) their examples of how to do the mental processing. Regarding the means, all teachers were rated on (1) the degree to which the mental processing was modeled, (2) the extent to which they directed the students' attention to the salient features of the mental processing, (3) whether they consistently helped students focus on the mental processing or helped them refocus their attention during confusion, (4) the extent to which they provided a review of the mental process being taught; (5) the appropriateness of the individual practice provided after the presentation, and (6) the degree to which students were helped to apply the mental processing in connected text. Students' responses to the interview questions were rated according to the quality of the response. High ratings were given if the response to the question of what was being learned included a specific reference to the language task and an example; if the response to the question of why it was important specified both the context in which it will be useful and what they are able to do in that context; and if the response to the question of how to do it included an example of how one does the mental processing associated with successful completion of the task.

Findings. The findings for the second study are presented in terms of the two research questions. First, the relationship between the explanation behavior and the reading outcomes of the students is reported. Second, the qualitative instructional differences noted among the teachers are discussed.

Regarding the relationship between teachers' explanation behaviors and pupil outcomes, it is necessary to start with Teacher C. Contrary to the expectations we had set when we selected the teachers for the study, Teacher C had a great deal of difficulty with classroom management. He constantly battled a discipline problem, he seldom kept children on task, and there was a good deal of confusion in the classroom. Consequently, his response to our interventions regarding teacher explanation behavior was less than desirable. He received relatively low ratings for teacher explanation behavior in all lessons, and the student awareness of the mental processing needed to successfully complete the skill was erratic. In effect, the findings for Teacher C served only to reinforce once again the importance of good classroom management skills as a prerequisite to any explanation behavior.

Fortunately, Teachers A and B provided a richer data base. As seen in Figure 18.1, Teacher A did provide more explicit explanation in some lessons and, generally speaking, student interview responses tended to be higher when lesson ratings for explicitness of the explanation were high. Teacher B responded very well to the interventions and consistently received high ratings for his explanation. His student interview responses were also consistently high. Both the pupils in Teacher A's class and Teacher B's class made considerable achievement growth.

TEACHER A

Lesson	1	2	3	4	5	6
Teacher [a] Explanation	A–18.1% B–36.3%	A–27.2% B–40.9%	40.9%	54.5%	A–27.2% B–31.8%	22.7%
Student [b] Awareness	A– 6.3% B–12.5%	A–10.4% B–29.1%	12.5%	38.8%	A–12.5% B–29.1%	25%

		pre scores	post scores	gain
Reading Achievement[d]	Intervention Group	3.0	3.75	+.75
	Control Groups	4.5	4.4	−.1

TEACHER B

Lesson	1	2	3	4	5	6
Teacher Explanation	18.1%	77.3%	90.9%	68.2%	54.5%	77.3%
Student Awareness	19.4%	81.3%	75%	66.7%	46.7%	75%

		pre scores	post scores	gain
Reading Achievement	Intervention Group	3.5	4.5	+1.0
	Control Groups	3.9	4.2	−.3

[a] Includes teachers' statements about the knowledge presented during the lesson regarding how to do the mental processing and the means used to explain the mental processing.
[b] Includes students' statements about what was learned, why it was important, and how to do it.
[c] The ratings were collapsed across categories; the percent represents the degree of explanatory explicitness or student awareness when all categories are considered.
[d] Scores are reported as grade equivalents and reflect the comprehension subtest of the Woodcock Reading Mastery Test.

Figure 18.1

These data suggest a relationship between the explicitness of the teacher's explanation and pupil outcomes. For instance, when Teacher B provided explicit explanation, the pupils tended to responds in terms of explicit responses. When teacher explanations were less clear, as can be seen with Teacher A, the pupils' interview responses tended to indicate less awareness. While we cannot put a lot of faith in the achievement test results because of the limited sample size, it nevertheless is interesting that Teacher B (who was the most explicit in his instruction) produced the most growth, that Teacher A (who was somewhat explicit) produced the next level of growth, and that Teacher C (who never did get to teacher explanation behavior) was the only teacher whose students did not exceed the control group in growth.

The relationship between what teachers say during instruction and how pupils respond during interviews was particularly dramatic. For instance, when Teacher C was teaching a lesson on drawing conclusions, the following interchange occurred:

T: Would you look at your goals, please? What is the first goal, Sylvia?
C: Do you want me to read it?
T: Please.
C: (*inaudible.*)
T: Obvious. Would you write above "obvious" for me, please? Would you write "easy to see"? Obvious. It means easy to see. All right. What does obvious mean, Todd?
C: Obvious means easy to see.
T: Easy to see, all right. I want you to write above it, "easy to see."
C: Where?
T: Right above it. "Easy to see." Would you, please?
C: I'm going to write "obvious."

Following this lesson, when Teacher C's pupils were interviewed about what they learned, each said, "Obvious." Only after probing were two of the children able to provide any response beyond this.

In contrast, Teacher B taught a lesson in R-controlled words (Lesson 2) that received a percentage rating of 77.3 percent out of a possible 100% for explicitness of explanation. The following pupil interview response is illustrative of the degree of pupil awareness:

I: What were you learning to do today?
C: We were learning about the E–R, the U–R and the O–R and the E–A–R and they mean the same, they're UR (sound like UR).
I: How do you use that?
C: Well, you just look at the U–R and you go, like it, say it's *curl* and you can't figure it out, you never heard it before. You look at it and you say, you know that's – ER and you go "ccuurrll."
I: Why were you learning this?
C: So when we read stories we can understand words we've never seen before.

In summary, there seems to be a relationship between the explicitness of teachers' explanation and both pupils' awareness of what they are learning and their general comprehension achievement. Consequently, regarding our first research question, we can say that there appears to be enough data to justify more extensive examination of the relationship between direct explanation and pupil outcomes.

The second major set of findings examines the nature of explanation itself. What explains why some explanations were more explicit than others? By comparing Teacher B's explicit explanations with Teacher A's less explicit explanations, we were able to identify five components of explicit instruction.

The first related to the two teachers' ability to break away from the typical format of the basal text and its associated dependence upon turn taking. For instance, Teacher A was never able to break completely from the pattern of having pupils read orally from the basal and then, in an isolated and unrelated way, complete a skill lesson in which no reference is made to the story just completed or any other future connected text. This tendency is seen in her introduction to the lesson on similies (Lesson 3). She said:

> All right, we are finished with the first thing we were going to do. We were going to talk about the story and discuss it. We've done that. Now I'd like you to close your books. We're going to think about something that will help you in writing stories.

It apparently never occurred to Teacher A that the two activities could be related. Similarly, she never got completely away from limiting instruction to turn taking. Despite the five interventions and some indication in Lesson 3 and 4 that she was using sustained teacher talk to make her instruction more explicit, she reverted in Lessons 5 and 6 to a straight turn-taking model in which no explanation or modeling was provided. The following excerpt from Lesson 6 is typical:

> *T*: All right, now here are some possibilities. "A Trip Downtown." "The New Shirt." "The Shirt That Didn't Fit." Let me read them again. "A Trip Downtown." "The New Shirt." "The Shirt That Didn't Fit." Now those three possibilities, which one would go best? Angela?
> *C*: A Trip Downtown.
> *T*: O.K. Troy, what do you think?
> *C*: The New Shirt.
> *T*: David, what was your choice?
> *C*: The New Shirt.
> *T*: Suzanne, how about you?
> *C*: The New Shirt.
> *T*: I think the girls decided on The Trip Downtown and the boys liked The New Shirt. Mainly what was the story about?
> *C*: A trip downtown.
> *C*: Getting a new shirt.
> *T*: Getting a new shirt, wasn't it?

In contrast, after his first lesson, Teacher B never reverted to the standard turn-taking format for conducting instruction. Instead, he explained clearly at the beginning what was being taught and gradually moved to a turn-taking pattern once the students began to understand how to do the skill. He massed his instructional talk at the beginning of the lesson and began assigning turns only when pupils has a reasonable chance to answer correctly. In all his lessons, Teacher B first taught a skill, then provided practice, and finally talked about how to apply the skill to stories in the basal, thereby bringing a sense of internal flow to the instructional sequence.

Second, Teacher B's explanation seemed to be more explicit because he was able to provide good explanation regarding why it was useful to learn the skill—

similar to what Lipson calls the "why bother" aspect.[5] For instance, when Teacher B talked to his students about learning an inferencing skill (Lesson 6), he said:

> I want you to underline some of the key words that you need to pay attention to and again, when I do it here, it is for the purpose that when you get back to your own reading, whether you are reading a text book or some fun reading or a newspaper, you are able to pick out these clues yourself.

Teacher B routinely presents skills within the context of how children will use them in real reading. In contrast, Teacher A seldom makes any attempt to justify the value of a skill for students. When asked what she hoped the ultimate outcome of a skill lesson would be, she typically answers: "I would hope that they would be able to do the workbook page successfully." The level of meaningfulness is obviously different between Teacher A's instruction and Teacher B's. This appears to be one of the components that made Teacher B's instruction more explicit. Specifically, because students received explicit information about why the skill was useful, they had a reasonable rationale for pursuing the learning. Perhaps the best example of Teacher B's facility for making clear the value of learning occurred several days following a comprehension lesson on fact and opinion (Lesson 4). Two pupils in the class began arguing about whether the movie *Raiders of the Lost Ark* was boring. Teacher B intervenes as follows:

> *T*: Remember what we talked about last time? Fact and opinion?
> *C*: Yes, and that was my opinion.
> *T*: That was your opinion, but it sounded like you were saying that she was wrong.
> *C*: No, but I don't think it was boring.
> *T*: OK, different people have different opinions. Is there any fact to any of those?
> *C*: I know one fact. They both have opinions.

A third component of explicit instruction relates to the specificity of the teacher's instructional talk. The more specific the teacher is, the more explicit instruction becomes and the more aware pupils are of what is being learned and how to do it. For instance, note what Teacher B says when he opens a lesson on inferencing:

> Today we are again studying something about comprehension, a comprehension skill of being able to read clues in a paragraph and make a reasonable guess of what is going to happen next—what the author has in mind. Okay, let me say that again. Today we are working on a skill that involves paying attention to what you are reading. We call them clues that help you get what is going to happen before you read. They call that making inferences, based on the information that you have.

Teacher A, in contrast, opened a lesson on syllables by saying, "Today we are going to learn about syllables." During the remainder of the lesson, she made no overt attempt to explicate the lesson content beyond this statement.

Specificity continues to be important as the lesson progresses. Teacher A, in teaching a lesson on making short sentences longer (Lesson 4), highlighted the need to underline verbs and nouns without specifying the thinking one does about the nouns and verbs in order to expand sentences. When pupils were interviewed following the lesson, the responses tended to be like the following:

I: Okay, and how do you make a short sentence a little longer?
C: Well, you add a couple more words that you think would sound good with the sentence and then you have a longer sentence.
I: Okay, that's good. Did the teacher given you some steps to follow when you were doing that?
C: What do you mean, like steps?
I: Well, like, when she was teaching you how to make short sentences into longer sentences, did she give you some steps to follow?
C: You mean, like how to do it?
I: Uh-huh.
C: Like you could circle and underline.
I: Okay, once you have the word circled or underlined, then what do you do?
C. Then you just add some words and that makes a longer sentence.

In contrast, such vagueness was not associated with the pupil interview responses of the children in Teacher B's low group, perhaps because his explanations continued to be specific throughout the lesson. Note, for example, the specificity of the modeling he provided in a lesson on diphthongs (Lesson 3):

Okay, let me tell you how I would do this if I were reading alone. Let's suppose I was reading along and I came to the word "out" and I had never seen the word before, which is really possible. I see an "ou" and I know "ou" has the sound of ow, like Gracie said, it sounds like a *w* is in there— *owwwww*—and I know it has a *t* at the end and the *t* sounds like *t–t–t* so I hav *ou–t, out.*

Fourth, it apparently is not only important that explanations be specific; they should also be consistent. For instance, Teacher B's talk pattern in lesson after lesson reflected a continual return to the theme of the lesson; he reviewed and elaborated in a consistent, almost redundant, pattern. In contrast, the teacher talk pattern for Teacher A is less consistent. She often emphasized different things from minute to minute, was sometimes distracted from the salient features of the task, and once something had been said, she rarely came back to it.

The fifth and final component of explicit instruction related to the teacher's ability to continue to explain during the turn-taking sessions. This is particularly important when one considers that each student is likely to process the teacher's explanation in terms of his or her unique prior knowledge. Such restructuring becomes evident when students respond to turns. If they restructure the explanation in a way that helps improve their reading ability, the teacher should respond with appropriate feedback. If they restructure the explanation in a way that is harmful to their improved reading ability, the teacher should respond with appropriate explanatory feedback. The differences between Teacher A and Teacher B in this regard are dramatic. On the one hand, Teacher A provides no explanatory feedback at all when confronted with misunderstandings during turn-taking. The following example from a lesson on apostrophes (Lesson 5) is illustrative:

T: When you add an apostrophe *s* to boy, it shows that the boy has something. Can you make up a sentence for kittens? Something belongs to the kittens.
C: There's a basket full of kittens.

T: That's what Jennie was doing over here. You added just an *s*. That's more than one kitten. This time make it ownership. Something belongs to this right here. Troy?

C: The kitten always owns the basket.

T: All right, but can you change your sentence around? You're saying the kitten owns the basket. Let's use kitten and basket.

C: Kitten basket.

T: But with the aposthrophe *s*.

C: The kitten's basket.

T: The kitten's, that's the kitten's basket. All right. What belongs to the kitten, Troy?

C: The basket.

T: The basket. All right, let's try it with dolphins.

In contrast, note the explanatory assistance Teacher B embeds in his feedback to pupils during the turn-taking section of a lesson on inferencing (Lesson 6) in which he wants them to use clues in the text to determine that the story is set in a department store:

T: What is another important clue in this sentence, David?

C: Clerks, selling.

T: Selling would be an important clue. What about the second sentence?

C: Counters.

T: Is there anything else in that sentence that might be a clue? That might give you an idea of where you are? Wendy pointed out counters. What about counters? What kind of counters?

C: The counters that we set things on.

T: Set things on. Okay. Just the fact that it had counters tells you something about where it is. That is very good.

C: Covered with glass.

T: Covered with glass is important, too. Where do you see counters covered with glass mostly?

C: In a department store.

Summary of the Research

No firm conclusions or generalizations can be based on descriptive studies of just five teachers. Nevertheless, the two studies reported here help clarify the nature of instruction. They dramatize the limitations of the direct instruction model, which emphasizes efficiency and time on task; they highlight the potential of explicit teacher explanation of reading processes, both for increasing reading achievement and for heightening student awareness of how the reading process works; and they suggest some components of the teacher's instructional talk which seem particularly important in expediting student outcomes. As such, the two studies provide the basis for continued study of the impact of direct explanation of comprehension processes.

CONCLUSIONS

The studies reported here have three kinds of implications for practitioners charged with improving classroom instruction of comprehension. The first relates to the issues, the second relates to trial use of direct explanation, and the third relates to the importance of one aspect of proactive teacher behavior.

The line of research reported here raises four issues of which practitioners should be aware. First, these studies raise the issue of just what constitutes instruction. Is it enough for teachers to provide opportunity to learn through intensive time on task, or are teachers responsible for more? If more, is it some form of direct explanation? Second, these studies raise the issue of the importance of a teacher's instructional talk. Can instruction be improved if we attend more carefully to the instructional content of teacher talk? Should a teacher mass explanation early in a lesson before providing for turn taking? Should we be attending more carefully to the specificity, consistency and clarity of what teachers say to pupils during such explanation? Third, should reading comprehension focus on the skills of comprehension, making pupils consciously aware of how such skills can be activated to resolve and make sense of problems of text? Or should comprehension instruction focus on the content of stories so that students can invent for themselves the strategies of comprehension? Finally, these studies raise the issue of how to get teachers themselves to be metacognitive about what they are teaching. How can we promote the sense-making ability exhibited by Teacher B in which he convinced children of the value of skills and the logical way in which they can be applied to reading compared to the mechanistic approach exhibited by Teacher A in which skills were taught for no utilitarian purpose and instruction was a process of getting right answers during turn taking?

Regarding the classroom use of direct explanation, practitioners need first to be aware that more research must be conducted to delineate fully the relationship between direct explanation of reading comprehension processes and pupil achievement and awareness outcomes. However, direct explanation can be given a trial. If this is done, the following steps should be emphasized:

1. Think about skills as a mental process which students use when they encounter problems which interfere with meaning getting during reading. As such, students need to be consciously aware of the situation in which the skill is useful and the thinking one goes through in applying the skill to eliminate the barrier to meaning getting.
2. Think of teaching as the explanation you provide to the students about what the skill is, its value, and the secret to using it successfully when encountering problems of meaning in real text.
3. Think of the traditional materials of instruction as something that is used after your direct explanation of the skill. The workbook page, worksheet, or instructional game can be used after explanation to give pupils an opportunity to practice the skill in a controlled situation. Then, the basal text story can be used to show students how the skill works in real connected text.
4. Regularly interview your students to determine their awareness of what is being learned in reading, why it is of value, and how to do it successfully.
5. Persist in this instructional concept despite the fact that traditional materials, accountability standards, and other constraints of classroom life may seem to force you to minimize your instructional talk and to emphasize mechanized rather than metcognitive skill acquisition.

Finally, practitioners interested in teacher explanation of the kind described here must understand the crucial importance of teachers' own conscious awareness of the function and utility of the skill being taught and their ability to use this awareness to emphasize salient features of the skill that are really important and to create linkages between the skill and "real reading." This is distinct from teacher knowledge *about* reading skills, their ability to correctly identify such skills or their competence as readers. The key here is a consciousness about the *thinking* one goes through in using a skill to make sense out of a problem encountered in text, not simply the ability to perform the skill oneself. This aspect of proactive teacher behavior appears to be most crucial to effective explanation, and practitioners must attend to it most if this research is to be translated into practice.

NOTES

1. A. Collins and E. Smith. *Teaching the process of reading comprehension.* Technical Report No. 182. Center for the Study of Reading, University of Illinois, September 1980.

2. L. Baker and A. Brown. *Metacognitive skills and reading.* Technical Report No. 187. Center for the Study of Reading, University of Illinois, November 1980. S. G. Paris. *Combining research and instruction on reading comprehension in the classroom.* Paper presented at the annual conference of the International Reading Association, Chicago, April 28, 1982.

3. For details regarding research design, see G. Duffy L. Roehler, and D. Reinsmoen. *A descriptive study of two styles of direct instruction in teaching second grade reading and language arts.* Research Series No. 100. Institute for Research on Teaching, Michigan State University, 1981.

4. For details regarding research design, see G. Duffy, L. Roehler, and C. Book, and R. Wesselman. *A pilot study of the effects and characteristics of direct explanation in reading.* Unpublished paper, Institute for Research on Teaching, Michigan State University, October 1982.

5. M. Y. Lipson. *Promoting children's metacognition about reading through direct instruction.* Paper presented at the annual conference of the International Reading Association, Chicago, April 28, 1982.

REFERENCES

Beck, I. L., Omanson, R. C., & McKeown, M. G. An instructional redesign of reading lessons: Effects on comprehension. *Reading Research Quarterly*, 1982, *17* (4), 462–481.

Brophy, J. How teachers influence what is taught and learned in classrooms. *Elementary School Journal*, in press.

Brown, A. L., Campione, J. C., & Day, J. D. Learning to learn: On training students to learn from texts. *Educational Researcher*, 1981, *10* (2), 14–24.

Gibson, E. J. Trends in perceptual development: Implications for the reading process. In A. Pick (Ed.), *Minnesota Symposia on Child Psychology*, 1974, *8*, 24–54.

Mosenthal, P. The influence of social situation on children's classroom comprehension of text. *Elementary School Journal*, in press.

Roehler, L., & Duffy, G. Classroom teaching is more than opportunity to learn. *Journal of Teacher Education*, 1981, *32* (6), 7–13.

Tharp, R. G. The effective instruction of comprehension: Results and description of the Kamehameha Early Education Program. *Reading Research Quarterly*, 1982, *17* (4), 462–481.

19

Verbal Patterns of Teachers: Comprehension Instruction in the Content Areas

Kathleen J. Roth,
Edward L. Smith, and Charles W. Anderson

What is comprehension instruction in the content areas? For many elementary science teachers, it is the program materials. Lesson planning and daily instruction are dictated by the sequence of activities described in the teacher's guide. Like many tourists whose trips are planned by travel companies and conducted by tour guides telling them where to go and when, students are taken through science units by teachers who follow the program with little flexibility. "If it's Monday, this must be photosynthesis."

While teachers seem to believe that the program will instruct the students, our classroom observations of fifth-grade science teachers (see Chapter 13) have convinced us of the crucial role of the teacher. What the teacher says, how sensitive the teacher is to the students' response to instruction, and how the teacher responds to what the students say are critical in comprehension instruction whether the instruction is textbook or activity based.

In this chapter the verbal interaction strategies of four science teachers are used to illustrate common verbal patterns of teachers and the student responses they elicit. Drawing from our observations of these teachers and from what we have learned from related research, a model of comprehension instruction is described. The underlying premise of this model is that teachers must engage students *intellectually* with the task and with actively processing information. Having students physically busy manipulating science materials, filling out worksheets, or reading through a content-area textbook is not enough.

THE CASE STUDIES

As reported in Chapter 13, our two-year study on fifth-grade science instruction has shown that students are not changing their thinking and understanding of science concepts as a result of instruction. They failed to learn in spite of the carefully planned instructional materials used by their teachers. Just like tourists, these students can come home and tell all about where they have been ("We did plants today!"), but they have no real understanding of what it was all about. Their trip through science class may have exposed them to new ideas and aroused their curiosity, but it has not changed their way of thinking about important science concepts. One can say that these students did not comprehend the content-area material and that the instruction provided by the teachers failed to produce such comprehension.

Why is this so? What was the nature of the instruction provided by those teachers, and what hypotheses can we generate regarding how their instruction could have resulted in greater comprehension? To answer these questions, we provide brief descriptions of four teachers, based on the case studies developed in conjunction with our research. The first two descriptions are of teachers who rely on activity-based instruction. Ms. Ross used a program with the standard teacher's guide, while Mr. Kinney used a teacher's guide that had been revised by researchers to help the teacher focus more explicitly on the cognitive thinking involved in the content. The second two descriptions are of teachers who used a textbook-centered approach to science instruction. Ms. Lane used an unaltered textbook, while Ms. Ramsey used the textbook and a supplementary set of materials, again designed by researchers to help the teacher focus more explicitly on the cognitive thinking needed to understand the content.

Activity-Based Content-Area Instruction

Ms. Ross and the original program materials. Ms. Ross was observed planning and teaching a unit on the oxygen-carbon dioxide cycle (Smith & Sendelbach, 1982) from the Science Curriculum Improvement Study SCIS 1978). This program is an activity-based science program in which students are engaged in a series of experiments with plants and animals over a seven- to eight-week period. To simplify a densely packed teacher's guide (Knott et al. 1978), Ms. Ross's verbal interactions with students focused on the procedures for carrying out the experiments. She was an instruction giver. During experimental work, she encouraged students to verbalize their observations, but she did not use this time to explore students' ideas or encourage students to think critically about the experiment.

After experiments, Ms. Ross often ignored suggestions in the teacher's guide to hold a discussion about the experiment, and as a result students were seldom given the opportunity to draw conclusions from their experimental work. Thus, Ms. Ross had her students *doing* experiments, but she had little knowledge about what her students were thinking or even whether they were thinking about the meaning of the experiments.

How did her students respond to this verbal pattern? Not surprisingly, her students did not achieve the learning outcomes intended by the curriculum. Their talk was focused instead on carrying out the experiments properly: "You're supposed to put *twelve* drops of BTB in the water" or "I'll put the drops in and you blow through the straw." As the experiments progressed, students would also talk to each other about their observations. The teacher rarely challenged them to think about the meaning of the experiments, and few students uncovered the meaning of this seemingly arbitrary sequence of experiments on their own.

Although students were *physically* engaged on task, their tasks seldom required *intellectual* engagement. They learned how to use indicators to test for the presence of carbon dioxide but missed the important concepts about the oxygen-carbon dioxide cycle.

Mr. Kinney and the revised teacher's guide. Based on analysis of the planning and teaching of Ms. Ross and other teachers using the SCIS program and on analysis of student learning in these classrooms, Smith, Berkheimer, and Anderson developed a revision of a portion of the SCIS teacher's guide.[1] The revised unit (Photosynthesis) more explicitly but concisely defined for teachers:

1. The learning goals of the activities.
2. The common student misconceptions about photosynthesis that were making learning more difficult.
3. Definite indications about when to conduct discussions, what questions to ask in these discussions, expected student responses to the questions, and general advice about how to address student response.

Mr. Kinney used the revised teacher's guide. How did his verbal interactions differ from those of Ms. Ross? Following the discovery mode of learning that he interpreted as the philosophy of the SCIS program, Mr. Kinney's discussions with the class as a whole were generally idea-collecting exercises. Typically, Mr. Kinney would pose a question, and the students would given their own "theories." Whether the students were making predictions before an experiment or explaining results after an experiment, Mr. Kinney generally accepted all answers, acknowledging each one with an "O.K." and a call for other ideas. He worried that students would go home with incorrect beliefs, but he purposely avoided closure in his discussions. He expected that the experimental evidence would soon become so overwhelming that the students would "put it all together" on their own.

Beyond asking questions, Mr. Kinney did not say very much. He considered it a "betrayal" of the program to tell the students anything. Because of this view of the program, he ignored suggestions in the teacher's guide to "present the following ideas to the students" or to "direct the discussion toward the concept that cotyledons are the food source for young plants." The revised teacher's guide helped him be more sensitive to his students' thinking but did not convince him to say anything directly to the students about their misconceptions or about the intended learning outcomes. Mr. Kinney acted as an interested bystander, waiting to see if "the program" could change his students' ideas about photosynthesis.

Unlike Ms. Ross, then, Mr. Kinney did stimulate his students to talk about the "whys" of their activities, and he learned a lot about how his students were responding to the instructional program. He asked important questions that focused students on the "whys" of the activities, requiring them to make predictions, draw conclusions, and support their ideas with observational evidence.

How did Mr. Kinney's students respond to what Mr. Kinney said during instruction? Throughout the unit, theories abounded in this enthusiastic and able group of students. But on the final day of the unit, Mr. Kinney presented his last question to the students, "So, do plants get food from the soil?" Looking around the room, Mr. Kinney saw heads nodding yes. Dismayed, he ended the unit with a surprised and disappointed, "You're not convinced!" In spite of his many "why" questions, his students continued to cling to their preconceptions or an elaboration of them.

In always encouraging open-ended responses from students without probing for evidence and clarification, Mr. Kinney left students with the impression that their ideas were correct and that no one answer was better than the others. That any answer was "right" or "better" was never explicitly stated. The students thought about the meaning of the experiments, but they did not have a useful way of deciding whose ideas were most appropriate. In a postinstruction interview, one of his students expressed her confusion, noting that "Mr. Kinney never explains anything."

In Ms. Ross' activity-based classroom, then, verbal interactions between teacher and students focused almost exclusively on procedures and observations. Mr. Kinney was more sensitive to what his students were thinking, and he focused talk more on "why" issues. However, he had difficulty knowing how to handle such discussions so that learning would occur. His attitude was that the teacher's role is only to stimulate thinking.

Textbook-Centered Content-Area Instruction

Ms. Lane and the textbook. During our observations, Ms. Lane's class was studying light and seeing, using the Laidlaw *Exploring Science* text (Blecha, Gega, and Green 1979). Typical of many teachers using this textbook, Ms. Lane's statements to the class related directly to what was written in the textbook. Daily instruction consisted of round-robin oral reading of the text, with pauses to answer questions posed in the text or watch demonstrations or perform experiments suggested by the text. The teacher's verbal pattern was to call on students when a question arose in the text, to indicate when a student had answered correctly, and to rephrase or repeat ideas that seemed difficult. Incorrect student reponses were either passed over or rejected by the teacher. The teacher often accepted incorrect approximations of the answer as if they were correct. The teacher did not probe to elicit improvement of incorrect or half-correct student answers.

Discussions in Ms. Lane's class were determined by what page they were on in the text. Since the text presented one idea after another without emphasizing important ideas, without relating one idea to another, and without challenging students' common misconceptions,[2] Ms. Lane's presentation followed the same pattern. In one class period, for example, Ms. Lane introduced the following concepts: light as energy, light for seeing, light travels fast, speed of light, atoms, photons, sources of light (artificial vs. natural), bioluminescence, uses of light, animals that give off light, reasons light travels fast, lightning, amplitude, wavelengths, light travels in straight lines, intensity of light, pioneer uses of candles, electricity provides artificial light, watts, volts, fluorescence, and light cannot bend. Ms. Lane did not give any overall structure to help students assimilate this barrage of new information.

Ms. Lane's students did not learn much about the goal concepts from this kind of verbal interaction. Although they were almost always "on task," that task was rarely to think about the meaning of the text. They followed along as their fellow students read orally, and they gave brief answers to the teacher's questions. Most of the student talking that was longer than a word or a phrase was the relating of a personal experience that was in some way (often vaguely) related to the topic at hand. Ms. Lane's students became aware of idea after idea about light, but they were not stimulated to think about the meaning of these ideas. They viewed science as a mass of information to be memorized. Ms. Lane's absorption with the textbook and the suggested answers to questions given in her teacher's edition prevented her from focusing on what her students were really saying and thinking.

Ms. Ramsey and the transparency set. Another textbook-centered teacher took a different approach to classroom talk. In this part of the study, teachers were supplied with a set of transparencies to be used with the text.[3] These transparencies were designed to break the "read and answer the questions" cycle of instruction by first presenting a problem to elicit student misconceptions about light and seeing. Students could then contrast their answers directly with a more scientific answer given on an overlay. The teacher's guide to the transparencies described common student misconceptions and an explanation of the goal conception. Armed with this knowledge, Ms. Ramsey created a very different verbal environment.

In Ms. Ramsey's classroom, round-robin reading was eliminated, and daily discussions included much student talk as students explained their ideas. Ms. Ramsey was sensitive to these student explanations and frequently readdressed questions to a student to get a clear understanding of what the student was saying. The teacher praised students for precise, careful use of language: "I like *that* word better. Why is it better?" Ms. Ramsey often used the transparencies to give students practice applying newly learned concepts. In contrast to Ms. Lane's class, student answers were lengthier, and the teacher was more likely to interact with a single student repeatedly before posing a new question. She would also come back to a student after other students had spoken to see if she could get the student to restate a position more precisely using what other students had said. This careful probing of student answers enabled Ms. Ramsey to uncover student misconceptions even when the students' initial answers sounded "pretty good" and could easily have been accepted as close enough approximations of the "correct" answer.

Another feature of verbal interaction in Ms. Ramsey's class was redundancy. Key ideas were repeated by the teacher in different contexts. Different students were given opportunities to answer the same question. The transparencies were reviewed periodically throughout the unit. Students kept written lists of "summary statements" in their notebooks.

Did these differences in the verbal climate make a difference in student learning? On the posttest, 60 percent of Ms. Ramsey's students understood how we use light when we see. This is in stark contrast to the 12 percent in Ms. Lane's class[4]. Ms. Ramsey's students were challenged to think about and state their ideas clearly and to give evidence for their ideas. Ms. Ramsey not only knew what questions to ask but also had a sensitivity to her students' thinking that enabled her to elicit, analyze, and respond to student talk effectively. Ms. Ramsey's students were intellectually engaged in the difficult process of changing their ideas about light.

Summary of the Case Studies

These four teachers are representative of a number of case studies we have conducted as part of our research (see Chapter 13 of this volume and notes 2, 5, and 6 at the end of this chapter). It seems clear from these studies that the teachers' verbal strategies as well as teacher-student verbal interactions are important and that certain patterns are more successful in facilitating student comprehension than others. A model that builds on these insights follows.

A MODEL OF COMPREHENSION INSTRUCTION IN A CONTENT AREA

The knowledge about teaching and learning accumulated from our study of science teachers suggests that comprehension instruction in content areas should engage students intellectually (rather than just physically) and get them to relinquish or modify naive preconceptions in favor of well-structured scientific views. To do so, instruction is viewed as a set of components that are logically designed and interrelated to induce conceptual change in learners. The teacher must be actively involved in diagnosing student misconceptions, in presenting content in such a way that students are intellectually engaged and in guiding students to change naive preconceptions to more scientific views. The teacher must *think* about students' thinking rather than merely provide opportunities for students to learn on their own, and must say things to help students go beyond what they can learn independently. In short, the responsibility for instruction belongs to the teacher and *not* to the curriculum materials.

Research Base for the Model

Beyond our own research, the model draws from recent research in a variety of fields that all emphasize the importance of being sensitive to students' intellectual processing of instruction. Numerous studies in cognitive psychology and instructional psychology, for example, have revealed that students do not always process information from instruction in the intended manner (Anderson 1981, Doyle 1979, Winne and Marx 1980).[7] What the teacher says may cue students to perform certain behavioral tasks, but it does not always result in student learning (Anderson 1981). Other studies have revealed that students' naive views of the world (preconceptions) make the learning of content more difficult (Champagne 1980, Cole and Raven 1969, Davis 1980, Erlwanger 1975, Leboutet-Barrell 1976, Rosnick and Clement 1980, Rowell and Dawson 1977, Rumelhart 1977). Thus, changing students' preconceptions is a more difficult task than pouring knowledge into an empty vessel. Research efforts have also suggested the benefits of teaching students how to monitor their internal mental processing. This ability, termed metacognition by the cognitive psychologists, has been shown to improve learning, retention, and transfer in several studies (Brown, Campione, and Barclay 1979; Day 1980; Chapter 17 in this volume).[8]

While studies such as the above have been influential, the conclusions drawn from our own research have directly shaped our model and influenced our concept of comprehension instruction. These are presented here as four principles.

Teachers need to be sensitive to their students' misconceptions, and they need to continually consider how these misconceptions are influencing students' responses to instruction. Ms. Ross and Ms. Lane were so absorbed with following the program materials that they failed to track their students' thinking. Mr.

Kinney and Ms. Ramsey both were sensitive to their student's misconceptions. However, Mr. Kinney's failure to use this awareness of the students' thinking to improve student learning suggests that awareness of student misconceptions is not enough.

Teachers need to focus what they say and what their students are saying on the "whys" of science. Ms. Ross' students had little opportunity to learn the meaning of their science experiments because they were only directed to think and talk about experimental procedures and observations. In her class, students learned all about "doing" science, while the students in Ms. Lane's class became acquainted only with concept after concept at a factual level. In both these classes, as well as in Mr. Kinney's class, information was presented without making explicit the importance of the information and how it fit together. Science was presented as a string of seemingly unrelated abstract ideas or observations.

In contrast, Ms. Ramsey focused on the "whys" by insisting that students give explanations for their observations and ideas and by frequent repetition of important ideas. Class discussions were used to refine student explanations, with the teacher emphasizing and repeating key points. Repetition, when properly focused and organized to emphasize key concepts in different situations, can be used to help students develop structural frameworks that will enable them to incorporate and retain new knowledge more effectively. Redundancy, then, is one important focusing strategy.

Teachers need to know more than just what questions to ask; they also need to know how to respond to student statements. Mr. Kinney asked all the important "why" questions. However, he failed to use these questions and the student responses they elicited to effect student learning. He frequently commented to researchers that he could use more guidance in handling student ideas. In contrast, Ms. Ramsey said things in response to student statements that got them to think more carefully about the meaning of the science content. This ability clearly enhanced her instructional effectiveness.

There must be a balance between open-ended verbal interactions and directed, structured discussions that lead to closure and consensus. Slavish devotion to one verbal interaction pattern was not successful. Mr. Kinney stimulated students to think and talk about their ideas, but without direct guidance from him, his students failed to change their ideas. Ms. Ramsey, on the other hand, was able to elicit student ideas and then provide direct, structured discussion to lead the students to develop more scientific views. Ms. Ramsey realized that while there were times to encourage students to think creatively and divergently, there were also times to directly explain scientific ideas. She was not afraid to distinguish among poor answers, good answers and best answers, and she clearly communicated to students why certain answers were better than others. Often, through careful questioning, she was able to get the students themselves to make these distinctions.

The Model

Figure 19.1 diagrammatically depicts the components of the proposed model for comprehension instruction in content areas. It is essentially a division between two crucial instructional functions: The outer ring represents the indirect components of instruction that ensure a proper environmental setting, and the core represents the sequence designed to elicit active student processing of the content material.

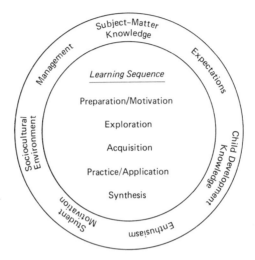

FIGURE 19.1 A Model of Science Instruction.

The outer ring prerequisites include:

1. The presence of good classroom *management*.
2. The teacher's sound understanding of the *concepts* being taught.
3. High teacher *expectations* for the students.
4. Teacher knowledge about *child development*.
5. Teacher *enthusiasm* in presenting the material.
6. Teacher sensitivity to the *social needs* of students.
7. The teacher's ability to *motivate* students.

Once the prerequisites are in place, as was largely the case with the four teachers we have described, the teacher must then implement an instructional sequence designed to result in an active student cognitive response. The sequence involves five steps adapted from Gagne (1979). These steps demand that the teacher's roles and strategies change as the students progress. The teacher acts as a facilitator, a diagnostician, or a director, depending on what is needed to keep students actively thinking. In each case, the teacher's verbal patterns are essential, particularly as they relate to student responses.

Preparation. During this initial phase of the instructional sequence, the teacher provides an overview and gives background information for the unit. Students are made aware of the learning goals for the unit through explicit presentations by the teacher. Such presentations might include pictorial representations that show the students the territory that will be covered. Motivational activities may also be used to encourage students to be willing to think about the subject matter. The goal of deeper processing by students will never be attained if students have no desire to think about the content. During this phase students get mentally set for instruction, relevant schema or frames are called to mind and background information crucial to comprehension of the subject matter is explained. At this point, the teacher's planning is based on consideration of *likely* student responses.

Exploration. During this stage, the teacher provides an opportunity for students to explore and become more aware of their own ideas. Use of hands-on experiences is an important exploratory tool because it provides motivation to get students actively involved in defining their own views. Not all science experiments can be considered good exploration activities, however; they must be practical in terms of materials and duration. Other exploratory activities include open-ended discussions, problem-solving opportunities, open-ended expository writing, or free reading. These activities are all characterized as being invitations to students to express their own views. Teacher verbal patterns in this stage must challenge students to think and must create some internal mental conflict. The teacher's response is to accept and acknowledge all answers. The exploratory phase is a critical idea-collecting process in which conflicting ideas will surface as preconceptions that the teacher must catalogue and consider in planning for the next phases of instruction.

Acquisition. Once the students' ideas have been challenged by the exploratory activity, the teacher's verbal statements make explicit this conceptual conflict and further verbal patterns direct the students in resolving the conflict through conceptual change. Direct instruction by the teacher is crucial to ensure that each student receives an explanation of the scientific phenomena that is in clear contrast to the misconceptions elicited during the exploration stage and that is reasonable and understandable to students. At this point, the teacher might use classroom discussions that grow from the exploratory activity but that are now carefully structured to lead the class away from incorrect preconceptions and toward specific scientific conclusions. At this stage of the lesson, the teacher

1. Asks more closed questions.
2. Discourages divergent student comments.
3. Provides key explanations.
4. Models the desired thinking processes.
5. Emphasizes important points by frequent repetition of key concepts in new situations.
6. Carefully relates theories to observations.

Teacher-student interaction is characterized by the teacher's careful probing and shaping of student statements with an insistence on sound reasoning and careful use of language. Misconceptions are systematically refuted by scientific evidence. This phase of instruction is demanding on the teacher; it requires meticulous care in the planning of a series of statements, questions, or tasks that will lead students to the desired understanding.

Practice/application. Acquiring knowledge of the goal concept is not sufficient for students to reorganize their internal conceptual framework. It is also essential that students use the new concepts until they become their own. This requires that instruction provide opportunities for students to practice using and applying their newly acquired knowledge in new situations.

Some ideas about effective ways to present such opportunities include

- Recitation discussions where students practice talking about the ideas, with other students and the teacher providing correctives and feedback.
- Experiments and other hands-on activities that deal with new but related problems
- Small group problem solving sessions
- Directed expository writing experiences that force students to explain the concepts in an applied situation
- Student creation of concept maps

Traditional fill-in-the-blanks worksheets, in which everyone fills in the same answer, will rarely get students to think about the subject matter; more often, students will confer with their neighbors to get the correct answers and complete the sheet. Even as a reinforcer of vocabulary, these worksheets are probably of little value.

This stage of instruction may lead back to the acquisition phase if it becomes clear that students have not acquired the intended learning. For example students may write papers that reveal the persistence of misconceptions. At such times, the teacher must again take instructional leadership and explicitly point out the differences between the students' ideas and those of the scientific community. This may involve working with a few individual students, holding a brief whole-class session to clear up a few issues, or a major reorganization of the planned sequence.

The teacher has multiple roles during the practice phase. As facilitator, the teacher presents the opportunities for practice and supports students as they work. As diagnostician, the teacher elicits information about how completely students have given up misconceptions and about how well they have integrated new knowledge into their schema. The teacher then uses this information in deciding when it is necessary to once again become the director of instruction in planning additional practice opportunities, in providing prompt corrective feedback, and in helping students learn how to monitor their own learning.

Synthesis. Once the students have had sufficient practice and reinforcement to make the new knowledge their own, they need to synthesize the information so that they will continue to retrieve such information in preference to their old, incorrect ideas. The synthesis process will help the students fit smaller pieces of learning into an overall framework or schema for the particular topic of study. One way the teacher may help students accomplish this synthesis is by filling in details on a pictorial overview that was initially presented during the preparation phase. Helping students get the big picture will require direct teacher instruction and some kind of evaluation. Evaluation measures, including formal testing and informal assessments, should focus on how well students have processed the information. How accurate are they in recognizing the ideas? How well are they able to produce the ideas? Can they use the ideas in new situations? How thoroughly and systematically have they integrated the new knowledge in their memory?

Summary

The case studies presented earlier in this chapter illustrate how teachers can become so totally absorbed with one *part* of instruction that they fail to include instructional steps crucial to student learning. In activity-based programs, for example, teachers like Ms. Ross and Mr. Kinney provided the opportunity to explore using manipulative materials, but did not follow up on the activities to ensure acquisition and did not allow for practice and application. The teacher was purely a facilitator, hoping that the activities themselves would lead students to "discover" important science principles. Unfortunately, the majority of students in such programs do not learn the intended objectives and do not give up their preconceptions. They learn to view science as a fun activity where everybody's ideas are equally valid. Students are physically engaged on task, but the lack of intellectual engagement results in a waste of precious instructional time.

In textbook-centered programs, to the other hand, students are rarely given the opportunity to explore their ideas, and teachers have little idea of what their students think. Preparation is often neglected except for whatever attention is given to it on the first page of the unit in the text. Although time is spent in what could be called acquisition and practice, teachers' failures to consider the students' processing of instruction results in wasted instructional efforts. Teachers do not take charge of explaining ideas to students; they assume the text has done this for them. "Practice" consists of fill-in-the-blank worksheets that students can answer by referring to their textbooks or by conferring with their neighbors. Important opportunities for critical reading are missed. Instead of reading and thinking, students are reading and accepting at face value. Teachers typically evaluate the unit on the basis of student interest and acceptable performance on a unit test does not reveal what students are thinking.

In contrast to such teaching, content-area instruction needs to emphasize each of the phases of learning. There must be *balance* between preparation, exploration, acquisition, practice, and synthesis, and the teacher must alternatively play the role of facilitator, diagnostician and director. While the relative emphasis on each of these phases and roles should vary depending on the developmental needs of the student, classroom observational studies suggest that most content-area classrooms can benefit from increased emphasis on the acquisition phase in which the teacher's role as an active director of learning is emphasized.

CONCLUSION

A major goal in science education is for students to develop sound reasoning, thinking, and problem-solving skills and to gain a deeper understanding of their world. In order to achieve such goals, instruction must focus on engaging students intellectually. Learning gains can be significant if students are actively processing information and if teachers are sensitive to students' thinking. Instruction must provide a learning sequence designed to keep students actively processing ideas at each step. In providing such a well-balanced instructional program, the teacher cannot just be a tour guide following a predetermined itinerary. The teacher must instead be willing to change roles based on thoughtful consideration of how students are responding to instruction. Decisions on when to allow exploration and when to give very direct, explicit explanation, should be based on what is needed to help students become mentally involved in the learning task and to help them build a well-structured understanding of scientific phenomena. Once the decision is made to provide direct explanation, the teacher's verbal patterns become crucial in structuring the lesson and in responding during teacher-student interaction.

NOTES

1. E. L. Smith, G. D. Berkheimer, and C. W. Anderson. *SCIS revised teacher's guide*. East Lansing: Elementary Science Project, Institute for Research on Teaching, Michigan State University, 1982.

2. J. F. Eaton, C. W. Anderson, and E. L. Smith. *Student preconceptions interfere with learning: Case studies of fifth-grade students*. Paper presented at the annual meeting of the National Association for Research in Science Teaching, Fontana, Wisconsin, 1982.

3. C. W. Anderson and E. L. Smith. *Transparencies on light: Teacher's manual*. East Lansing: Elementary Science Project, Institute for Research on Teaching, Michigan State University, 1982.

4. C. W. Anderson and E. L. Smith. *Student conceptions of light, color, and seeing: Phase 1 test results*. Paper presented at the annual meeting of the National Association for Research in Science Teaching, Fontana, Wisconsin, 1982.

5. E. L. Smith and C. W. Anderson. *Plants as producers: A case study of elementary school science teaching*. Paper presented at the annual meeting of the National Association for Research in Science Teaching, Fontana, Wisconsin, 1982.

6. L. Slinger, C. W. Anderson, and E. L. Smith. *One view of fifth-grade text-based science instruction*. Paper presented at the annual meeting of the National Association for Research in Science Teaching, Fontana, Wisconsin, 1982.

7. L. Anderson. *Students' responses to seatwork: Implications for the study of students' cognitive processing*. Research Series No. 102. East Lansing: Institute for Research on Teaching, Michigan State University, 1981. W. Doyle. *Student mediating responses in teaching effectiveness. Final Report*. Denton, Tex.: North Texas State University, March 1980. P. H. Winne. Treatment design for research on teaching. In L. Corno (Chair), *Students' cognitive processing during teaching*. Symposium presented at the annual meetings of the American Educational Research Association, Los Angeles, 1981. P. H. Winne and R. W. Marx. *Students' and teachers' views of thinking processes for classroom learning*. Research Report No. 81–05. Instructional Psychology Research Group, Simon Fraser University, British Columbia, Canada, 1981.

8. A. L. Brown and J. D. Day. *The development of rules for summarizing texts*. Unpublished manuscript, University of Illinois, 1980.

REFERENCES

Anderson, L. Student short-term responses to classroom instruction. *Elementary School Journal*, 1981, *82* (2), 97–108.

Blecha, M. K., Gega, P. C., & Green, M. *Exploring science*, green book. Teachers' edition. River Forest, Ill.: Laidlaw, 1979.

Brown, A. L., Campione, J. C., & Barclay, C. R. Training self-checking routines for estimating test readiness: Generalization from list learning to prose recall. *Child Development*, 1979, *50*, 501–512.

Champagne, A. B. Klopfer, L. E., & Anderson, J. H. Factors influencing the learning of classical mechanics. *American Journal of Physics*, 1980, *48*, 1074–1079.

Cole, H., & Raven R. Principle learning as a function of instruction on excluding irrelevant variables. *Journal of Research in Science Teaching*, 1969, *6*, 234–241.

Davis, R. B. The postulation of certain specific explicit, commonly-shared frames. *Journal of Mathematical Behavior*, 1980, *3* (1), 167–201.

Day, J. D. *Training summarization skills: A comparison of teaching methods.* Unpublished doctoral dissertation, University of Illinois, 1980.

Doyle, W. Classroom tasks and students' abilities. In P. Peterson and H. Walberg (Eds.), *Research on teaching: Concepts, findings and implications.* Berkeley: McCutchan, 1979.

Erlwanger, S. H. Case studies of children's conceptions of mathematics. Part I. *Journal of Children's Mathematical Behavior*, 1975, *1* (3), 157–183.

Gagné, R. M. *The conditions of learning.* New York: Holt, Rinehart and Winston, 1970.

Knott, R., Lawson, C., Karplus, R., Thier, H., and Montgomery, M. *SCIIS Communities teacher's guide.* Chicago: Rand McNally, 1978.

LeBoutet-Barrell, L. Concepts of mechanics in young people. *Physics Education*, 1976, *11* (7), 462–466.

Rosnick, P., & Clement, J. Learning without understanding: The effect of tutoring strategies on algebra misconceptions. *Journal of Mathematical Behavior*, 1980, *3*, 3–27.

Rowell, J. A., & Dawson, C. J. Teaching about floating and sinking: An attempt to link cognitive psychology with classroom practice. *Science Education*, 1977, *61* (2), 243–251.

Rumelhart, D. E., & Ortony, E. A. The representation of knowledge in memory. In R. C. Anderson, R. Spiro, and W. Montague (Eds.), *Schooling and the acquisition of knowledge.* Hillsdale, N.J.: Erlbaum, 1977.

Smith, E. L., & Sendelbach, N. The program, the plans, and the activities of the classroom: The demands of activity-based science. In John Olson (Ed.,), *Innovation in the science curriculum: Classroom knowledge and curriculum change.* New York: Nichols, 1982.

Winne, P. H., & Marx, R. W. Matching students' cognitive responses to teaching skills. *Journal of Educational Pscyhology*, 1980, *72*, 257–264.

Summary of Part IV

Comprehension Instruction as Verbal Communication

The five chapters in this section have much in common regarding the nature of comprehension instruction. It is agreed that classroom management, while crucial as a prerequisite to effective instruction, is not the essence of teaching. Instead, there seems to be a consensus that the heart of instruction communication is the verbal communication between teacher and student. Further, there is agreement across all five chapters that this communication requires an active, not passive, teacher role; that teachers have a responsibility for being explicit in their comprehension instruction; and that the outcomes of comprehension instruction should include teaching students to monitor their understanding of text as well as the raising of their achievement level.

In addition to the agreement noted above, this section also raises a significant issue. Pearson stated one side of this issue in the opening chapter of the section when he made the distinction between *what* is comprehended (content) and *how* it is comprehended (process), saying that "I know of no data base that would allow us to determine the independence of content . . . and process . . . factors." In the next two chapters, Raphael and Gavelek and Palinscar, while not explicitly stating it, imply their agreement with Pearson's reluctance to separate content and process. As a result, all three of these chapters report studies that focus on comprehension *strategies*—techniques that reflect the principles of how comprehension works without explicitly stating for students what processes or skills are used to do the comprehension. In contrast, Duffy and Roehler (Chapter 18) take a different position regarding the content-process controversy by attempting to directly teach students the mental processing involved in performing comprehension skills and then showing students how such processing can be used to interpret text. Roth, Smith, and Anderson take a similar position in Chapter 19 by arguing for explicit explanation of the significance of science concepts.

Hence this section presents some common principles on which comprehension instruction can be based. Nevertheless, questions remain. Not the least of these is the relative emphasis to be placed on strategy training as opposed to explanation of the content and processes of comprehension.

294

SELECTED BIBLIOGRAPHY, PART IV

Allington, R. L. *Poor readers don't get to reach much.* Occasional Paper No. 31. East Lansing: Institute for Research on Teaching, Michigan State University, 1980.

Allington, R. Teacher interruption behavior during primary grade oral reading. *Journal of Educational Psychology,* 1980, *72,* 371–377.

Anderson, L., Evertson, C., & Brophy, J. An experimental study of effective teaching in first grade reading groups. *Elementary School Journal,* 1979, *79,* 193–222.

Beck, I., McCashen, E., & McKeown, M. Basal readers' purpose for story reading: Smoothly paving the road or setting up a detour? *Elementary School Journal,* 1981, *81,* 156–161.

Beck. I, & McKeown, M. G. Developing questions that promote comprehension: The story map. *Language Arts,* 1981, *58* (8), 913–918.

Beck, I. L., Omanson, R. C., & McKeown, M. G. An instructional redesign of reading lessons: Effects on comprehension. *Reading Research Quarterly,* 1982, *17* (4), 462–481.

Brophy, J. *Teacher behavior and its effects.* Occasional Paper No. 25. East Lansing: Institute for Research on Teaching, Michigan State University, September 1979.

Brophy, J. Successful teaching strategies for the inner city child. *Phi Delta Kappan,* 1982, *63* (8), 527–529.

Brown, A. L., Campione, J. C., & Day, J. D. Learning to learn: On training students to learn from texts. *Educational Researcher,* 1981, *10* (2), 14–24.

Case, R. A developmentally based theory and technology of instruction. *Review of Educational Research,* 1978, *48* (3), 439–463.

Duffy, G., & Roehler, L. Instruction as sense-making: Implications for teacher education. *Action in Teacher Education,* 1982, *4* (1), 1–7.

Durkin, D. What classroom observations reveal about reading comprehension instruction. *Reading Research Quarterly,* 1978–79, *14,* 481–533.

Engleman, S., & Carnine, D. Cognitive learning: A direct instruction analysis. *Educational Technology,* in press.

Fisher, C., Berliner, D., Filby, N., Marliave, R., Cahen, L., & Dishaw, M. Teaching behaviors, learning time and student achievement: An overview. In C. Denham & A. Lieberman (Eds.), *Time to Learn.* Washington: National Institute of Education, May 1980.

Hodges, C. Commentary: Toward a broader definition of comprehension instruction. *Reading Research Quarterly,* 1980, *15* (2), 299–306.

Pearson, D., & Spiro, R. Toward a theory of reading comprehension instruction. *Topics in Language Disorders,* 1980, *1,* 71–88.

Roehler, L., & Duffy, G. Classroom teaching is more than opportunity to learn. *Journal of Teacher Education,* 1981, *32* (6), 7–13.

Rosenshine, B. Classroom instruction. In N.L. Gage (Ed.), *The psychology of teaching methods.* Seventy-fifth Yearbook of the National Society for the Study of Education. Part I. Chicago: University of Chicago Press, 1976.

Rosenshine, B. Content, time and direct instruction. In. S. Walberg & P. Peterson (Eds.), *Research on teaching: Concepts, findings and implications.* Berkeley: McCutchan, 1979.

Tharp, R. G. The effective instruction of comprehension: Results and description of the Kamehameha Early Education Program. *Reading Research Quarterly*, 1982, *17* (4), 462–481.

Part V

Implications for Research and Practice

20

A Practitioner's Model of
Comprehension Instruction

Jana Mason, Laura R. Roehler, and Gerald G. Duffy

The preceding chapters have presented various perspectives on comprehension instruction intended to provide practitioners with research on comprehension instruction in a form that can be used to improve classroom practice.

In a broad way, the book has been separated into three aspects of instruction. It first describes ways in which comprehension instruction is constrained and suggests that teachers—because of environmental conditions—are not always free to do whatever they want in teaching comprehension. Then it describes certain conditions of text itself and how, depending on the way text is structured, the teacher's efforts to present instruction can be simplified or complicated. Finally, it describes a variety of strategies for teaching comprehension that can be adapted and applied to classroom practice.

The very act of distinguishing three aspects of instruction reveals the varying influences on comprehension instruction. There are at least four. First, comprehension instruction is heavily influenced by cognitive psychology generally and by the schema-theoretic view of comprehension described in Chapter 3 in particular. This is evident in the emphasis throughout the book on comprehension as active processing, which stands in contrast to earlier notions of drill, massed practice, and objective measures of learning in the emphasis on congruence between text content and reader background; and in the emphasis on metacognition and readers' possessing executive control of their comprehension. Second, comprehension instruction is viewed from the perspective of the realities of the classrooms in which such teaching occurs. As a result, the majority of the research reported in this book has been conducted in real classrooms that are subject to all the ecological constraints of the real world of teaching rather than in laboratories or research centers. Third, simplistic explanations of how to improve comprehension instruction are avoided. This is evident in the discussions of effective instruction, in the analyses of written materials, and in the explanations of why instructional procedures and materials need to be tried out in the classroom. Finally, there is a viewpoint that advocates examining what teachers think and do when teaching comprehension. This is reflected in analyses of teacher presentation of strategies, teacher ability to plan and to implement plans through interactive decision making, and teacher skill at responding to student restructuring with appropriate explanations.

As a result of both the broad messages and the varying influences reported here, the purposes of the book as they were stated in Chapter 1 have been met. The first purpose was to describe a "common ground" that could be used as a foundation for building effective instructional programs. This "common ground" has been provided by advocating (1) that instructional improvement in comprehension must be initiated within the framework of the realities of schools (including teacher thinking, classroom environments and school contexts); (2) that a fundamental ingredient of comprehension instruction is "considerate" text, whether the text is instructional (such as basals or workbooks) or content-related (such as textbooks or trade books); and (3) that the essence of comprehension instruction is the communication between teachers and students regarding the strategies and/ or content to be learned. The second purpose of the book was to provide suggestions that can be used to create improved comprehension instruction. These suggestions are evident throughout the book, ranging from Lezotte's (Chapter 9) findings of school effects research and Davison's (Chapter 10) treatment of the limitations of determining what text to use by applying traditional readability formula to explications of instructional strategies provided in Part 4.

In addition to meeting its stated purposes, the information in the book has raised issues and stimulated insights that go beyond the "common ground" and "instructional suggestion" purposes anticipated at the outset. Distinctions heretofore ignored have been raised; also, a broader instructional context has been suggested. This more extensive definition of comprehension instruction indicates the need for clarification of basic concepts regarding instruction. It also leads to the realization that our models of reading comprehension instruction have been inadequate. Consequently, in the remainder of this chapter we outline the conceptual distinctions we believe are critical to instruction. Following that, we propose a new model of reading comprehension instruction for school practitioners and teacher educators.

CONCEPTUAL DISTINCTIONS IN COMPREHENSION INSTRUCTION

Because the book is a marriage between researchers of instruction and researchers of comprehension, it is not surprising that conceptual distinctions can be categorized in terms of these two fields. Instructional distinctions are discussed first, followed by distinctions about reading comprehension. For each we attempt to extrapolate and clarify significant issues in comprehension instruction. We then synthesize these in a summary based on our understanding of where we have been and where we will be going in the near future. This synthesis serves as the background to the model of comprehension instruction that follows.

Instructional Distinctions

There are three instructional distinctions that we believe need to be presented. The broadest is discussed first and the narrowest is discussed last.

The first distinction places in perspective the notion of "inner grounding" and "outer grounding" for thinking about comprehension instruction. The inner grounding is comprehension instruction as it is actually occurring. It focuses on what teachers say to students, the strategies used and the content taught. As such, it has a temporal dimension: We can point to a certain incident or series of incidents in a classroom and say, "What's happening right now is comprehension instruction." The outer grounding, in contrast, is the larger context within which the instruction occurs. As such, it is not temporal; it is constant. It considers the implicit and explicit mandates about what will be taught and how it will be taught; the constraints posed by the collective nature of schooling and the fact that most instruction takes place with groups of students rather than with individuals; the techniques which must be imposed on groups in order to ensure order, engagement, and smooth activity flow; the organization and recordkeeping associated with managing accountability aspects of instruction; the climate of the school and the classroom; and others. Both the inner and the outer groundings are crucial to comprehension instruction. The important distinction, however, is that the outer grounding is in effect a prerequisite condition to the inner grounding. We are all, to one degree or another, products of our environment; we are what we are because of the way our context has shaped our lives. It is not any different for comprehension instruction. What happens when a teacher interacts with students about comprehension instruction is largely shaped by the context in which that instruction is conducted. Consequently, when considering comprehension instruction, the inner grounding does not exist in isolation but as a product of a complex set of contextual conditions that constitute the outer grounding of comprehension instruction.

The second distinction focuses on the teacher's role during instruction. There has long been a tradition in American schooling that comprehension is essentially unteachable and that the most teachers can do is set the stage for learning to occur. Comprehension instruction from this perspective was very limited since one learned to comprehend on one's own: It was totally self-regulated. Recently, Vygotsky (1979) has presented an alternative to this position that gives instruction a larger role. Vygotsky's theory of cognitive development is based on the concept of internalization. Vygotsky argues that thinking strategies are originally developed in social situations in which adults (mostly parents) and children interact. Children first experience active problem-solving activities with others, but gradually they become independent problem solvers. This process of internalization is gradual; first the adult or adultlike person controls and guides the child's activity. Gradually, the adult and child share the responsibilities, with the child taking the lead and the adult guiding the child's responses and providing correctives when the child has erred. Finally, the adult gives the child the full range of responsibilities and provides support. This progression from other-regulation to self-regulation in the development of problem solving is an appropriate way to consider comprehension instruction. In schools, teachers are the adults and the classroom is the social situation. Teachers develop students' self-regulation of comprehension activities by providing a decreasing level of assistance. Responsibility for monitoring and evaluating comprehension is gradually transferred to the student. The internalization of comprehension ability occurs within the student's "zone of proximal proximal development," defined as the distance between the student's level of independent problem solving and the level of potential development as determined through problem solving under adult guidance. If one takes a Vygoskyian view, one of the teacher's primary functions is to provide instruction that leads from other-regulation to self-regulated situations. This position is distinct from the traditional view that comprehension is essentially unteachable.

The third distinction focuses on the differences among instruction in *the nature of* a skill or strategy, instruction in *practicing* a skill or strategy, and instruction in *using* a skill or strategy. While the three are certainly tied together and all lead to the ultimate goal of use in "real reading," they are nevertheless distinct and need to be distinguished in the classroom. Instruction in the *nature* of a skill or strategy requires the teacher to "regulate" students' text processing so as to create a conscious awareness that (1) a particular comprehension problem can be eliminated through use of a particular skill or strategy, and (2) the skill or strategy can become part of a repetoire of mental structures that students possess for dealing with confusions in text; instruction in *practicing* the skill or strategy requires the teacher to provide students with a text controlled by task pursued and by comprehension difficulty (but not by formulaic measures of readability) and to provide students with multiple opportunities to respond by using their newly learned skill or strategy; instruction in *using* a skill or strategy requires the teacher to provide students with multiple opportunities to do "real reading" in which the text has not been modified or controlled relative to the particular comprehension difficulty but for which an expectancy has been set that the skill or strategy will be consciously applied as needed. In sequence, the progression is from instruction in the nature of the skill or strategy, to its practice, to its use. The distinctions among these three forms of instruction are important because of the implications both for the sequence of comprehension instruction and for the type of Vygotskian "regulation" called for by each. The absence of such instructional variation explains, at least in part, why the current studies of classroom practices in comprehension instruction reported in Chapters 1 and 4 are so disturbing.

COMPREHENSION DISTINCTIONS

Like instruction, there are three distinctions about comprehension. The first, the distinction in reading between decoding and meaning getting, has been verbalized for years but has not significantly influenced practice. The emphasis has remained on word identification. However, in the light of schema-theoretic and cognitive processing approaches to comprehension, this distinction takes on new importance. Comprehension is no longer simply a matter of accepting text meaning with word recognition, by implication, being a prerequisite to this end. Comprehension and decoding are defined interactively—and in terms of active processing of text information using one's own knowledge. The reader uses knowledge about the graphemes printed on the page (decoding) and knowledge that he or she has stored in the form of schemata accumulated from prior experience (comprehension) to construct an interpretation of the author's message. This distinction is crucial for instruction because we can no longer perceive the outcome of reading instruction as decoding or comprehension, nor can skills or strategies for decoding or comprehension be taught in isolation from the goal of constructing the author's message. A reading strategy is useful only if it results in a sensible interpretation, so the decision to teach one or another comprehension strategy lies with its potential for sense making.

A second comprehension distinction is between comprehending text and *strategies* for comprehending text. Both are part of comprehension instruction, but they imply different pedagogical views. When the frame is comprehending text, the *content* of text takes priority. The teacher's goal is to have students understand the text content so that the pedagogy is directed toward assuring that understanding has occurred. The Directed Reading Lesson used with standard basal text selections is an example of pedagogy directed toward understanding text. Because strategy development assumes that a self-monitoring *process* underlies the comprehension of text content, the explication of this process takes priority when teaching strategies for comprehending text; the goal is to have students understand the process and *then* transfer it for use in understanding the content of text. The pedagogy is directed toward presenting the strategy and making the transfer. This distinction is crucial to understanding comprehension instruction since much of the debate about how best to conduct instruction is based in differences regarding whether the undergirding process strategies must be directly taught or whether strategies for comprehending text develop naturally as a consequence of comprehending text.

A third comprehension distinction is between metacognition and automaticity. Metacognition refers to the reader's executive control over what is read; automaticity refers to the reader's ability to process text without hesitation. Currently, metacognition is associated with comprehension and automaticity with word recognition. Both terms apply to comprehension instruction, however, since the issue raised is unconscious or habit formed processing of text versus directed thinking and conscious analysis of text.

Summary of Distinctions

The fact that distinctions such as the above can be made is indicative of the distance we have come in recent years in understanding comprehension instruction. It was not unusual five years ago to discuss instruction with little reference to contextual influence, with little acknowledgement of the regulatory function of teachers, and with little distinction between instruction in the nature of a strategy, its practice, and its application. Similarly, there was little understanding five years ago of the interaction between word recognition and comprehension, of the pedagogical distinctions between views of comprehension as strategy development or as text understanding, and of the teaching of comprehension as a metacognitive or an automatized process.

Because these distinctions are relatively new, there are no truly definitive ways to resolve the questions raised by each. Nevertheless, as a step toward improving practice, tentative answers must be provided. We do so here with the understanding that the following four suggestions must be accepted or rejected by reference to research.

First, the complexity of reading and of classrooms is fundamental to comprehension instruction and the way in which the "inner" activities of classroom instruction are shaped by the context of the "outer" environment must be considered by any practical model of comprehension instruction.

Second, effective comprehension instruction depends not upon choosing whether one should teach to understand text or to develop strategies, or that one should choose between teaching about strategies, practicing strategies, or applying them. Clearly, comprehension is too complex a process to be confined to one goal. Instead, a model of comprehension instruction should include all, but should do so with a conscious awareness of the conceptual differences between each and the pedagogical differences required as a result.

Third, there can be little question regarding the role of the teacher in comprehension instruction. It must be an active one. Whether Vygotsky's perception of instruction ultimately proves to be accurate or not, it is becoming increasingly more clear that we cannot leave students to develop comprehension spontaneously. There must be some form of assistance within the zone of proximal development that moves students from teacher-regulated to self-regulated behavior.

Finally, the apparent conflict between metacognitive and automatized outcomes calls for a synthesis. Under normal circumstances in which the reader is reading text that poses no difficulty of any kind, we would expect the processing to be automatic. However, what do we want to happen when the reader encounters a comprehension problem—a blockage in the form of a topic for which there is insufficient prior knowledge or an unknown word or an inability to construct an inference? We suggest that at the point where the reader encounters dissonance because sense making is breaking down, the metacognitive aspects of comprehension should come into play. The reader, at this point, becomes conscious of the breakdown in meaning and consciously searches his or her repertoire of skills, strategies, and understandings relative to comprehension to find a means for removing the blockage and proceeding with the reading. During this time, the reader is consciously in control of the reading process and deliberately attempts to activate what is known to alleviate the problem. Once the blockage is removed, an automatic mode can be reinstated in which understanding the text predominates, not how the process of comprehension works.

These distinctions form the basis for our model of comprehension instruction.

A MODEL OF COMPREHENSION INSTRUCTION

The model described next and displayed in Figure 20.1 considers reading comprehension instruction within multiple contexts and considers a variety of influences. It is hierarchical, consisting of four layers, with each layer affecting directly the next inner layer. The outer layer, describing school effects and teacher preparedness, provides grounding for instruction. Discussed by Lezotte in Chapter 9, schools are found to be more or less effective depending on the leadership role played by the school principal; the presence of safe and orderly classrooms; and evidence of regular, ongoing assessment of learning. Teacher preparedness is the other component of the outer layer. Noted in Chapters 13 and 19, it is depicted by three characteristics: knowledge about lesson content, classroom management techniques, and child development and social-context principles.

This outer, backgrounding layer constrains the second layer, defined as two characteristics: classroom milieu for classroom instruction and instructional materials. That is, effective schools and competent teachers are likely to use and select good materials, have satisfactory attitudes about the job and a willingness to persevere and to work with other staff members, and be able to organize and carry out effective instruction. Aspects of the instructional milieu are described in Chapters 5, 6, 7, and 8; instructional materials are discussed in Chapters 10, 11, 12, 13, and 14.

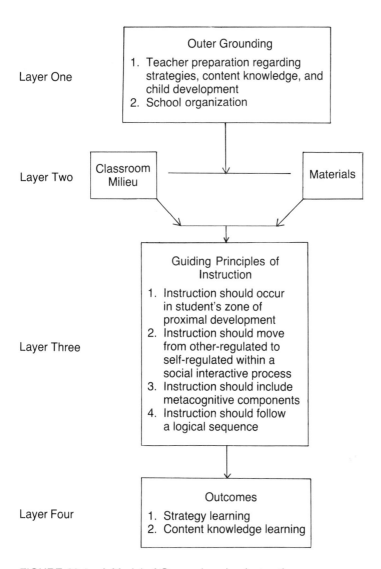

FIGURE 20.1   A Model of Comprehension Instruction.

Classroom milieu and materials directly affect the third level, the act of instruction. Instruction is represented by a number of basic principles for planning, sequencing, communicating and implementing a learning task. Not intended as an inclusive listing, the principles, discussed more broadly in Chapters 15, 16, 17, and 18, have been coalesced in the model into four characteristics of comprehension instruction.

The act of instruction leads to the fourth level: learner outcomes. We believe instruction should focus on two outcomes: (1) the development of students' awareness about how comprehension occurs and (2) the development or expansion of students' knowledge about what is being read. The first outcome is related to learning to read and centers on making students more aware of procedures to understand, analyze or evaluate how comprehension occurs. The second outcome is related to reading to learn; the instructional goal is for students to construct or extend their content knowledge frames. Either goal should be clearly stated to students and organized by the teacher in terms of student gains and steps to achievement.

Layer One: School and Staff Constraints

Schools do make a difference. This can be seen from observations of students working in classrooms; from interviews of staff, parents, and students; and from standardized tests that measure progress of low-achieving as well as high-achieving students. Schools are more or less effective depending on the climate set for learning and the competency of staff members. Effective schools project a sense of purposefulness, a shared commitment to learning, an expectation that all students will make achievement gains, a belief that they are expert instructional or administrative leaders, and a willingness to evaluate themselves through measures of student progress.

How can the work on schools and staff be related to a model of reading comprehension instruction? Reading comprehension is a cornerstone to the curriculum of a school. As noted in Chapters 3 and 4, because comprehension instruction seldom has been explained satisfactorily and is frequently not taught well or often enough, it is particularly important to have an effective environment for reading, learning and studying. A common goal of staff members ought to be instruction that stresses the meaningfulness and usefulness of reading. Principals ought to provide leadership that favors reading comprehension instruction. Teachers ought to have sound background knowledge in content-area topics they teach. Students should be measured on their reading comprehension knowledge. In general, all students ought to have opportunities to learn how to comprehend what they read and how teachers can help them learn.

Layer Two: Classroom Constraints

Constraints on reading comprehension instruction at the classroom level are described from two perspectives: (1) teachers' planning for and decisions about instruction and (2) quality and content of instructional materials. Each is affected by school and staff characteristics, which in turn affect the act of instruction.

Planning and decision making by teachers As Clark (Chapter 5) and Brophy (Chapter 6) explained, teachers plan instruction at several times during the year and at different levels of specificity. General ideas about content, routines, and procedures are worked out before school begins; resources for the content and an instructional sequence are typically dealt with at the unit planning level; and learning situations and specific content are decided on by the week or day. More plans are made about pupil activities and instructional content than about learning objectives. Interviews with teachers indicate that decision making also occurs while they are teaching but that at that time it is "more reactive than reflective, more intuitive than rational, and more routinized than conscious" (p. 72 this volume).

The research indicates that while teachers have plans regarding what and how to teach, their plans can become inflexible routines. They may establish such a well-formed expectancy about the flow of activities and the response of students that unexpected events or responses by students become interruptions in the planned routine. These unexpected situations, which could serve as excellent "teachable moments," require teachers to make a decision and take some action—exploit and teach from the situation, give a brief answer but return to the plan, or ignore the moment. Teachers seldom deviate from their plans to exploit the situation, even though student achievement is higher on higher-level cognitive objectives when they do. Nevertheless, since effective reading comprehension instruction frequently requires students to explain, evaluate, interpret, or generalize about the content of a text, which by itself can lead to unexpected situations, teachers should learn to accept variations in their plans or even to build flexibility into their plans.

Effective reading comprehension also requires that the teacher emphasize to students the understanding and usefulness of lessons. Yet, as Anderson found (Chapter 7), teachers seldom tell students what is to be learned and how it is related to other work. Instead of discussing strategies for thinking or ways to figure out answers, they emphasize the procedure for work, correctness, neatness, and completeness.

Florio and Clark (Chapter 8) discussed writing rather than reading, but their underlying instructional theme matches one characteristic of an effective reading comprehension program. It is that active engagement by students in thinking and learning can be fostered through informal procedures, providing the teacher sets up opportunities for such learning. Student-initiated reading as well as writing projects could be encouraged in a classroom. By encouraging a milieu in which students can initiate, use, or expand their reading activities, they will become more involved in reading as an act of understanding rather than as an exercise.

Structure and content of instructional materials   Obviously, textbooks for school-children are written to be understood and appreciated by them as well as to provide important information. As such, the texts must be written in a manner that makes the new information accessible and retains students' interest and attention to the learning tasks. The traditional approach to keeping texts from being too difficult to read is to impose vocabulary and sentence-length constraints on what is read. Divison discussed in Chapter 10 the use of shortcomings of these readability guidelines.

Other factors that affect text understanding and learning were described in Chapters 11–14. Chapters 12 and 14 provided guidelines for evaluating text structures and their relationship to content and lessons. Chapter 11 described a way to analyze the substantive content of text information, while Chapter 13 described how readers' preconceptions can interfere with reading.

The first point to be made is that poorly written stories and poorly conceived workbook tasks constrain students' understanding and limit their opportunity to learn. Guidelines for identifying well-written textbooks ("considerate" texts) were suggested by Armbruster. They can be classified as four suggestions: (1) Use global coherence characteristics (e.g., match content with structure and organize the structure so that it clarifies significant information and is meaningful); (2) use standard signaling devices (e.g., titles, subtitles, introductions, topic sentences); (3) use linguistic devices to tie sentences together (e.g., pronouns, conjunctions) and use a natural or temporal sequence of events; (4) be aware of characteristics that affect learning (e.g., type and stress of information and type of questions). Guidelines for identifying well-organized workbook tasks were suggested by Osborn. They can be expressed under four characteristics: (1) Workbook tasks should be functional and interesting to students and related to other learning tasks; (2) workbook tasks should employ language consistent with that appearing in text and lesson material and should utilize layouts that help rather than hinder understanding; (3) task procedures should involve reading and writing, should be unambiguous, easy to follow, and accurate, and should use a limited number of student response modes; (4) tasks should be tried out on students before their publication.

Both Armbruster and Osborn found a large number of poorly written, poorly conceived, inconsiderate lesson materials intended for elementary school children. Hence, teachers who must teach from the materials and educators who decide which set of materials to choose for a school district may find the suggestions useful. They can be used not only to understand why some learning materials are hard for students to follow but to evaluate and choose texts and workbooks.

Information in textbooks needs to be studied and evaluated not only on structural dimensions but also on content dimensions. Anderson and Smith (Chapter 15) reiterate a point made in Chapter 3 and elsewhere in this volume, namely that comprehension of written information must be interpreted in the light of readers' prior experience and understanding of the world. Scientific and mathematical principles are not obvious or easy to understand when the underlying concepts conflict with naive explanations. Textbook writers and teachers need to be aware of incorrect perceptions. Students are likely to misinterpret written information and practice exercises and be unable to acquire new concepts unless some portions of textbooks are more clearly written.

A more general point about text content was made in Chapter 11 through an analysis of basal readers from grades 2, 4, and 5. Three dimensions of content were looked for in the texts: (1) subject matter (presence or not of theories or facts or of an undergirding concept about individual or social life); (2) function (information that leads to understanding about process, reasoning, or interpretation); and (3) ethos (a position taken about virtue or moral behavior). Over 20 percent of the selections were judged to contain no substantive content and over 60 percent seemed to provide content on only one dimension.

Since the presence of substantive content can be assumed to add meaningfulness and usefulness, it is apparent that many textbook selections constrain students' opportunities to learn. The three content dimensions suggested by Schmidt et al. indicate yet another important approach for selecting, evaluating, and rewriting textbooks.

In summary, textbooks and workbooks can and ought to be evaluated on more than a measure of difficulty based on readability formulas. Textbooks and the lessons in which they are embedded represent a complex system for instructing students. Educators and textbook writers need to be aware of as many dimensions of text complexity as possible, otherwise the text information or the way it is presented will unwittingly constrain rather than facilitate students' comprehension.

Layer Three: The Instructional Act

Layer three of the model embodies the instructional act. Surrounding and guiding the actual act of instruction are instructional principles that we feel are crucial for successful comprehension instruction and high levels of student understandings. As stated earlier in this chapter, our listing of principles is not inclusive and new principles will be added as research shows them to be applicable.

The principles are as follows: (1) Instruction should occur within the students' zone of proximal development; (2) instruction should move from other-regulated to self-regulated within a social interactive process; (3) instruction should include metacognitive components; and (4) instruction should follow a logical sequence. A brief discussion of each of the principles follows.

Principle One. Instruction should occur within students' zone of proximal development. Teachers, as they are planning instruction in the problem-solving strategies used to understand text, should use the students' zone of proximal development as a major guide. Vygotsky (1979) defines the zone of proximal development as "the distance between the actual development level as determined by independent problem solving and the level of potential development as determined through problem solving under adult guidance or in collaboration with more capable peers." For the purposes of instruction, teachers must distinguish between these two developmental levels and the kinds of instruction each requires. When an instructional activity is presented at the student's actual developmental level (one where they can use problem-solving strategies independently), the teacher's task is simply one of setting and clarifying purposes and making connections between the students' background experiences and the content of the reading material. However, when an instructional activity is presented within the students' zone of proximal development, that area where the student cannot complete the task independently, the teacher's task becomes much more complicated. Not only does the teacher need to set and clarify purposes and make connections between students' background experiences and the content of the reading material, the teacher must assume an additional role. Since students cannot do the new strategy by themselves, the teacher becomes an assistant during the learning of the new skill or strategy. The teacher's task is one of coaching students through the problem-solving strategy. The teacher understands and knows how to do the strategy and through directions and questions coaches students toward using the new strategy independently. When students reach the independent level, they can use that strategy with no assistance, and the teacher can begin to prepare the next strategy to be learned.

This concept of having students in an instructional situation where they must "stretch" mentally while the teacher provides adequate assistance for the stretching to be successful is found in each of the chapters that deals with instructional communication. Pearson (Chapter 15) argues for a mental stretching of the students while they are learning strategic techniques that will help them understand the demands of the reading task. Likewise, Palincsar asks students to stretch mentally during the learning of the comprehension monitoring fostering activities she described in Chapter 17, and Raphael and Gavelek also discuss questioning strategies within the proximal level of difficulty in Chapter 16. Roehler and Duffy advocate that instruction for comprehension strategies occurs within the zone of proximal development; while Roth, Anderson, and Smith argue for new science understanding to be presented in the zone of proximal development, with the teacher playing an active assistance role.

Principle Two. Instruction should move from other-regulated to self-regulated within a social interactive process. Wertsch (1977) has stated that one of the most important functions of adults is to provide the strategy assistance needed to carry out a task. Before students begin to function as independent learners, they must provide the strategic support needed to be successful. This progression from needing instructional assistance to not needing outside help is called moving from other-regulated to self-regulated learning.

Self-regulated learning grows out of social interaction. According to Vygotsky (1979), human abilities (i.e., comprehension strategies) emerge first on the interpsychological plane of functioning and then on the intrapsychological plane of functioning. At an early age, children, through social interaction provided by parents, develop thinking strategies. The learning of these strategies begins within social interactions and gradually moves to the point where children can use them independently. Other-regulated learning situations allow students to participate in a problem-solving effort within a social interactive system that carries out the process of cognitive functioning. Out of the social interaction comes self-regulated learning. Classroom comprehension instruction should follow the same progression.

Again, each of the chapters in the section on instructional communication deals with learning in a social interactive process that moves from other-regulated to self-regulated. Pearson discussed Raphael's questioning-answering study in which students were moved from other-regulated to self-regulated situations through an instructional design that progressed from modeling to guided practice to independent practice. Palincsar not only had students involved in the process of moving from other-regulated to self-regulated learning, she also involved the teachers in her study in a training process that moved from other-regulation to self-regulation. Raphael and Gavelek developed a conceptual framework for understanding the development of questioning that drew heavily on the movement from other-regulated to self-regulated learning or the movement from an interpsychological plane of function to the intrapsychological plane. Roehler and Duffy have also embedded the principle of moving from other-regulated to self-regulated learning in their study on explicit explanations for comprehension skills. Finally, Roth, Smith, and Anderson also included a move from other-regulated to self-regulated in their instructional sequence regarding the learning of science content.

Principle Three. Instruction should include metacognition components. Flavell has described metacognition as follows:

> Metacognition refers to one's knowledge concerning one's own cognitive processes and products or anything related to them. . . . For example, I am engaging in metacognition . . . if I notice that I am having more trouble learning A than B; if it strikes me that I should double check C before accepting it as a fact; if it occurs to me that I had better scrutinize each and every alternative in any multiple-choice type task situation before deciding which is the best

one; if I sense that I had better make a note of D because I may forget it. ... Metacognition refers, among other things, to the active monitoring and consequent regulation and orchestration of these processes in relation to the cognitive objects or data on which they bear, usually in the service of some concrete goal or objective. (1976, p. 232)

In comprehension instruction, the reader must be metacognitive about his or her understanding of text and the processes used to understand. The reader carries out self-monitoring throughout the comprehension task by mentally consulting a "master plan" to see what's next, by knowing when a subtask is completed, and by knowing how to determine what to do next. As the student reads connected text and encounters a problem, he or she runs through the repertoire of strategies that might solve the problem, selects a strategy from the repertoire, implements it, and then evaluates the usefulness of the strategy (i.e., was it successful?).

Since neophyte readers are not naturally metacognitive, they need to be placed in an instructional setting where they can learn to be. As Wertsch (1979) explains, students do not first master a strategy and then begin to act; they act first and then begin to master the strategy that guides the action. Awareness of the metacognitive function emerges in the transition from other-regulated to self-regulated learning where the students become aware of what has already been occurring for some time under the direction of a teacher.

The following steps can be followed by teachers who plan to develop metacognitive functions during reading comprehension instruction:

1. Teachers should understand the goal of the instructional task, the usefulness of the task, and the means for achieving the task.
2. Teachers are responsible for alerting the students about the goal of the instructional task, the usefulness of such a task, and the ways to complete the task.
3. Teachers arrange the instructional task so students can deal with each step of the instructional task separately. The teacher might identify the separate pieces before beginning the task.
4. Teachers spend a great deal of instructional time reminding students where they are in the learning of the instructional task, why their correct responses are correct, and where they have erred in their incorrect responses.
5. Teachers close an instructional task with shared statements of what was learned, its usefulness, and the means used to accomplish the task.

These types of metacognitive components are heavily discussed in Chapters 17 and 18.

Principle Four. Instruction should follow a logical sequence. After choosing learning that is within the students' zone of proximal development, developing instructional activities that move from other-regulated to self-regulated within a social interactive situation and incorporating metacognitive components, the teacher must place these activities into a logical instructional sequence.

The first activity in the sequence is the activation of the students' background information. Such activation allows for linkages to occur between the old knowledge and the new knowledge that is to be presented. This step includes the strategies described by Roth (Chapter 19) for discovering students' misconceptions regarding scientific concepts and by Raphael and Gavelek (Chapter 17) for activating students' schema.

The second activity is the focusing activity where the aim is to present knowledge. The students are given something to think about. This step includes goal-setting explanation. This activity is included in all the chapters on instructional communication.

The third activity is the modeling of the use of the strategy. Roehler and Duffy, Raphael and Gavelek, and Palincsar all describe this strategy. Thinking out loud, a type of modeling activity, was a successful technique used in Roehler and Duffy's work.

The fourth activity is the expressing activity where students use the strategy just presented and modeled. This activity includes practice. The reciprocal teaching strategy described by Palincsar (Chapter 17) and the synthesis described by Roth (chapter 19) focus on this kind of activity.

Summary   The instructional act is guided by instructional principles. While we do not attempt to discuss them all, we have discussed those that are particularly relevant for our model of comprehension instruction. Instruction should occur within the students' zone of proximal development; should move from other-regulated to self-regulated learning within a social interaction system; should include meta-cognitive components that eventually allow students to monitor their own learning; and should follow a logical sequence of activating, focusing, modeling, and expressing-type activities.

Layer Four. Outcomes of Instruction

Layer four of our model incorporates the outcomes of instruction. Two major kinds of outcomes are developed. The first relates to strategy learning, the second to content knowledge. The outcomes related to strategy development will be discussed first.

All instruction on strategies should prepare students to *use* the strategy while reading in order to create meaning. The outcome has two parts. First, students must become aware of what strategies are available for understanding and remembering text. We encourage instruction that sets out to make students consciously aware of how skills and strategies work in solving real reading problems and have as a desired outcome that students understand what they are doing when they use a skill to solve a reading problem. For instance, we need instruction that helps students learn such complicated and diverse skills as locating information, determining relationships, generalizing, and drawing conclusions. Palincsar discussed studies that had as an outcome the development of reading strategies, namely question generating, summarizing, predicting, and clarifying. These outcomes were best achieved when the instructional principles discussed in layer three of our instructional model were present. Similarly, Roehler and Duffy described a study designed to develop in students conscious awareness and use of the problem-solving strategies of comprehension. The results of this study also favored instruction that closely relates to our model of comprehension.

After comprehension strategies and skills are learned, they need to be used in controlled reading situations where the focus is on practicing them until they are a part of the student's available repertoire of comprehension strategies. While the learning of the use of comprehension strategies has to occur in connected text, the emphasis is still on the strategies, not on the content of the material. The ultimate outcome is the creation in students of strategies that can be called upon when the need arises during the understanding and remembering of texts. Both Pearson and Raphael and Gavelek based their chapters on studies in which the outcome was the use of comprehension strategies in order to understand and remember text.

The second kind of outcome focuses on the learning of content knowledge. Here the strategies previously learned play a secondary role as the focus is on the construction and expansion of content knowledge. The ultimate outcome is to understand and remember that knowledge that our culture has deemed worthy of transmitting to new generations. Strategies assist in that transmission but the focus is on content knowledge. Roth et al. (Chapter 19) had this outcome in mind; they hoped to further understand about science, not to create strategies to be used in processing text.

Reading for remembering (studying) involves all the strategies for understanding and more. In order to remember, the students must take purposeful action to ensure that content is remembered as well as understood. This kind of reading, comprehension, and monitoring involves the ability to concentrate on the main ideas, to introduce deliberate tactics that aid learning and the ability to self-test the effectiveness of the study strategy as a means for remembering important information.

In summary, our model has two major outcomes. The first is the learning and use of strategies that focus on the processes involved in comprehending. The second outcome is the understanding of the knowledge embedded in the content.

CONCLUSION

In the foreword to this volume, Shulman and Anderson note that "marriages of insufficiencies," which bring together specialists from different fields, are disciplined collaborations that can result in levels of understanding and utility that go beyond what either group could produce alone. This volume, we feel, is a good example of the importance of marriages. The various chapters, whether considered individually or collectively, provide valuable insights on the problems of reading and teaching that, when combined, provide the promise of improving comprehension instruction.

The key words here are "insights" and "promise." There are no "answers" or "guarantees." This final chapter is evidence of this. The distinctions cited provide insights; the model offered holds promise. While they move forward our understanding of comprehension instruction, they are not likely to be viewed as revelations. Such is the reality of schooling. Improved classroom comprehension instruction results from a longitudinal effort of which this book generally (and this chapter in particular) is just a beginning. To achieve the ultimate goal of improved comprehension instruction, marriages such as the one that stimulated this book must continue to be performed to bridge the gap between various research emphases, and marriage between researchers and practitioners must be performed in order to bridge the gap between research and practice.

REFERENCES

Flavell, J. H. Metacognitive aspects of problem solving. In L. B. Resnick (Ed.), *The Nature of Intelligence*. Hillsdale, N. J.: Erlbaum, 1976.

Vygotsky, L. S. Mind in Society: The Development of Higher Psychological Processes. Cambridge, Mass.: Harvard University Press, 1979.

Wertsch, J. V. From social interaction to higher psychological processes: A clarification and application of Vygotsky's theory. *Human Development*, 1979, 22, 1–22.